M000251302

PRESENT AT SINAI: THE GIVING OF THE LAW

Commentaries selected by S . Y . AGNON

PRESENT AT SINAI
THE GIVING OF THE LAW

Commentaries selected by S. Y. AGNON

TRANSLATED BY MICHAEL SWIRSKY
WITH AN INTRODUCTION BY JUDAH GOLDIN

THE JEWISH PUBLICATION SOCIETY
PHILADELPHIA · JERUSALEM   5754 · 1994

Originally published in Hebrew under the title
Atem Re'item
Copyright © 1959 by Schocken Publishing House Ltd.,
Tel Aviv, Israel
This edition copyright © 1994 by
The Jewish Publication Society
Introduction © 1994 by Judah Goldin
First English edition   All rights reserved
No part of this publication may be reproduced or transmitted
in any form or by any means, electronic or mechanical, including
photocopy, recording, or any information storage or retrieval
system, except for brief passages in connection with a critical
review, without permission in writing from the publisher:
The Jewish Publication Society, 1930 Chestnut Street, Philadelphia,
PA 19103.

Manufactured in the United States of America

Library of Congress Cataloging-in-Publication Data
Atem re'item.   English
    Present at Sinai : the giving of the Law / commentaries selected
by S.Y. Agnon ; translated by Michael Swirsky ; with an introduction
by Judah Goldin.
        p.   cm.
    Includes bibliographical references and index.
    ISBN 0-8276-0503-X
    1. Revelation on Sinai.   2. Bible. O.T. Exodus XIX–XX—
Commentaries.   3. Midrash—Translations into English.   4. Aggada—
Translations into English.   I. Agnon, Shmuel Yosef, 1888–1970.
II. Swirsky, Michael.   III. Title.
BM612.A8813   1994   93-46215
296.1′4—dc20   CIP

Designed by Adrianne Onderdonk Dudden
Typeset in Bembo and Goudy Modern by ComCom

The publication of this volume was made possible
through a generous gift from
Gerald Cohn, Seymour Graham, and Sidney Klemow
in honor of
MARTIN D. COHN
President of the Board of Trustees of
The Jewish Publication Society
1990–1993

CONTENTS

FOREWORD:
OF SINAI AND AGNON

JUDAH GOLDIN

In the glossary of classical Hebrew (often in post-classical, too) a number of words enjoy a noteworthy currency, and they shape the character and ideals of the whole tradition of Israel. Consider, for example, *mitzvah*. It means a commandment; it also means a good deed. (Note by the way that in Hebrew one does not speak of the Ten Commandments [*mitzvot*] but of the Ten Proclamations, Ten Declarations [*dibrot*].) A mitzvah therefore is not only a particular halakhah—a statutory ruling to be obeyed or performed (or if a negative ruling [*lo ta'aseh*] is intended, a prohibition, something to be avoided)—but also an act that increases the practice of goodness. One cannot have too much of that. This is how the Holy One, blessed be He, wished to add to the merit of Israel, as the Mishna says; give them more and more commands.

Consider, too, the term "holiness." Leviticus instructs: "Be ye *holy*" (19:2). Again and again and again, "holiness" is invoked as noun and as conjugated verb. When it is joined to other nouns, a sacred dimension is added to them; thus, by way of a few examples at random, the holy Sabbath, the holy of holies, the holy language, the holy land, the holy spirit, the holy ark, and so on. Such frequency of definition and association testifies to a fixation, not just a rhetorical refrain or homiletical slogan; it affects one's diet, the rhythm of the week and year, the relations between men and women, groom and bride, native and stranger.

Additional eloquent terms—"covenant," "shalom"—likewise deserve honorable mention. But in the dialect of law-givers and prophets and advocates of Wisdom, all such terms fall short of the level of praise reserved for Torah. Its reach is limitless. And yet—it always comes as a shock that the Great Hallel, Psalm 136, does not mention Torah!

Torah, as we know, refers to the Five Books of Moses, to the Holy Scriptures as a whole, to what is called the Oral Torah (Midrash and Talmud), to the whole corpus of interpretation and codification of the Written and word-of-mouth legacy. The roots of every imperative are in the soil of the Torah, even if no more exalted than the requirements of good manners and civilized conduct. What is attributed to it is even more. Before the world was created it had already been brought into being; the Torah served as the blue-print God consulted like an architect to bring the universe into existence. In heaven God himself conducts Torah seminars.

This representation of Torah derives from citation, of course, or to put it accurately, from a combination of citations from the Midrash. The example is meant to illustrate, however faintly, Agnon's method—what he does, not only with midrashic sayings but with reflections and teachings from the enormous library of Hebrew literature produced by Israel's intellectual spokesmen in the course of a long history, that is, until the arrival of Modernism. Although Agnon does quote two or three 19th-century scholars in this collection, he does so only because their observations are in keeping with the temperament of earlier masters and thinkers. By and large, modern generations have too often lost sight of the relevance and inspiration of their predecessors. At best they have been reduced to middlemen of ornamental *bons mots*. By contrast, Agnon prefers to make the words of the pre-modern visible once more. He resurrects them. And he does this in several ways.

In the first place, he reproduces what these ancient teachers said. He does not paraphrase, he will not summarize; though he translates from the Aramaic when need be, he will not modernize or deconstruct to make them sound up to date. Without rehearsal he lets them speak for themselves. And the reader gradually—sometimes even rapidly—discovers that what the ancients or ancestors or great-grandfathers are talking about is not meaningless even in our times. Even their fantasies are intelligible, especially in a period that has been disillusioned with its own fantasies. Only rarely does he interrupt, as when he explains that a text as popularly published is a misreading, owing to the hand of the censor.

Like every editor, Agnon selects and excludes. Some of what he has not included, he tells us, are not rejections. They may be too longwinded; he simply had no room for them, although he does not hesitate to quote at length. What he did select was what was most appealing to him personally as he reviewed the contents of his files; naturally he hopes that they will appeal also to his twentieth-century readers; and to later ones, no less. In his choices of material—from midrashic-talmudic rabbis down to hasidic charismatics—and in his delight in half-playful/half-earnest interpretations refracted by the numerical value of consonants that make up a word (gematria) or their somersaults ('very', *m'd* = 'man,' *'dm*), we can glimpse his learning, his sensitivity, his sophistication, his seriousness, and his appreciation that even solemn doctrine benefits from the light touch. And who knows how much piquancy is covered up by his piety.

But it is not only content that attracts him. The way the table is set is as important as the food. Thus, patterns of presentation are not to be detached or erased from the passages quoted. Form is not immaterial or an afterthought. If there is repetition and then expansion of what has already been reported in one source, Agnon likewise will repeat without apology. So these different teachers spoke; let them. They also were reacting to what they had learned; they liked the taste of quotation on their tongue. He does, too, with relish.

More telling: Like the compilers of the tannaitic (first two centuries C.E.) and subsequent "exegetical" midrashim and the Bible commentators in post-talmudic centuries, Agnon adopts the very order of the verses in the biblical chapters as his framework. Therefore, he presents verbatim what is recorded in chapters 19 and 20 of Exodus (his base), each verse in its reserved place, and follows their sequence faithfully. Then come the correlated sections of commentary.

Not quite—and this is not insignificant. We begin with chapter 19 and enter into the first verse of chapter 20. At that point, from verse 2 through verse 17, the biblical text is not interrupted, for these verses are the body and soul of the Revelation. These verses may not be parted one from the other; they are the climax to which other verses lead and later follow from. Agnon, I think, wishes to insist that the Commandments which, following the Greek, we call the Decalogue, constitute One indivisible logos. (Unlike human beings, God can say two and more things at the same time.) Perhaps he is also eager to imply that despite a few variations in the version of the Commandments as drawn up in Deuteronomy 5:16–18, it is unjust to discriminate between the Exodus text and that of Deuteronomy. (Of course, this is guesswork on my part; I can almost overhear Agnon's rebuke: Please spare me your hindsight.) At all events, verses from Exodus 20:18 through 20:22 reappear as framework after the commentary on the Commandments in twenty (twice ten!) subdivisions.

Furthermore: Agnon uses biblical verses as more than framework. Within the citations themselves, biblical verses are employed as proof-texts. Thus, as already noted by the translator of the volume, Michael Swirsky, Agnon adopts a favorite practice of post-talmudic poets and writers: to leave traces of their names by means of acrostics, in order to escape anonymity. In the overture to his volume, he so arranges a number of verses from Psalm 119 so that their first letters spell out his name. In translation this is not apparent; in the Hebrew original it is unmistakable: "Shmuel Yosef Agnon ha-Levi, Hazak" (Samuel Joseph Agnon, the Levite, More power to you! See verses 165, 99, 46, 8, 92, 77, 44, 117, 135, 125, 18, 105, 47, 109, 34, 93, 41, 80, 64, 50, 151 in the Hebrew Bible). Agnon's choice of Psalm 119 is not arbitrary. That psalm, the longest in the Book of Psalms, comprising 176 verses drawn up in alphabetic acrostic, may be described as a celebration of Torah. The first-person tone of voice of the psalm-verses is a music of autobiography.

Similarly, the headings Agnon provides for the biblical verses and the commentary accompanying them are often phrases (sometimes brief clauses) borrowed from the specific verse that serves as a jumping-off place for the selections that follow. Sometimes the headings may be loan words from elsewhere or Agnon's formulation echoing classical terminology. We may call all these "sub-headings," but they are not facile auxiliary attachments to the quoted texts. They are themselves inventions, clefs for the score and setting of the expository contents. We are always within hearing distance of the classical idiom.

Thus: WE WILL DO AND WE WILL HEAR is the head line of the section on Exodus 19:7–9 (in actuality, the last two Hebrew words of Exodus 24:7). In the subsection on verse 19:8, "All the people answered as one, saying, All that the Lord has spoken we will do! And Moses brought the people's words to the Lord," Agnon has created nine units with the following rubrics: (1) "One voice"; (2) "All the people"; (3) "the Secret of the Word"; (4) "the Integrity of the Upright"; (5) "In order to Hear and to Carry out"; (6) "Bless the Lord, ye angels"; (7) "Everything that the Lord spoke"; (8) "the Practive and Contemplative"; (9) "the Words of the People." Each of these phrases is introductory to texts that the headings exemplify in miniature. Through these signposts, he has brought cohesion to what otherwise might seem indiscriminate borrowings. Yet they are anything but that! The selections are planned associations.

The juxtaposition of the assembled commentary-texts transforms them from ready-made collector's acquisitions into original compositions that transcend anthological gatherings. Particularities have merged into a unity. The views are many, but the voice is the voice of Agnon.

Let an abbreviation of one section on Exodus 19:17 represent (with a few minor deviations from the translation before us) Agnon's approach to source material. The subject this time is Mount Sinai as model of humility:

A. Rab Joseph said: A person should always learn from what his Creator had in mind. For note, the Holy One, blessed be He, turned away from all the mountains and hills and caused his Shekinah to rest on Mount Sinai, and He forsook all the splendid trees and caused His Shekinah to rest on the thorn bush.

B. (From Leviticus Rabba): God took the measure of all the mountains and found no mountain save Mount Sinai worthy of serving as the place where Torah should be given. Humility is learned from Sinai; from it let all Torah-students learn humility; for the Holy One, blessed be He, turned away from all the mountains and brought His Shekinah to rest on Mount Sinai—for it is low-lying.

C. "The Lord came from Sinai." The giving of the holy Torah was an example of the nature of humility, for that is the lesson of Sinai, the lowest of the mountains. By virtue of (our) humility, He extends His loving kindness to us and teaches us the way to live.

. . .

D. (Passover Haggadah) Because of the humility they learned from Mount Sinai, they were stripped of all corporeal concerns and were purified to such a degree that they could acquire the whole Torah even prior to its being given. This is the intent of the saying of the author of the Haggadah, "Had He brought us nigh to Mount Sinai, it would have been enough even if He had not given us the Torah." For it was because of His love of Israel, that He gave the Torah to them, in accordance with what is taught, Greater is he who puts into practice what he has been commanded to do than he who puts into practice what he has not been commanded.

E. "His cheeks are like beds of spices, banks of perfume; his lips are lilies, they drip myrrh which keeps flowing." You find that when the Holy One, blessed be He, revealed Himself on Mount Sinai, the whole world was filled with perfume; as is written, 'Banks of perfume'; 'His lips drip myrrh which keeps flowing.' Whereto? The Holy One, blessed be He, has put it into storage in the Garden of Eden for the righteous.

F. "You are beautiful, My beloved." It is to this that the following verse refers: 'Truly, Ephraim is a dear son to Me.' The Holy One, blessed be He, said to Israel, Ever since I spoke to you at Sinai I recall that presence of yours. Say, therefore, 'Even when I have spoken against him, I have still not dismissed him from My Mind.'

. . .

G. Rabbi Joshua ben Levi said: Each and every day a Voice issues from Mount Horev and cries out with the words, Woe to mankind for their contempt of the Torah. For whoever does not engage in Torah-study is called Reprobate.

H. Reprobate, that is he who is reproved by God.

I. Mount Horev is one of the five names of Mount Sinai. And why was it called Horev? Because when the Torah was offered, the Nations of the

World refused to accept it; then destruction (hurva) came down on them. Hence the name Horev.

J. In our times many withdraw from study of the Torah with alibis that they have to make a living. Actually this was the alibi of the idol worshipers at the time of the giving of the Torah, that they could not accept the Torah because it conflicted with their livelihood. Therefore, when Israel spoke up and said with one accord, We will do and obey, obviously they accepted it even when it interferes with their pursuit of a livelihood.

K. The Sages say, So long as people neglect the study of Torah, the Holy One, blessed be He, seeks to destroy the world.

Too repetitive? Likely, if one were planning arguments for debate or condensation for a treatise or essay on logic. But Agnon, like the pious authorities he summons, loves the flavor of these words, loves the return and recurrence of the vocabulary that leads away from the commonplace and the mediocre polemic.

Two more selections follow the eleven above, and they too repeat but as usual provide nuances of their own. And this is typical of the whole volume. As a result, the comments bring us into contact with imagery, concepts, parables, exhortations, and supplications that exemplify Israel's universe of discourse, passions, and never-abandoned hopes. These make up the sounds and silent meditations of Torah, which in turn reactivate the details, down to the particles, of the biblical sentences.

Torah is fire—don't get too close to it, you'll be burned; don't get too far away from it, you'll freeze. Sinai, which teaches humility, is the station where Israel congregates. God offered the Torah to the Nations of the World— the descendants of Esau, the Moabites, the Ishmaelites—but they turned it down because it was contrary to their curricula and profession. Israel, however, reached out for it enthusiastically; well, not necessarily enthusiastically, for another version has it that at first Israel hesitated. If God had not threatened them—Take it or I'll turn this mountain upside down and under its lid bury you alive—they too might have refused. There are times when a spirit of holiness stirs up a person by a voice that pierces the ear of his soul. Human figures of speech are employed to describe the supernatural because the Torah speaks in human terms and metaphors.

Thus the Midrash teaches:

Moses rushes back directly to the children of Israel before stopping to take care of his personal needs.

When the impulse to evil threatens, drag it to the study house.

A wife complains: When we were first married, my husband told me I was beautiful; now that I've grown old, he criticizes me for being ugly. O God, is that Your attitude toward Your people?

Whatever commandments Israel gave up their lives for under oppression, they still keep; what they did not give up their lives for, they tend to neglect.

Don't be like slaves who serve their master on condition that they receive an allowance, and let the fear of Heaven be upon you.

In the Temple they used to recite the Ten Commandments every day; we no longer do so because of the heretics who say that only these were given to Moses at Sinai.

Oh, how God loves Israel! Their relationship to each other is nuptial: see the Song of Songs.

The Ten Commandments correspond to the ten divine utterances at the creation of the world.

What a maidservant in Israel beheld at the Revelation, even the greatest of prophets and visionaries did not see.

At the Revelation, none in Israel was blind, for it is said, 'And all the people saw.' None were mute, for it is said, 'Together all the people responded.' None were deaf, as it is said, 'Everything God said, we will carry out; we hear.' None was lame, as it is said, 'They stood up straight at the bottom of the mountain.' And none were mentally defective, as it is said, 'From what you were shown you were to learn.'

In human experience one does not see a sound, but at Sinai they saw the sounds as well as flames of fire. Even as they saw the flames, so they saw the sounds, for it is said, 'And the people saw.' What did they see? They saw the Great Glory *(doxa)*.

The sound travelled from one end of the world to the other: this is to teach you that the Glory of the Lord and His holy words are not confined to some single place but fill the whole wide world and in one moment embrace all the ends of the earth.

And much more of the same, all calculated to emphasize that the experience at Sinai was not an event for the Generation of the Wilderness exclusively but a permanent summons to everyone in every century and millennium. None of it is transitory, and the biblical verses are not a haphazard assortment. Everyone heard and hears according to his capacity: the old according to their capacity, the young according to their capacity; youngsters according to theirs, infants according to theirs, women according to theirs. Even Moses, according to his capacity, as it is said, 'Moses would speak and God would reply by voice,' that is, by a sound that he could bear. So too it says, 'The voice of the Lord is with might.' It does not say, with *its* might, but 'with might,' that is, a might within the capacity of every single one. Even pregnant women heard according to their might. Say then, every single one according to his own might. . . . The same is true of the manna, each to his taste.

The fact that Agnon does not organize his citations chronologically, early texts first and later ones later, is indeed his deliberate design. It is not historical or critical literary development that he is after, even when a later source quotes an earlier one before stretching it further. It is not that Agnon wishes to ignore such things, but that he is uninterested in the notion that the calendar can tell you more than the date. Not *Zeitgeist* but *Geist* is what he seeks. The spell he is under is the unanimity of assent to the exuberance at the foot of Mount Sinai. From the top of the mountain the Voice came down, audible to ancestors and descendants. Therefore, they can collaborate. Both share the frame of mind that welcomes such proclamations.

But one can't compare hearing to seeing with one's own eyes. To be sure, the whole camp of Israel was thunderstruck as God announced the first two and Moses recited the next eight Commandments, but God ordered him to remind the people: You *saw* that I spoke to you from heaven, not only heard. For Agnon this is the heart of the matter—You saw, You were eyewitnesses of this unique phenomenon. Hence the title of the volume, *Atem Re'item,* You yourselves were eyewitnesses—it's not by report from someone, it's not simply a message delivered by an intermediary. An immediacy was experienced here. At Sinai the Revelation was witnessed: in the sight of all "I spoke from heaven." And "all" equals the more than 600,000 recently emancipated from bondage and all who came after them. All the generations of Israel were in attendance. The verse reads "You" (You saw) and Agnon means, as the tradition maintains, you, and you, and you; in other words, "we" too.

The title of the Hebrew volume being what it is, and *eyesight* being insisted on, Agnon can't resist closing with the supplication, not from Exodus this time but Deuteronomy (26:15), *"Look* down from Your holy abode, from heaven." Even as we beheld with our eyes, so You keep Your eye on us. The final citation is therefore twin commentary and prayer. "Look down from Your holy abode, from heaven, and bless Your people Israel and the land You have given us as You swore to our fathers. . . ." "Look down from Your holy abode, from heaven, and bless Your people Israel"—Do it for us. "The land," Do it for our land; "Which You gave us"—Do it by virtue of our Torah. "As You swore to our fathers"—Do it for the sake of Your great Name which has been called forth to be upon us, as it is said, "Yet You are in our midst, O Lord, and Your Name is attached to us"—Do not forsake us!

TRANSLATOR'S PREFACE

Present at Sinai: The Giving of the Law is not a completed book. Agnon himself tells us that he originally prepared a larger work, of which the present book constitutes but the first part. The remainder, approximately the same length and covering several related themes, has never been published. But even in its abbreviated form, the present book seems an important one to make accessible to readers of English.

For one thing, the book is a testimony to Shmuel Yosef Agnon, to the extraordinary sweep of his Jewish erudition and Jewish sympathies, and to his skill as an anthologist. Even more significant is the subject matter: the materials Agnon brought together for us here illuminate what has always been, together with the Exodus from Egypt, the core of Jewish religious consciousness—*Ma'amad Har Sinai* (the Sinai Event), as memory and continually renewed experience. The unique encounter between God and humankind, the great once-and-for-all yet endlessly unfolding revelation upon which these texts reflect is the very fountainhead of Judaism itself.

There is one more good reason for making this book available to a wider audience. There is no genre or epoch in Jewish theological tradition—I mean, simply, Jewish thinking about God—that does not concern itself with Sinai. The subject, therefore, is a particularly apt prism with which to view that tradition as a whole. The sampler Agnon gives us is not an exhaustive one—for example, not much of a philosophical nature, either medieval or modern, is included—yet it is amazingly wide-ranging, encompassing biblical and talmudic texts and commentaries, the whole sweep of the Midrash, Kabbalah, Hasidism, and homiletical and pietistic writings of various periods down to our own time. What is more, the book introduces us to the subject of Jewish theology, not in an abstract, systematic way, but in the way to which Judaism is partial: commentary, verse by verse and word by word, on a sacred text.

It would not be quite accurate to describe *Present at Sinai* as a mere anthology. While the bulk of it consists simply of excerpts from other books (that is, sources cited in their original form), Agnon has also altered some sources—abridged, amplified, even paraphrased altogether—without necessarily making us aware of it. In addition, he sometimes interjects comments entirely of his own. No attempt has been made in the present translation to untangle the skeins of the text, separating original from reworked material; I have simply followed Agnon's design and left the responsibility for it on his very broad shoulders. Those wishing to study the texts in greater depth are well advised to consult the original books, a few of which are available in English. Some day a "critical edition" of this book, based on closer scrutiny of the sources it cites, may be prepared; this translation should not be mistaken for such an edition.

Like all Jewish sacred texts, those cited in this book are rarely transparent. They require explication—some of them, such as the mystical texts, require quite a lot—and this, too, has not been attempted here except to a very limited degree. Scattered throughout the translation are hidden (unbracketed) interpolations that serve to fill in merely rhetorical gaps in the original language. Less frequently, bracketed interpolations appear, designed to supply much-needed additional information that is not in the original, as unobtrusively as possible. Finally, where the uninitiated reader could otherwise make no sense at all of a text, occasional footnotes are provided. (All these are my own, unless otherwise indicated.) Of course, a certain amount of interpretation is inevitably effected by the translation itself. But my point is that the serious reader will in many instances want to seek out a teacher and/or proper commentary.

Although some of the works cited in this book have previously been translated from Hebrew (or Aramaic) into English, the present translation is entirely new, with one exception: the biblical passages are generally taken from the New Jewish Publication Society Version (abbreviated here as NJPSV).* Even in this case, some retranslation had to be done, where a given midrash† hinged on a reading of a biblical word or phrase different from the reading selected by the NJPSV translators. Occasionally, where a midrashic reading was particularly fanciful, I stayed with the NJPSV in translating the prooftext and simply supplied a transliteration of the key Hebrew term to show the point of departure of the midrashic version.

The following key has been used in transliteration, including that of most proper names: ḥ = ח; kh = ך, כ; z = צ, ז. The letter ע is always indicated by

---

*TANAKH (Philadelphia: Jewish Publication Society, 1962–82).
†Rabbinic amplification of a biblical passage (see Glossary).

' as is the letter א when it begins a syllable in the middle of a word. The spellings of names in biblical passages have been retained from the NJPSV. In spelling names that are not of Hebrew origin, I have followed the *Encyclopaedia Judaica* wherever I could find them there.

The citations indicate the title of the book from which a given excerpt is drawn and/or its author. Where both author and title are given, the author comes first and is separated from the title by a comma. Two titles separated by a comma indicate the name of a book and the name of a chapter (frequently, a *parashah* or weekly scriptural reading). Names or titles separated by a semicolon are independent sources of the same passage. A single number following the title is a volume or chapter or section number. When two numbers are separated by a colon, the first is a volume or chapter number, the second a paragraph or verse number. Passages from the Babylonian Talmud are identified only by tractate and folio number. In some instances, Agnon identifies a passage by a few introductory words at the beginning rather than a citation at the end, but in most cases I have placed the citations at the ends of the excerpts. Passages in bold, with no identifying citation are the words of Agnon himself.

An attempt has been made, within the limits of standard English and the meaning of the original, to avoid gender-specific terms. Thus: "human being" instead of "man," "ancestors" instead of "forefathers." However, I am afraid these departures from conventional translation usage will not be sufficiently thoroughgoing for many readers. I apologize ahead of time and plead innocent of any prejudicial intent.

I would never have dared undertake this translation without the assistance of others far more learned than myself in the classical sources. In particular, I would like to thank Dr. Aryeh Strikovsky, of the Pardes Institute and the Israel Ministry of Education, a patient teacher and true *talmid hakham,* for the many hours during which we studied these texts together. It was for me an extraordinary learning experience. Wise counsel was also generously given over a period of many weeks by Professor Jacob Elbaum, of the Hebrew University, who supported me in this project from the outset and whose great erudition was responsible for innumerable improvements in the translation. Both were kind enough to read the entire manuscript and offer detailed comments. In addition, Hayim Yehudah Yaron, Agnon's son-in-law, went over my work with special care and was of particular help in the preparation of the bibliography. Of course, I alone am responsible for any errors that remain. My thanks to Beth

Uval for her diligence and good cheer in the otherwise thankless task of transcribing the biblical passages from the existing translation. And last but not least, my appreciation to Dr. Ellen Frankel and Rabbi Michael Monson of The Jewish Publication Society for agreeing to entrust this project to my unworthy hands.

Michael Swirsky
Jerusalem
'Erev Shavu'ot

PRESENT AT SINAI: THE GIVING OF THE LAW

Commentaries selected by S. Y. AGNON

THE MAKING OF THIS BOOK

I

It was not in a haughty or self-assured spirit that I approached the task of preparing a book about the Sinai Event and the Giving of the Torah. Rather, since the Torah itself speaks only briefly about these occurrences, and I had not been able to find any book that dealt especially with them, I resolved to search out what the scriptures tell us and what the sages had discovered as to the sequence of events. At length I summoned the courage to set down in writing some of what they said, in order to clarify for myself and others like me what had transpired on that sacred occasion, the like of which had never taken place before nor has it taken place since. And although the task was beyond my abilities, I felt confident that, if there were a need for such a book, Heaven's help would be forthcoming.

Initially I had intended to make the book all of a piece, in a uniform language and style, so that one could read it straight through from beginning to end without encountering any repetition of subject matter from one chapter to the next. But in order to accomplish that I would have had to chop and cut and extract and edit and combine one interpretation with another and one statement with another. The result would have been outwardly attractive but inwardly a jumble. I have thus cited the sources in their original form, just as they have been handed down to us from their authors. For while they may be many and various, in spirit they are all one. Some sources may say one thing, other sources another; nevertheless, all were given to us by our rabbis, may their memory be a blessing, from the mouth of the Lord of all Works, may He be blessed.

When things first appear in the midrashim of the Earlier Authorities* but are interpreted in later midrashim, I have cited the later versions, be the books from which they are drawn well known or esoteric. Whatever was pertinent I copied here, and what was not pertinent I left out. Things originally written in Aramaic I have translated into the holy language [Hebrew], for most of our people are not familiar with the Aramaic tongue. As I did for the Sages [of the

---

*Heb. *rishonim;* codifiers of Jewish law between the close of the Talmud and the compilation of Rabbi Yosef Caro's *Shulhan Arukh,* in the sixteenth century. The Later Authorities *(ahronim)* are those who followed Caro.

Talmud], so did I do with later teachers. But in the case of the latter I was concerned more with content than with language. In any event, I have included words that enrich the language, even though there is no mention of them in the dictionaries.

Biblical verses cited by the Sages I have copied according to the Masoretic text. Where they interpret the latter part of a verse but cite only its first words, I have cited the entire verse. Sayings of the Sages that the Later Authorities cite allusively or with a change of wording I have cited in their original form and indicated their sources. I have kept cross-references to a minimum, but where such a reference can shed light on a particular text I have included it. I have made scant use of honorific titles; the words of the righteous are their titles.

This book is based on the four levels of meaning: the plain sense *(peshat)*, the allegorical *(remez)*, the homiletical *(derash)*, and the esoteric *(sod)*.* The words of the living God contain many mysteries and endless hidden things. There are scriptural passages that do not fit when understood literally and so cry out for interpretation, for the uncovering of their allusions and the probing of their secrets. The words of the Torah are both revealed and hidden, and however much one examines them one never penetrates more than a small part of their mystery.

There are some books that I have cited frequently and others, such as the works of the preachers, that I have not had the opportunity to cite at all. These latter make their point in sermons, which tend to rely on lengthy expositions involving questions and answers, introductions and perorations, problems and solutions, surprises and riddles, doubts and their resolution, parables and metaphors, and the like. These expositions cannot be reported except in their original form, for if anything is omitted, the form is impaired. Furthermore, since most of what they say is based on midrashim of the Sages, and I have cited the latter in all the expected places anyway, and it is not appropriate to repeat the same thing many times in one book—there being many midrashim and aggadot that all the preachers use—I have been compelled to omit them altogether, knowing full well that the book would have been greatly improved by their inclusion.

Some of what I have not managed to do in this book I will do in the books that follow, for *Atem Re'item*† is to be in four volumes, all named after the verse, *"You yourselves saw that I spoke to you from the very heavens"* [Exod. 20:19].

The first volume is called *The Book of the Story of the Giving of the Torah*. The second is called *The Book of the Ten Commandments*. The third is called *On the Tablet of Your Heart*, after the Tablets of the Law; this volume

---

*A reference to the well-known acronym *PaRDeS*, meaning, literally, "garden" or "orchard," but figuratively referring to the realm of sacred knowledge.

†*You Yourselves Saw*, the original title of the book.

also deals with the making of the Ark, the Cherubim, the Curtain, the Cover, the enumeration of the Commandments, Moses, and "Remember the Torah of Moses." The fourth volume is about the Torah, its subdivisions and chapters, the standard emendations of the text, its punctuation and vocalization, the scribal tradition, the ornamentation of the letters, and stories about the Torah.

Blessed be God, who has aided me from the outset. May He help me to finish what I have begun.

In all these books I have cited only the words of believers in God, concerning whom, and concerning the like of whom, it is said, "That which the veteran scholar shall some day teach . . . was already told to Moses at Sinai" (Palestinian Talmud, Pe'ah Ch. 2).

II

What makes a book like this more than just a collection of excerpts, strung together interchangeably? What makes it a *book*? If I were to say it had been a matter of selection, who would venture to choose among the words of the Sages, pronouncing some of them acceptable and some not? And if I were to say I had based this composition on the books I happened to own, why, nowadays, when great treasure houses of books are open to all, no author of a book such as this could claim to have done the job by relying only on what was at hand. Thus the question remains. And the answer is: when I set about to compile this book I saw that it would be impossible to make it all of a piece, in a uniform style; and as for making a review of the literature, there is no end to the books that have been written or the views expressed by the Sages of the Torah, from the time of Moses our Teacher until now. And in some cases these views are quite far apart, but this should not be cause for dismay, for all are for the sake of heaven, and all are the words of the living God, as if each had direct access to revelation, to the words of Moses himself, as explained by the Maharshal, may his memory be a blessing, in the introduction of *Yam shel Shlomo* [*Solomon's Sea*], his book on Tractate Baba Kama. There he writes:

> Though Moses never uttered a contradiction, the Sages in their study of the text drew different and sometimes contradictory conclusions, either through the exercise of logic or on the basis of tradition handed down from Moses at Sinai, one to another. But all these conclusions are legitimate. How can this be? The Kabbalists explained it this way: All souls were at Mount Sinai and received [the revelation] through forty-nine conduits—being seven times seven, purified twice seven times over. These were the [heavenly] voices they not only heard but also saw [Cf. Exod. 20:15]. And all Israel saw the voices, meaning the proclamations dissemi-

nated through the conduits, each seeing through his own conduit according to his ability to comprehend and according to the capacity of his
higher soul to be elevated or diminished, one widely differing from
another.

III

I would like to make mention here of a number of books that provide a link
from the Written to the Oral Torah, and from the Oral to the Written. Some
cite the sources in their original form, while others summarize them; some refer
to specific locations in the texts, while others follow the order of the *Parashiot**
or go according to topic. I refer to them here one after the other as they occur
to me:

Damesek Eli'ezer (Pressburg, 1880; Paks, 1881–86), by Rabbi Zusman Eli'ezer
Sofer, including midrashim by Earlier and Later Authorities as well as mystical
midrashim, arranged according to the order of the *Parashiot,* with aggadic and
moralistic commentaries.

Torah Temimah [*The Pure Torah*] on the Pentateuch and the Five Megillot
(Vilna, 1902), drawn from the Written Torah together with the Oral Torah,
according to a compilation of homilies and sayings of the Sages, in regard to
Halakhah and Aggadah, in the Babylonian and Palestinian Talmudim, the *Sifra*
and *Sifrei,* the Tosefta, the *Mekhilta, Avot de-Rabbi Natan,* and the Minor
Tractates, with an extensive commentary on the scriptural basis of the homilies,
and with novellae and comments clarifying the halakhah; by Rabbi Barukh
Halevi Epstein.

Humash Torah Shelemah [*Pentateuch: The Whole Torah*] (Jerusalem, 1927; New
York, 1954), consisting of the Written Torah together with the commentary
of the Oral Torah, including commentary on the Torah from the time of its
giving until the beginning of the Gaonic period, drawn from all the works of
the Sages, the works attributed to them, and the Targumim, as to the plain
sense, the Halakhah, the Aggadah, the homilies, the scriptural supports for
Rabbinic enactments, the traditions, and the allusions—marshaled for every
verse, word, and letter of the Torah, with a commentary, cross-references,
notes, and novellae, by Rabbi Menahem Mendel Kasher.

*The sections into which the Pentateuch is divided for the purpose of the weekly
public readings in the synagogue.

Yefeh 'Einayim [*He of the Beauteous Eyes*], by the great sage Aryeh Leib Yellin, on the Babylonian Talmud (and printed in the Vilna edition of the Talmud, 1880), including cross-references to the Palestinian Talmud, the Midrashim, *Yalkut, Sifra, Sifrei, Mekhilta, Pirkei de-Rabbi Eli'ezer,* and *Pesikta Rabbati,* with notes and novellae concerning variant readings and differences between the Babylonian and Palestinian Talmudim.

Yalkut Reuveni [*The Compilation of Reuben*] on the Torah (Amsterdam, 1700)— essays and midrashim, old and new, compiled by Rabbi Reuven ben Rabbi Hoeshke Katz, citing short essays from *Targum Yonatan, The Book of the Bahir,* and the Zohar, as well as from a number of kabbalistic works and *The Book of the Hasidim.*

Yalkut Eli'ezer [*The Compilation of Eliezer*] (Pressburg, 1864–71), gleaned from the Palestinian Talmud, Midrash Rabbah, *Mekhilta, Sifra, Sifrei, Tanhuma, Shoher Tov,* Tosefta, *Tana Devei Eliyahu, Pesikta, Pirkei Rabbi Eli'ezer, Yalkut Shim'oni, Yalkut Reuveni, Aggadat Bereshit, Tadshe, Midrash Hane'elam,* minor midrashim, and those found in other books. The entries are arranged alphabetically, with the compiler's commentary.

Toldot Aharon [*The Story of Aaron*], by Rabbi Aharon of Pissaro, being a key and index to the biblical verses expounded in the Babylonian Talmud. To this, Rabbi Ya'akov Sasportas, in his book *Toldot Ya'akov* [*The Story of Jacob*], added a cross-index to the Palestinian Talmud.

In the same vein but adding a further dimension is the work *Beit Aharon* [*The House of Aaron*], by Rabbi Aharon ben Rabbi Shmuel, a key to all the verses in the Bible cited in the Babylonian and Palestinian Talmudim and the Midrashim, the works of Kabbalah and homiletics, and some of his commentary on the Masorah.

Adding to this from seventy other books is Rabbi Avraham David ben Rabbi Yehudah Leib Lavat, in his book *Beit Aharon Vehosafot* [*The House of Aaron and Addenda*] (Vilna, 1881).

Similar but superior in its arrangement is *Sefer Torah Haketuvah Vehamesurah* [*The Book of the Torah as Written and Transmitted*] on the Torah, Prophets, and Writings (Tel Aviv, 1937–38 and 1940), by Rabbi Aharon ben Rabbi Mordekhai Heimann, which supplies the verses in large letters, most of them without abridgement.

Sefer Ziun Laderash [*The Book of the Mark of Interpretation*] (Krotoszyn, 1858) is a key to the teachings of the Sages of the Babylonian and Palestinian Talmudim as cited in the work *'Ein Ya'akov* [*The Well of Jacob*], or in some cases, if not cited there, arranged alphabetically by topic; by Rabbi Shraga Feibush Frankel.

An even greater achievement is that of Rabbi Moshe David Gross in his three-volume work, *Ozar Ha'aggadah* [*The Treasury of Aggadah*] (Jerusalem, 1954–55). He cites the Mishnah, the Tosefta, the Talmudim, the Midrashim, and the Zohar, but not lesser-known midrashim printed recently, unless their contents are included in *Yalkut Shim'oni*. The work includes statements outside the realm of Aggadah, tending toward that of Halakhah.

An earlier work is *Sefer Zikhron Torat Moshe* [*The Book of the Remembrance of the Torah of Moses*] (Prague, 1623), which encompasses all the teachings of the Babylonian and Palestinian Talmudim and the references to them in the *Guide of the Perplexed*, the homilies of the Ran, *'Akedat Yizḥak* [*The Binding of Isaac*], *Sefer Ha'ikkarim* [*The Book of Principles*], *Derekh Emunah* [*The Way of Faith*], and *Neveh Shalom* [*Oasis of Peace*]. Its author is Rabbi Moshe ben Rabbi Yosef.

Following this is the book *Naḥalat Shim'oni* [*Simeon's Portion*] (Wandsbeck, 1738), which lists all the names in the Torah, the Prophets, and the Writings in alphabetical order and quotes everything said about them in the Babylonian Talmud and Midrash Rabbah. The author is Rabbi Shim'on ben Rabbi Yehudah Leib Feizer of Lissa.

The finest of all from a stylistic point of view is *Sefer Ha-Aggadah* [*The Book of the Aggadah*] (Tel Aviv, 1948), a selection of the aggadot in the Talmud and the Midrashim, arranged topically and annotated by Rabbi Ḥayim Naḥman Bialik and Rabbi Y. H. Rawnitzki. Most of the contents can be related back to the scriptures. [The work has been translated into English by William Braude as *The Book of Legends* (New York: Schocken, 1993).]

I would like to make mention of one more work, *Mevo Hamidrash* [*Introduction to the Midrash*] (Lemberg, 1877), a collection of teachings, stories, and parables from Midrash Rabbah and the midrashim on the Five Megillot, by Rabbi Shlomo Wolf ben Rabbi Yeshaya Yosef of Drohobycz.

Finer still is the book *Yalkut Sippurim Umidrashim* [*An Anthology of Stories and Midrashim*] (Warsaw, second edition, 1923), which includes stories and aggadot of the Tannaim on the Pentateuch and on the Book of Esther, collected and arranged by Rabbi Ze'ev Wolff ben Rabbi Moshe Aharon Greenwald, with notes gleaned from the greatest of the commentators and a list of sources for all citations from our Rabbis, may their memory be a blessing.

Even I, in my unworthiness, have made a collection of aggadot of the Sages on the Pentateuch, apart from the stories and aggadot I collected from the works of the Later Authorities. I have included most of the former in the present work.

Many other works, great and small, old and new, have brought the teachings of our Sages, may their memory be a blessing, to bear on the verses of the Torah, the Prophets, and the Writings, as signposts to their understanding. First and foremost is the book *Yalkut Shim'oni* [*Simeon's Compilation*], by Rabbi Shim'on, the greatest of the expounders. All who seek to know the Torah, its interpretations, its allusions, its homiletical elaborations, and its secrets will find this book edifying.

Signposts have also been set up to help in understanding the books of the Zohar, some dealing with the secrets of the verses according to the order of the *Parashiot*, some in the form of keys to the topics, arranged alphabetically. To the extent that they are known to me, I list them herewith:

Mekor Hokhmah [*The Source of Wisdom*] (Prague, 1611), a key to the Zohar according to the *Parashiot* of the Torah. It was written by Rabbi Yissakhar Baer, son of Rabbi Moshe Petahyah of Kremnitz. The book is printed, with minor changes, in *Sefer Hazohar* (Amsterdam, 1728). The author is the one who wrote *Sefer Imrei Binah* [*The Book of Insightful Sayings*] (Prague, 1611), a short dictionary of all the foreign terms in the Zohar, arranged according to the *Parashiot*.

Maftehot Hazohar [*The Keys to the Zohar*] (Venice, 1744), by Rabbi Shmuel (surname unknown). The book has two parts. The first part deals with topics mentioned in the Zohar, the second with biblical verses scattered throughout the Zohar. The latter part was written by Rabbi Yisrael Berakhiah Fontanella, son of Rabbi Yosef Yekutiel of Reggio.

Midreshei Hazohar [*Midrashim of the Zohar*] (Philadelphia, 1934), on the Torah, the Prophets, and the Writings, according to the order of the *Parashiot* and the verses, selected and arranged with notes by Rabbi Nehemiah Shmuel Leibovitch.

Petah 'Einayim Nispah Lesefer Hazohar [*The Opening of the Eyes: An Appendix to the Zohar*] (Sulzbach, 1684), possibly identical with *Sefer Petah 'Einayim* (Cracow, 1607), by Rabbi Eli'ezer, son of Rabbi Menahem Mannes, is a key to biblical verses cited in the Zohar and in *Tikkunei Hazohar*. Though the latter work is mentioned by bibliographers, I myself have not seen it.

Mafteah Hazohar [*The Key to the Zohar*] (Amsterdam, 1710), by Rabbi Moshe, son of Rabbi Mordekhai Galante: keys to the scriptural passages expounded in the Zohar, arranged according to topic.

Beirurei Hamiddot [*Explanations of the Virtues*] (Jerusalem, 1923), by Rabbi Aharon Shlomo Maharil, son of Rabbi Katriel; essays on certain positive attributes and upright modes of behavior, which laws are to be observed at all times according to the Talmud and the Codes, their explanation, and their hidden meaning as set forth in the Zohar; arranged according to topic.

Aggadot Hazohar [*Legends of the Zohar*] (Warsaw, 1923), by Rabbi A. N. Frank, selected and arranged, translated and explained.

Would that an exacting editor, someone learned in the Torah and of good taste, wise and knowledgeable, might come and gather all the commentaries together. It would be a worthy task to collect everything the Sages of Israel throughout the generations have said about the Holy Scriptures: Halakhah and Aggadah, the plain meaning and the homiletical, the allegorical and the esoteric.

IV

Thus, when I saw that there was no end to books and no end to opinions—and, in any case, what joy is there in merely copying from one book to another?— I said to myself, It is not even your task to *begin*, and I wanted to put this work aside.

I wanted to put this work aside, yet my imagination had already been captivated by it, so that I could not look at any thing or any book without being reminded of what happened at Sinai. Each day I personally fulfilled the commandment to remember the Sinai Event, which ought to be called to mind every day, as in the words cited by the prayer books: "Remember the day when you stood before the Lord your God at Horeb, lest you forget what your eyes have seen." And when I recalled what happened at Sinai I recalled the scriptural texts describing it. And every verse had its interpretations and commentaries, its explanations and reasons, its allusions and numerological meanings, first and foremost the halakhic and aggadic midrashim. Things I had read as a child, as a young man, and in the previous year or two all leapt out of the pages. New books seemed to come my way only for the sake of the references to Sinai they contained. Whenever I saw something new on the subject I underlined it, and I did the same with books I had read earlier, which I went back over, not yet realizing that I was preparing something already prepared, that everything was in fact falling into place of its own accord.

At that time I was given an edition of the Zohar with the commentary *Hasulam* [*The Ladder*], by the Kabbalist Rabbi Yehudah Halevi Ashlag, may his memory be a blessing. I reread the Zohar together with the commentary, and I am indebted to the commentator, may his memory be a blessing, for helping me with a number of passages.

One day, as I was looking over my things, I came upon a box full of notes for my book *Sefer, Sofer, Vesippur* [*Book, Author, and Story*].* It was originally a short book that I had drafted in five weeks. Now, twenty years later, it had expanded greatly and took up quite a bit of space. I thought, How much longer is it going to lie in this box? I'll take five or six months and prepare it for publication. Truth to tell, even though I have a special fondness for this book, with its stories of most of the writers from Moses' time to our own and how their books were written, and I am constantly adding to it tidbits that I come across, I also have a certain interest in readying this book for publication. I am an old man, and my house is near the frontier, and if, God forbid, there should be a war and I have to flee, I shall not have the strength to carry with me a big box full of notes. So I set aside time and began the work of editing the book, in order to get it published and thereby relieve myself of the responsibility of keeping it. And since the book began with the Torah, I planned to add to it some of the things with which I had of late been so fully taken up.

One thing leads to another, and before long these things turned into a whole separate book. That is how *You Yourselves Saw*, with its four parts, came into being. I did not include in this book all the things I had written down. There were many good and precious things I had to leave out. To have included them as they were would have been impossible, because they were too deep. Yet I was not able to explain them in such a fashion that anyone could read them easily.

"After these faithful deeds" [2 Chron. 32:1], I think I can say that this book reflects, not merely a selection of what I like, but what the years have yielded for me. Books I have read ever since childhood have stood me in good stead in the preparation of this work. And it is not I who have made the choice but the years themselves. At the same time, whoever is interested can easily go beyond the sources I have read and cited here. There are many great and worthy commentaries, early as well as late, that I did not have the good fortune to see, including some I have probably not even heard of. As we learn in *Shnei Luḥot Habrit* [*The Two Tablets of the Covenant*], the Torah has 600,000 interpretations, corresponding to the 600,000 souls [of the Israelites who stood at Sinai], each of whom received one interpretation as his portion. With the little strength at my disposal I have assembled, in the four parts of this book, a tiny bit of four thousand books. May we each find, in the books we write, the very interpretations our souls received as their portion.

Throughout my work I kept in mind the injunction of the *Guide of the*

*Jerusalem, 1938; dedicated to Salman Schocken on his sixtieth birthday; printed in 120 copies at Ha'arez Press, Tel Aviv.—S.Y.A. Reissued Jerusalem and Tel Aviv, 1978.— *Translator*

Perplexed (Part 2, chapter 34, as translated by Rabbi Yehudah Alharizi) that it is not proper to break through the bounds and say too much about the secrets of Mount Sinai . . . for this is among the hidden aspects of the Torah.

In the midrash *Meor Ha'afelah* [*Illumination of the Darkness*], it says, "Like the awakening at Mount Sinai, so shall be the awakening of the Messianic age." May it be God's will that we merit seeing the latter speedily and soon, amen.

Shmuel Yosef Agnon,
son of Rabbi Shalom Mordekhai Halevi,
may the memory of the righteous
be a blessing

Jerusalem, may it be rebuilt and re-established;
Friday, the eve of the Sabbath of the portion
in which we read "that I may remain alive thanks to you"
[Lekh-Lekha], 5718 [1957].

Those who love Your teaching enjoy well-being; they encounter no
    adversity.
O how I love Your teaching! It is my study all day long.
I will speak of Your decrees, and not be ashamed in the presence of
    kings.
I will keep Your laws; do not utterly forsake me.
Were not Your teaching my delight I would have perished in my
    affliction.
May Your mercy reach me, that I might live, for Your teaching is my
    delight.
I will always obey Your teaching, forever and ever.
Sustain me that I may be saved, and I will always muse upon Your
    laws.
Show favor to Your servant, and teach me Your laws.
I am Your servant; give me understanding, that I might know Your
    decrees.
Open my eyes, that I may perceive the wonders of Your teaching.
Your word is a lamp to my feet, a light for my path.
I will delight in Your commandments, which I love.
Though my life is always in danger, I do not neglect Your teaching.
Give me understanding that I may observe Your teaching and keep it
    wholeheartedly.
I will never neglect Your precepts, for You have preserved my life
    through them.

May Your steadfast love reach me, O Lord, Your deliverance, as You
  have promised.
May I wholeheartedly follow Your laws so that I do not come to
  grief.
Your steadfast love, O Lord, fills the earth; teach me Your laws.
This is my comfort in my affliction, that Your promise has preserved
  me.
You, O Lord, are near, and all Your commandments are true.*

---

*Following the ancient Jewish tradition of the acrostic, these twenty-one verses from
Psalm 119 have been arranged by the author so that their first letters (in Hebrew) spell:
Shmuel Yosef Agnon Halevi (the Levite), Hazak (may he be strong).—*Translator*

BEFORE CREATION

IN THE BEGINNING GOD CREATED

In His love for us and in faithfulness to the oath He had sworn to our ancestors, the Lord singled us out from among the nations and gave us His Torah, with which He had created His world and which had been His tool, as our teachers, may their memory be a blessing, expounded in Genesis Rabbah:

Rabbi Oshaya began his discourse with the words, "[When He fixed the foundations of the earth, wisdom] was with Him as a confidant *(amun)*" (Prov. 8:30). The Torah declares, "I was the tool *(kli omanuto)* of the Holy One, blessed be He." It is common practice that when a human king builds a palace he does it, not according to his own conception, but according to that of an architect. The architect, in turn, does not work off the top of his head but uses plans and diagrams to figure out where to put the rooms and the doorways. Thus did the Holy One, blessed be He, consult the Torah when creating the world. And when the Torah says, "In the beginning *(bereshit)* God created" (Gen. 1:1), it means "with me, to begin with *(bi reshit)*, God created," for *reshit* always refers to the Torah itself, as in the verse, "The Lord created [wisdom] as the beginning *(reshit)* of His course" (Prov. 8:22). —GENESIS RABBAH [1:4]

Rabbi Berakhyah said: The entire world was created solely for the sake of Israel, . . . which is called the first of His fruits *(reshit tevuato)*, as in the verse "Israel was holy to the Lord, the first fruits of His harvest *(reshit tevuato)*" (Jer. 2:3); and for the sake of the Torah, as in the verse "The Lord founded the earth by wisdom" (Prov. 3:19) and the verse "The beginning *(reshit)* of wisdom is the fear of the Lord" (Ps. 111:10); and for the sake of Moses, as in the verse "He saw the best choice *(reshit)* for himself, [for there was the portion of an honored leader]" (Deut. 33:21). —[LEVITICUS RABBAH 36:4]

Rabbi Shim'on ben Lakish said: Why in the description of the Creation does it say "a first day," "a second day," "a third day," "a fourth day," "a fifth day," and then "*the* sixth day"? Why the extra "the"? It comes to teach us that the Holy One, blessed be He, stipulated with the works of Creation, saying, "If Israel accepts the Torah [with its five books* you shall survive], but if not, I shall return you to chaos." —TANHUMA on Genesis; SHABBAT 88a

The Sages taught: For 974 generations before He created the world, the Holy One, blessed be He, sat and studied and researched and refined and checked every last word of the Torah 248 times, corresponding to the 248 parts of the human body, before setting them all in place in His Torah, . . . as scripture says, "The words of the Lord are pure words, silver purged in an earthen crucible, refined sevenfold" (Ps. 12:7). It was only then that a word could be set in place in His Torah. And if it had been even slightly out of place, it might have brought about the destruction of the whole world. —SEDER ELIYAHU ZUTA 10

Rabbi Eli'ezer ben Horkanos began his discourse with the words, "Who can tell the mighty acts of the Lord, proclaim all His praises?" (Ps. 106:2). Is there indeed anyone living who can give expression to the might of the Holy One, blessed be He, or praise Him adequately? Even the ministering angels cannot do so. But we can at least recount some small part of His mighty deeds, of what He has done and what He will do, so that the name of the Holy One, blessed be He, may be exalted among the creatures He made, from one end of the world to the other, as in the verse "One generation shall laud Your works to another" (Ps. 145:4).

Until the world was created there was only the Holy One, blessed be He, and His great Name. Whenever He thought about creating the world, He would draft a design for it, but it never seemed workable. To what may this be compared? To a king who wants to build himself a palace. He does not begin to build until he has drawn on the ground the outline of its foundations, its entrances and exits. Thus did the Holy One, blessed be He, design the world, but it was not workable until He created repentance.

Seven things were created before the world. What were they? The

*The definite article is indicated in Hebrew by the letter ה, which has the numerical value of 5.

Torah, hell, paradise, the Throne of Glory, the Temple, repentance, and the Messiah's name.

How do we know about the Torah? Because it is written, "The Lord created [wisdom] as the beginning of His course, as the first of His works of old" (Prov. 8:22). Why "first"? Because it preceded even the creation of the world.

How do we know about hell? Because it is written, "The Tophet* has long been ready for him" (Isa. 30:33). What is "long"? Before the world was created.

How do we know about paradise? Because it is written, "The Lord God planted a garden in Eden, in the east *(mikedem)*" (Gen. 2:8). That is, *mikodem* (before), before the world was created.

How do we know about the Throne of Glory? Because it is written, "Your throne stands firm from of old" (Ps. 93:2). What is "of old"? Before the world was created.

How do we know about the Holy Temple? Because it is written, "O Throne of Glory exalted from of old" (Jer. 17:12). What is "from of old"? Before the world was created.

How do we know about repentance *(teshuvah)?* Because it is written, "Before the mountains came into being, . . . You return *(tashev)* man to dust; [You decreed, 'Return *(shuvu),* you mortals!']" (Ps. 90:2–3). What is "Before"? Before the world was created.

How do we know about the name of the Messiah? Because it is written, "His name precedes the sun" (Ps. 72:17). And elsewhere in scripture it is written, "And you, O Bethlehem of Efrath,† least among the clans of Judah, from you shall come forth to rule Israel for Me—one whose origin is from of old" (Mic. 5:1). What is "of old"? Before the world was created.

Thereupon the Holy One, blessed be He, consulted the Torah, whose name is wisdom *(tushiah),* as to the creation of the world. It answered Him, saying, "Sovereign of the Universe, if a king has no army and no camp, of what is he king? And if a king has no people to praise him, what majesty does he have?" The Lord of the World heard these words and was pleased by them. Said the Torah, "The Holy One, blessed be He, has consulted me as to the creation of the world, as it is written, 'Mine are counsel and wisdom *(tushiah)' "* (Prov. 8:14). —PIRKEI RABBI ELI'EZER 3

---

*In biblical times, a place of human sacrifice by fire, identified with Gehinnom (hell). (See 2 Kings 23:10.)

†The line of David, hence of the Messiah.

It is said that while the Torah and the Throne of Glory were created [before the world itself], the other things were merely contemplated. . . . But that still leaves the question of which came first, the Torah or the Throne of Glory. Said Rabbi Abba bar Kahana: The Torah preceded the Throne of Glory, as it is written, "The Lord created [wisdom] as the beginning of His course, as the first of His works *(kedem mif'alav)* of old *(me'az)*" (Prov. 8:22), that is, before *(kodem)* that of which scripture says, "Your throne stands firm from of old *(me'az)*" (Ps. 93:2). —YALKUT YIRMIYAH 298; GENESIS RABBAH I

And thus did Rashi, may his memory be a blessing, write in his hymns: "Then, before [the heavens] were stretched out, . . . seven things [were created] . . . : the Law and the Throne and the spiritual healing of wayward sons"— *first the Law, which means the Torah, then the Throne of Glory.*

You will find it is God's way to give precedence in time to that which is dearer to Him. Being dearest of all, the Torah was created first, as it is written, "The Lord created me as the beginning of His course, as the first of His works of old" (Prov. 8:22). And scripture continues, "In the distant past I was fashioned, at the beginning, at the origin of the earth" (Prov. 8:23). —SIFREI, 'Ekev

THE BEGINNING OF HIS COURSE

"The Lord created me as the beginning of His course, as the first of His works of old" (Prov. 8:22). This verse refers to the Torah as a whole, which was the beginning of God's way. For the Torah was created two thousand years before the world itself. So said Rabbi El'azar: "Seven things were created before the world. What were they? The Torah, hell, paradise, the Throne of Glory, the Temple, the Messiah's name, and repentance" (Nedarim 39b; Pesaḥim 54a). He used the Torah to create the world, as it is written, "The Lord made me as the beginning of His way. . . . " This is what is meant by the first words of the Torah: "*With* the beginning God created." Said Rabbi Yehudah: See how different the Torah is from the world, for the world was created in only six days, but the Torah took forty days and forty nights. —MIDRASH HANE'ELAM

THE TOOL OF THE HOLY ONE

When the Holy One, blessed be He, decided to create the world, He looked at the Torah, at each and every word, and fashioned the world accordingly. For all the words and deeds of all the worlds are contained in the Torah, and so the Holy One, blessed be He, looked at it when creating the world. It is not that the Torah itself created the world, but that God, looking at the Torah, created it. . . .

This is how the Holy One, blessed be He, consulted the Torah: It is written, "In the beginning God created the heavens and the earth." Looking at this word [i.e., heavens], God created the heavens. In the Torah it is written, "God said, 'Let there be light.' " He looked at this word and created light. And so it went, with each and every word in the Torah: the Holy One, blessed be He, looked at the word and created the thing to which it referred. . . .

Once the world was created, it could not have been sustained had it not occurred to the Divine Will to create human beings, who would engage in the study of Torah, for the sake of which the world would be sustained. Now, those who delve into the Torah and engage in its study are as if they sustained the whole world. Just as the Holy One, blessed be He, looked into the Torah and created the world, human beings look into it and sustain the world. The entire world is thus both made and sustained by the Torah. Therefore, happy are they who engage in the study of Torah, for they are upholding the world.
—ZOHAR, Exodus 161a–b

Why did the Holy One, blessed be He, use the Torah to create the world? It is unthinkable that He *needed* the holy Torah to create the world. Rather, He wished to demonstrate to the world the Torah's greatness and the importance of fulfilling it; for whole worlds could be created with it, just as He Himself, may His Name be blessed, had done. —HASHAVAH LETOVAH, citing Rabbi Hanokh Hakohen of Alexander

WHO PRESSED FORWARD BEFORE THEIR TIME

"[Wicked men] who pressed forward before their time" (Job 22:16). Rabbi Shim'on the Pious taught: These are the 974 generations that pressed forward to be born before the world was created. The Holy One, blessed be He, arose and planted them in [subsequent] generations, and it is they who are the insolent ones of each generation. —HAGIGAH 13b

During the two thousand years by which the Torah preceded the world, these [974] generations were originally to have been created, as we learn from the verse, "the promise He gave to the thousandth generation" (Ps. 105:8).* But the Holy One, blessed be He, foresaw that the world could not endure so long without the Torah, and so He postponed the creation of these generations, incorporating them into the twenty-six that followed creation [up until the time the Torah was revealed]. The thousand generations referred to in the psalm were thus reduced by 974. —RASHI on Shabbat 88b

During the twenty-six generations that the world was without the Torah, the Holy One, blessed be He, sustained it with His kindness and benevolence, saving the Torah for a people who would be worthy of it. This we learn from Tractate Pesaḥim (118a): "Said Rabbi Yehoshu'a ben Levi: To what do the twenty-six repetitions of the refrain 'His steadfast love is eternal' [in Ps. 136] correspond? To the twenty-six generations that the Holy One, blessed be He, brought into the world before giving the Torah. These He sustained by freely bestowing His lovingkindness upon them." What then to do with the verse, "The promise He gave to the thousandth generation" (Ps. 105:8), which indicates that the Torah was given to the thousandth generation [and not the twenty-sixth]? This apparent contradiction the Sages resolved by maintaining that the Torah was kept hidden for the length of 974 generations before the creation of the world. —MENORAT HAMA'OR 3

AND WHY WAS THE TORAH NOT GIVEN AT THE BEGINNING OF THE CREATION?

And why was the Torah not given at the beginning of the Creation, when the Holy One, blessed be He, made all things and established their order? After all, the Torah is itself the order of all created things, and there is nothing random. The answer is that only Israel was fit to receive this Torah, and the people of Israel had not yet come into being.

If it was Israel alone that would be fit to receive the Torah, why then did Israel not come into being at the time of the Creation? This question, too, can easily be answered: it was not fitting that the Patriarchs, or indeed the people

*The verse implies that one thousand generations passed between the creation of the Torah and its revelation. According to scripture, twenty-six of these generations came after the creation of the world.

[Israel] itself, be created at the beginning but rather at the end of the process of creation, after all the other peoples had come into being. This is in the nature of things, for the human being, the highest of the animals, the one for whom all the others were created, was created last. And you cannot find a single case of a people created after Israel; all preceded it. Even Edom and Ishmael, even Ammon and Moab were already great nations before Israel became a people, as if this were built into the natural order. For that which represents the acme of all things ought to come as the completion of them. Just as human beings, the pinnacle of creation, came last, so too did Israel, the pinnacle of humankind, come last. That is what is meant by the saying, "You are called human, but those who deny the Divine Name are not called human" (Yevamot 61a). All things being in their proper order, it is thus obvious why Israel was not created at the beginning of the creation of the world.

One might well ask, however, why, if the Torah deserved to be given only to the seed of Abraham, it was not given to Abraham himself, who did, after all, receive the commandment concerning circumcision, or to Jacob, who received the commandment concerning the sinew of the thigh. But the Torah, which is God's eternal, unchanging plan, could only be given to someone who was himself unchanging. An individual is prone to change, unlike a people, whose name is fixed forever. It is for this reason that the Torah was given to Israel only after they came out of Egypt and became a people called by this name, a name with which they would be stamped to the end of time. Then the Torah, being eternal and changeless, was suited to them, whereas they could not have been given it as long as they were merely a collection of individuals. He did give the commandment of circumcision to Abraham and that of the thigh sinew to Jacob, but only because these commandments applied specifically to them as individuals and because they needed them; but He did not give the Patriarchs the rest of the Torah, because as individuals they were changeable. When Abraham died there would be no more Abraham, and the same for Isaac and Jacob, but the Torah, being God's eternal plan, is only for one who does not change, who bears forever the name of the collectivity. The name of a people could not yet be applied to Abraham, Isaac, and Jacob. Only when Israel came out of Egypt did they become a people. They were then sixty times ten thousand in number, and [as was explained in the book *Gevurat Hashem*] the number sixty connotes wholeness.* A part may change, but not the whole. Thus the Torah, which is eternal and unchanging, was only given when an unchanging recipient came along. —Maharal of Prague, TIF'ERET YISRA'EL 17

---

*Space being fully defined by six directions: up, down, right, left, forward, and back.

HE RESERVES WISDOM FOR THE UPRIGHT

Rabbi Yoḥanan said, quoting Rabbi Yose the Galileean: The Holy One, blessed be He, skipped over 974 generations in order to give the Torah to the Wilderness Generation, because they were upright, as scripture says, "He reserves wisdom for the upright" (Prov. 2:7). —TANḤUMA, Lekh Lekha

"Happy are those whose way is blameless, who follow the teaching *(Torah)* of the Lord" (Ps. 119:1). This refers to the Wilderness Generation. Said Ḥizkiyahu bar Ḥiyya: The Holy One, blessed be He, foresaw that no generation after the Flood would be as receptive to the Torah as this generation would, so He put it aside for them, as we learn from the verse, "He reserves wisdom for the upright."

Said Rabbi Berakhyah, in the name of Rabbi Ḥanina bar Abahu: Both scripture and the Holy One, blessed be He, have praise for this one generation, as we learn from the verse, "He is ever mindful of His covenant, the promise He gave to the thousandth generation" (Ps. 105:8). . . . You can be sure they obeyed unquestioningly: when they got to the sea and He told them to go in, they did; and [when He told them to set off] into the wilderness, they did. When He told them to accept the Torah, they did; and even before He told them to accept it they said, "All that the Lord has said, we shall do and obey" (Ex. 24:7). . . .

Another comment on the verse, "Happy are those whose way is blameless": the Wilderness Generation were a devoted lot *(hasidim)*. So said Rabbi Eli'ezer: [It is they to whom the following verse refers:] "Bring in My devotees *(hasidai)*, [who made a covenant with Me over sacrifice]" (Ps. 50:5) . . . [because] they accepted the Torah unquestioningly. . . . Indeed, they accepted [the commandments] without asking what the reward would be for fulfilling them. That is why scripture says, "Happy are those whose way is blameless." —MIDRASH ON PSALMS

"He stood and measured the earth" (Hab. 3:6). Said Rabbi Shim'on bar Yoḥai: The Holy One, blessed be He, took the measure of all the peoples and did not find any worthy of receiving the Torah except Israel. He took the measure of all the generations and found none worthy of receiving the Torah but the Wilderness Generation. He took the measure of all the mountains and did not find any worthy of having the Divine Presence rest upon it but Mount Moriah. He took the measure of all the cities and did not find any worthy of having the Temple built in it but Jerusalem. He took the measure of all the mountains and did not find any on which the Torah could be given but Mount Sinai. He took the measure of all the lands and did not find any worthy to be given to Israel but the Land of Israel, as we learn from the verse, "He stood and measured the earth; He glanced and made the nations tremble." —YALKUT SHIM'ONI

"He took the measure of all the generations and did not find any worthy of receiving the Torah but the Wilderness Generation" (Leviticus Rabbah 13). Said the Ari,* may his memory be a blessing: The soul of that whole generation was derived from Knowledge,† on the level of Moses our Master, may he rest in peace; and that is an exalted level. That is why the Wilderness Generation is called a Generation of Knowledge, and that is why they were worthy of receiving the Torah, which is Knowledge.

The Ari, may his memory be a blessing, said further: The soul [of humanity] had been refined and purified by the [experience of] the generations of the Flood, Babel, Sodom, and Egypt. "Israel encamped there [in front of the mountain]" (Ex. 19:2)—refined and pure. And there, at Sinai, they were disciplined and chastened again and again. Thus, He could not have found a generation worthier than the Wilderness Generation to receive the Torah. —PENEI DAVID, Yitro

Why was [the Torah] given in the wilderness? To teach you that, if you do not set yourself free, like the wilderness, [of all worldly bonds], you do not deserve the Torah. And just as the wilderness is without end, so is Torah without end, as it is written, "Its measure is longer than the earth and broader than the sea" (Job 11:9). And just as Torah is endless, so is its reward, as it is written, "How abundant is the good that You have in store for those who fear you" (Ps. 31:20). —PESIKTA DE-RAV KAHANA, Bahodesh Hashelishi

Who is she that comes up from the wilderness, leaning upon her beloved? Under the apple tree I roused you; it was there your mother conceived you, there she who bore you conceived you. Let me be a seal upon your heart, like the seal upon your hand. For love is strong as death, jealousy is mighty as She'ol. Its darts are darts of fire, a blazing flame. Many waters cannot quench love, nor rivers drown it. If a man offered all his wealth for love, he would be laughed to scorn. —SONG 8:5–7

*Lit., "lion." An acronym for Ha-elohi Rabbi Yizhak (the divine Rabbi Yizhak), the name by which the great Safed mystic Yizhak Luria (1534–72) is known.
†Da'at, one of the ten Sefirot (Divine emanations or manifestations), which form a central doctrine in Kabbalah.

"Who is she that comes up *('olah)* from the wilderness . . . ?" This verse refers to Israel coming up from the wilderness to the land of Canaan, as scripture says: "[Who is she that comes up from the wilderness like columns of smoke,] in clouds of myrrh and frankincense?" (Song 3:6)—this is the fragrance that rested upon [Israel] at the time of the giving of the Torah. And as for the "columns of smoke" *(timrot 'ashan),* this corresponds to what is described in the verse, "[Already wickedness has blazed forth like the fire, devouring thorn and thistle. It has kindled the thickets of the wood,] which have turned into billowing smoke *('ashan)*" (Isa. 9:17). And the Sages use the phrase *metamer ve'oleh** to mean "it rises straight up," as in the case of a burnt offering *('olah).* —RABBI YOSEF KIMḤI

"Who is she that comes up from the wilderness, leaning upon her beloved?" The Holy One, blessed be He, and His court say of the assembly of Israel: "Who is she?"—How esteemed must that one be to have been raised up out of the wilderness by all manner of precious gifts, to have been raised up by the gift of the Torah and the company of the Divine Presence. The love she enjoys is evident. And being still in exile, she is "leaning on her beloved"—that is, she snuggles up against Him. . . .

"Under the apple tree I roused you." Thus does she say when seeking the affections of her beloved: "Under the apple tree I roused you." Remember that at the foot of Mount Sinai, which arched over [Israel] like an apple tree, "I roused you." This language evokes the affections of a young wife, who rouses her beloved at night, when they are asleep in bed, embracing and kissing him. . . .

"Let me be a seal"—because of that love, seal me upon Your heart, so that You do not forget me; and You will see that "love is strong as death"—my love for You outweighs my [fear of] death, for I am prepared to die for You.

"Jealousy is mighty as She'ol"—that is the resentment the other nations vent against me on account of You. . . .

"Many waters cannot quench love." "Many waters" refers to the nations. "Rivers" refers to their kings and princes. "Drown it"—by force or intimidation or even seduction.

"If a man offered all his wealth" to persuade You to betray Your love, "he would be laughed to scorn."

In all these ways do the Holy One, blessed be He, and His court testify that the assembly of Israel "[leans] on her beloved." —RASHI

*Cf. Yoma 28b.

"Who is she that comes up from the wilderness?" "[S]he" *(zot)* is the Torah, of which scripture says, "And this *(ve-zot)* is the Torah" (Deut. 4:44).

"Comes up from the wilderness"—the Torah was given in the wilderness, as scripture says, "and from Midbar [lit., the wilderness] to Mattanah [lit., a gift]" (Num. 21:18).

"Leaning upon her beloved"—the Torah clings and holds fast to those who cherish it and study it. —SIAḤ SEFUNIM

"He found him in a wilderness region" (Deut. 32:10)—this refers to Israel, as scripture says, "I found Israel as grapes in the wilderness" (Hos. 9:10).

"And in an empty, howling waste" (Deut. 32:10)—in a place of trouble, a place of marauding bands, a place of robbers.

"He engirded him *(yesovevenhu)*" (Deut. 32:10)—at Mount Sinai, as scripture says, "You shall set bounds to the people round about *(saviv)*" (Exod. 19:12).

"He instructed him" (Deut. 32:10)—in the Ten Commandments. This teaches us that a commandment would issue forth from the mouth of the Holy One, blessed be He, and Israel would look at it and know how many interpretations and laws, arguments *a fortiori* and arguments from analogy it contained.

"Guarded him as the apple of His eye" (Deut. 32:10). Though each time He spoke they shrank back twelve miles,* they would return, undeterred by the sound of the thunder and lightning. —SIFREI, Ha'azinu

"Who is she that comes up out of the wilderness . . . ?" (Song 3:6). Was it in fact out of the wilderness that they came up or out of Egypt? The point is the praise Israel gave the Holy One, blessed be He, for taking notice of them in the wilderness and providing them with all good things, as scripture says, "He found them in a desert region" (Deut. 32:10). —Avigdor Kohen-Zedek, COMMENTARY ON THE SONG OF SONGS

THIS IS THE BOOK OF ADAM'S LINE

Said Rabbi Yehudah ben Rabbi Simon: The first man was worthy of being the giver of the Torah. Why? [Because it is written,] "This is the book of Adam's line" (Gen. 5:1). Said the Holy One, blessed be He: "He is the work of My hands; shall I not give it to him?" But then the Holy One, blessed be He, had

---

*The mile *(mil)* referred to here was 2,000 cubits or about 3,000 feet in length. Hence, in modern terms the distance would be about seven miles. Tradition has it that the camp of Israel at Sinai was twelve "miles" across.

second thoughts and said: "I have given him six commandments, and he has not upheld them; how then can I give him 613, 248 positive and 365 negative?" [Hence it is written,] "He said *la-adam**" (Job 28:28)—"Not to Adam shall I give them but to his offspring," as it is written, "This is the book of Adam's line." —GENESIS RABBAH 24

He went first to the children of Esau. He said to them, "Will you accept the Torah?" They replied, "Master of the Universe, what is written in it?" He said to them, "You shall not murder." They said to Him, "Our father promised us our very existence would depend upon the sword"—as it is written, "By your sword you shall live" (Gen. 27:40)—"so we cannot accept the Torah."

Then He went to the children of Ammon and Moab. He said to them, "Will you accept the Torah?" They replied, "Master of the Universe, what is written in it?" He said, "You shall not commit adultery." They said to Him, "Our very existence derives from adultery"—that is what is implied by the verse, "Thus the two daughters of Lot came to be with child by their father" (Gen. 19:36)—"so we cannot accept the Torah."

Then He went to the children of Ishmael. He said to them, "Will you accept the Torah?" They replied, "Master of the Universe, what is written in it?" He said, "You shall not steal." They said to Him, "Our very existence derives from theft and robbery"—that is what is implied by the verse, "He shall be a wild ass of a man; his hand against everyone, and everyone's hand against him" (Gen. 16:12)—"so we cannot accept the Torah."

Then He came to Israel. They said, "We shall do, and we shall hear" (Exod. 24:7). This is what is implied in the verse, "The Lord came from Sinai; He shone upon them from Seir; He appeared from Mount Paran, and approached from Rivevot-kodesh, lightning flashing at them from His right" (Deut. 33:2).

Said Israel to the Holy One, blessed be He, "Master of the Universe, 'Hurry away, my beloved, swift as a gazelle or a young stag, to the hills of spices!' (Song 8:14). 'Hurry away, my beloved'—hurry away from the foul smell and come to the fragrance of the 'hills of spices.'

" 'With *('alei)* a ten-stringed harp *('asor)'* (Ps. 92:4)—it is incumbent upon us *('aleinu)* to accept the commandments, including the Ten *('aseret)* Commandments. 'And with *('alei)* a psaltery *(navel)'* (Ps. 92:4)—we shall have *('aleinu)* to endure humiliation *(lehitnabel)* because of it *('aleha)* in times of religious persecution."

*"To the man" or "to Adam" but here read *lo adam,* "not Adam."

Rabbi Shim'on ben Levi said [they accepted it] gladly; the other sages said: not against their will. And when the Holy One, blessed be He, saw that it was Israel's intention to ask for the Torah in love and affection, in awe and fear, trembling and quaking, He began with the words, "I am the Lord, *your* God" (Exod. 20:2). —PESIKTA RABBATI, 'Aseret Hadibrot

THE EARTH TREMBLED

"When He stands, He makes the earth shake; when He glances, He makes nations tremble" (Hab. 3:6). Rabbi Shim'on ben El'azar said: If the children of Noah could not abide by the seven commandments they accepted, how much less likely would they have been to obey all the commandments in the Torah. It is like a king who appoints two custodians, one for a storehouse full of straw and one for a storehouse full of silver and gold. When the straw disappears the one appointed over it is suspected; yet he not only disclaims responsibility but protests at not having been appointed to look after the silver and gold instead. The one appointed over the silver and gold says to him, "Worthless man! Seeing how readily you have disclaimed responsibility for the straw, think how much more readily you would have done so with the silver and gold." It is a matter of *a fortiori* reasoning: if the children of Noah could not abide by the seven commandments they were given, how much less would they have been able to abide by all the other commandments in the Torah. —MEKHILTA

Rabbi Yose said: "When You came forth from Seir, advanced from the country of Edom, the earth trembled" (Judg. 5:4)—When the Holy One, blessed be He, came back from Seir [Edom], they having refused the Torah, "the earth trembled, etc." Why did it tremble? Because it was on the point of reverting to chaos. For the Holy One, blessed be He, had stipulated with the world that if the Israelites accepted the Torah, it would be all well and good, but if not He would return the world to chaos. When the earth saw that the Holy One, blessed be He, had summoned each of the peoples and asked them to accept the Torah, and that none had accepted it, leaving Israel as one last possibility, the earth assumed that Israel, too, would refuse, and so it trembled. But as soon as the Israelites said, "We shall do, and we shall hear," the earth calmed down. That is the meaning of the verse, "The earth was affrighted, then became quiet" (Ps. 76:9): at first it was afraid, but then it calmed down. —ZOHAR, Numbers 193a

Rabbi Ḥiyya began his exposition with the verse, "When You came forth from Seir, advanced from the country of Edom, the earth trembled; the heavens dripped" (Judg. 5:4). Consider this: Israel is deemed worthy both in this world and for the world to come, for the Holy One, blessed be He, desires them, and they cleave to Him. Thus they are called holy, a holy people, and so on, until they are elevated to the point known as "consecration" (kodesh), for it is written, "Israel was consecrated (kodesh) to the Lord, the first fruits of His harvest" (Jer. 2:3). This is as we have explained: from their eighth day [the day of circumcision] on, Jews cleave to Him and to His Name, are marked with His Name, and belong to Him, as you can see from the verse, "Who is like Your people Israel, a unique nation on earth . . . ?" (2 Sam. 7:23). The other peoples do not cleave to Him and do not walk in His ways, and they do not bear the holy mark. On the contrary, they cleave to the powers of evil, which are not holy.

Consider further: When the Holy One, blessed be He, wanted to give the Torah to Israel, He summoned the children of Esau and said to them, "Do you want to receive the Torah?" At that moment the Holy Land flew into a rage and threatened to jump into the great abyss. She said to Him, "Lord of the World, is the Torah, which served Your pleasure for two thousand years before the world was created, now to be given to these uncircumcised ones who do not bear the seal of Your covenant?" The Holy One, blessed be He, said to her, "By My throne, a thousand such nations shall perish before they are allowed to enter into the covenant of the Torah!" This is what is meant by the verse, "When You came forth from Seir, advanced from the country of Edom, the earth trembled." Certainly it is because the Torah could not be given to anyone who had not entered into the covenant of consecration. And whoever teaches Torah to one who is uncircumcised betrays two covenants: the covenant of the Torah [made at Sinai] and the covenant of the Righteous Assembly of Israel; for the Torah was given here and nowhere else.

Rabbi Abba said: He betrays three higher entities—the Torah, the Prophets, and the Writings. We know he betrays the Torah because it is written [in the Torah], "This is the Torah that Moses set before the Israelites" (Deut. 4:44). We know he betrays the Prophets because it is written [in the Prophets], "And all your children shall be disciples of the Lord" (Isa. 54:13)—they and no one else. And it is written, "Seal the instruction (torah) with My disciples" (Isa. 8:16)—with them and no one else. We know he betrays the Writings because it is written [in the Writings], "He established a decree in Jacob, ordained a Teaching in Israel" (Ps. 78:5), and it is written, "Only the righteous shall praise

Your name" (Ps. 140:14). Who are "the righteous"? The Righteous Assembly of Israel. For one who is not circumcised and has not entered into the covenant [of Israel] will not praise His holy Name, which is the Torah.

Said Rabbi Hiyya: As soon as the Holy One, blessed be He, revealed Himself on Mount Sinai in order to give the Torah to Israel, the earth subsided and grew calm. That is what is referred to in the verse, "The earth was affrighted, then became quiet" (Ps. 76:9). —ZOHAR, Leviticus 91

GIFTS

Consider this: It is written, "When You came forth from Seir, advanced from the country of Edom, the earth trembled, etc." When the Holy One, blessed be He, sought to give the Torah to Israel, He first approached the children of Esau, but they would not accept it. This is how you must understand the verse, "The Lord came from Sinai; He shone upon them from Seir" (Deut. 33:2)—but they would not accept it. He went to the children of Ishmael, but they would not accept it, as it is written, "He appeared from Mount Paran" (Deut. 33:2). Because they were unwilling, He went back to Israel. That is what we have learned.

Now we must raise a question, for we have learned that there is no sin in examining the fine points of the Torah very carefully and asking questions to illuminate them. Our scriptural passage ["He shone upon them from Seir"] is problematical, and we must ask, When the Holy One, blessed be He, went to Seir, to what prophet did He reveal Himself? And when He went to Paran, to what prophet did He reveal Himself? If you claim He revealed Himself to the whole people, we have never found this to be the case except with Israel and through the agency of Moses. Therefore it is said that the verse ought to read, "The Lord came *to* Sinai, and shone forth *to* Seir, appearing *to* Mount Paran," for what could be meant by "*from* Seir," and "*from* Mount Paran"? This must all be clarified by further inquiry. But I have inquired, and so far I have not received an answer that puts my mind at ease.

When Rabbi Shim'on came, he asked him the same question. Rabbi Shim'on said to him: This question can be answered as follows: The Lord came from Sinai, as you find it written, "I will come to you in a thick cloud" (Exod. 19:9)—it was from Sinai that He came and revealed Himself to them. "He shone upon them from Seir" (Deut. 33:2)—hearing the refusal of the children of Seir brought Him to shine upon Israel and give them additional light and great love. In the same way He appeared from Mount Paran and gave light to Israel from there, as a result of hearing the refusal of the children of Paran; from this came the extra love and light Israel received.

As for your question about through whom He revealed Himself to them, it is a supernal secret that you must uncover yourself. The Torah came from the supernal secret sealed up in the King's head. When it reached the left arm, the Holy One, blessed be He, saw that bad blood had accumulated there. He said: "I must purify and cleanse this arm, for if I do not, this bad blood will proceed downward and harm all the rest. No, it is here that I must avert the damage." What did He do? He called Samael [the guardian angel of Esau], and when he came before Him, He said to him, "Do you want My Torah?" He replied, "What is in it?" He said, "You shall not murder." (The Holy One, blessed be He, had skipped to the particular passage He needed to make His point.) He said, "Heaven forfend! This Torah is Yours and must remain Yours. I do not want it."

Samael pleaded with Him again, saying, "Master of the Universe, if You give this to me, my whole kingdom will be undermined, for it is based on murder, and there will be no war; my kingdom, being under the sign of Mars, will simply pass out of existence. Master of the Universe, take Your Torah; I want no part of it. But if You see fit, there is a people, the children of Jacob, to whom it is suited." And he thought what he had said would work to their detriment. This is what is meant by "He shone upon them from Seir"—it was from Seir itself that the light shone upon Israel. Samael had said to himself: "If the children of Jacob accept it they will certainly disappear and never gain dominion." But the Holy One, blessed be He, replied, repeating His words several times, "You are the first-born, and it is to you that it is suited." Samael said, "Let Jacob have my birthright. It has been sold to him with my consent." "Since you want no part of it," God replied, "leave it in its entirety." "All right," said Samael.

"In that case," God said, "how would you advise Me to persuade these children of Jacob you mentioned to accept it." Said Samael, "Master of the Universe, they have to be bribed. Take some of the light of the heavenly hosts and bestow it on them; then they will accept it. Here, take mine first." And he peeled off the light that covered him and gave it to Him to give to Israel. This is what is meant by the verse, "He shone upon them from Seir"—literally from Seir, that is from Samael, as it is written, "Thus the goat *(hasa'ir)* shall bear on him" (Lev. 16:22)—that is, for him, for Israel.

Having rooted out the evil and purged His left arm of the bad blood, He turned to His right arm.* There He saw the same. He said, "This arm, too, must be purged of bad blood." He then summoned Rahab [the guardian angel of Ishmael] and said to him, "Do you want My Torah?" He said, "What is

*Identified in Kabbalah with Abraham. The "bad blood" would be Abraham's son Ishmael.

written in it?" Skipping over the rest of the [commandments], He said, " 'You shall not commit adultery.' " Rahab said to himself, "Woe is me. If the Holy One, blessed be He, bequeathes me this legacy, it will be a bad one, one that will bring down my whole domain; for I have received the blessing of water, the blessing of the fish of the sea, as it is written, 'Be fertile *(peru)* and increase [. . . and rule the fish of the sea] (Gen. 1:28), and it is written, 'I will make him fertile *(vehifreti)* and exceedingly numerous, etc.' (Gen. 17:20), and it is written, 'He shall be a wild ass *(pere)* of a man' (Gen. 16:12)" [all of which implies unlimited sexual license]." So Rahab began to plead with his Master. He said to Him, "Master of the Universe, Abraham had two sons, [not only Ishmael but also] Isaac and his sons. Give it to them; it is suited to them." "I cannot do that," God replied, "for you are the first-born, and it is fitting that you get it." Rahab pleaded with Him again, saying, "Master of the Universe, let him have my birthright; and as for this light that I inherited by virtue of the birthright, give that to him as well." And so He did. That is the meaning of the verse, "He appeared from Mount Paran" [that is, from being with Rahab/Ishmael].

Why in the case of Samael does scripture say He "shone" and in the case of Rahab only that He "appeared"? In the former case, God took the light Samael had stripped off, and He gave [it to Israel in the form of] the right to kill and wield the sword, as it is written, "[O happy Israel! Who is like you, a people delivered by the Lord,] . . . your Sword triumphant" (Deut. 33:29)— even though this right had not originally been Jacob's. But God took [only] part of the blessing of which Rahab had stripped himself, the blessing of being fruitful and multiplying. Therefore, concerning Rahab it says, "[God] *appeared* from Mount Paran" [that is, a lesser manifestation] and not "He shone."

When He had taken these gifts from the two guardian angels, He summoned all the myriad angels appointed over the other peoples, and they all answered Him the same way. He received gifts for Israel from all of them. It can be compared to a physician who had one portion of a life-giving potion and kept it to give to his son. Being a wise man, the physician said to himself, "There are wicked people in my household. If they find out that I am giving my son such a gift they will try to kill him out of spite." What did he do? He took a small amount of poison and smeared it on the rim of the vial. Summoning his servants, he said to them, "Would you who are so faithful to me like some of this potion?" They answered, "Can we try it?" They took the vial, but no sooner had they gotten a whiff of it than they thought they would die. They said to themselves, "If he gives this potion to his son, he will surely die, and we shall be our master's heirs." So they said to him, "Sire, only your son is worthy of this potion. We decline your offer of a reward for our labors. Go and induce him to accept the potion." It was thus with the Holy One, blessed be He: being a wise physician, He knew that if He gave the Torah to Israel before informing the other nations, they would persecute Israel for it relentlessly and eventually kill him. But by going to the other nations first, He got them to give Israel gifts and contributions to induce him to accept the Torah. All these, Moses received in order to pass on to Israel. That is what is meant by, "You went up to the heights, having taken captives, [having received tribute because of man]" (Ps. 68:19). Thus Israel was able to inherit the Torah without arousing any condemnation or complaint. Blessed be He, and blessed be His Name for ever and ever. —ZOHAR, Numbers 192–193

THE NATIONS AND THEIR GUARDIAN ANGELS

Because at the time of the giving of the Torah the Holy One, blessed be He, revealed Himself to the guardian angels of Esau and Ishmael, Esau and Ishmael in turn were granted a measure of holiness: they were allowed to rule over Israel. —SHNEI LUHOT HABRIT

Even though the nations had refused the Torah, the fact that the Holy One, blessed be He, sought to persuade them all to accept it enabled them to achieve holiness in some measure: a few of their number then became converts. —YALKUT DAVID

Why did the Holy One, blessed be He, invite the guardian angels of Esau and the rest of the seventy nations of the world to Mount Sinai at the time of the giving of the Torah? So that the holy souls living under the rule of the seventy nations would be able to convert. Had He not done so they would not have converted, for the Israelites would have said to them, "The Torah is a legacy handed down to us by our ancestors, and you have no part of it." —VAYELAKET YOSEF, quoting Kli Hemdah

LIKE A LILY AMONG THORNS

"Like a lily among thorns, so is my darling among the maidens" (Song 2:2). Rabbi 'Azaryah said, in the name of Rabbi Yehudah, son of Rabbi Simon: It can be likened to a king who had an orchard—with a row of fig trees, a row of grapevines, a row of pomegranate trees, and a row of apple trees—and he leased it to a tenant farmer and went on his way. Some days later, the king came back and looked into the orchard to see what had become of it, and he found it overgrown with thorns and thistles. He ordered woodsmen to come and chop it down. Then he looked at the thorns and spotted among them a single rose. He plucked it and smelled it, and his mind was put at ease. Said the king, "For the sake of this rose, let the whole orchard be saved." In the same way, the world as a whole was only created for the sake of the Torah. After twenty-six generations, the Holy One, blessed be He, looked at His world to see what had become of it, and He found it full of wickedness: the generation of Enoch was full of wickedness, the generation of the Flood was full of wickedness, and the generation of the Tower of Babel was full of wickedness. So He ordered woodsmen to come and cut it down, as it is written: "The Lord returns* to the Flood" (Ps. 29:10). And He saw a single rose, namely Israel, and He plucked it and smelled it—when He gave them the Ten Commandments. And His mind was put at rest—when they replied, "We shall do and we shall hear." Said the Holy One, blessed be He, "For the sake of this rose, let the whole orchard be saved—by the merit of the Torah and Israel shall the whole world be rescued." —LEVITICUS RABBAH 23:3; SONG OF SONGS RABBAH 2:3

HIS SPLENDOR FILLS THE EARTH

"God is coming from Teman, the Holy One from Mount Paran. His majesty covers the skies, His splendor fills the earth" (Hab. 3:3). Here the prophet is describing the great and awesome sights God showed Israel in the wilderness, sights He will show them again when they are brought back from exile but which He first showed them when He gave them the Torah. This is what is meant by "God is coming from Teman," as the Torah says, "He shone upon them from Seir" (Deut. 33:2), for Seir is Teman. Similarly, "from Mount Paran," as the Torah says, "He appeared from Mount Paran" (Deut. 33:2).

"His majesty covers the skies"—this refers to the lightning they saw illuminating heaven and earth on the day of the Giving of the Torah. "His majesty" means "His glory." "His splendor *(utehilato)*" means "His radiance," as in the verse, "when His lamp shone *(behilo)* over my head" (Job 29:3). Seir and Paran are mentioned because they are near Mount Sinai.

"It is a brilliant light" (Hab. 3:4)—this is what the Torah is referring to when it says, "The Presence of the Lord appeared . . . as a consuming fire on the top of the mountain" (Exod. 24:17). "Which gives off rays *(karnayim)* on

*Reading *yashuv* instead of *yashav*.

every side, and therein His glory is enveloped" (Hab. 3:4)—this is what we find in the verse "how radiant *(karan)* the skin of Moses' face was" (Exod. 34:35). In other words, this radiance of Moses came from God, and the dual form *karnayim* is used because the face has two sides. Others explain this as referring to the tablets He gave to Moses, which were two in number and which shone both outwardly and inwardly.

"And therein His glory is enveloped"—there, at Sinai, what had been hidden since the beginning of time was revealed, for never was there such a day either before or since, on which the blessed God, in His great glory, was revealed on Mount Sinai in the sight of all Israel. Others interpret "His glory is enveloped" as referring to the Ark, as we read, "You and Your mighty Ark" (2 Chron. 6:41), for the Ark was where the tablets were kept. —RADAK

"God is coming from Teman." By all rights You should remember to have mercy on Israel. After all, when You came from Teman to Edom, to [persuade the latter to] accept Your Torah—"the Holy One from Mount Paran"—and when You came in Your holiness from Ishmael, he too having refused the yoke of Your Torah, nonetheless "[Your] splendor [filled] the earth" when Israel accepted the Torah. "[There was] a brilliant light"—the light on Mount Sinai on the day of the Giving of the Torah was as brilliant as the light of the Seven Days of Creation—"which gives off rays on every side"—that brilliance, coming from the Holy One, blessed be He, pierced through the firmament and came down in two separate rays to illumine Mount Sinai—"and therein His glory is enveloped"—there on Mount Sinai He gave Israel the glory of the Torah, which He had kept hidden in His shadow for two thousand years.

"Pestilence marches before Him, and plague *(reshef)* comes forth at His heels" (Hab. 3:5)—harmful creatures *(benei reshef)*, angels of destruction, preceded Him, intent on destroying the world if Israel did not accept the Torah. —RABBI YOSEF KARA

GOOD INSTRUCTION

[Rabbi 'Akiva] would say: Beloved is man, for he was created in the Divine image. It is an extra measure of love that he was told he was created in the Divine image, as it is written, "For in the image of God was man created" (Gen. 9:6).

Beloved are [the people] Israel, for they are called children of the Omnipresent. And it is an extra measure of love that they were told they were to be called children of the Omnipresent, as it is written, "You are the children of the Lord your God" (Deut. 14:1).

Beloved are [the people] Israel, for they were given a precious instrument. And it is an extra measure of love that they were told they had been given a precious instrument, with which the world had been created, as it is written, "For I give you good instruction; do not forsake my teaching" (Prov. 4:2). —AVOT 3:18

Said Rabbi Ze'ira (and some say it was Rabbi Ḥanina bar Papa): Note that ordinary mortals are not like the Holy One, blessed be He. In the case of ordinary mortals, when one man sells something [he values] to another, the seller is sad and the buyer happy. But the Holy One, blessed be He, is different: He gave the Torah to Israel and rejoiced, as it is written, "For I give you good instruction; do not forsake my teaching." —BERAKHOT 5a

"The seller is sad"—because he was forced to sell and part with something that was of value to him. "And [God] rejoiced"—we learn this from the fact that the Holy One, blessed be He, warned Israel against abandoning the Torah and praised it to them as "good instruction" that they had been given. —RASHI

Rabbi Yiẓḥak began, "When the morning stars sang together and all the Divine beings shouted for joy" (Job 38:7)—Fortunate are the people Israel that the Holy One, blessed be He, gave them the holy Torah, which is a joy to all. It is also a joy to the Holy One, blessed be He, a place for Him to amble, as it is written, "I was . . . a source of delight every day" (Prov. 8:30).

The Torah as a whole is one of the names of the Holy One, blessed be He, and with the Torah He created the world, as it is written, "I was with Him as a confidant" (Prov. 8:30). Read not "confidant" *(amun)* but "craftsman" *(oman).*

And it was with the Torah that human beings were created, as it is written, "And God said, 'Let us make man'" (Gen. 1:26)—the Holy One, blessed be He, said to the Torah, "I want to create man." Said she to Him, "Some day that man will sin and anger You; and if You are not patient with him, how will he survive in this world?" He said to her, "You and I together will sustain him in this world, for it is not for nothing that I am called longsuffering." —ZOHAR, Leviticus 35b

Rabbi Simai says: From the heavens come the bodies and souls of all the creatures created from the heavens, and from the earth come the bodies and souls of all the creatures created from the earth, except for man, whose soul is from the heavens and whose body is from the earth. Thus, if man fulfills the Torah, doing the will of his Creator, he is very much like the heavenly creatures, as it is written, "I had taken you for Divine beings, sons of the Most High, all of you" (Ps. 82:6). But if he does not live by the Torah and the will of his Father in heaven, he is like all the other earthly creatures, as it is written, "You shall die as men do" (Ps. 82:7). —SIFREI, Ha'azinu

Rabbi El'azar said: Without the Torah, neither heaven nor earth could have endured, as it is written, "Were it not for My covenant day and night, I should not have instituted the laws of heaven and earth" (Jer. 33:25). —PESAHIM 68b

The people Israel are obliged to occupy themselves with the Torah. How do we know this? "Let not this Book of the Teaching cease from your lips" (Josh. 1:8). For if the Holy One, blessed be He, had not known that Israel would accept the Torah, He would not have created the world, as it is written, "Were it not for My covenant day and night, I should not have instituted the laws of heaven and earth" (Jer. 33:25). —OZAR MIDRASHIM, She'ilta on Vezot Haberakhah

"Pour out your heart like water in the presence of the Lord" (Lam. 2:19)—Just as these waters give life to all the inhabitants of the world and all His handiwork in this world, so do the words of the Torah preserve the House of Israel—may I suffer in their stead—wherever they live.

Another interpretation of "Pour out your heart like water": just as water means life for the world, so are the words of the Torah life for the world. Just as the world cannot be built up without water, cannot be developed without water, cannot persist without water, so too do heaven and earth depend for their survival on Israel and the Torah, as it is written, "Were it not for My covenant day and night, I should not have instituted the laws of heaven and earth" (Jer. 33:25). And it is written, "This is the covenant I will make with the House of Israel. . . ." (Jer. 31:32). —SEDER ELIYAHU RABBAH 18

A TIME IS APPOINTED FOR EVERYTHING

"A time is appointed for everything" (Eccles. 3:1). A time was appointed for Adam to enter the garden of Eden—"The Lord God took the man and placed him in the garden of Eden" (Gen. 2:15)—and a time was appointed for him to leave it—"He drove the man out" (Gen. 3:24). A time was appointed for Noah and his sons to enter the ark—"Go in to the ark, you and all your household" (Gen. 7:1)—and to leave it—"Come out of the ark" (Gen. 8:16). A time was appointed for circumcision to be given through Abraham—"As for you, you shall keep My covenant [. . . . Every male among you shall be circumcised]" (Gen. 17:9)—and times were appointed for his sons to be circumcised in two different places, in Egypt and in the wilderness. "And a time for everything under heaven" (Eccles. 3:1)—said Rabbi Berakhiah: There is something over heaven that is given under heaven. What is it? The Torah. When? In the third month. —PESIKTA DE-RAV KAHANA, Baḥodesh Hashelishi

"On the third new moon after the Israelites had gone forth from the land of Egypt, [on that very day, they entered the wilderness of Sinai]" (Exod. 19:1)—Why was the Torah not given as soon as they left Egypt? Did He not say to Moses, "When you have freed the people from Egypt, [you shall worship God at this mountain]" (Exod. 3:12)? Said Rabbi Yehudah bar Shalom: It is to be likened to a prince who recovered from an illness. His father said, "We will give him three months to recover fully, and then I shall take him to the rabbi's house to study Torah." In the same way, when Israel went out of Egypt, there were among them those who had been crippled by enslavement. Said the Holy One, blessed be He, "I will wait until they are healed, and then I will give them the Torah." —TANḤUMA, Yitro

The Midrash says, "Why was the Torah not given as soon as they left Egypt? It is to be likened to a prince who recovered from an illness. His father said, 'We will give him three months to recover fully, and then I shall take him to the rabbi's house to study Torah.' In the same way, when Israel went out of Egypt, there were among them those who had been disabled by enslavement. Said the Holy One, blessed be He, 'I will wait until they are healed, and then I will give them the Torah' " (Tanḥuma, Yitro; Ecclesiastes Rabbah 3).

Said Rabbi Menahem of Kotsk: Does engaging in the study of Torah not bring healing to the body, and if so, should the Torah not have been given immediately in order to help them recover? In fact, their sickness was such that they did not recognize the disablement that had been caused by their enslavement in Egypt, that place of defilement. The blessed Lord waited three months for them to come to their senses and recognize their disability. Having seen their impairment, they could then be healed by the holiness of the Torah, as it is written, "Listen, you who are deaf; you blind ones, look up and see!" (Isa. 42:18). —'AMUD HA'EMET

The Israelites ought to have been given the Torah as soon as they left Egypt; why wasn't this done immediately after the Exodus and the parting of the Reed Sea? In fact, had they received it after the parting of the sea, it would have seemed as though they had accepted the Torah because of the miracles done for them. This is why the Holy One, blessed be He, waited for them a little while. Little by little, they forgot the miracles that had been performed for them, as it is written, "And the people grumbled. . . ." (Exod. 15:24). Then they received the Torah and said, "We shall do and we shall hear." From this we learn that they received the Torah out of love. —KEDUSHAT LEVI

"More desirable than gold, than much fine gold" (Ps. 19:11)—we do not know who uttered these words, Israel or the other nations of the world. Then Solomon came and explained it: "I [Israel] delight to sit in his [God's] shade" (Song 2:3). —MIDRASH ON PSALMS

THE TORAH THE HOLY ONE, BLESSED BE HE, GAVE TO MOSES

Rabbi Pinhas said in the name of Rabbi Shim'on ben Lakish: the Torah the Holy One, blessed be He, gave to Moses was in the form of white fire inscribed on black fire—that is, fire mingled with fire, carved from fire, and given from fire. This is the meaning of the verse, "Fire flashing at them from His right" (Deut. 33:2). —PALESTINIAN TALMUD, Shekalim 6:1

"Fire *(esh dat)* flashing at them"—had law *(dat)* not been given along with it, no human being could bear up under it. —SIFREI, Vezot Haberakhah, according to the versions of Rabbenu Hillel and the Yalkut

We find that when the Holy One, blessed be He, gave the Torah, it was all fire, as it is written, "Fire flashing at them from His right." Said Resh Lakish: The Torah was made of fire. Its parchment was of fire. Its script was of fire. Its stitching was of fire, as it is written, "Fire flashing at them from His right." The face of the go-between [Moses] turned to fire, as it is written, "And they shrank from coming near him" (Exod. 34:30). The angels who came down with him were made of fire, as it is written, "He makes the winds His angels, [fiery flames His servants]" (Ps. 104:4). "The mountain was burning with fire" (Deut. 4:11, 5:20, 9:15). The Torah was given out of fire consuming fire, as it is written, "For the Lord, your God, is a consuming fire" (Deut. 4:24) and "on earth He let you see His great fire" (Deut. 4:36). And even the spoken words themselves came out of fire. When they had seen the lightning and all these fiery things, the Holy One, blessed be He, said to them, "Do not think these are numerous deities." That is why He began with "I [am the Lord . . .]; you shall have no [other gods beside Me]" (Exod. 20:2–3). —TANHUMA, Yitro

IN THE BOSOM OF THE HOLY ONE, BLESSED BE HE

Where was the Torah kept until the world was created? Rabbi Eli'ezer, the son of Rabbi Yose the Galileean, said: For 974 generations before the world was created, the Torah, which had been written down, was kept in the bosom of the Holy One, blessed be He, where it recited songs of praise together with the ministering angels, as it is written, "I was with Him as a confidant, a source of delight every day, . . . rejoicing in His inhabited world" (Prov. 8:30–31). —SIFREI, 'Ekev

We find that before the world was created there was no parchment on which to write the Torah, for the animals had not yet come into being. How then was it written? By the arm of the Holy One, blessed be He, in black fire on white fire; and the Holy One, blessed be He, took it and set it before Himself to gaze at. —MIDRASH 'ASERET HADIBROT

THE DISCIPLES OF THE LORD

Said Rabbi Yonah, the father of Rabbi Mana, quoting Rabbi Levi, who had quoted Rabbi Abba: The Torah need not have been given to Israel in this world. Why? Because in the Next World everyone will learn Torah from the mouth of the Holy One, blessed be He. Why then was it given to them in this world? So that when the Holy One, blessed be He, comes to teach them in the Next World, they will all know which passage He is speaking about. —TANHUMA, Tavo

"And all your children shall be disciples of the Lord" (Isa. 54:13). Said the Holy One, blessed be He, "In this world the people Israel learn Torah from teachers of flesh and blood. That is why they forget what they learn, for the Torah was given through Moses, who was also flesh and blood. And just as creatures of flesh and blood pass away, so too does their learning, as it is written, "You see it, then it is gone" (Prov. 23:5). But in the Time to Come Israel will learn only from the mouth of the Holy One, blessed be He, as it is written, "And all your children shall be disciples of the Lord." Similarly, scripture says, "No longer will they need to teach one another" (Jer. 31.34). And just as God is everlasting, so is His teaching: what they learn from Him they will never forget, as it is written, "The House of Jacob shall dispossess those who dispossessed them (morasheihem)" (Obad. 1:17). Now morasheihem can only refer to the Torah, as we read, "When Moses charged us with the teaching as the heritage (morashah)" (Deut. 33:4). —YALKUT SHIM'ONI, Isaiah, Remez 479

"A happy mother of children" (Ps. 113:9)—Blessed be the Omnipresent, blessed be He, who rejoices greatly over Israel forever. For just as the people Israel fulfill the Torah in this world and rejoice in it, so does the Torah itself rejoice in them in the World to Come, as it is written, "A happy mother of children (em habanim semehah)" ı henceforth to be read, "[We are] a people in whom He rejoices (am banu simhato)." —SEDER ELIYAHU RABBAH 5

THE ORDER OF THE GIVING OF THE TORAH

"No man can set a value on it" (Job 28:13)—Said Rabbi El'azar: the various sections of the Torah were not given in their proper order, for if they had been, whoever read it could create a world and bring the dead to life and perform wonders. That is why the proper order of the Torah is hidden. But it is known to the Holy One, blessed be He, as it is written, "Who like Me can read and tell and set a value on it for Me?" (Isa. 44:7). —MIDRASH ON PSALMS 3

Rabbi [Yehudah Hanasi] said: Many passages that are next to each other in the Torah are as far apart [in content] as east is from west. —SIFREI, Balak 131

Yet we reckon it to the merit of our Sages that they sorted out earlier and later passages in order to pass down to us the correct order of the text.

The Holy One, blessed be He, began by commanding Moses, "You shall set bounds for the people" (Exod. 19:12)—that he make a boundary around the mountain that the people would be forbidden to cross. That is what was meant when Moses said to the Holy One, blessed be He, "You warned us saying, 'Set bounds about the mountain and sanctify it'" (Exod. 19:23), for the boundary around the people was in fact a boundary around the mountain. Then he warned them to avoid defilement for three days and required immersion of them, as it is written, "[Moses] purified the people, and they washed their clothes (Exod. 19:14)."

And on the morning of the third day—that is, the sixth of Sivan—there was "thunder, and lightning, and a dense cloud upon the mountain, and a very loud blast of the horn" (Exod. 19:16). But the Shekhinah had not yet come down, as we find elsewhere in scripture: "There was a great and mighty wind, splitting mountains and shattering rocks by the power of the Lord; but the Lord was not in the wind. . . ." (1 Kings 19:11).

Israel was seized with trembling at the sound of the thunder, as it is written, "And all the people . . . trembled" (Exod. 19:16). Moses encouraged the people and led them out to meet God, and they lined up at the foot of the mountain. And as they stood at the foot of the mountain trembling in expectation, the blessed Lord descended in fire onto the mountain, and "the smoke of it rose" to the heart of heaven in darkness, cloud, and thick fog. The mountain itself trembled and shook. This is the same as what David described: "The earth trembled, the sky rained because of God, yon Sinai, because of God, the God of Israel" (Ps. 68:9). In other words, flame poured down from the sky because of Sinai. We find the same in the case of the Prophet Deborah, who said, "O Lord, when You came forth from Seir, advanced from the country of Edom, the earth trembled; the heavens dripped, yea, the clouds dripped water" (Judg. 5:4).

Similarly, scripture says, "Mountains skipped like rams. . . ." (Ps. 114:4). And this is not merely a metaphor, just as "the sea saw them and fled. . . ." (Ps. 114:3) is not. And so said Jeremiah, "As surely as Tabor is among the mountains and Carmel is by the sea, so shall this come to pass" (Jer. 46:18). This our Sages, may their memory be a blessing, interpreted as meaning that at the time of the Giving of the Torah these mountains were set down in the Land of Israel, Carmel having been transported across the sea.

Now you must know that the episode when "all the people witnessed the thunder . . . , and when the people saw it they fell back" (Exod. 20:15) took place before the Giving of the Torah. It was at that moment that they said to Moses, "You speak to us, and we will obey" (Exod. 20:16). For they were close to fainting away from the terror of what they were seeing and hearing and did not have the strength to listen to the voice of God Himself, for fear they would die. But Moses encouraged them, saying, "Be not afraid; for God has come only in order to test you, etc." (Exod. 20:17). The people obeyed Moses and "remained at a distance" (Exod. 20:18), keeping back from the boundary line.

Moses drew near to the thick darkness, but he did not enter it. Then God uttered the Ten Commandments.

Why were the Ten Commandments not uttered at the beginning of the Torah? [The Sages] explained this with a parable: Someone arrives in a foreign country and says to the people, "I wish to be your king." They say to him, "Have you done anything for us that would entitle you to this?" What does he do? He builds a wall for them; he provides them with water; he wages wars for them. Then when he says, "I wish to be your king," they reply, "Yes, yes!" So it was with the Omnipresent: He took Israel out of Egypt, split the sea for them, rained down manna for them, brought water forth from the well for them, flew the quail to them, made war for them against Amalek, and then when He said to them, "I wish to be your king," they answered, "Yes, yes!"

—MEKHILTA 5

IN THE THIRD MONTH

EXODUS 19:1
*In the third month after
the Israelites had gone forth from
the land of Egypt, on this very day,
they entered the wilderness of Sinai.*

"In the third month after the Israelites had gone forth from the land of Egypt"—from this we learn that the months are counted from the Exodus from Egypt.

But I might think that it was only months; what about years? This is intimated by the verse, "In the second year following the exodus from the land of Egypt" (Num. 1:1).

But I might think that it was only done at that time; what about later? This is intimated by the verse, "In the fortieth year [after the Israelites had left the land of Egypt]" (Num. 33:38).

But these instances were all before they entered the Land; what about after they entered it? This is intimated by the verse, "In the four hundred and eightieth year after the Israelites left the land of Egypt" (1 Kings 6:1).

But all these instances were before the Temple was built; how do we know that a new era begins with its construction? This is intimated by the verse, "At the end of twenty years from the time Solomon constructed the House of the Lord" (2 Chron. 8:1).

And if, [acknowledging their sin and punishment,] they did not want to count from the building of the Temple, they could count from its destruction, as it is written, "In the twenty-fifth year of our exile, [the fourteenth year] after the city had fallen" (Ezek. 40:1).

And if they did not want to count using their own [landmark events], they could count using others', as it is written, "In the second year of the reign of Nebuchadnezzar, Nebuchadnezzar had a dream" (Dan. 2:1); and it is written, "In the second year of King Darius" (Hag. 1:1); and it is written, "If you

do not know, O fairest of women, [go follow the tracks of the sheep]*" (Song
1:8); and it is written, "Because you would not serve the Lord your God
. . . you shall have to serve your enemies" (Deut. 28:47–48). —MEKHILTA

"In the third month"—Why in the third and not in the second or the seventh
or any other month? Our Sages explained that Rabbi Oshaya said: Rabbi Ḥiyya
the Great taught me as follows. A female convert who has been taken captive
and then freed is not to be married or even engaged until three months have
elapsed. [The people] Israel, too, are called converts (gerim), as it is written, "For
you were strangers (gerim) in the land of Egypt" (Lev. 19:34); and captives
(shevuyim), as it is written, "They shall be captors (shovim) of their captors" (Isa.
14:2); and freedmen, as it is written, "I the Lord am your God who brought
you out from the land of the Egyptians to be their slaves no more" (Lev. 26:13).
Said the Holy One, blessed be He: I shall allow them three months and then
give them the Torah. —TANHUMA HAYASHAN, Yitro

"Like an apple tree among trees of the forest, so is my beloved among the
youths" (Song 2:3). Rav Huna and Rav Aḥa said in the name of Rabbi Yose
ben Zimra: Why an apple tree? Everyone avoids them during the sirocco.
Why? Because they give no shade under which to sit. Similarly, all the nations
of the world fled from sitting in the shade of the Holy One, blessed be He, on
the day of the Giving of the Torah. And what about Israel? The answer is to
be found in the verse, "I delight to sit in his shade" (Song 2:3)—I delighted in
Him, and so I sat down; I am the one who delighted in Him, and not the other
nations.
    Rav Aḥa, son of Rabbi Ze'ira, said two things. The first thing he said was:
The apple tree blossoms before it produces leaves. The people Israel are like
this: in Egypt they believed even before they heard, which is what is meant by
the verse, "The people were convinced, and when they heard that the Lord had
taken note, etc." (Exod. 4:31). Rav Aḥa, son of Rabbi Ze'ira, also said: Just as
the apple tree blossoms before it produces leaves, so too did Israel in Sinai
express willingness to act even before they heard what action was to be taken,
as it is written, "We shall do, and we shall hear" (Exod. 24:7).
    Rabbi 'Azaryah said two things: Just as the apple tree's fruit does not ripen
until the month of Sivan, Israel did not give off a fragrance† until Sivan [when

*Interpreted to mean, "follow the gentiles."
†I.e., only then did they begin to give the Lord special pleasure.

they accepted the Torah]. Rabbi 'Azaryah also said: Just as it takes fifty days from the time the apple tree blossoms until its fruit is ready, so it was fifty days from the time Israel left Egypt until they received the Torah. And when did they receive it? "In the third month after the Israelites had gone forth" (Exod. 19:1). —SONG OF SONGS RABBAH 2; PESIKTA DE-RAV KAHANA, Bahodesh Hashelishi

"On the third new moon"—This is what is meant by the verse, "Indeed, I wrote you down for a threefold lore, wise counsel" (Prov. 22:20). Said Rabbi Yehoshu'a, son of Rabbi Nehemiah: This refers to the Torah, whose letters are divided into three.* And all the rest is likewise threefold. The scriptures are threefold: Torah, Prophets, Writings. The Mishnah is threefold: interpretation, law, and lore. God's agents are threefold: Miriam, Aaron, and Moses. The liturgy is threefold: evening, morning, and afternoon. The Chorus of Sanctification is threefold: "Holy, holy, holy." Israel is threefold: priests, prophets, and ordinary Israelites. The letters of Moses' name *(MoShE)* are threefold, and he was from the tribe of Levi, whose letters are threefold *(LeVI)*. Israel came from the threefold seed of Abraham, Isaac, and Jacob. In the three-month period of Nisan, Iyar, and Sivan they journeyed to Mount Sin [Sinai], whose letters are threefold *(SIN)*, as it is written, "And they encamped in the wilderness of Sin" (Num. 33:11); and they were to purify themselves over a period of three days, as it is written, "Be ready for the third day" (Exod. 19:15).

Rabbi Yehoshu'a bar Nehemiah said: The third is always the most beloved. Adam had three sons, Cain, Abel, and Seth, and Seth was the most beloved, as scripture says, "This is the record of Adam's line" (Gen. 5:1), and then, "He begot a son in his likeness after his image, [and he named him Seth]" (Gen. 5:3). Noah had three sons—as scripture says, "Noah had three sons: Shem, Ham, and Japheth" (Gen. 6:10)—and although Japheth was the eldest, it is not he who is recognized as being pre-eminent, but Shem. Amram had three children: Miriam, Aaron, and Moses, and it is written, "Had not Moses His chosen one. . . ." (Ps. 106:23). Among the tribes of Reuben, Simeon, and Levi, Levi was the most beloved, as scripture says, "At that time the Lord set apart the tribe of Levi" (Deut. 10:8). Among the kings Saul, David, and

*See the comment of *Zayit Ra'anan,* below. Abudarham suggests, alternatively, that what is meant is that the Hebrew alphabet is customarily divided into three groups of letters according to value: the first nine represent units (1 to 9); the next nine represent tens (10 to 90); and the last four represent hundreds (100 to 400). See A. J. Wertheimer, ed., *Abudarham Hashalem* (Jerusalem, 1963), 114. (I am indebted to Jacob Elbaum for drawing this source to my attention.)

Solomon, it was Solomon who was most beloved, as scripture says, "Solomon successfully took over the throne of the Lord as king [instead of his father David]" (1 Chron. 29:23). Among the months, it is the third that is most beloved, as it is written, "In the third month" (Exod. 19:1). —TANḤUMA, Yitro

"Whose letters are divided into three"—[what the midrash means is] that there are twenty-seven letters* in the alphabet used to write the Torah, a number that is divisible into groups of three: *aleph-bet-gimel, dalet-he-vav,* etc. —ZAYIT RA'A-NAN

WHY WAS THE TORAH GIVEN IN THE THIRD MONTH?

Rav Nehorai began his discourse as follows: It is written, "In the third month." Why the third? Because its sign, Gemini, is human in form, and it is the only month to have such a sign. Thus scripture says, "Your breasts are like two fawns, twins of a gazelle" (Song 4:5). —PESIKTA ḤADETA

"Because its sign, Gemini, is human in form"—*and in Pesikta Rabbati, Para-shat 'Aseret Hadibrot, the Sages say:* This is the reason the Holy One, blessed be He, gave the Torah in the month of Sivan. The sign of Sivan is Gemini, and Gemini is human in form. *They say further there:* Man has a mouth with which to speak. *And in the Zohar it is stated:* None of the other signs has a mouth or a tongue, but this one has both rolled into one. Therefore, "Recite it day and night" (Josh. 1:8)—that is, recite the book of the Torah, "day" referring to the tongue and "night" referring to the mouth. And the two are rolled into one and joined in the mystery of Gemini. Joined in the mystery of Gemini—meaning the Written Torah and the Oral Torah.

"In the third month"—Why was the Torah given in the third month? Because that month's sign is Gemini *(te'omim),* and it was in that month that the Holy One, blessed be He, and the Israelite people became twins [*nit'amu*]. That is what is meant by the verse, "Only one is my dove, my perfect one *(tamati)*" (Song 6:9). Read not *tamati* but *te'omot* (twins). —Midrash cited in TORAH SHLEMAH

*Including the five alternate forms used at the ends of words.

"In the third month"—Why was the Torah given in the third month? So as not to give the nations of the world an opportunity to say, "Had He given us the Torah, we would have obeyed it." Said the Holy One, blessed be He, "See in which month I gave the Torah: the third, whose sign is Gemini (the twins), for if the evil Esau* should decide to convert and do penitence and come and study Torah, he could come and study, and I would accept him. That is why I gave it in the third month." —PESIKTA DE-RAV KAHANA

"Under the sign of Gemini" —because Jacob and Esau were twins.

And the Rosh [Rabbenu Asher ben Yehiel], may his memory be a blessing, wrote: This is the reason He waited until the third month, for Gemini was rising at the beginning of the day on which He gave the Torah, and the Holy One, blessed be He, was waiting to see if the children of Esau, Jacob's twin brother, would do penitence and accept the Torah. But they turned a deaf ear. —TOSFOT HAROSH

"In the third month after the Israelites had gone forth from the land of Egypt, on this very day, they entered the Wilderness of Sinai" (Exod. 19:1)—This month's sign is Gemini, for the Holy One, blessed be He, is like a twin brother, as it were, to those who do His will. And just as scholars have written that when one twin fares poorly so does the other, and if one fares well so does the other, because, having been created at the same moment, they have the same sign, so is the blessed Creator like a twin to those who do His will. This is why Israel (yisra'el) is called yeshar el—that is, equal to God—though in reality He rules over the Israelites. That is why He brought them before Mount Sinai in the third month and revealed Himself to them and spoke with them as one does with his own brother, as it were. —'AVODAT YISRA'EL

"In the third month"—that is the month of Sivan, the numerical value of which is the same as that of the word 'anav† (humble). And Moses, too, is called 'anav, as in the verse, "Now Moses was a very humble man ('anav)" (Num.

---

*Israel's twin, the ancestor of the Edomites and of the archvillain Amalek; also often identified in the Rabbinic literature with Rome.

†According to the hermeneutical method of gematria, in which the first letter of the alphabet equals 1, the second 2, etc.

12:3). And the numerical value of the last letters of each of the five books of the Torah is the same as that of *'anav*. Hence: an *'anav* will come and receive *'anav* in the month of *'anav!* —NAHAL KEDUMIM, quoting Rabbenu Efraim

"In the . . . month *(baḥodesh)*"—on the new moon, as in the phrase, "Tomorrow will be the new moon *(ḥodesh)*" (1 Sam. 20:18). —HIZKUNI

The word *ḥodesh* has two meanings. One is the time from one new moon to the next—that is, a month. The other is the first day of the month, as in, "Tomorrow is the new moon *(ḥodesh)*" (1 Sam. 20:5). And in fact, Israel came to the Wilderness of Sinai on the new moon. —MIKHLAL YOFI

"In the third month after the Israelites had gone forth from the land of Egypt. . . ."—Throughout the Torah, new topics are connected by the *vav* consecutive* with those preceding them. Yet here the text begins, "In the third month," as if describing a completely separate topic, not related to the one that came before. This confirms the statement of the Mekhilta: " 'Then He said to Moses' (Exod. 24:1) came before the Giving of the Torah, and 'Then he took the record of the covenant' (Exod. 24:7) refers to the part of the Torah from the Creation up to the Giving of the Torah, [i.e.,] up to the phrase 'In the third month,' which came before the Giving of the Torah. The part beginning 'In the third month' was written after the Giving of the Torah." That is why this section begins as though it were launching into something new, like "When God began to create . . ." (Gen. 1:1) [which is similarly lacking the *vav* consecutive]. —MESHEKH ḤOKHMAH

"In the third month"—The early commentators explained why the language here differs from that in other passages describing [Israel's] journeys: from the very outset of the Exodus from Egypt, the destination was synonymous with the objective of the Exodus itself, namely, to come to the Mountain of God to receive the Torah. Thus, scripture informs us that "in the third month" they were deemed worthy to achieve this goal. —HA'AMEK DAVAR

*Often translated, "And. . . ."

AFTER THE ISRAELITES HAD GONE FORTH FROM THE LAND OF EGYPT

"After the Israelites had gone forth from the land of Egypt"—Rabbi Levi said in the name of Rabbi Shim'on ben Ḥalafta: Like a king whose son has been taken captive, who in a vindictive mood goes out and redeems his son and then announces the inauguration of a new era from the time of his son's redemption, so the Holy One, blessed be He, said, "Inaugurate a new era from the time of the Exodus from Egypt." —PESIKTA DE-RAV KAHANA

ON THIS VERY DAY

"On this very day they entered the Wilderness of Sinai" (Exod. 19:1)—It does not say "on that very day" *(bayom hahu)* but rather "on *this* very day" *(bayom hazeh),* as if to say, they entered the Wilderness of Sinai today. What this means is that on whatever day you engage in Torah, it is as if you received it that same day. And so scripture says, "The Lord your God commands you this day to observe. . . ." (Deut. 26:16). —TANḤUMA HAYASHAN, Yitro; see also PESIKTA, Baḥodesh Hashelishi

"On this very day they entered the Wilderness of Sinai"—Rashi explains: "The only reason for the phrase *bayom hazeh* ('on *this* very day') is to tell you that the words of the Torah should always be as new to you as if they had been given today."

Now his holy words seem to hint at something deeper, that in truth what was revealed then is continually revealed each day of each year, throughout eternity. It is similar to what happens on Passover: just as our ancestors left Egypt at that time, so do Jews leave Egypt [ritually] every year. Likewise in the case of this month: since our ancestors drew near to Mount Sinai at this time, it is revealed to us that we, too, can come closer to the Holy One, blessed be He, that we can receive the Torah and draw near to Mount Sinai.

"Sinai" is related to the word *sin'ah* (hatred)—it "hates" all evil. This is what our Sages, may their memory be a blessing, said: "Sinai is the place where hatred of idolaters came down."

Hence, from the new moon of Sivan to the feast of Shavu'ot,* everyone should read the Torah and partake of the holiness that was revealed "on this

*Pentecost, the anniversary of the Giving of the Torah.

very day." This is the meaning of Rashi's comment "that the words of the Torah should always be as new to you as if they had been given today."

"They entered the Wilderness of Sinai"—they made themselves like that wilderness, which is empty and bare; that is, they saw themselves as a wilderness, as if they had not even begun to worship the Lord. —'AVODAT YISRA'EL

THE WILDERNESS OF SINAI

"They entered the Wilderness of Sinai"—where hatred for all those who do not observe the precepts of the Torah descended. This is what Rabbi Yose used to say [concerning Isaiah 45:19]: "I did not speak"—to the Israelites—"in secret, . . . in a land of darkness"—when I gave the Torah to Israel, I did not give it in secret or in a land of darkness. "I did not say to the stock of Jacob"—for the Torah is yours—" 'Seek Me out in a wasteland' "—I did not simply enjoin it upon you [arbitrarily], but rather provided its own reward along with it. "I am the Lord, who bespeaks righteousness"—I speak of the righteousness of Israel—"who tells of uprightness"—I tell what they do before Me out of love. "He did not do so for any other nation" (Ps. 147:20) [because they were not deserving. Yet what could the nations of the world have been expected to do [to be more deserving], not having learned Torah? "Of such rules they know nothing" (Ps. 147:20)—I did give them the seven [Noahide] commandments, but even these they could not keep. —MEKHILTA DE-RABBI SHIM'ON BAR YOHAI

"The Wilderness of Sinai"—said Rabbi Yose, son of Rabbi Hanina: It has five names: the Wilderness of Zin, because Israel was commanded (sheniztavu) there; the Wilderness of Kadesh, because Israel was sanctified (shenitkadshu) because of it; the Wilderness of Kedemot, because the Primordial (kedumah) [Torah]* was given there; the Wilderness of Paran, because Israel was fruitful (paru) and multiplied there; and the Wilderness of Sinai, because the hatred (sin'ah) of idolaters descended there. And what is its true name? Horeb is its true name. In this they disagreed with Rabbi Abbahu, who said: Its true name is Mount Sinai. Why then is it called Mount Horeb (horev)? Because the destruction (hurvah) of idolaters descended there. —SHABBAT 89b

*Or, "a pre-eminence" (that of Israel).

EXODUS 19:2

Having journeyed from Rephidim,
they entered the wilderness of Sinai
and encamped in the wilderness;
Israel encamped there
in front of the mountain.

"Having journeyed from Rephidim, they entered the Wilderness of Sinai"—
But are we not also told this in the section dealing with their journeys [Num.
33:15]? Why does the Torah have to tell us here as well, "they entered the
Wilderness of Sinai"? In order to point out an analogy between their departure
from Rephidim and their arrival in the Wilderness of Sinai: just as their arrival
was accompanied by repentance, so was their departure.

Another analogy between their arrival in the Wilderness of Sinai and their
departure from Rephidim: just as at Rephidim they had angered God but then
briefly repented and were forgiven, so too at Sinai they angered God but then
briefly repented and were forgiven.

Rabbi El'azar ben Rabbi Yose the Galilean said: Note that scripture says,
"In distress you called and I rescued you; I answered you from the secret place
of thunder; I tested you at the waters of Meribah, *selah"* (Ps. 81:8)—Even as
I began to answer you and shield you and crush the whole world for your sake,
I knew what you would do at the waters of Meribah.

Abba Sha'ul said: Note that scripture says, "I answered you from the
secret place *(beseter)* of thunder"—you call out secretly *(beseter),* and I answer
you openly, with thunder that fills the world.

Rabbi Yehudah ben Lakish said: Note that scripture says, "God saw the
Israelites" (Exod. 2:25)—He saw that they had repented, but they did not see
this in one another—"and God knew about them" (Exod. 2:25)—He knew
that they had repented, but they did not know this about each other.

Rabbi Eli'ezer said in the name of Abba Yose ben Dormaskit: Note that
scripture says, "[God heard their moaning and God remembered His cove-
nant]. . . . God saw the Israelites" (Exod. 2:24–25)—He foresaw clearly that one
day they would anger Him, that one day they would offend Him. Why then
[did He take note of their suffering]? Because of the vigor of their repentance.

In a similar vein, Rabbi Eli'ezer ben Yose taught: "In all their troubles
He was troubled. . . ." (Isa. 63:9), "and He said, 'Nevertheless, they are My
people, [children who will not play false]' " (Isa. 63:8)—Was it not already

known to Him that they would one day prove false? That is why scripture says "nevertheless"—it was known to Him. And the words, "So He was their deliverer" (Isa. 63:8), can only mean that He did not redeem them as people destined to offend Him but rather as [though they were] people who would never betray Him. So scripture says, "They deceived Him with their speech, lied to Him with their words; their hearts were inconstant toward Him; they were untrue to His covenant" (Ps. 78:36–37); and yet, "He, being merciful, forgave iniquity" (Ps. 78:38), and further, "Soften that people's heart" (Isa. 6:10)—and it will do penitence—"it will repent and save itself" (Isa. 6:10).
—MEKHILTA

"Because of the vigor of their repentance." But another version has it, "because of the timeliness of their repentance"—that is, He only took note of the penitence they did at that time, knowing that one day they would sin; for timely repentance is a great thing. Another version [that of *Hagahot Eifat Zedek*, a commentary on the Mekhilta] has it, "because of the severe oath [He took to their ancestors]." Even though the Holy One, blessed be He, foresaw that they would offend Him—"God knew about them"—nevertheless, because of the oath, "God remembered His covenant. . . . [and God took notice of them]" (Exod. 2:24–25). We find the same idea in Exodus Rabbah, at the end of this passage: "God saw the Israelites, and God knew" (Exod. 2:24–25)—the Holy One, blessed be He, knew He was bound to redeem them for His own Name's sake, because of the covenant He had made with their forefathers. And so it is written, "God remembered His covenant"; and thus Ezekiel says, "I acted for the sake of My Name" (Ezek. 20:14).

Another interpretation of "God saw": according to Rabbi Levi, He saw that they were going to rebel at the Sea of Reeds, as it is written, "They rebelled at the sea, at the Sea of Reeds" (Ps. 106:7). "And God knew" that one day they would say, "This is my God" (Exod. 15:2). Rabbi Yehoshu'a ben Levi said: He foresaw that one day they would say [concerning the Golden Calf], "This is your God, O Israel" (Exod. 32:4), but also that they would say, "We shall do" even before saying "We shall hear."

But the Sages said: "God saw" that they had repented; both the wicked and those who were neither very good nor very bad were considering repentance, as it is written, "The green figs form on the fig tree" (Song 2:13). "And God knew"—they did not even know each other's intentions; only the Holy One, blessed be He, did. Each of them resolved to repent, and then they all repented. Nonetheless, although they had repented, they would not have gotten out of there had it not been for the merit of their ancestors, for the Divine Attribute of Strict Justice was accusing them of the sin of the Golden Calf they would one day commit.

"Having journeyed from Rephidim, they entered the Wilderness of Sinai"—Why is it necessary to state this? Are we not told elsewhere [in Num. 33] of their journey from Rephidim and their encampment in the Wilderness of Sinai? Why then did the Torah have to tell us this here? In order to make an analogy between their journey from Rephidim and their encampment in the Wilderness of Sinai. Just as at the time of their journey from Rephidim they were trying and quarrelsome—"Is the Lord present among us or not?" (Exod. 17:7)—so were they trying and quarrelsome when they encamped in the Wilderness of Sinai—[where they undoubtedly also said,] "Is the Lord present among us or not?" This is to teach us the power of repentance, for the moment Israel repented they were forgiven.

"And [they] encamped in the wilderness"—the Torah was given to them in the most deserted place in the world; for had it been given in the Land of Israel the inhabitants of the land would have said, "It is ours!" and had it been given somewhere else the inhabitants of that place would have said, "It is ours!" Therefore it was given in the most deserted place in the world, where whoever wanted to take it could do so.

Another interpretation: just as a wilderness lacks refined pleasures, so the words of the Torah cannot be fulfilled unless one refrains from refined pleasures. Thus, scripture says, "from Midbar [wilderness] to Mattanah [a gift]" (Num. 21:18)—the Torah cannot be fulfilled except by one who makes of himself a wilderness. —MEKHILTA DE-RABBI SHIM'ON BAR YOHAI

ISRAEL ENCAMPED THERE

"Israel encamped there in front of the mountain"—later [e.g., in Num. 21 and 33] it says the Israelites "journeyed" (vayis'u) and "encamped" (vayahanu), [the plural forms implying that] when they journeyed they were divided, and when they encamped they were divided; whereas here it says "they encamped (vayi-han) there" [in the singular, implying that] they had been given to feel a shared kindliness (hanayah), so that they could love one another and thus be able to receive the Torah.

Another interpretation of "[Israel] encamped there": He told them they would have to stay there a long time; and indeed we find that, in the end, they stayed ten days short of twelve months. —MEKHILTA DE-RABBI SHIM'ON BAR YOHAI

"Israel encamped there"—wherever it says "they journeyed" and "they encamped" [in the plural], it means they journeyed and encamped divided among themselves. But here they were made to feel of one mind, and so it is written [in the singular], "Israel encamped there." —MEKHILTA

The *Mekhilta* says: just as they came to the Wilderness of Sinai contritely, so they journeyed contritely. Said Rabbi Menahem of Kotsk: Whence did [the Rabbis] derive this interpretation? From the fact that it is written [in the singular], "Israel encamped there." And Rashi comments: As one person and of one mind; for each person examined his own failings and decided that the others were better than he; and this is the greatest form of repentance. —'AMUD HA'EMET

All the encampments had been characterized by division and strife, but here when they encamped they were of one mind. What does it mean to say that all the encampments had been characterized by division? They were of two minds: the evil inclination and the good inclination, as our Sages, may their memory be a blessing, said concerning the verse, "You must love the Lord your God with all your heart" (Deut. 6:5)—with your evil inclination as well as your good inclination. And this is always the source of strife, as King David, may he rest in peace, said, "There is . . . no wholeness in my bones *(be'azmi)* [because of my sin]" (Ps. 38:4)—within myself *(be'azmi)* there is no wholeness, because I am at war with myself. But at Mount Sinai, when Israel said "we will do" before they said "we will hear," the evil inclination was rooted out of their hearts, and they all became like angels. For so it is written of [angels], "[and let me fetch a morsel of bread] that you may refresh yourself" (Gen. 18:5), and Rashi cites concerning this verse: "Rabbi Hama said: 'It is not written, "yourselves *(levavkhem)"* but "yourself *(libkehm),"* implying that the evil inclination has no dominion over angels, so that they are of but one mind.' " —KOL YEHUDAH

"Israel encamped there in front of the mountain"—since all the souls of Israel to the end of time were present there, and it is well known that all souls derive from a single source, therefore it is not fitting to speak of souls in the plural. Thus the singular is used, for scripture is not speaking merely of the physical bodies that were there but of all the souls. —YADAV SHEL MOSHE

"Israel encamped there"—This is related to the verse, "Her ways are pleasant ways" (Prov. 3:17). The Holy One, blessed be He, wanted to give the Torah to Israel when they came out of Egypt, but they were arguing with one another and saying the whole time, "Let us head back for Egypt" (Num. 14:4). And while it is written, "They journeyed *(vayis'u)* from Succoth and encamped *(vayaḥanu)* at Etham" (Exod. 13:20), [the plural verbs] implying that they were quarreling while both journeying and encamped, when they got to Rephidim they were in accord with one another and united. How do we know this? Because it is written, "Israel encamped there in front of the mountain," and it does not say *vayaḥanu* [the plural form of "encamped"] but *vayiḥan* [the singular]. Said the Holy One, blessed be He, "The Torah is all about peace; to whom then shall I give it? To a people that loves peace." Hence, "All her paths are peaceful" (Prov., loc. cit.). —TANHUMA HAYASHAN

IN FRONT OF THE MOUNTAIN

"Israel encamped there in front of the mountain"—"in front of *(neged)* the mountain" means against *(neged)* the evil inclination, which is called a mountain—as our Sages, may their memory be a blessing, said, "To the righteous, [the evil inclination] will seem like a mountain" (Sukkah 52a)—and which forever yearns to stir up controversy in Israel. Here, however, "[Israel] encamped," all of one mind, "in front of the mountain"—that is, in defiance of the mountain. —APIRION, quoting Rabbi Natan Adler

"Israel encamped there in front of the mountain"—against the evil inclination; for "to the righteous, it will seem like a mountain" (Sukkah 52a). And this is what our Sages, may their memory be a blessing, meant when they spoke of Israel being of one mind. For man's two hearts, the foolish on the left and the wise on the right, became one: one subdued the other, and only one was left, with which they could repent. It is as the poet says in the Rosh Hashanah hymn, "Your people depend on repentance to be united with You, their two hearts turning as one to You, the One." When they do this, their enmity ceases and they become like ministering angels, who, as we know, have but one heart, as it is written, "And let me fetch a morsel of bread] that you may refresh *yourself* [singular]" (Gen. 18:5).

Now the righteous are able to control themselves [lit., "have their hearts in their hands"]. This is what is meant by the verse, "Having journeyed from *Rephidim*": whereas at first they were lax *(berifyon yadayim)*, they left this [laxity] and "encamped . . . in front of the mountain"—against the evil inclination, which can loom like a mountain, God forbid, if one is unworthy; and "[Israel] encamped," as one person. —MAHAZEH AVRAHAM

"Israel encamped there in front of the mountain"—Rabbi Moshe of Kubrin said: When Israel is "encamped"—in the singular, that is, when they are of one mind—then they are "in front of the mountain"—they can stand up to the mountain, that is, the evil inclination, which is compared to a mountain. —OR YESHARIM

"Israel encamped there in front of the mountain"—Rashi says: as one. Clearly, "encamped (vayihan)" [being in the singular] suggests unity. Hence the plural form (vayahanu) is not used here, as it is in other instances of encampment. And there is a sign of this meaning in the word yihan (encamped) if we take it as an acronym for the verse, "Ya'akov hevel nahalato," [literally], "Jacob's portion is a rope" (Deut. 32:9): just as a rope is plaited from a number of fibers that are intertwined, so must we Israelites intertwine with one another and cleave to one another, as one, with one mind, in our attachment to our heavenly Father. —DEVASH HASADEH, quoting Rabbi Yeshaya Asher of Ropshitz

"Israel encamped there in front of (neged) the mountain"—In everything that involves his being Israel, obstacles as big as mountains loom before him (negdo). —BEIT AHARON

"Israel encamped there in front of the mountain"—the author of the Haggadah says, "Had He brought us before Mount Sinai and not given us the Torah, it would have sufficed." The point is this: the performance of every precept requires preparation, and the greater the precept the greater the preparation. And sometimes the preparation is even more important than the performance. Thus, the people Israel were given the Torah by the Holy One, blessed be He, but the preparation for receiving it was something they had to do themselves. When? On the day after the battle with Amalek, of which it is written, "[Remember what Amalek did to you on your journey,] . . . when you were famished and weary, he being undeterred by fear of God" (Deut. 18:25). It was immediately after that that "[Israel] encamped [there] in front of the mountain," being united and of one mind. —BINYAN SHLOMO, quoting Rabbi Avraham Ya'akov of Sadgora

"Israel encamped there"—Rashi explains this to mean: being united and of one mind. Thus did they prepare to receive the Torah: by cultivating love for one another in their hearts. Similarly, the Sages say: "What is the straight path for a man to follow? Rabbi Eli'ezer says, a benevolent eye" (Avot 2:9)—the ability to rejoice in another's good fortune, even when one lacks what the other has.

And what was their reward? "All the people witnessed the thunder and lightning" (Exod. 20:15): even though there were simple people among them who would not otherwise have been able to see this, their benevolent eye made it possible for them to do so, for each rejoiced in what his neighbor saw, they being all united and of one mind.

And one cannot attain this virtue except by including himself in the collectivity of Israel and not holding himself apart from the others. One only counts as a part of the Assembly of Israel. As the Ari, may his memory be a blessing, wrote: before beginning to pray, one must take upon himself the precept, "Love your neighbor as yourself" (Lev. 19:18); for if one is not a part of the Assembly of Israel, how can he pray to the blessed Lord? But when all Israelites are fully united, all their human desires are directed to one place, to the main object of what is desired. The unity of Israel in their encampment was also wrought by the blessed Lord. And so it is with all the commandments: human beings are helped to fulfill them. Now, all this happened at the time of the receiving of the Torah; but no doubt it applies equally now, that each year at the new moon of Sivan we must awaken and raise ourselves to the level of the encampment [at Sinai] and the preparation [for the revelation]; for these things are eternal. —HIDDUSHEI HARIM; GUR ARYEH

FROM THE TIME ANYTHING EXISTED, I WAS THERE

As the commentators have pointed out, scripture says at the beginning [of the verse], "They encamped [plural] in the wilderness," whereas here [at the end of the verse] it says "[Israel] encamped" [singular]—that is, the very same verse begins in the plural and ends in the singular. What we have here is an allusion to the saying of the Sages, may their memory be a blessing, that all future souls came to Mount Sinai to receive their portion, as the verse says, "From the time anything existed, I was there" (Isa. 48:16). In the world of souls there is complete unity; it is only in this world that there is separation. Thus, when it says "they encamped [plural] in the wilderness," [the Torah] refers to the Jews of that particular generation, body and soul; and when it says "Israel encamped [singular] there," it is alluding to the souls of [all the generations of] Israel. It also makes a point of saying, "[Israel] encamped there in front of the mountain," for that was the place where God was to be found, and since they were pure souls they had an affinity for the kingship of heaven. —ZEKAN AHARON

AND MOSES WENT UP TO GOD

EXODUS 19:3
And Moses went up to God.
The Lord called to him from the mountain, saying,
"Thus shall you say to the house of Jacob
and declare to the children of Israel."

"And Moses went up to God"—How fortunate was Moses to have merited this honor, to which the Torah itself attests. Consider how different Moses is from other mortals. With them, "going up" means being elevated to wealth, to greatness, to power; but when Moses goes up, what does scripture say of him? "And Moses went up to God." How fortunate he was.

Rabbi Yose said: the Haverim* deduce from this verse that "one who comes to be purified is helped" ('Avodah Zarah 55a). For it is written, "And Moses went up to God," and what is written right after that? "The Lord called to him." One who wishes to draw near should be brought near.

"The Lord called to him from the mountain . . ."—Rabbi Yizhak began his discussion of this verse with the verse, "Happy is the man You choose and bring near to dwell in Your courts" (Ps. 65:5)—Happy is that man whom the Holy One, blessed be He, desires and brings near to Him, to dwell inside the Holy Palace. For whomever He desires for His service receives a citation on high, to make it known that he has been chosen by the holy and exalted King to dwell in His own quarters. And whoever bears this citation is granted passage through all the heavenly gates and never detained.

Rabbi Yehudah said: How fortunate was Moses. Of him it is written, "Happy is the man You choose and bring near," and of him it is written, "Moses approached the thick cloud [where God was]" (Exod. 20:18), and "Only Moses shall come near the Lord, but they shall not come near" (Exod. 24:2). —ZOHAR, Exodus 79b

*Originally, in the tannaitic period, members of a group that took upon itself extra stringency in the observance of the laws of tithes and purity; later, scholars in general.

"And Moses went up"—His spirits were lifted when he saw that Israel was united, for he knew then that they were worthy of the Torah and of being elevated in every way. He "went up" because of the elevation of Israel. —SIFTEI KOHEN on the Torah

"And Moses went up to God"—while Israel tended to the necessities of making camp, Moses went up and prepared himself for prophecy. —SFORNO

"And Moses went up"—on the second of the month, which was a Tuesday. And he did not ascend of his own accord but because "the Lord called to him from the mountain, saying, 'Thus shall you say,' " from which we learn that he only went up because he had been given permission to do so. But some interpret it that he did go up of his own accord, to ask the Holy One, blessed be He, how they were to worship Him, thus fulfilling what he had been told previously: "When you have freed the people from Egypt, you shall worship God at this mountain" (Exod. 3:12). And the Holy One, blessed be He, told him, "Thus shall you say to the house of Jacob . . . If you will listen to Me . . . ," (Exod. 19:3–5)—that shall be My worship. Nevertheless, we see that at the Giving of the Torah "they offered burnt offerings and sacrificed bulls as offerings of well-being [to the Lord]" (Exod. 24:5), [beyond what was commanded]. HIZKUNI

"The Lord called to him"—by his name, Moses, as He had done in Egypt. And he answered, "I am here," just as we have learned [in regard to the summons] at the beginning of Leviticus. But it would be incorrect to interpret it that at this point he was summoned to the top of the mountain, for that is said further on, in verse 20—"The Lord called Moses to the top of the mountain"—and it is explained that up until then he had not ascended to the top of the mountain. Rather, [in the first instance,] He called to him, and he stood halfway up the mountain. —HA'AMEK DAVAR

"And Moses went up to God . . ."—to the place where the wings of the Shekhinah were spread, as in the verse, "He bent the sky and came down. . . . He mounted a cherub and flew, gliding on the wings of the wind" (Ps. 18:10–11). —ZOHAR, Exodus 78b

"And Moses went up to God . . . "—the Sages taught: When Moses went up on high, a cloud came down to him, and Moses did not know whether to climb onto it or to take hold of it. The cloud then opened its mouth, and Moses went

inside, and he was able to ride it through the heavens the way one walks on earth. Thus the Torah says, "Moses went inside the cloud" (Exod. 24:18).
—PESIKTA RABBATI; MA'AYAN HAHOKHMAH; PIRKEI HEKHALOT

WHEN MOSES WENT UP ON HIGH

And Rabbi Yehoshu'a ben Levi said: When Moses went up on high, the ministering angels said to the Holy One, blessed be He, "Master of the Universe, what is a creature born of woman doing among us?" He said to them, "He has come to receive the Torah." They said to Him, "That precious treasure, which You kept hidden away for 974 generations before the world was created, You now propose to give to a creature of flesh and blood? 'What is man that You have been mindful of him, mortal man that You have taken note of him?' (Ps. 8:5). 'O Lord, our Lord, how majestic is Your name throughout the earth, You who have given the heavens Your splendor!' (Ps. 8:2)."

Said the Holy One, blessed be He, to Moses, "You answer them." He said to Him, "Master of the Universe, I am afraid they will scorch me with their breath." He said to him, "Take hold of My throne and give them an answer." For it is written, "He takes hold of the front of His throne, and He spreads [parshez] His cloud over him" [Job 26:9]; and Rabbi Nahum says, this verse teaches us that the Almighty spread the glory [perash ziv] of His Shekhinah and His cloud over him.

Said he to Him, "Master of the Universe, what is written in this Torah that You are giving me?" God replied, " 'I the Lord am your God who brought you out of the land of Egypt' (Exod. 20:2)." So Moses said to the angels, "Have you been down to Egypt? Have you been enslaved to Pharaoh? Why then should you have the Torah?"

Again he asked, "What is written in it?" " 'You shall have no other gods' (Exod. 20:3)." Said Moses to the angels, "Do you then dwell among idolatrous peoples?"

And again he asked, "What is written in it?" " 'Remember the Sabbath day and keep it holy' (Exod. 20:8)." "Do you do any work, then, that you have need of rest?"

And again he asked, "What is written in it?" " 'You shall not take (tissa) [the name . . . in vain]' (Exod. 20:7)." "Is there any business (massa umatan) among you?"

Again he asked, "What is written in it?" " 'Honor your father and your mother' (Exod. 20:12)." "Do you then have fathers and mothers?"

Again he asked, "What is written in it?" " 'You shall not murder. You shall not commit adultery. You shall not steal' (Exod. 20:13)." "Is there any jealousy or lust among you?"

Forthwith they admitted their error to the Holy One, blessed be He, by repeating the words, "O Lord, our Lord, how majestic is Your name [throughout the earth]" (Ps. 8:10). But the words they added previously, [in verse 2,] "You who have given the heavens Your splendor" [implying that the Torah should remain in heaven], do not appear this time. Then each of them showered Moses with affection and gifts, as it is written, "You went up to the heights, having taken captives, having received tribute because of man" (Ps. 68:19)—meaning, as compensation for your having been called a mere man, you received gifts. And even the Angel of Death presented him with a gift, as it is written, "[As Moses had ordered . . . Aaron] put on the incense and made expiation for the people; he stood between the dead and the living [until the plague was checked]" (Num. 17:12). If the Angel of Death had not told Moses to have Aaron do this, how would he have known? —SHABBAT 88b–89a

Rabbi Yehoshu'a ben Levi said further: When Moses came down from being with the Holy One, blessed be He, Satan came and said to Him, "Master of the Universe, where is the Torah?" He said to him, "I have given it to Earth." So he went to Earth and said to her, "Where is the Torah?" She said to him, " 'God understands the way to it' (Job 28:23)." He went to the Sea, who said to him, "I do not have it." He went to the Deep, who said to him, "It is not in me"—as it is written, "The Deep says, 'It is not in me'; the Sea says, 'I do not have it.' . . . Destruction and Death say, 'We have only a report of it' " (Job 28:14, 22).

So he went back to the Holy One, blessed be He, and said, "Master of the Universe, I have searched the world and not found it!" Said He to him, "Go to the son of Amram." He went to Moses and said to him, "Where is the Torah which the Holy One, blessed be He, gave you?" He said, "Who am I that the Holy One, blessed be He, should give me the Torah?" Said the Holy One, blessed be He, to Moses, "Moses, you are a liar!" "Master of the Universe," said Moses, "how can I lay claim to this precious treasure in which You take delight, day in, day out?" Said the Holy One, blessed be He, to him, "Since you have been so modest, it shall be named after you, as it is written, 'Be mindful of the Torah of My servant Moses' (Mal. 3:22)."

Rabbi Yehoshu'a ben Levi also said: When Moses ascended on high, he found the Holy One, blessed be He, tying crowns on the letters [of the Torah, but he kept silent]. God said to him, "Moses, where you come from do people not greet one another?" Said he, "Should a servant then greet his master?" He replied, "You would have given Me encouragement!" Straightway he said, "Now, I pray, let my Lord's strength be great, as You have declared" (Num. 14:17). —SHABBAT 89a

---

"Tying crowns on the letters"—spikes. Three vertical strokes must be added to the letters *shin, 'ayin, tet, nun, zayin, gimel,* and *zadi,* as we are told in Menaḥot 29b.

"Where you come from do people not greet one another?"—is it not customary where you live to extend greetings? "He said to Him"—the next time he went up—" 'Now, I pray, let my Lord's strength be great.' " —RASHI

"Where is the Torah?"—Did Satan not know about the Giving of the Torah? No, says the Midrash, the Holy One, blessed be He, chased him away at the time the Torah was being given, so that he would not argue, "You are giving the Torah to a people destined to sin after forty days by building the Golden Calf?" And this Satan was in fact the Angel of Death. Similarly, they say in the Gemara [Baba Batra 17a] and in Sanhedrin 26b that the Torah was given in secret because of Satan. —TOSAFOT

WHEN THE ANGELS ASKED FOR THE TORAH, WHAT WERE THEY AFTER?

When the angels asked for the Torah, what were they after? Did they intend to observe the commandments? Hardly, since most of the commandments refer to bodily acts, [and angels do not have bodies]. Rather, the Torah is divided into two parts, the Written and the Oral, and most of the Oral Torah consists of the rules and principles by which the Written Torah is to be interpreted. These rules and principles assist not only in the interpretation of the Written Torah but also in the endless spinning out of new laws and rulings. And as for the verse, "The Lord gives a command *(omer);* the heralds are a great host" (Ps. 68:12), what it means is that a single phrase *(amirah)* in the Written Torah can give rise to a number of interpretations and detailed laws, that a single passage of scripture can have a number of explanations. That is the meaning of "the heralds are a great host." Now the Torah was given to Israel that they might engage in interpreting it, and whatever agreement they came to, based on the principles, would be definitive. As we find cited in Baba Mezia (19b), "It is not in the heavens" (Deut. 30:12) but rather as the earthly court decides. That is why the angels asked that the Torah be given to them rather than man: so that the interpretations would be theirs and not his. That, too, is the meaning of "What is man that You have been mindful of him, mortal man that You have taken note of him *(tifkedenu)*" (Ps. 8:5). What they are saying is, Man is not worthy of Your attention; how much less is he worthy of being appointed custodian *(pakid)* [of Your Torah]. "You have made him master over Your handiwork, laying the world at his feet" (Ps. 8:7)—You have made him the ruler as well!

Herein lies the answer to the question posed by the Magen Avraham as to how we can refer to the festival of Shavu'ot, [which falls on the sixth of the month of Sivan,] as "the Anniversary of the Giving of Our Torah" when the Torah was in fact given on the seventh of the month. The answer is that scripture says, "Warn them to stay pure today and tomorrow" (Exod. 19:10), and Moses our Teacher added one more day on his own initiative, as it says in the Tractate Shabbat, page 87a; and the Holy One, blessed be He, approved, so that the Shekhinah did not descend until the following day.

Now the Giving, in which Israel not only was granted the Torah but also the right to interpret it, took place on the sixth of Sivan, when the Shekhinah had not yet come down. This is what is called "the *Giving* of the Torah," when the Torah was presented as a gift. What took place on the seventh was the *Receiving* of the Torah, when Israel accepted it. But the Giving was on the sixth.

That is why Shavu'ot is called the Anniversary of the Giving of *Our* Torah and not the Anniversary of the Giving of *the* Torah. "Our Torah" means it is up to us to interpret it. This refers to the Oral Torah and Israel's homiletical literature. As it says in the introduction to Lamentations Rabbah, " 'They have rejected the Torah of the Lord' (Isa. 5:24) refers to the Written Torah, while '[They have] spurned the word of the Holy One of Israel' (Isa. 5:24) refers to the Oral Torah." That explains the verse, "The Lord gives a command; the heralds are a great host" (Ps. 68:12), for one passage of scripture can be interpreted to yield many new insights and laws. "The kings *(malkhei)* and their armies are in headlong flight" (Ps. 68:13) means that it was precisely this with which the angels *(mal'akhim)* took issue, wanting themselves to have the power to derive new insights from the interpretation of scripture. "Housewives are sharing the spoils" (Ps. 68:13) means that Israel won out over them and received the Oral Torah.

It was on account of this that the Sages instituted the recitation of two benedictions over the Torah at the public reading, one before the reading—

"[Blessed are You, Lord, our God, King of the World,] who has chosen us from among the peoples and given us His Torah"—which is for the Written Torah, and one after the reading—" . . . who has given us the Torah of truth and planted eternal life in our midst"—which is for the Oral Torah. For it was granted to us that our Sages' interpretations would constitute the truth of the Torah. This is the meaning of "who has given us the Torah of truth and planted eternal life in our midst": the Torah is a planting that continues indefinitely to yield new insights. A similar interpretation is given in Tractate Ḥagigah, page 3b, to the verse, "The sayings of the wise are like goads, like nails fixed [in prodding sticks]" (Eccles. 12:11): "just as a goad is used to guide a cow down a furrow in order to produce life for the world, the words of the Torah guide those who study them away from the paths of death to the paths of life, . . . ; and just as this planting is fruitful and prolific, so are the words of the Torah fruitful and prolific." —BEIT HALEVI

THE ENVY OF THE ANGELS

Rabbi Aharon Maggid Mesharim of Zhitomir writes in *Toldot Aharon,* citing Rabbi Levi Yizhak of Berditchev:

Why did the angels protest only at the time of the Giving of the Torah, saying, "You who have given the *heavens* Your splendor" (Ps. 8:2)? Was the Torah not already to be found on earth? Adam, Enoch, Methuselah, Noah, Abraham, and all the Patriarchs had already studied the Torah; why had the angels not protested in their day? The answer is that before, the angels were not envious of mortals because they did not have to conduct themselves according to the mortals' understanding [of the Torah]; rather, they studied the Torah according to their own level [of understanding and acted accordingly]. However, when Moses received the Torah, we were given authority such that all the worlds had to conduct themselves thenceforth according to Israel's understanding. Thus the angels became envious and said, "Give the heavens, rather, Your splendor!" —TOLDOT AHARON, Vayak-hel

"When Moses went up on high, the ministering angels said to the Holy One, blessed be He, 'Master of the Universe, what is a creature born of woman doing among us?' He said to them, 'He has come to receive the Torah' " (Shabbat 88b). Said Rabbi Yisra'el Me'ir, author of *Hafez Hayyim:*

It is not that the angels belittled Moses; after all, the Holy One, blessed be He, Himself had said that of all the members of His household he was the most faithful. Rather, what they said was that since he spent all his time among people of flesh and blood, dickering and negotiating with them, his mental powers had been diminished, and he would not be able to attain higher illumination, like a schoolteacher in a small town who has taught youngsters all his life and had to settle their petty quarrels, so that over time his intelligence is diminished and he can no longer probe deeply into matters of wisdom. But the Holy One, blessed be He, replied that, nevertheless, Moses had come to receive the Torah, and He told Moses to answer them, [which he did in such a fashion that] they yielded to him and came to love him. —HAFEZ HAYYIM on the Torah

---

The Hafez Hayyim would often explain the Giving of the Torah with the following parable: It is generally accepted that when a person is going to buy something he does not know how to evaluate, he needs to consult those who do. And if he sees that the most knowledgeable person is bidding on the same merchandise, he can be sure that it will be a profitable purchase. Our Sages, may their memory be a blessing, tell us the angels said, " 'Give the heavens Your splendor' (Ps. 8:2)." And since angels are all spirit and no flesh—as scripture says, "He makes His angels of spirits" (Ps. 104:4)—clearly they would have the greatest understanding of the value of the Torah, which is entirely spiritual. In the end, Moses our Teacher, may he rest in peace, won out over the angels and received the Torah. Now we must reflect on the greatness of its Giver and on the preciousness of the Torah itself, which we have been privileged to receive in order to meditate upon it, for it is our life and the length of our days.

ONE WISE MAN GAINED ASCENDANCY
OVER A CITY OF WARRIORS

"One wise man gained ascendancy over a city of warriors" (Prov. 21:22)—"A city of warriors" refers to heaven, which is the "city" of the angels. "One wise man gained ascendancy *('alah)"* refers to Moses, who went up *('alah)* to heaven. "And brought down its mighty stronghold *('oz)"* (Prov. 21:22) refers to the Torah. And how do we know the ministering angels are referred to as warriors? Because it is written, "[Bless the Lord, O His angels,] warriors who do His bidding" (Ps. 103:20). And how do we know that Moses ascended on high? Because it is written, "And Moses went up to God" (Exod. 19:3). And how do we know that the Torah is called a stronghold *('oz)?* Because it is written, "The Lord shall give strength *('oz)* to His people" (Ps. 29:11). —MIDRASH ON PROVERBS

"And Moses went up to God"—The Holy One, blessed be He, made the heavens for heavenly beings and the earth for earthly beings, as it is written, "The heavens belong to the Lord, but the earth He gave over to man" (Ps. 115:16). Along came Moses and made the earth a place for heavenly beings and heaven a place for earthly beings, as it is written, "And Moses went up to God. . . . The Lord came down upon Mount Sinai" (Exod. 19:3,20). —DEUTERONOMY RABBAH 10:2

HAVING TAKEN CAPTIVES

"You went up to the heights, having taken captives" (Ps. 68:19). This is what is meant by the verse, "One wise man gained ascendancy over a city of warriors and brought down its mighty stronghold" (Prov. 21:22). This refers to Moses, as it is written, "And Moses went up to God" (Exod. 19:3). "To take gifts for man" (Ps. 68:19) refers to the Torah, which was given freely to Israel. "But the rebellious must live in a parched land" (Ps. 68:7) refers to the nations of the world, who refused to accept it. "Even [among] those who rebel the Lord God takes up abode" (Ps. 68:19) refers to Israel, who rebelled, but when they accepted the Torah, the Shekhinah came to dwell among them. —MIDRASH ON PSALMS 68

Concerning the verse, "You went up to the heights, having taken captives, to take gifts for man," the Midrash asks: Might Moses, having "captured" the Torah, not be said to have seized it without payment? Lest we think so, scripture says "to take *(lakahta)* gifts," meaning that it was given to him through an act of acquisition *(bilekiha)* on his part. And lest we think that payment was required, scripture says "gifts"—it was given to him as a gift.

Rabbi Menahem of Kotsk, may his memory be a blessing, interpreted it this way: "Might Moses, having 'captured' the Torah, not be said to have taken it without payment?"—meaning, simply by touching it. "Lest we think so, scripture says 'to take,' " implying that the recipient had to take it, to take it with all his strength. "Lest we think that payment was required"—meaning that he would only deserve it to the exact measure that he grasped and understood it—"scripture says 'gifts' "—the words of the Torah were gifts from the Giver. For what are the deeds of flesh and blood worth to the Blessed One that man can repay Him for His kindness with them? Rather, the Torah must be seen purely as a gift. —'AMUD HA'EMET

ONE TO ANOTHER

"This is my God, and I will enshrine Him" (Exod. 15:2)—This one will come to receive this from this one for this people. This one (zeh) will come—namely, Moses, as it is written, "that man (zeh) Moses" (Exod. 32:1)—to receive this (zot)—namely, the Torah, as it is written, "This (zot) is the Torah" (Deut. 4:44)—from this one (zeh)—namely the Holy One, blessed be He, as it is written, "This (zeh) is my God, and I will enshrine Him"—for this people ('am zu)—namely, Israel, as it is written, "the people ('am zu) whom You have ransomed" (Exod. 15:16). —MENAḤOT 33b

[The people] Israel were fortunate to have Moses the Prophet among them, for it was for him that the Holy One, blessed be He, wrought all those wonders. . . . And the Holy One, blessed be He, did not make His covenant with the other peoples, so as to form a bond with them, but with Israel. For they were the children of Abraham, of whom it is written, "[I will maintain My covenant between Me and you,] and your offspring to come, as an everlasting covenant throughout the ages" (Gen. 17:7); and it is written, "And this shall be My covenant with them, said the Lord: My spirit which is upon you . . . shall not be absent from your mouth, [nor from the mouth of your children, nor from the mouth of your children's children . . . for all time]" (Isa. 59:21). "Blessed is the Lord forever, amen and amen" (Ps. 89:53). —ZOHAR, Numbers 184b

THUS SHALL YOU SAY TO THE HOUSE OF JACOB

"Thus shall you say to the House of Jacob and declare to the children of Israel." "Thus shall you say"—in the holy tongue [Hebrew]. "Thus"—in this sequence. "Thus"—concerning this matter. "Thus"—without adding or detracting. —MEKHILTA

"Thus shall you say to the House of Jacob and declare to the children of Israel"—The Holy One, blessed be He, said to him, "Tell them all that you have seen." —PESIKTA ḤADETA

"Thus shall you say to the House of Jacob [and declare to the children of Israel]"—Originally he was called Jacob, but now he was privileged to take the great name Israel, "for you have striven with God (ki sarita 'im elohim)" (Gen. 32:29). —MEKHILTA DE-RABBI SHIM'ON BAR YOHAI

"Thus shall you say to the House of Jacob"—through the merit of Jacob—"and declare to the children of Israel"—through the merit of Israel. —MEKHILTA

"Thus shall you say to the House of Jacob"—state plainly to the people. "And declare (vetagged) to the children of Israel"—The verb haggadah always connotes getting to the essence of something, beyond its plain meaning. "To the children of Israel"—Though this expression always refers to the people as a whole, it may sometimes take on a more specific meaning from the context: the greatest minds [of Israel]. There are a number of words in the holy tongue that sometimes refer to an entire class of things and sometimes to particular members of that class. —HA'AMEK DAVAR

"Thus shall you say to the House of Jacob"—to the women speak gently, telling them only the main points. "And declare to the children of Israel"—when you speak to the men go into the fine points. —MEKHILTA

"Thus shall you say to the House of Jacob"—meaning the women. God told Moses to tell them only the main points, which they could understand. "And declare to the children of Israel"—meaning the men. God told Moses to give them the finer points, which they could understand.

Another interpretation: why does He speak of the women first? Because they are quicker to fulfill the commandments. Alternatively: so that they can begin teaching their sons Torah.

Said Rabbi Taḥlifa of Caesarea: The Holy One, blessed be He, said, "When I created the world I commanded Adam and only afterwards Eve, and she transgressed and spoiled the world. This time, if I do not call upon the women first, they will abrogate the Torah." That is why it is written, "Thus shall you say to the House of Jacob." —EXODUS RABBAH 28

Another reason the Holy One, blessed be He, commanded Moses to speak first to the women and only then to the men is that if He had commanded him to address them the other way around, the women could have claimed they were not accepting the Torah wholeheartedly but only in order to please their husbands. For if a man sells some property, his wife, even if she consents at the time, can always demand alimony from the buyer unless she herself made the sale, for she can claim she was only consenting in order to please her husband. Here too the women can make this claim. That is why the Holy One, blessed be He, commanded Moses to address the women and then the men, to avoid giving the women an excuse to say this. —Rabbi Natan of Grodno, SUPERCOMMENTARY ON RASHI

Why did He put the women first? Because men follow their wives' way of thinking, as it is written, "Manoah followed his wife" (Judg. 13:11). Furthermore, it is the women who raise their sons to study Torah. —TORAH SHLEMAH

He put the women first because it was by virtue of righteous women that Israel had been redeemed from Egypt. And because He honored the women in this way, they were reluctant to contribute their earrings for the making of the Golden Calf. —TORAH SHLEMAH

How did the women merit being put first? Rabbi Moshe of Narbonne—may the memory of the righteous be a blessing—used to expound that it was because of Leah's virtue that they were addressed first. She would wear over her heart a gold plate, inscribed with the verse, "Moses charged us with the Torah [as the heritage of the congregation of Jacob]" (Deut. 33:4), and she would meditate on it day and night. That is why "Leah had weak eyes" (Gen. 29:17): they were weakened by the gleam of the gold. And that is why her descendants merited receiving the Torah first. —MOSHAV ZEKENIM, cited in TORAH SHELEMAH

"Thus shall you say to the House of Jacob"—meaning the women—"and declare to the children of Israel"—meaning the men. Rabbi Shim'on said: "Thus (koh) shall you say" is like "Thus (koh) shall you bless" (Num. 6:22). And it is written, "Your faithful ones shall bless You (yevarekhukha)" (Ps. 145:10)—that is, shall bless thus (yevarekhu koh).*

"Thus shall you say (tomar) to the House of Jacob"—"saying" (amirah) comes from the Divine Attribute of Judgment. "And declare (vetagged) to the children of Israel"—this is like the usage in the verse "He declared (vayagged) to you the covenant" (Deut. 4:13) and in the verse "I declare (higgadeti) this day before the Lord your God" (Deut. 26:3), [where the verbs suggest the Divine Attribute of Mercy]. "To the children of Israel"—the men, who derive from the realm of Mercy.

Rabbi Yose [other versions: Rabbi Yizhak] said: Since we have brought up this passage, why does it say, "I declare this day before the Lord your God"? It should have said "before the Lord our God." Rabbi Shim'on replied: Why will only the latter expression do? Is it not written, "For the Lord your God is bringing you into a good land" (Deut. 8:7); "[the good land] that the Lord your God is giving you" (Deut. 4:21); and "the Lord your God is a consuming fire" (Deut. 4:24)? And there are many other instances. But in this instance the reason we have learned for the usage is this: one who lives in the Land of Israel is as if he had God, while one who lives outside the Land of Israel is as if he were without God. Why? Because the holy seed [Israel] makes its way up to the Land of Israel, and the Shekhinah dwells there, and the one depends on the other. Thus Moses only said "your God" to those who had been summoned to go up to the Holy Land to receive the Shekhinah. —ZOHAR, Exodus 79b

"Thus (koh) shall you say to the House of Jacob and declare to the children of Israel"—The word koh alludes to all blessings—as it is written, "Thus (koh) shall you bless" (Num. 6:22) and "So (koh) shall your offspring be" (Gen. 15:5). And most people lack sustenance and material comfort. Therefore our Creator, may His name be blessed, said, "Thus (koh) shall you say to the House of Jacob"—meaning, to these masses, called by the name Jacob, shall you draw abundance from the power of koh, which is the source of blessings and material plenty.†

"And declare to the children of Israel"—these are the distinguished people, called by the name Israel, to whom you must draw the higher light; you

*The letters כה can be read as koh, "thus," or kha, "you."
†Koh may also be understood to refer to the sefirah of Sovereignty (malkhut) in the kabbalistic system.

must bring love and awe into their hearts from the higher worlds. [The verb-root used here for "declare"] has the connotation of "draw": you must draw down from the higher worlds what they need at their level to worship the blessed Lord. —NO'AM ELIMELEKH

"Thus shall you say to the House of Jacob and declare to the children of Israel"—According to the interpretation of our Rabbis, may their memory be a blessing, "Thus" means: no more and no less. Is it conceivable that Moses would have been tempted to change the revealed word, so that such a warning was needed? As we know from Maimonides, may his memory be a blessing, Moses our Teacher, may he rest in peace, was concerned only with the essence and purpose and higher value [of the Torah], and the material rewards meant nothing to him. Thus the blessed Lord thought, as it were, that Moses might change something and tell the people only the purpose and essence of the Torah, even though Israel had not yet gained any understanding of it. That is why He warned him with the words, "Thus shall you say": no more and no less. —NO'AM MEGGADIM

"And declare *(vetagged)* to the children of Israel"—things that are as distaste- ful as wormwood *(gidim)*. This interpretation is substantiated by the fact that nowhere else in scripture is [the verb *vetagged*] ever spelled, [like *gidim*,] with the letter *yod*. It should be pointed out further that the words "thus shall you say *(tomar)*" refer only to the larger headings. Proof is to be found in the verse "He related *(amar)* the headings" (Daniel 7:1). "Declare *(vetagged)*," then, refers to all the subtopics and penalties and warnings. It can be demonstrated with a verse concerning Samson, "He has confided *(higgid)* everything in me" (Judg. 16:18); and, similarly, from the verse, "Tell me *(vehagged)* what you have done; do not hold anything back from me" (Josh. 7:19); and the verse, "Declare *(vehagged)* to My people their transgression" (Isa. 58:1), [the verb in all three cases connoting detailed disclosure].

AND DECLARE

The extra letter *yod* [in the word *vetagged,* "declare"] is for the Ten Command- ments that were to be given to them.* —MIDRASH LEKAH TOV, Yitro

---

*The numerical value of the letter *yod* is ten.

NOW JACOB, NOW ISRAEL

When the Holy One, blessed be He, blessed Jacob, saying, "You shall be called Jacob no more" (Gen 35:10), He did not mean the name Jacob should be discarded, but rather that at times he would be called Jacob and at times Israel, as expounded by our Rabbis, may their memory be a blessing. For the angel, too, blessed him in this way, saying, "Your name shall no longer be Jacob" (Gen. 32:29); but the angel's intention was to get rid of the name Jacob and then to accuse him of usurping the birthright, saying, "It was to Jacob that Esau sold his birthright, and you are Israel!" So when the Holy One, blessed be He, came to bless Jacob, He said, "You shall be called Jacob [alone] no more, but [also] Israel"—now Jacob, now Israel—in order to prevent Esau's guardian angel from accusing him concerning the birthright. —LEV ARYEH

THE DIFFERENCE BETWEEN JACOB AND ISRAEL

The difference [in the numerical value of the letters] between "Jacob" [182] and "Israel" [541] is 359, corresponding to the word "Satan." For it is through the accusations of Satan that Israel could become Jacob, Jacob being a term of lowliness and Israel being a term of greatness. Satan accuses Israel in order to turn him into Jacob. Thus when Jacob is victorious over Satan, the latter says to him, "Your name shall no longer be Jacob, but Israel." Because Satan cannot get the better of Jacob, the latter is called Israel. —SHEM SHMUEL

JACOB AND ISRAEL

Know that Jacob is Israel, for the name Jacob alludes to the value of the Torah and its observance in this world—as in, "Observe faithfully [the Torah . . . with which I charge you] *today*" (Deut. 7:11)—while the name Israel alludes to the exalted reward in the Next World for engaging in Torah and observing it. "Jacob" leads to "Israel"; for "the reward for fulfilling a commandment is the commandment itself" (Avot). In other words, by fulfilling a [physical, this-worldly] commandment, one gains access to its spiritual [other-worldly] side. "Jacob" *(Ya'akov)* implies fulfilling the commandments "today," for "in obeying them there is much reward *('ekev)*" (Ps. 19:12). Even seemingly neglible commandments must be observed.

"Jacob" is the ultimate purpose ["end" being another meaning of *'ekev*]; and the ultimate purpose, the true goal, is as described in the verse, "Revere

God and observe His commandments, [for this is the whole purpose of man]"
(Eccles. 12:13). That refers to the *'ekev* that is part of the word *Ya'akov* (Jacob).
It is this understanding of "Jacob" that is alluded to earlier, when the Holy One,
blessed be He, says to Isaac, "I will make your descendants as numerous as the
stars of heaven" (Gen. 26:4). That this alludes to Jacob we can see from the
verse, "It is through Isaac that offspring shall be continued for you" (Gen.
21:12)—through Isaac's descendants, but not all of them (Nedarim 31a). This
is also what is meant by "I will . . . give to your offspring all these lands" (Gen.
26:4), that it was Jacob who was to inherit the Land. And later when it says,
"inasmuch *('ekev)* as Abraham obeyed Me and followed My mandate: My
commandments, My laws, and My teachings" (Gen. 26:5), the word *'ekev*
alludes to Jacob. Moreover, there are ten words in this verse, corresponding to
the Ten Commandments, while in the Ten Commandments there are 172
words, corresponding to the numerical value of the word *'ekev*—so writes the
author of the *Turim*. In short, the name Jacob is alluded to in *'ekev,* because the
Ten Commandments are equivalent to *'ekev*. That is the import of the name
Jacob.

But you may be thinking, Why in that case was he not just called 'Ekev?
The answer is alluded to in the verse, "[Then his brother emerged,] his hand
grasping the heel *('ekev)* of Esau; [so they named him Jacob]" (Gen. 25:26).
Jacob's heel belongs to holiness; he is the end, in the sense of true purpose. But
Esau's heel *('ekev 'esav)* belongs to the realm of the Fiery Serpent; it is the end
in the sense of the final destruction at the End of Days, as in the verse, "At the
end He plunges all in darkness" (Job 28:3). [So Jacob had to be distinguished
from *'ekev 'esav* by the addition of the letter to 'ekev in the formation of his
name.]

Concerning the verse, "They shall strike at your head *(rosh)*, and you [the
serpent] shall strike at their heel" (Gen. 3:15), the Zohar writes: [The serpent]
was referred to as *rosh*, because the first letter [*rosh*] of the name *Ya'akov*, the
letter *yod*, [whose numerical value is ten,] represents the Ten Commandments,
and it is with them that "they shall strike at your head." But "when you [Esau]
grow restive" (Gen. 27:40), and throw off the [commandments represented by
the] *yod* [of *Ya'akov*], "you shall strike at their heel." Thus he was called
Ya'akov, because of the *'ekev* (heel), which is derived from Samael the Accuser;
to avoid arousing the latter, the letter *yod* must be added, making the name
Ya'akov. This is the hidden meaning of "his hand *(yado)* grasping the heel of
Esau."

The word *yado* has the same letters as the word *yod*, alluding to the
joining of the letter *yod* with *'ekev* to make the name *Ya'akov*. And it was by

virtue of this name that Jacob merited the name Israel, following the chastening
he underwent in his difficulties with Esau and the fear he had felt.

Now, the name Israel is more exalted than that of the angels, and he was
given this name for "having been made a ruler* along with God" (Gen. 32:29),
translated by Onkelos as "You are more important than all others in the sight
of the Lord."

Now I shall explain the hidden meaning. When he still bore the name
Jacob, he came deviously, cleverly, to take the blessings, meaning to supplant
Esau. Satan the Accuser was holding on to him from above. For Esau [Satan]
is Edom, who in turn is the foul and accursed primordial serpent. "Now the
serpent was the shrewdest [of all the wild beasts]" (Gen 3:1); therefore Jacob
had to approach him shrewdly, to subdue him with his own devices, just as they
slew Balaam with a sword, which was his own accustomed weapon. (We learn
this from Rashi's comment on the verse, "They also put Balaam son of Peor
to the sword" [Num. 31:8].) The Zohar tells us they could only have killed
Balaam with his own sword.

The Targum translates the phrase "a skillful hunter" (Gen. 25:27) [into
Aramaic] as nahash-yarkhan. According to [the commentary of Rabbi Mena-
ḥem] Ẓioni the hidden meaning of this is that there was a serpent (nahash)
tattooed on [Esau's] thigh (yerekh). Samael [Esau's guardian angel] tried to touch
the hollow of Jacob's thigh [to transfer to it the evil power on Esau's thigh].
But he could not do it, for "there is no serpent [nahash†] in Jacob" (Num.
23:23).

Now the fruit of Jacob's thighs is a holy race, and Esau derives from the
cursed serpent. Jacob and his offspring are "a stock the Lord has blessed" (Isa.
61:9). Therefore, Jacob came to take the blessing, but he did so in a roundabout
(be'okvah), devious way, with the cunning of the serpent. 'Ormah, "cunning,"
can also mean prudence, as we see in the verse, "I, Wisdom, live with prudence
('ormah)" (Prov. 8:12).

Later on, when Jacob takes hold of the source of his blessings on high,
he is called Israel, for he goes up to God, to the Hidden Place. Israel's level is
an exalted one; he is among the angels and attains to heights even they cannot
reach. We speak here of ascent step by step to a place hidden even from the
highest ministering angels. Hence Onkelos's translation: "You are more important than all others in the sight of the Lord."

All this becomes clear in the verse, "Lo, there is no augury (nahash) in

---

*An alternative reading of sarita, usually understood to mean "you have wrestled."
†Usually understood to mean "augury" (see below).

Jacob, no divining *(kesem)* in Israel: Jacob is told at once, yea Israel, what God has done *(mah pa'al el)"* (Num. 23:23). At the outset Jacob drives out the serpent *(nahash),* with all its powers, so that there is not even any divining in Israel. (The latter is at bottom something minor, as in "Remove the toothpick [*kisam*] from between your teeth" [Arakhin 16b].) He then rises step by step, until there comes a time when the ministering angels ask Jacob, who has now become Israel and has been given precedence over them, "What has God done *(mah pa'al el)?"* That is the interpretation of our Rabbis, may their memory be a blessing, as cited by Rashi in his commentary on the portion Balak [Num. 22:2–25:9].

The name Israel was not new. It had occurred [to God] before the world was created. But it was only down below [in the created world] that Jacob came to be *called* Israel, by virtue of his ascent to the level of the Eternal Israel, to which our Rabbis, may their memory be a blessing, allude in their esoteric writings. All the Patriarchs were likewise called Israel, each according to his degree of ascent. —SHNEI LUḤOT HABRIT, Torah Shebikhtav 288

MEN WILL HALLOW THE HOLY ONE OF JACOB AND STAND IN AWE OF THE GOD OF ISRAEL

"Listen to Me, O Jacob, Israel whom I have called. . . . [My own hand founded the earth, My right hand spread out the skies]" (Isa. 48:12–13). This is what is meant in the verse, "You have seen what I did. . . . Now then, if you will listen to Me" (Exod. 19:4–5)—you have only come to Me in order to listen to Me; hence, "Listen to Me, O Jacob."

Rabbi Abbahu said: In the Time to Come, all shall stand amazed before those who obeyed the Holy One, blessed be He, saying, "What is this? So-and-so, who did not study a day in his life, is now sitting and talking with the Patriarchs?" And the Holy One, blessed be He, shall say to them, "Why should you be amazed? These people are deserving because in their lifetimes they listened to Me, as it written, 'He whose ear heeds the discipline of life lodges among the wise' (Prov. 15:31)." Hence, "Listen to Me, O Jacob."

Another interpretation of "Listen to Me, O Jacob": this is what is meant by the verse, "But you have not called upon Me, O Jacob" (Isa. 43:22). It can be likened to a king who had a friend, a poor man. This poor man made a feast one day, to which he invited his children. The king went uninvited and, once inside the poor man's house, said to him, "You invited all your children, but me you did not invite; do I not love you?" He said to him, "If it please your majesty, I am a poor man, and I was not making a feast worthy of your majesty, so that I was ashamed to invite you." Said the king to him, "My good man, do not be ashamed! Any feast you make means more to me than those prepared for me in my own palace."

Similarly, at the hour of his death, our Father Jacob summoned his children to read them his will, and he blessed them and parcelled out the Land among them. At that moment, the Holy One, blessed be He, revealed Himself to him and said, "Jacob, do you not summon Me as well? 'You have not called upon Me, O Jacob!' " He said to Him, "Master of the Universe, I was ashamed to summon You, for I am poor." Said God to him, "Do you not know that when a poor man calls upon Me, I listen, as it is written, 'Here was a poor man who called and the Lord listened' (Ps. 34:7)? You should have summoned Me along with your children!" "I would have been ashamed," Jacob said. God replied, "Heaven forbid you should be ashamed, as it is written, 'No more shall Jacob be shamed' (Isa. 29:22)." When Jacob's children saw this, they began to praise the Holy One, blessed be He, for His humility in not despising those who stand in awe of Him. And what is written next? "When . . . his children behold what My hands have wrought in his midst, they will hallow My Name. Men will hallow the Holy One of Jacob and stand in awe of the God of Israel" (Isa. 29:23). Therefore, "Listen to Me, O Jacob."

Another interpretation of "Listen to Me, O Jacob": those who are slain while calling upon My Name, as it is written, "It is for Your sake that we are slain" (Ps. 44:23), and "Though He slay me, yet will I trust in Him" (Job 13:15); those who call upon Me year after year, as it is written, "I raise the cup of deliverance and invoke the name of the Lord. . . . I came upon trouble and sorrow and I invoked the name of the Lord" (Ps. 116:13, 3–4)—these generations said to Him,

Master of all Worlds, earlier generations had fathers whose merit stood them in good stead, but "we have become orphans, fatherless" (Lam. 5:3). Yet You instructed the prophet to say, "In You alone orphans find pity" (Hos. 14:4) and "You have ever been the orphan's help" (Ps. 10:14). Often in Your Torah You command us concerning orphans: "When you gather the grapes of your vineyard, [do not pick it over again]" (Deut. 24:21); "When you reap the harvest [in your field and overlook a sheaf . . . , do not turn back to get it]" (Deut. 24:19); "When you shake [the fruit from your olive trees, do not go over them again]" (Deut. 24:20). And to whom [are these things to be left]? "The stranger, the fatherless, and the widow." We are fatherless; have mercy on us, as it is written,

"In You alone orphans find pity"! Obadiah's house was blessed when his children were orphaned. When was Isaac blessed? When his father left him, as it is written, "After the death [of Abraham,] God blessed [his son Isaac]" (Gen. 25:11). So it was with the tribes: "Joseph died" (Gen. 50:26) "and the Israelites were fertile" (Exod. 1:7). Your eyes are on the orphans; "In You alone orphans find pity."

Said He to them, "Repent, and I shall heal your afflictions."
The Holy One, blessed be He, says,

Even before they repented I agreed to heal their affliction, as it is written, "Turn back, O rebellious children; I will heal [your afflictions]" (Jer. 3:22), and it is written, "I will heal their affliction, generously will I take them back in love" (Hos. 14:5). I love you unceasingly. Isaac called Esau his firstborn, and I call Jacob My firstborn; [Esau's] birthright was annulled, but Jacob's was fulfilled. Isaac loved Esau—as it is written, "Isaac loved Esau" (Gen. 25:28)—and I love Jacob. Isaac's love ended, but [Mine for Jacob] did not. How the nations of the world have tried to make Me hate him, but they have not been able to do so, as it is written, "Vast floods cannot [quench love]" (Song 8:7)—these are the nations of the world, who are compared to water, as it is written, "Ah, the roar of many peoples that roar as roars the sea" (Isa. 17:12).

Moreover, some of the nations kill Jews in order to drive the Jewish people away from the Holy One, blessed be He; but the Assembly of Israel says to them, "I cannot deny Him, as it is written, 'My heart was stirred for him. . . . I was faint because of what he said' (Song 5:4, 6)—as soon as He spoke to me at Mount Sinai, my soul took heed—and my heart is sick for Him, as it is written, 'I am faint with love' (Song 2:5)."
The nations of the world said to [Israel], "How is your beloved better than another?" (Song 5:9), and she said to them,

I shall recount to you in detail His praiseworthy deeds, so that you understand that it is not for nought that I court Him: "My beloved is clear-skinned (zakh) and ruddy" (Song 5:10)—clear-skinned to Jacob and ruddy to Esau, as it is written, "[Who is this coming from Edom, in crimson garments . . . ? 'It is I, who contend victoriously. . . . '] Why is your clothing so red?" (Isa. 63:1-2). "Pre-eminent among the throng" (Song 5:10)—in the hosts of heaven there is none like Him. "His head is finest gold" (Song 5:11)—this refers to the Torah, as it is written, "[The judgments of the Lord are true, . . .] more desirable than gold, than much fine gold" (Ps. 19:11). "His locks are curled" (Song 5:11)—these are the chapters of the Torah, which are made up of verses. "Black as a raven" (Song 5:11)—that is the writing. Another interpretation of "black": this refers to the Assembly of Israel, as it is written, "I am black, but comely" (Song 1:5). "His eyes are like doves" (Song 5:12)—the sun and the moon. "His hands are rods of gold" (Song 5:14)—the rainbow. "His belly a tablet of ivory" (Song 5:14)—the air.

"His legs are like marble pillars" (Song 5:15)—the mountains. "Set in sockets of fine gold" (Song 5:15)—the foundations of the Sanctuary. "He is majestic as Lebanon" (Song 5:15)—the Temple. "Stately as the cedars" (Song 5:15)—for He walks with the righteous, as it is written, "I shall walk in your midst" (Lev. 26:12). "His mouth is delicious" (Song 5:16)—at the time of the Giving of the Torah. "And all of him is delightful" (Song 5:16)—when He takes back the penitent.

The nations of the world replied, "Since He takes back the penitent, 'Whither has your beloved gone, O fairest of women? Whither has your beloved turned? Let us seek him with you' (Song 6:1)." Said the Holy One, blessed be He, "The nations of the world are trying to make Me hateful to My children, while My children are trying to make [the nations] love Me, as much as if I had given them a hundred worlds full of the love I have given My children, as it is written, 'If a man offered all his wealth for love, they would yet laugh him to scorn' (Song 8:7)." —AGGADAT BERESHIT; SHTEI YADOT

YOU SHALL BE TO ME A TREASURED POSSESSION

EXODUS 19:4

You have seen what I did to the Egyptians,
how I carried you on eagles' wings
and brought you to Me.

"You have seen"—It is not through tradition that I am speaking to you, nor am I sending you a written message, nor am I summoning witnesses; rather, "you have *seen* what I did to the Egyptians." —MEKHILTA

"What I did to the Egyptians"—Although the Egyptians are idolaters and fornicators and killers, I did not punish them except on your account and for your sake. —MEKHILTA DE-RABBI SHIM'ON BAR YOHAI

"What I did to the Egyptians"—How I pleaded with them to repent their evil ways. For I do not desire the death of the wicked but rather that they abandon their evil ways and live [Cf. Ezek. 33:11]. But since they were stubborn, I had to multiply My signs and wonders in their midst and destroy them. —SFORNO

HOW I CARRIED YOU

"How I carried you"—The provision of a person's livelihood and needs is called "carrying," as when we say that a nurse "carries" an infant. To be sure, there are two kinds of carrying: when the child cannot yet walk and must be carried in one's arms, and when the child can walk but must still be lifted by the hands over thresholds and obstacles. This is the way the Holy One, blessed be He, sustains Israel throughout the generations: they work, like all people, independently plying their trades, yet He watches over their progress. This is akin to the second manner of "carrying" and is alluded to in the verse, "They

will carry you *(yisa'unkha)* in their hands" (Ps. 91:12). Here the extra letter *nun**
indicates that it is not literally carrying—that is, holding in the arms—but
merely holding up by the hands. The verse is interpreted as meaning that there
is Divine supervision "lest you hurt your foot on a stone" (Ps. 91:12)—that is,
run into trouble. But when the Holy One, blessed be He, sustains a man
without his working at all, it is called real carrying. Such was the carrying in
the wilderness, of which it is written, "how I carried you." As for "on eagles'
wings," it is explained that the sustenance was of a supernatural kind, lofty like
the wings of eagles. —HA'AMEK DAVAR

ON EAGLES' WINGS

"How I carried you on eagles' wings"—Rabbi Eli'ezer said: This refers to the
event at Mount Sinai, while "brought you to me" refers to the Temple.

Another interpretation of "on eagles' wings": The ear is told what it is
capable of hearing. Rabbi Eli'ezer, son of Rabbi Yose the Galileean, said: It is
written, "Like an eagle who rouses his nestlings" (Deut. 32:11). Eagles hover
over their young with their wings outspread so that they are not afraid. In the
same way, when the Omnipresent revealed the Torah to Israel, He did not
reveal it from one direction only but from all four, as it is written, "The Lord
came from Sinai; He shone upon them from Seir; He appeared from Mount
Paran" (Deut. 33:2). And what was the fourth direction? "God is coming from
Teman" (Habakkuk 3:3).

Another interpretation of "on eagles' wings": Birds keep their young
between their knees for fear of those that are stronger than they are [and
therefore fly higher], but the eagle, which does not fear any stronger creature,
puts its young on its shoulders. Why not in its claws? Because what it fears are
the pellets and arrows people throw at it, and therefore it makes its body a
barrier to protect its young against them. So does the Omnipresent make the
ministering angels into a barrier protecting Israel from the Egyptians, as it is
written, "The angel of God . . . [followed behind them]" (Exod. 14:19). And
just as the eagle spreads its wings and retracts them from time to time, so was
Israel buffeted twelve miles back and forth by each Divine pronouncement.†
So scripture says, "You grew more and more beautiful, and became fit for

*The word would normally be *yisa'ukha.*
†See note, p. 24.

royalty" (Ezek. 16:13)—just as the eagle ascends quickly from below to on high, so does Israel ascend quickly from below to on high. And just as [Israel's] ascent was supernatural, so was their descent. Thus it says, "When they go, I will spread My net over them, I will bring them down like birds of the sky; I will chastise them when I hear their bargaining" (Hos. 7:12). —MEKHILTA DE-RABBI SHIM'ON BAR YOHAI

"How I carried you on eagles' wings"—What makes the eagle different from other birds? They all carry their young in their claws, fearing other birds that might fly down upon them from above, but the eagle fears only man, who might shoot an arrow at it. It says, "It is better that it hit me and not my young." It may be compared to one who was walking along with his son in front of him when highwaymen came along and tried to kidnap him from the front. At this, the man put his son behind him. Then along came a wolf and tried to tear the lad away from behind, so he put him back in front of him. With highwaymen in front and a wolf behind, he put the child on his shoulders, as it is written, "in the wilderness, where you saw how the Lord your God carried you, as a man carries his son" (Deut. 1:31). —MEKHILTA

"How I carried (va'esa) you"—This refers to the day Israel came to Ramses. For they were dispersed throughout the land of Goshen, and in preparation for their departure they were all assembled briefly at Ramses. Onkelos translates va'esa as though it were va'asi'a—"I transported you, [as if on eagles' wings]"—a revision more respectful to the Most High. —RASHI

"On eagles' wings"—I carried you over the sea, the way eagles cross seas by flying, and you were unharmed, as it is written, "Like an eagle who rouses his nestlings, gliding down to his young, [so spread He His wings and took him, bore him along on His pinions]" (Deut. 32:11). —RASHBAM

"How I carried you on eagles' wings"—That is to say, I raised you up on high, elevated you to greatness, in that I took you out of slavery and brought you to Me, to worship Me, the King of Kings. What a great elevation this is for you, as if I had lifted you on the wings of eagles, which fly higher than all the other birds. "On eagles' wings" refers to the fact that the eagle bears its young aloft on its wings, and they are not afraid, either of arrows from below or of other birds from above, because the eagle flies higher than them all. So did the Holy One, blessed be He, for Israel, placing the pillar of fire before them and the [pillar of] cloud behind them, "the waters forming a wall for them on their right and on their left" (Exod. 14:22), and they had no fear of any foe. —BEKHOR SHOR

"You have seen what I did to the Egyptians, how I carried you on eagles' wings"—Said Rabbi Yehudah: out of compassion, as it is written, "Like an eagle who rouses his nestlings." This is the hidden meaning expounded by Rabbi Shim'on: "How an eagle makes its way over the sky" (Prov. 30:19)— what is meant by "over the sky"? Out of compassion. Just as an eagle shows compassion to its young and harshness toward others, so does the Holy One, blessed be He, show compassion toward Israel and harshness toward the idolatrous nations.

Rabbi El'azar was walking from Cappadocia to Lydda, and Rabbi Yose and Rabbi Hiyya were with him. They arose at daybreak and went on their way. Said Rabbi Hiyya: I see before me what is described in the verse, "Each of the four had the face of a lion on the right; each of the four had the face of an ox on the left; and each of the four had the face of an eagle" (Ezek. 1:10). The lion is to the right and the ox to the left, but where is the eagle? Rabbi El'azar replied: In Jacob's place [the place of compassion].* Why? Because the eagle combines the two, showing compassion toward its young and harshness toward others. Thus does the Holy One, blessed be He, guide Israel in mercy and treat others with strict judgment, as it is written, "I carried you on eagles' wings" and "Like an eagle who rouses his nestlings."

How do we know the eagle is called Mercy? Because it is written, "How an eagle makes its way in the heavens" (Prov. 30:19)—literally, in heaven [the place of the *sefirot,* including Beauty, which is mercy]. And that is why the lion is to the right, the ox to the left, and the eagle in between, drawing them together. Man includes all, and all are included in him, as it is written, "Upon this semblance of a throne there was the semblance of a human form"† (Ezek. 1:26). —ZOHAR, Exodus 80b

Rabbi Shim'on said: Of the three creatures in the chariot, the lion, the ox, and the eagle, none is as compassionate as the latter. That is why He said to Israel, "How I carried you on eagles' wings and brought you to Me." —TIKKUNIM 25

*A reference to the *sefirah* of Beauty *(tif'eret).*
†A reference to the *sefirah* of Sovereignty *(malkhut).*

Rabbi Yishma'el said: Metatron, the guardian angel of the innermost court, He-Who-Dwells-in-the-Highest, said to me,

> How numerous are the chariots of the Holy One, blessed be He! He has chariots of cherubim, as it is written, "He mounted a cherub and flew" (2 Sam. 22:11). He has chariots of wind, as it is written, "gliding on the wings of the wind" (Ps. 18:11). He has chariots of light clouds, as it is written, "Mounted on a light cloud, [the Lord will come to Egypt]" (Isa. 19:1). He has chariots of thick clouds, as it is written, "I will come to you in a thick cloud" (Exod. 19:9). He has chariots of altars, as it is written, "I saw my Lord standing upon the altar" (Amos 9:1). He has chariots of myriads, as it is written, "God's chariots are myriads upon myriads, thousands upon thousands" (Ps. 68:18). He has chariots of the Tent of Meeting, as it is written, "The Lord spoke to him from the Tent of Meeting" (Lev. 1:1). He has chariots of the Ark cover, as it is written, "He would hear the Voice addressing him from above the cover [that was on top of the Ark]" (Num. 7:89). He has chariots of sapphire, as it is written, "Under His feet there was the likeness of a pavement of sapphire" (Exod. 24:10). He has chariots of eagles, as it is written, "I carried you on eagles' wings and brought you to Me."
>
> —SEDER RUḤOT 5:177

AND BROUGHT YOU TO ME

"And brought you to Me"—to Mount Sinai. Rabbi 'Akiva said: This refers to the day of the Giving of the Torah. . . . —MEKHILTA

"And brought *(ve'avi)* you to Me"—The word *ve'avi* is missing the [usual] letter *yod* [whose numerical value is ten], for they had not yet received the Ten Commandments. —SEKHEL TOV

"And brought you to Me"—to be your God; for all the earth and all peoples are Mine, but you alone have I chosen. —RASHBAM

"And brought you to Me"—["You"] has two meanings: first, the masses, whom He had brought to be His people; and second, the leaders of Israel, whose awareness He had raised so that they could attain the holy spirit and Divine power. And before taking up the matter of conditions, He speaks of what He has already done [for us], in order to show us that it is in our interest to be connected to Him, may He be blessed. For His powers are greatly exalted, as we have seen. —HA'AMEK DAVAR

WHAT WAS IS WHAT SHALL BE

Rabbi Naḥman said: What was is what shall be. Just as the Holy One, blessed be He, raised Israel up into clouds of glory and encompassed them and carried them along—as it is written, "I carried you on eagles' wings"—so will He do for them in the future, as it is written, "Who are these that float like a cloud" (Isa. 60:8). —MIDRASH ON PSALMS 48

"You have seen what I did to the Egyptians"—to the guardian angel of Egypt, as in the verse, "[The Israelites caught sight of] the Egyptians advancing upon them" (Exod. 14:10), where the verb is [the singular] *nose'a*, referring to their guardian angel, rather than the plural [*nos'im*]. He was brought down at the height of his powers, on the fifteenth of Nisan, for that is when [the constellation] Aries, an Egyptian god, is at its height, and the Holy One, blessed be He, humiliated him, as it is written, "I will mete out punishments to all the gods of Egypt" (Exod. 12:12). "I carried you on eagles' wings" means I took you out from under his rule and did not give you over to any constellation or angel but rather lifted you up above them. Thus the Holy One, blessed be He, said to our Father Abraham, "Look *(habet)* toward heaven [and count the stars. . . . So shall your offspring be]" (Gen. 15:5); and *habata* always means looking down. "While the sandal is on your foot, trample the thorns; [he who is placed below (the stars) fears them, but you (Abraham) are placed above them]" (Genesis Rabbah 44:12); that is, our Father Abraham was not under the control [of the stars]. Similarly here, "I carried you on eagles' wings" [means "I lifted you above eagles' wings," and] refers to heavenly eagles, as in the comment of the author of *'Akedat Yizḥak* on the verse, "Our pursuers were swifter than the eagles of heaven; they chased us in the mountains, lay in wait for us in the wilderness" (Lam. 4:19)—Israel was about to be destroyed at the hands of its enemies, and the Holy One, blessed be He, despoiled them and raised Israel above them.

"And brought you to Me"—so that I, and no one else, might watch over you. —SHEMEN TOV

"You have seen what I did to the Egyptians, how I carried you on eagles' wings and brought you to Me. Now, if you will heed Me and keep My covenant, you shall be to Me a treasured possession among all the peoples. Indeed, all the earth is Mine, but you shall be to Me a kingdom of priests and a holy nation. . . ." (Exod. 19:4–6). Although you have not yet received the Torah, I have already raised you up from the lowest to the highest—"I carried you on eagles' wings

and brought you to Me"—so that you would be attached to Me. "Now
then"—if you want to remain at this exalted level, you must resolve to do two
things: "obey Me faithfully," which is equivalent to "we shall hear" (Exod.
24:7); and "keep My covenant," which is equivalent to "we shall do" (Exod.
24:7). Then, "you shall be My treasured possession among all the peoples. . . .
You shall be to Me a kingdom of priests and a holy nation." This is the degree
of elevation meant by "and brought you to Me." —MEI MAROM

EXODUS 19:5
Now, if you will heed Me
faithfully and keep My covenant,
you shall be a treasured possession
to Me among all the peoples.
Indeed, all the earth is Mine.

IF YOU WILL HEED ME FAITHFULLY

"Now, if you will heed Me." "Now"—You might as well undertake these
things now, for all beginnings are difficult.

"If you will heed"—From here derives the saying that if you heed one
commandment, you can be told many others, as it is written, "If you will heed
(shamo'a tishme'u)"; whereas, if you forget one commandment, you can be
made to forget many others, as it is written, "If you do forget *(shakhoah tishkah)*"
(Deut. 8:19).* —MEKHILTA

"Now, if you will heed Me . . . you shall be to Me a treasured possession among
all the peoples"—This [status] is retroactive. And, *a fortiori,* if I was willing to
perform all these miracles for them even before they had accepted the Torah
and begun to observe the commandments, how much more so afterward.

Another interpretation of "if you will heed Me": we learn from this that
all beginnings are difficult, but once one begins to pay heed, it all becomes easy.
One who heeds a little can be told much more; one who heeds the Torah can
be taught the words of the Scribes. —MEKHILTA DE-RABBI SHIM'ON BAR YOHAI

---

*Both verses use the emphatic, double form of the verb, which appears to imply one
action leading to other, similar ones.

"If you will heed Me"—observing My commandments and performing My service, you shall be exalted above all the other nations. For they are all Mine, but I shall raise you up above them all. "Indeed, all the earth is Mine," and thus it is in My power to exalt you above them. —BEKHOR SHOR

"Now, if you will heed Me"—Since humankind is part of the material world, and two opposites cannot be joined except by some common element, [God] resolved that in order to unite [Israel] with His great Name He would have to prepare them a bit [by giving them the Ten Commandments] and then guide them Himself. This is the meaning of "Now, if you will heed Me": you will hear the Ten Commandments directly from Me rather than through a prophet, so that you yourselves become prophets and fall under Divine guidance.

"And keep My covenant"—by physically observing the commandments—"you shall be to Me a treasured possession among all the peoples"—Divine guidance and inspiration shall come [first] to you, and only then to all the other peoples.

"Indeed, all the earth is Mine"—and it is through you that Divine bounty shall come to the others, after the fashion described in the verse, "Who gives rain to the earth and sends water over the fields" (Job 5:10), namely, that it is from the dregs of the Land of Israel that all the other lands shall be given to drink. —SHEMEN TOV

"Now, if you will heed Me. . . ."—Once, in one of the holy talks he gave at his pure table, Rabbi Simḥah Bunem of Przysucha said, quoting the Ba'al Shem Tov, that a difficulty arose from the saying of the Sages, may their memory be a blessing, that "each day a heavenly voice issues forth from Mount Horeb saying, 'Woe to men for the affront to the Torah.' " How are we to understand this? If the voice comes to rouse Israel to repentance, we should be able to hear it [yet we do not]! And if no one can hear it, what is the voice for? In fact, said Rabbi Simḥah Bunem, it is to be compared to a man who went on a business trip during the summer accompanied by his young son. As they drove through a forest, the boy began asking if he could climb down from the wagon and go off into the forest to gather berries. His father replied, "Son, if you go off to gather berries and I drive on, you are bound to get lost in the forest, God forbid." Said the boy, "I will go slowly, and you continue on, and every so often I will call you, and when you answer I will be able to follow your voice, so that I will know where you are and not get lost; and once I have gathered some berries I will rejoin you." The boy climbed down from the wagon and went off to gather berries, and his father went on. The father called out, "My son, my son," but the boy did not hear him. Said the father, "This is all well and good as long as you hear my voice, but if you do not, you are bound to get lost, God forbid." —SIAḤ SARFEI KODESH

"In heaven You pronounced sentence, [the earth was numbed with fright]" (Ps. 76:9)—Said the Holy One, blessed be He, "If Israel accepts the Torah, well and good; but if they do not, I shall return [the world] to chaos." This is what is meant by "now then": if right now, as I give you the Torah, "you heed Me" by accepting it, "you shall be to Me a treasured possession among all the peoples"— your merit will carry much weight, for only by virtue of it will "all the earth [be] Mine," that is, [only by virtue of you] will [the other nations] survive; if not, I will return them to chaos. Therefore, you shall be rewarded for all their sakes by being made "to Me a treasured possession." —ZEKAN AHARON

YOU SHALL BE TO ME A TREASURED POSSESSION

"And keep My covenant"—Rabbi Eli'ezer says: This refers to the covenant of circumcision. Rabbi 'Akiva says: It refers to the covenant of the Sabbath. And the Sages say: It refers to the covenant [against] idolatry.

"You shall be to Me"—consecrated to Me, to the study of My Torah and the performance of My commandments. Thus scripture says, "[You shall be holy to Me, for I the Lord am holy,] and I have set you apart from other peoples to be Mine" (Lev. 20:26)—as long as you are set apart from the other peoples you are Mine, but if not, you belong to Nebuchadnezzar and his friends.

"A treasured possession among all the peoples"—just as a person's most treasured possession is beloved of him, so Israel is beloved of Me; just as a person's most treasured possession is precious to him, so Israel is precious to Me. Concerning this a parable is drawn: To what may the matter be compared? To a person who has inherited a great deal of land but nevertheless goes out and buys an additional field, which becomes his favorite. Why? Because he bought it himself. Similarly, although the whole world belongs to Him-Who-Spoke-and-the-World-Came-Into-Being, He only loves Israel. Why? Because He Himself took them out of Egypt and redeemed them from the house of bondage. That is why it says, "You shall be to Me a treasured possession among all the peoples."

Rabbi Yehoshu'a ben Korḥah says: "A treasured possession"—but you should not get the wrong idea. A woman, being her husband's treasured possession, can seclude herself from all but him; and a son, being his father's treasured possession, can seclude himself from all but him. Should [the people] Israel thus seclude themselves from the other nations of the world? This is why scripture tells us, "All the earth is Mine"—[meaning, you will still be part of it]. —MEKHILTA DE-RABBI SHIM'ON BAR YOHAI

Meruzeh 'alav [translated here as "beloved of him"] should be understood in the sense of *meruzeh bo* ("[he is] pleased with him"), and the same with the plural forms.

"Now, if you will heed Me"—to take upon yourselves the Torah and the commandments—"and keep My covenant"—which I shall make conditional upon your acceptance. This is the covenant He made after they said, "We shall do, and we shall hear": "This is the blood of the covenant that the Lord now makes with you concerning all these commands" (Exod. 24:8)—so that I will not have to do to you what I did to the Egyptians.

"You shall be to Me a treasured possession among all the peoples"— And although the entire human race is dearer to Me than the lower creatures—as our Rabbis, may their memory be a blessing, said, "Dear is man, for he was created in the [Divine] image"—nonetheless, you shall be My particular treasure.

"For all the earth is Mine"—Your difference from them is only a matter of degree, for the whole world is Mine, and the righteous of the other nations are dear to Me as well; nevertheless, I shall treasure you above them all. —SFORNO

THE CHAIN OF BEING

All being depends on the word of the Blessed One, in a chain ascending from one level to the next. As the foundations of the world draw their existence one from another, the inanimate gives rise to plant life, plant life gives rise to animal life, the speaking animal [human being] is higher still, and the angel represents yet a higher spiritual stage. There are also intermediate stages: as has been said in the name of Rabbi Yizhak Abrabanel, the intermediate stage between the human being—who is the speaking animal—and the angel, who is a spiritual being, is the Jewish people, which is a creature that speaks Divine words, so that it provides a spiritual link [between God and] humanity as a whole.

This is the import of the verse, "you shall be My treasured possession among all the peoples." For "all the earth is Mine"—that is, all life flows from Me and to Me—yet My plenitude can only reach down to other living things through you; your mediation is essential to the existence of the world. As scripture says, "If the heavens above could be measured, [and the foundations of the earth below could be fathomed,] only then would I reject all the offspring of Israel for all that they have done to Me—declares the Lord" (Jer. 31:37).* This is also the meaning of the verse, "[but the Lord's portion is His people,] Jacob His own allotment *(hevel nahalato)*" (Deut. 32:9)—that is, the chain of being.† The ladder our Father Jacob, peace be to him, saw also alludes to this.
—ZEKAN AHARON

Rabbi Yehoshu'a of Sakhnin said in the name of Rabbi Levi: [The people] Israel are called the treasured possession of the Holy One, blessed be He, as it is written, "You shall be to Me a treasured possession." When one's treasured possessions are defective, one tries to correct the defect. In the same way, it is hard for the Holy One, blessed be He, to cause any harm to Israel. Thus, [for example,] you can be sure that their losses [to the plague] in the days of David were made up for in the days of Solomon, as it is written, "Judah and Israel were as numerous as the sands of the sea" (1 Kings 4:20).

Just as a treasured possession can be the most precious thing a person owns, Israel is more precious to the Holy One, blessed be He, than all the other nations, as it is written, "The Lord your God will set you high above all the nations of the earth" (Deut. 28:1); and it is also written, "You shall be blessed above all other peoples" (Deut. 7:14).

Rabbi Abin said, in the name of Rabbi Yehoshu'a: "You shall be to Me *(li)*"—*Lamed* [the first of the two letters of the word *li*] is the largest of the letters, and *yod* [the second of the two letters] is the smallest: the greatest takes pleasure in cleaving to the smallest. "Great is our Lord and full of power" (Ps. 147:5); and "You are the smallest of peoples" (Deut. 7:7). The greatest takes pleasure in cleaving to the smallest. —PESIKTA RABBATI, Yehudah Veyisra'el

"You shall be to Me"—You shall be devoted entirely to Me, engaged in the study of the Torah and nothing else. —MEKHILTA

---

*Li, "to Me," can also be read "for Me."
†In addition to meaning a strip of land, *hevel* can mean a rope or strand.

"You shall be to Me a treasured possession *(segulah)*"—The Holy Jew of Przysucha explained this verse as follows: just as a talisman *(segulah)* is effective in ways that cannot be explained rationally, so did He promise to keep us close to Him, may He be blessed, regardless of any rational justification. —TORAT EMET

"You shall be to Me a treasured possession"—Rabbi Moshe of Kubrin said: "You shall be to Me [a treasured possession]" is the greatest of all privileges. "You shall be to Me a treasured possession among all the peoples. Indeed, all the earth is Mine"—all the peoples of the earth belong to Me, yet I shall set you apart from them to be Mine.

Rabbi Marinos [Yonah Ibn Janah] said: The meaning of "all the earth is Mine" is: although all the earth belongs to Me. This interpretation is supported, in my view, by the verses, "Stiffnecked though this people be, [pardon our iniquity and our sin, and take us for Your own]" (Exod. 34:9), and "[O Lord,] . . . heal me, for I have sinned against You" (Ps. 41:5). —IBN 'EZRA

"Indeed *(ki),* all the earth is Mine"—Although the whole world belongs to Me, you shall be the most precious of all. *Ki* here means "although," as in "although *(ki)* Manasseh was the firstborn" (Gen. 48:14), and as in "[God did not lead them by way of the land of the Philistines,] although *(ki)* it was nearer" (Exod. 13:17). —HIZKUNI

"You shall be to Me a treasured possession among all the peoples. Indeed, all the earth is Mine"—This presents a difficulty, for it seems to imply that, even though all peoples are equal in God's sight, He, may He be blessed, grants Israel a special status beyond what is merited. But is it imaginable that the other nations, who did not accept the Torah, should be as highly regarded as Israel, who did accept it? Rather, what it means is, You shall be to Me a treasured possession in the Time to Come, understanding the word *ki* to mean "when": when all the earth is Mine. Similarly, scripture says, "For *(ki)* then I will make the peoples [pure of speech, so that they all invoke the Lord by name and serve Him with one accord]" (Zephaniah 3:9). And though at that time they will all call upon My name, you shall be on a higher rung and more precious than them all. It is like the higher station enjoyed by the priests and saints vis-à-vis the rest of the people, as scripture says, "You shall be called 'Priests of the Lord,' [and termed 'Servants of our God.' You shall enjoy the wealth of nations and revel in their riches]" (Isa. 61:6). —ZEKAN AHARON

"You shall be to Me a treasured possession among all the peoples. Indeed, all the earth is Mine"—Needless to say, this applies as long as the other nations are sunk in error and do not recognize the one Creator. But even when His name is One* and all know and recognize the truths of the blessed Lord, Israel will remain His treasured possession. This is what is meant by the phrase "all the earth is Mine"—even *when* all the earth is Mine, when everyone acknowledges the name of the Lord, "you shall be to Me a treasured possession among all the peoples." —MESHEKH HOKHMAH

"Now, if you will heed Me [and keep My covenant, you shall be to Me a treasured possession among all the peoples]. Indeed, all the earth is Mine"— Why does it say "Now"? When the Messiah comes, the other peoples, too, will learn that "all the earth is Mine"; but as for "Now, if you will heed Me [and keep My covenant,] *you* shall be to Me a treasured possession among all the peoples." —MA'AGELEI ZEDEK

"Now, if you will heed Me [and keep My covenant, you shall be to Me a treasured possession among all the peoples]. Indeed, all the earth is Mine"— Even though I have appointed a guardian angel for every people and tongue, you shall remain in *My* special care, and I shall not appoint over you either a ruler or a judge but rule you directly Myself. That is what is meant by the verse, "[When the Most High gave nations their homes and] set the divisions of man, He fixed the boundaries of peoples [in relation to Israel's numbers]. . . . For the Lord's portion is His people" (Deut. 32:8–9). Similarly, scripture says, "See, the guardian of Israel neither slumbers nor sleeps! [The Lord is your guardian]" (Ps. 121:4). —ZIYYONI

"My beloved is mine and I am his who browses among the lilies" (Song 2:16)—"My beloved is mine" when He says to me, "I am the Lord your God" (Exod. 20:2); "and I am his" when He says to me, "You shall be to Me a treasured possession." "Who browses among the lilies" refers to the Holy One,

_____

*In the End of Days, when all come to acknowledge the one God, "the Lord shall be one and His name one" (Zech. 14:9).

blessed be He, as it is written, "Give ear, O shepherd of Israel" (Ps. 80:2).
—Rabbi Avigdor Kohen-Zedek, COMMENTARY ON THE SONG OF SONGS

AND KEEP MY COVENANT

"And keep My covenant"—This is the principle of the Torah as a whole, as it is written, "Then he took the record of the covenant [and read it aloud to the people. And they said, 'All that the Lord has spoken we shall do and we shall hear']" (Exod. 24:7). —MIDRASH SEKHEL TOV

"Now, if you will heed Me and keep My covenant"—He who is commanded and carries out the commandment is more meritorious than he who is not commanded and yet carries it out. For this reason, even when the other nations come to invoke the Name and seek to uphold the Torah, they will not be equal to Israel, for they will not have been commanded to do what they do. This is why it says "if you will heed Me" and only then "keep"—in other words, having been commanded, you then observe—then "you shall be to Me a treasured possession." And lest you protest that this statement is redundant, for the other nations do not observe the [commandments of] the Torah at all, scripture goes on to say that even when "all the earth is Mine" and all heed My words and draw near to My service, "you shall be to Me" more important than them, "a kingdom of priests and a holy nation." —MA'AGELEI ZEDEK

"Now . . ."—These two verses [5 and 6], through the words "a holy nation," speak of condition and result: if [the Israelites] do such and such, they shall merit such and such. But looking at the passage more closely we find we can understand it in two different ways:

(a) "If you will heed Me and keep My covenant," then "you shall be to Me [a treasured possession]." According to this interpretation, "you shall be to Me a kingdom of priests" is neither condition nor result but a commandment in its own right.
(b) "If you will heed Me and keep My covenant" and "be to Me a treasured possession," then "you shall be to Me a kingdom of priests."

Now both interpretations seem forced, for if (a) is correct, it should have said *vetihyu* ["you shall be to Me," in the future tense, "a treasured possession"]; while if (b) is correct, the word *ve'atem* ["and as for you," preceding "you shall be to Me a kingdom of priests"] is redundant. But in fact, both interpretations are Divinely inspired.

Interpretation (a) is for ordinary people. According to this view, "now" means "from now on"; and "If you will heed Me" means by studying Torah, in order to understand My word in a precise manner. (We see in a number of scriptural passages that "heeding" means "pondering carefully.") The condition imposed here represents a departure from what was stated at the beginning of the passage—"[You have seen] what I did to the Egyptians, [how I carried you on eagles' wings] (Exod. 19:4)—where [God's assistance] was given freely and unconditionally. Henceforth, it will be given only "if you will heed Me"—only then shall I fight your battles. (It is well known that the study of Torah is Israel's sword.) "And keep My covenant" refers to the sacrificial rites, the covenant of sacrifice that is also the Covenant of the Pieces made with our Father Abraham: if you are careful to bring sacrifice at the proper time. This condition is in contrast to the unconditional character of "I carried you on eagles' wings"; henceforth, God says, I will do this only "if you keep My covenant."

Note that scripture does not say a word here about acts of kindness (gemilut hasadim), which the other nations, too, are obligated to perform so as to build a compassionate world. (Sodom was destroyed for not supporting the poor.) But the descendants of Abraham, Isaac, and Jacob are known for their kindness, for being merciful and compassionate. Therefore the Lord set as His conditions only the study of Torah and the performance of the sacrificial rites.

The result, beside the victory in battle and the sustenance [that had been promised earlier], will be that "You shall be to Me a treasured possession among all the peoples." Those who wish to serve the Lord and to remove themselves from the defilements of the nations of the world cannot do so except by joining you, the congregation of Israel, and accepting your Torah. This is the meaning of "treasured possession": a treasure drawn from all peoples. "For all the earth is Mine," and there are among the nations of the world some individuals who are worthy of being converted and worshiping the Lord, as Moses said in his blessing, "Then were, O lover of the people, [all His worshipers in your care; they followed your lead, accepted your precepts]" (Deut. 33:3). Until the Giving of the Torah they all worshiped the Lord in their own way, according to their own views. But henceforth they could no longer worship the Lord unless they entered the "treasure" of Israel and accepted the Torah in its entirety, as all Israel did. And so it was in regard to this promise that He said, "[how I carried you on eagles' wings] and brought you to me"—one cannot be a true servant of God without becoming one of you. —HA'AMEK DAVAR

REVIEWING THE WHOLE PASSAGE

"Thus shall you say to the house of Jacob and declare to the children of Israel: 'You have seen what I did to the Egyptians, how I carried you on eagles' wings and brought you to Me. Now, if you will heed Me. . . .' " Rashi explains that "the house of Jacob" refers to the women: speak to them gently; but "declare to the children of Israel," the men, the details of the laws and the penalties attached to them—that is, those things that are difficult as wormwood. Wherein lies the difficulty? The blessed Lord sometimes sends a person thoughts of repentance, and these thoughts elevate him and lead him to study and pray. But if he is wise, he will be concerned, knowing that he has not acted of his own accord but only as a result of penitent thoughts sent him by the Lord without any awakening from within. Consequently, the arousal may only be temporary, and afterward he may fall back. The main thing is what a person achieves himself, climbing from rung to rung.

This, then, is the meaning of "Thus shall you say to the house of Jacob"; it refers to the women, to whom you must speak gently. But to "the children of Israel," [the men,] who are hard-headed, these same words are as bitter as wormwood. "You have seen what I did to the Egyptians, how I carried you on eagles' wings and brought you to Me"—without any awakening from within; for in Egypt they did not lift a finger, and the Lord took them out all at once. But a wise person [under such circumstances] will be distressed and ashamed at what the blessed Lord has done, knowing that he does not deserve what was done for him and did not lift a finger to bring it about. "Now, if you will heed Me. . . ."—by drawing near to the service of the Lord through an awakening from within—"you shall be to Me a treasured possession among all the peoples." —BEIT YISRA'EL, quoting Rabbi Avraham Ya'akov of Sadgora

EXODUS 19:6

"But you shall be to Me
a kingdom of priests and a holy nation."
These are the words that you shall speak
to the children of Israel.

A KINGDOM OF PRIESTS

"You shall be to Me"—as if to say, I shall not set any ruler over you except Myself. Thus scripture says, "The guardian of Israel neither slumbers nor sleeps" (Ps. 121:4).

"A kingdom"—None of the nations of the world shall be given kingship but you. Thus scripture says, "Only one is my dove, my perfect one" (Song 6:9). —MEKHILTA

"You shall be to Me"—devoted to Me, engaged in the study of My Torah and the performance of My commandments.

"A kingdom"—Rabbi Eli'ezer, the son of Rabbi Yose the Galileean, says: In the Time to Come, each of you will have offspring as numerous as those who came out of Egypt, as we learn from the verse, "Your sons will succeed [i.e., replace in number] your ancestors" (Ps. 45:17). Lest we imagine that they will be poor, scripture says, "You will appoint them princes throughout the land" (Ps. 45:17). Lest we imagine that they will be mere captains of commerce, scripture says "a kingdom." Lest we imagine that they will be warrior kings, scripture says "of priests." If they are to be priests, we might think they would be idle, as in the verse "David's sons were priests" (2 Sam. 8:18) [implying they had nothing better to do]; hence, scripture tells us, "a holy [i.e., truly consecrated] nation." From this derives the notion that [the people] Israel were worthy of eating the consecrated offerings until they made the Golden Calf, at which time this privilege was taken away from them and given to the priests.

"Nation" teaches us that they were to be as one body and one soul. Thus scripture says, "Who is like Your people Israel, a single nation on earth?" (1 Chron. 17:21). If one of them sins, all are punished, as it is written, "When Achan son of Zerah violated the proscription, anger struck the whole community of Israel; he was not the only one who perished for that sin" (Josh. 22:20). When one of them is hurt, all feel it, as scripture says, "Israel are as scattered sheep" (Jer. 50:17). Just as a ewe feels pain in all parts of its body when one part is hurt, so does all Israel feel it when one Jew is hurt. But with the other nations, everyone rejoices in his neighbor's [misfortune].

Why does scripture say "[a] holy [nation]"? In line with what is written elsewhere: "You are a people consecrated to the Lord your God" (Deut. 7:6). What is meant by holiness? The holiness conferred by the commandments. For each time the Holy One, blessed be He, gives Israel another commandment, He adds to their holiness.

"These [are the words]"—in Hebrew and no other tongue. "These [are the words]"—dealing with these matters and no others. "These [are the words]"—in this sequence and no other. "These [are the words]"—divided into these verses and no others. "These [are the words]"—divided into these chapters and no others. "These [are the words]"—no more and no less.

"These are the words [things] that you shall speak to the children of Israel"—What things? The three crowns that were bestowed upon them: the crown of the Torah, the crown of the priesthood, and the crown of royalty. That of the Torah we learn about from the words, "If you . . . keep My covenant" (Exod. 19:5); those of the priesthood and of royalty from the words, "you shall be to Me a kingdom of priests" (Exod. 19:6). Rabbi Natan says: The crown of a good name surmounts them all. —MEKHILTA DE-RABBI SHIM'ON BAR YOHAI

"You shall be to Me a kingdom of priests"—to understand [My word] and teach the entire human race to call upon the name of the Lord and to serve [Me] as one, just as Israel is destined to do in the Time to Come, as it is written, "You shall be called 'priests of the Lord' " (Isa. 61:6), and it is written, "Torah shall come forth from Zion" (Isa. 2:3).

"You shall be to Me a kingdom of priests"—There are three crowns: that of the Torah, that of the priesthood, and that of royalty. None is hereditary except that of the priesthood, which fathers bequeath to their children, who then attain the same status. And we know that [the people] Israel inherit the holiness of their ancestors from the verse, "The Lord's portion is His people, Jacob His own inheritance" (Deut. 32:9). And the Lord chose Israel because they inherit the holiness of their ancestors. This is the meaning of "a kingdom of priests." —KEDUSHAT LEVI

AND A HOLY NATION

"You shall be to Me a kingdom of priests"—free of all kinds of bondage. And because these are physical things, He specified a spiritual reward for them as well, namely, that they were to be "a holy nation," as scripture says, "You shall be holy, for I . . . am holy" (Lev. 19:2). [They are to be holy] in such a way as to ascend to the level of angels, who are called holy. —ZEROR HAMOR

"A holy nation"—We find that many things are called holy: Israel is called holy, as scripture says, "You shall be to Me a kingdom of priests and a holy nation"; sabbaths are called holy, as scripture says, "You shall keep the sabbath, for it is holy for you" (Exod. 31:14). But lest we think that the holiness of

Him-Who-Spoke-and-the-World-Came-Into-Being is of the same order, scripture says, "There is no holy one like the Lord" (1 Sam. 2:2). —MIDRASH HAGADOL, Leviticus

"A holy nation"—imperishable, eternal, enjoying [in this world] the stature they will have in the Time to Come, as it is written, "Those who remain in Zion and are left in Jerusalem . . . shall be called holy" (Isa. 4:3). Our Sages, of blessed memory, said, "Just as the Holy One endures forever, they shall endure forever" (Sanhedrin, Ḥelek). The Exalted God's intention in giving Israel the Torah was to give them all good things [including eternal life], [which He would have done] had they not acted corruptly in making the Golden Calf: "So the Israelites remained stripped of their finery from Mount Horeb on" (Exod. 33:6). —SFORNO

"And you shall be to Me a kingdom. . . ."—in spite of yourselves and not because of your virtue, as in the verse, "I will reign over you with a strong hand, and with an outstretched arm, and with overflowing fury" (Ezek. 20:33). In spite of yourselves you shall be "a holy nation," set apart from lewdness. —MEI MENUḤOT

"A holy nation"—The other nations, too, will be hallowed by you, as it is written, "O House of Jacob! Come, let us walk by the light of the Lord" (Isa. 2:5), "And the many peoples shall go and shall say: 'Come, let us go up [to the Mount of the Lord], to the House of the God of Jacob, that He may instruct us in His ways, and that we may walk in His paths' " (Isa. 2:3). —DIVREI EMET

"And you shall be to Me a kingdom of priests and a holy nation"—The word "priests" alludes to grace and the word "kingdom" to mastery. This is the Blessed One's promise, that we shall have the mastery [over the higher worlds] that will allow us to choose among the heavenly benefactions. This is what scripture means by a holy nation: that Divine grace and influence and the capacity to be holy are already within our grasp, and all that we desire and yearn for is that we be able to distinguish false grace from the true grace that flows from the source of holiness. —TORAT EMET

"A kingdom of priests and a holy nation"—What is meant by "[The levitical priests] shall not gird themselves with anything that causes sweat" (Ezek. 44:18)? Abaye said: They must not gird themselves in a place where one perspires, as we learn, "When they gird themselves, they must not do it below their loins or above their elbows but rather just at the point where the elbow touches the body."

Rav Ashi said that Huna bar Natan had said: I was once standing before King Izgedar, and my sash was bound high up. He pulled it down, saying, "It is written concerning you, 'A kingdom of priests and a holy nation.'" When I came before Amemar, he said to me, "The verse 'Kings shall be your foster-fathers' (Isa. 49:23) has been fulfilled through you!" —ZEVAHIM 19a

"In a place where one perspires"—in a place where the flesh folds over upon itself, causing perspiration underneath. "When they gird themselves"—when the priests put on their sashes to perform their duties. "Below their loins"—the point where the midriff spreads out over the hips. "Above their elbows"— above the point on the body that is opposite the elbows, because here the arm is always resting on the ribs and causing perspiration. "Just at the point where the elbow touches the body"—over the ribs opposite the elbow.

Izgedar was a Persian king. Huna bar Natan had his sash bound above the level of his elbows, and the king lowered it in order to make him look better. He said, "It is written concerning you, 'A kingdom of priests'—so you must dress yourselves with the dignity befitting priests. For it is written, 'They shall not gird themselves with anything that causes sweat.'" —RASHI

"[A] Holy [nation]"—What does the Torah mean by this? It is as in the verse, "You are a people consecrated to the Lord your God" (Deut. 14:2). To what does this refer? To the holiness that comes from the commandments; for each time the Holy One, blessed be He, gives [the people] Israel another commandment, He adds to their holiness. —MIDRASH HAGADOL

[The people] Israel are called holy, as it is written, "You are a people consecrated to the Lord your God" (Deut. 14:2)—consecrated in that they have separated themselves from idolatry, as it is written, "You shall sanctify yourselves and be holy" (Lev. 11:44); from fornication, as it is written, "Speak to the whole Israelite community [and say to them: You shall be holy]" (Lev. 19:2); from eating unslaughtered flesh, as it is written, "You shall be men holy to Me" (Exod. 22:30); from eating creeping things, as it is written, "For I the Lord am your God: you shall sanctify yourselves" (Lev. 11:44); and from all impure things, as it is written, "Thus he shall cleanse it of the uncleanness of the Israelites and consecrate it" (Lev. 16:19).

The Holy One, blessed be He, also consecrates Israel for the Time to Come, as it is written, "The nations shall know that I the Lord do sanctify Israel" (Ezek. 37:28); and it is written "You shall be holy to Me" (Lev. 20:26)—in this world—"and I have set you apart from other peoples to be Mine" (Lev. 20:26)—in the World to Come.

Rabbi Ḥananiah ben Antigonos said: Had He said, "I have set the other peoples apart from you," the other peoples would have had no hope; not one person from among them could ever have converted. To what may this be compared? To one who culls bad things from good: he never goes back over the bad things. And when He says "I have set you apart from other peoples," He is leaving open the possibility of conversion. To what may this be compared? To one who culls good things from bad: he goes back over the bad things to make sure he hasn't overlooked something good. —MISHNAT RABBI ELI'EZER

"You shall be holy"—You shall be set apart—"for I, the Lord your God, am holy" (Lev. 19:2)—that is, if you sanctify yourselves, I shall account it to you as if you had sanctified Me; and if you do not sanctify yourselves, I shall account it to you as if you had not sanctified me. One might have thought it meant, If you sanctify Me I shall be sanctified, and if not I shall not be sanctified; hence the Torah says, "for I . . . am holy"—My holiness persists whether you sanctify Me or not.

Abba Sha'ul said: How should a king's entourage behave? It should imitate him. "A man [should revere his mother and his father]" (Lev. 19:3)—This teaches us only concerning men, but not concerning women. Hence the Torah says "revere" [in the plural], implying two. Why then does it say "a man"? Because men can dispose of their money as they see fit [and can thus provide for their parents] but women cannot, because others rule over them. —SIFRA, Kedoshim

How should a king's entourage, his troops, behave? They should imitate him. "You shall be holy, for I, the Lord your God, am holy" (Lev. 19:2). We find that the Holy One, blessed be He, is called holy, as it is written, "for I, the Lord . . . am holy." But in fact, no attribute can be ascribed to Him, may He be blessed, not even holiness. Rather, all descriptions of Him are actually of His works. Now creation was entirely for Israel's sake, and every virtue that Israel exhibits accrues to the good name of the Holy One, blessed be He. Hence scripture says, "You shall be holy, for I, the Lord . . . am holy"—sanctify yourselves so that the Lord's Name will be sanctified because of you. —DIVREI ḤAYYIM

"You shall be holy"—The Midrash says this is what is meant by the verse, "He shall send you help from the place of holiness" (Ps. 20:3): "You shall be holy" is the blessed Lord's promise to them that they *will* be holy. You might well ask, How can we sanctify ourselves? Hence the Midrash cites the verse "He shall send you help from the place of holiness"—help in achieving holiness shall come to you from the place of holiness; from on high, He will send you help in becoming holy. For it is written, "You shall sanctify yourselves and be holy" (Lev. 11:44); and what is the way to holiness? "For I the Lord am your God" (Lev. 11:44)—knowing and remembering the Lord always. "You shall faithfully observe My laws" (Lev. 20:8), and if you do, "I the Lord [shall] make you holy" (Lev. 20:8)—I shall send you help from on high to become holy.
—ZEKHUTA DE-AVRAHAM

"You shall be holy to Me, for I the Lord am holy" (Lev. 20:26). The Sages taught: "You shall sanctify yourselves and be holy" (Lev. 20:7)—If a person sanctifies himself a little, he is granted much sanctity. If he sanctifies himself below, he is granted sanctity from above. If he sanctifies himself in this world, he is granted sanctity in the next. —YOMA 39a

"You shall sanctify yourselves" (Lev. 20:7)—a little—"and be holy" (Lev. 20:7)—to a great degree. One who undertakes to purify himself is helped to do so. —RASHI

One who hallows himself a little is helped to become very holy. And once he becomes very holy by his earthly efforts, he is hallowed from above. And once he is hallowed from above in this life, he is hallowed for the Next World as well. —MAHARSHA

"You shall be holy" (Lev. 19:2)—The Midrash cites the parable of a king whose subjects made him three crowns. What did the king do? He put one on his head and the other two on his sons' heads. Similarly, each day the heavenly beings crown the Holy One, blessed be He, with the three proclamations of holiness [Isa. 6:3]. And what does the Holy One, blessed be He, do? He puts one on His head and the other two on the heads of Israel, as it is written, "You shall sanctify yourselves and be holy" (Lev. 20:7).

There are two kinds of holiness. One is the holiness given to Israel, as scripture says, "Israel was holy to the Lord" (Jer. 2:3). The other is the holiness they must achieve themselves from within, in order to attain the higher holiness. These are the two kinds of holiness Israel enjoys. "For I, the Lord . . . am

holy"—My holiness is higher than yours. In other words, His holiness—may
He be blessed—is enhanced by your holiness; Israel adds to the strength of the
heavenly entourage. In fact, the Holy One, blessed be He, has no need for our
holiness, but we are obliged to hallow that part of the Divine in ourselves that
comes to us from above. This is the [part of the] holiness of the Holy One,
blessed be He, that is lifted up by the acts of mortals. Afterward the Holy One,
blessed be He, infuses us with [more of] His holiness; but first there must be
an awakening from within. "I, the Lord" then refers to the Unification, the
unification of the Holy One, blessed be He, with the Shekhinah. —BEIT
AHARON

"You shall be holy" (Lev. 19:2)—The Midrash says: Lest we infer that this
means "like Me," the Torah adds, "For I . . . am holy"—My holiness is higher
than yours. Rabbi Menahem of Kotzk said: "Lest we infer that this means 'like
Me' "—unchanging like Me, as in the verse, "For I am the Lord—I have not
changed" (Mal. 3:6); just as I am unchanging, so must you always be standing
still. Lest we infer this, "the Torah adds, 'For I . . . am holy'—My holiness is
higher than yours." Thus, man must constantly move forward, for however
much he sanctifies himself, the holiness of God, may He be Blessed, looms ever
higher. This is the sense of "Ascribe might to God, [whose majesty is over
Israel]" (Ps. 68:35)—Israel only adds to the strength of the heavenly entourage.

   Rabbi Menahem of Kotzk said further: At times man thinks he has
fulfilled his obligation and has no further to go. Hence [the Midrash] says, "Lest
we infer that this means 'like Me,' the Torah adds, 'For I . . . am holy'—My
holiness is higher than yours." For no matter how much you sanctify yourself,
you must realize that My holiness is even greater, and you have not yet fulfilled
your obligation. It may be compared to one who enters the courtyard of a
king's palace. He is afraid, but when he enters the palace itself, he is even more
afraid; and when he enters the inner chambers of the palace his fear is greater
still. So it is with one who sanctifies himself and truly draws near: the nearer
he comes, the more he is afraid. —'AMUD HA'EMET

"You shall be holy, for I, the Lord your God, am holy" (Lev. 19:2)—The
preacher Rabbi Aharon Klivaner, may the memory of the righteous be a
blessing, related the following:

   In my childhood I studied in a yeshivah in Prague. In a small town in the vicinity
   there was a rich man who had one daughter, and she had come of age. He wanted
   to marry her off to a scholar, so he went to Prague and asked the principal of the

yeshivah to choose a good student for her. I was the one he chose. The man took me home, stripped off my shabby clothes, dressed me in the clothing of leisure and affluence, gave me his daughter in marriage, and showered me with gold. I grew fat and gross and restless and finally cast off the yoke of diligence in the study of Torah. When my father- and mother-in-law saw this, they were angry with me and set wise men over me to chastise me.

Now in those days it was customary for preachers to travel about from place to place preaching in public, and they would stay with my father-in-law, who was a rich, respected pillar of the community. He would ask each of these preachers to reprove me. When they did this, I replied, "Even if I were to lie idle for twenty years I would still be more knowledgeable than all the other students of Torah in this town." That's what I told these preachers.

One day a good, wise preacher came to stay with my father-in-law. When he began to reprove me, I answered him the way I always did. But he replied, "What you say may be true in relation to the students of Torah in this town, but what will you do when your father- and mother-in-law lose patience with you and take away your fine clothes and dress you in rags and send you back to the yeshivah from which you came? How will you look, and how will you answer the students there, who continued to ascend while you descended? Will you not be covered with shame?"

His words sank in, and it occurred to me that this was the meaning of the verse "You shall be holy, for I, the Lord your God, am holy." On the face of it, what similarity can there be between the holiness of mere mortals and that of the living God, the Creator of all the worlds? But a person might be tempted to say to himself, I can carry on as I please and still be holier than the best of the gentiles. Therefore, scripture says, in effect, In this world it may well be as you say, but what will you answer on the day of judgment, when your soul returns to its source, to the abode of the holiness of the Blessed One?

This, then, is the meaning of "You shall be holy, [for I . . . am holy]": it is to prevent you from saying, We are holier in any case than the best of the gentiles. For the reply to this indeed is, In this world it may well be as you say, but what will you answer when you reach the abode of My holiness? As soon as this interpretation of the verse occurred to me, I resolved to return to my studies with renewed diligence. —OR YESHARIM

[The people] Israel are privileged in that the Holy One, blessed be He, sees fit to honor them over all other people. First He told them, "You shall be to Me a kingdom of priests" (Exod. 19:6). But this did not exhaust His love, and He called them "a holy nation," which is greater. This, too, did not exhaust His love, and He said, "You are a people consecrated [to the Lord your God]" (Deut. 7:6). Nor did this exhaust His love, and He said, "You shall be men holy to Me" (Exod. 22:30), which is the highest honor of all. —ZOHAR, Exodus 121a

"I accounted to your favor the devotion of your youth, your love as a bride—how you followed Me in the wilderness, in a land not sown" (Jer. 2:2)—You have forgotten the kindness I did you in your youth, how I redeemed you from the suffering of Egypt and led you through the wilderness, supplying your needs there for forty years. Now I am reminding you of the kindness I did you in your youth, when you followed Me through the wilderness, to an unsown land, and I called you holy, as it is written, "You shall be to Me a kingdom of priests and a holy nation" (Exod. 19:6). This is the meaning of "Israel was holy to the Lord" (Jer. 2:3), that at that very same time I called you by this name [holy]. And should you wonder what value there is in having such a name, in being called "holy," know that it is something great; for whoever makes use of a consecrated thing is subject to the penalty of a guilt-offering, and, if you [Israel] had not desecrated your name by sinning, the same would be true of you: "All who eat of it [i.e., your persecutors] will be held guilty" (Jer. 2:3). —RABBI YOSEF KARA

"['You shall be to Me a kingdom of priests and a holy nation.'] These are the words that you shall speak to the children of Israel" (Exod. 19:6)—Rashi explains: You shall say no more and no less. For if one gives someone a conditional gift, the stipulation must be double;* if it was not, the gift will be irrevocable even though the condition has not been fulfilled. The blessed Lord said, "If you will obey Me faithfully and keep My covenant, you shall be My treasured possession"—without a double stipulation. But because Moses was concerned that they obey the Lord, he might have refrained from spelling out the reward for them—"You shall be My treasured possession"—or he might have gone further and made the condition double, so that if they did not obey, the gift would be cancelled. Hence the blessed Lord told him, No more and no less. For it was His will—may He be blessed—that even if, heaven forbid, they did not obey, the gift would remain valid nonetheless. —'AMUD HA'EMET

REVIEWING THE WHOLE PASSAGE

"Moses went up to God. The Lord called to him" (Exod. 19:3)—scripture suggests here the path of worship, that one begins with the fear of the blessed Lord—this is the meaning of "[Moses] went up to God"—and then the Lord

*If *a* then *b;* if *not a* then *not b;* i.e., the consequences of nonfulfillment must be spelled out.

is revealed to him—["The Lord called to him"]—which entails love and grace.*

"Thus shall you say to the house of Jacob and declare *(vetaggid)* to the children of Israel" (Exod. 19:3)—Our Sages, may their memory be a blessing, explained the verb *taggid* as connoting [the transmission of] things that are distasteful as wormwood *(giddin)* and also things that touch the heart the way a fable *(aggadah)* does. And undoubtedly, both these interpretations are the words of the living God [i.e., true]. When He revealed Himself to them, with a love born of holiness and in a great union that touched their hearts, it was [moving] like a fable; yet it was, at the same time, distasteful as wormwood—as those familiar with esoteric lore understand.

"I bore you on eagles' wings" (Exod. 19:4)—The sage Rabbi Levi Yizhak—may his memory be a blessing—explained that the eagle *(nesher)* is named for its behavior, for at regular intervals it molts *(nosher)* and grows new feathers. This is what is referred to in the verse, "Your youth is renewed like the eagle's" (Ps. 103:5), which is explained by Rashi as follows: like the eagle, which renews its wings, growing new feathers each year; and there is a *midrash aggadah* about a kind of eagle that, when it gets old, becomes youthful again. This was the gift the Holy One, blessed be He, gave His people Israel, who are spoken of [in Zech. 3:7] as moving and not standing still, even as concerns their attainments in the realm of spiritual awareness. And when their awareness becomes reduced, they immediately repent and turn over a new leaf and ascend again. This is [why Israel is compared] to the eagle, and this is the meaning of "I bore you on eagles' wings."

Now Rashi further explains the metaphor of the eagle as follows: the eagle fears only arrows from below and therefore carries its young on its wings, saying, Better the arrow should hit me than them. This image of our Creator's kindness toward us must be properly understood, for otherwise the notion of "better the arrow should hit me" will not make sense. Who, after all, can shoot an arrow or lift a hand to do harm without our Maker's permission? Rather, at the time of the Exodus from Egypt and the splitting of the Reed Sea, and indeed at all times, when the Creator, blessed be He, shows great kindness to His people Israel, there is an accuser who tries to spoil things. Thus the guardian

---

*The name *Elohim* (here translated "God") traditionally refers to the fearsome, judgmental aspect of the Divinity (the "Divine Attribute of Strict Judgment"), while the name *YHVH* (the Tetragrammaton, here translated "Lord") refers to His gracious, compassionate side (the "Divine Attribute of Mercy").

angel of Egypt said, "Both peoples are idolaters, so why favor Israel?" Such accusations are arrows shot from the tongue, as it is written, "Their tongue is a sharpened arrow" (Jer. 9:7). Nevertheless, the Holy One, blessed be He, is magnanimous toward us and takes up our cause, vindicating us and silencing our accusers. This is what is meant by the verse, "I bore you on eagles' wings" and the comment "Better the arrow should hit me." For the Holy One, blessed be He, fends off the accusations against His people Israel, lest the arrow strike them, taking upon Himself, as it were, their defense.

"Now then, if you will obey Me faithfully"—according to Midrash Rabbah, "now then (ve'atah)" always refers to repentance. This is a hint to those who would draw near to Him—may He be blessed—that they should not despair or be afraid to approach Him because of their previous transgressions. For in any event, the main thing is to come closer henceforth and not to sin any more. This is the meaning of "Now then, if you will obey Me faithfully"— it refers to the commandment to repent. And such is His great kindness that He wishes to bring the penitent closer and not remind him of his prior deeds.

"And keep My covenant"—Just as men are careful with their [sexual organs, which bear the mark of the] covenant, so as to avoid expending their potency in vain, so does God ensure that in the higher worlds the Divine plenitude is not, heaven forbid, dissipated among those outside [i.e., the powers of evil and impurity]. This is the meaning of "keep My covenant."

"You shall be to Me a kingdom of priests"—This is the meaning of "[He who rules men] justly, he who rules in awe of God" (2 Sam. 23:3) That is, [Israel] is elevated and exalted to the highest heights, to the point where he can direct even the archangels and assign them tasks according to his great wisdom. And as I heard the Ba'al Shem quoted as saying, when the new moon of Nisan, the new moon of kings [melakhim], arrives, [Israel] reviews the behavior of the angels [mal'akhim], and when he finds one to be less than upright, he appoints another in his place. This, then, is the meaning of the verse and the promise, "You shall be to Me a kingdom of priests"—you shall rule over the priestly angels on high and marshal them into their ranks. This is like the case of King Solomon, may he rest in peace: just as he ruled over earthly creatures he ruled over heavenly ones as well. —'AVODAT YISRA'EL

WE WILL DO AND WE WILL HEAR

EXODUS 19:7

*Moses came and summoned the elders of the people
and put before them all the words
that the Lord had commanded him.*

"Moses came"—This teaches us that he did not first go home or turn to other business.

"And summoned the elders of the people"—This teaches us that Moses showed respect for the elders; it teaches that the elders take precedence over all other Jews; and it teaches that Moses served the elders of his day.

"And put before them"—He enlightened them with [God's words]. Another interpretation of "put before them" is: he presented [things in the order he had received them:] first things first and last things last.

"All the words that the Lord had commanded him"—[those that applied] to the women as well. —MEKHILTA DE-RABBI SHIM'ON BAR YOHAI

"That the Lord had commanded him"—It does not say "that the Lord had commanded" but "that the Lord had commanded *him*," from which we learn that they listened [to Moses] as if they were being addressed by the Holy One Himself. And they would listen not only to him but also to the elders who were to come after him and to the prophets. Thus it is written, "[In order that the people may hear when I speak with you] and so trust you, too, thereafter" (Exod. 19:9). —MEKHILTA DE-RABBI SHIM'ON BAR YOHAI

"Moses came and summoned the elders of the people and put before them all the words"—in order to initiate them into the covenant. And he explained to them that they would have to prepare themselves further. That is the meaning of "Be ready [for the third day]; do not go near a woman" (Exod. 19:15). This is the main point: if a king's subjects are to accept his edicts, he should appear before them in person. Accordingly, the Torah says, "For on the third day the Lord will come down, in the sight of all the people" (Exod. 19:11).

There is also an allusion to this in the verse, "[If you will . . .] keep My covenant, you shall be . . . to Me a kingdom of priests" (Exod. 19:5–6), which teaches that He wanted to crown them with three crowns: the crown of Torah, the crown of priesthood, and the crown of kingship. The crown of Torah [is referred to in the verse], "If you will . . . keep My covenant, you shall be My treasured possession" (Exod. 19:5). The crowns of priesthood and kingship [are referred to in the verse], "You shall be to Me a kingdom of priests and a holy nation" (Exod. 19:6). And in reference to the crown of a good name, which is higher than them all, the Torah says, "You shall be My treasured possession among the nations." This teaches us that Israel was to be called God's treasured possession *(segulah)* among the nations because Israel had the Torah and the commandments, and these have marvelous properties *(segulot)*. "He did not do so for any other nation; [of such rules they know nothing]" (Ps. 147:20)—for Israel alone do the commandments have supernatural powers.

Thus we see that a prayer-leader can wrap himself in his prayer shawl when reciting the Thirteen Attributes [of God] and [the benediction] "He brings back the wind and sends down rain," and a plague will stop for no natural reason. There is no connection between [the prayer and the event in nature]; the effect is brought about by the marvelous properties of the Torah [from which the Thirteen Attributes are taken] and the commandments, which have the power of life and death, of bringing rain and stopping plagues. That is why Israel was called a wise and discerning people, as in the verse, "Surely, that is a great nation of wise and discerning people" (Deut. 4:6); and that is the meaning of the words, "Observe them faithfully, for that will be proof of your wisdom and discernment to other peoples" (Deut. 4:6)—when they see that you are able to do things, not by natural means but through [miraculous] effects. That is why it is written here, "Now then, if you will obey Me faithfully and keep My covenant, you shall be My treasured possession *(segulah)*"—even when you carry out the nonrational commandments, you shall be considered wise, because in carrying out the commandments you are able to achieve their wondrous effects *(segulah)*.

Another allusion in the verse "You shall be My treasured possession among the nations" is to the privileged position that Israel enjoys thanks to God's love for the Patriarchs. Here, [the Torah] is seeking to justify God's love for Israel, the reason the blessed Lord took them as His portion. For when the Lord—may He be blessed—divided the world among seventy guardian angels, Israel appeared to be included [simply as one among many]; what basis would we have, then, for saying that the Lord gave them a privileged position or took them for His very own? Hence the verse comes to tell us explicitly that He gave them a privileged position; for He is the King of Kings, and the whole world is His. —ZEROR HAMOR

"And put before them all the words." "Put *(vayasem)* before them"—as in the verse, "This is the Teaching that Moses put *(sam)* before the Israelites" (Deut. 4:44). And [Sa'adyah] Gaon tells us this is in accord with the verse, "Write down this poem and teach it to the people of Israel; put it *(simah)* in their mouths" (Deut. 31:19)—meaning the Oral Torah, which is the explanation of the Written Torah. —IBN 'EZRA

"Moses came and summoned the elders of the people"—Moses our Teacher— peace be unto him—told the elders to go and appeal to the people's sentiments, but the people anticipated them and said, "All that the Lord has spoken we will do" (Exod. 19:8)—and we do not need the exhortations of the elders. —MEI MENUHOT

EXODUS 19:8

All the people answered as one, saying,
"All that the Lord has spoken we will do!"
And Moses brought back the people's words to the Lord.

"All the people answered as one"—They did not try to be diplomatic, nor did they discuss the matter among themselves, [but rather answered spontane- ously]—"Saying, 'All that the Lord has spoken we will do!' "—We take it upon ourselves. —MEKHILTA DE-RABBI SHIM'ON BAR YOHAI

Even though we have not yet heard the commandments, we undertake to obey them. —MIDRASH LEKAH TOV

WITH ONE VOICE

All Israelites are responsible for one another, as it is written, "All the people answered with one voice, saying, 'All the things that the Lord has commanded we will do!' " (Exod. 24:3). Had even one person demurred, the Torah would not have been given. Hence we say [in the final benediction of the *'Amidah*], "Bless us, our Father, all of us as one, with the light of Your countenance." —SEFER ḤASIDIM 233

Rabbi [Yehudah Hanasi] said: When [the people] Israel stood at Mount Sinai, they were unanimous in accepting joyfully the rule of heaven, as it is written, "All the people answered as one. . . ." What is more, they vouched for one another's [commitment to fulfill the commandments]. At that hour, the Holy One, blessed be He, wanted to make a covenant with them concerning [collective responsibility for] both private and public acts. They said to Him, "We agree to [take responsibility for each other's] public acts but not for private ones, for it will not do for one person to sin in private and the whole community take the blame, as it is written, 'Concealed acts concern the Lord our God, [but with overt acts, it is for us and our children ever] to apply all the provisions of this Teaching' (Deut. 29:28)." Hence it says, "*God** spoke all these words" (Exod. 20:1). —TANḤUMA, Yitro

Rabbi El'azar said: When Israel said "We will do" even before they said "we will hear," a heavenly voice issued forth and said to them, "Who has revealed to My children this secret, which the ministering angels use, as it is written, 'Bless the Lord, O His angels, mighty creatures who do His bidding, ever listening to His word' (Ps. 103:20)—first doing, then listening?" —SHABBAT 88a

"The Lord came from Sinai; He shone upon them from Seir" (Deut. 33:2)— When Israel used the language "We will do and we will hear," it was in contradistinction to Esau and Ishmael, who did not want to accept the Torah. You will find it written in Genesis Rabbah, Vayeze (q.v.) that there are those whose names are beautiful and whose deeds are beautiful and those whose names are beautiful but whose deeds are ugly. Esau has a beautiful name [which can be read as] *'asu*, "did," but he does not [live up to it by] doing *('oseh)*. Ishmael's name connotes hearing *(shome'a)*, but he too does not do. Israel, however, stood juxtaposed with them and said, "We will do and we will hear"—"do" as opposed to Esau and "hear" as opposed to Ishmael. —ZERA' BAREKH

**Elohim*, i.e., God in His role as judge. (See note, p. 103.)

ALL THE PEOPLE

"All the people answered as one, saying, 'All that the Lord has spoken we will do!' "—He said to them, "Will you accept the Torah?" They answered, "What is written in it?" He said, "The Ten Commandments." They said, "Our ancestors already observed these: 'I [the Lord am your God]' and 'You shall not [make for yourself a sculptured image]' were observed by Jacob, as it is written, 'The Lord shall be my God' (Gen. 28:21), and as it is written, '[So Jacob said to his household,] . . . "Rid yourselves of the alien gods" ' (Gen. 35:2). 'You shall not swear falsely' and 'Remember [the Sabbath day]' were observed by Joseph. ['Honor your father']* was observed by Isaac, who stretched forth his neck to be slaughtered. 'You shall not murder' was observed by Judah, as it is written, '[Then Judah said to his brothers,] "What do we gain by killing our brother . . . ?" ' (Gen. 37:26). 'You shall not commit adultery' was observed by Joseph. All the tribes observed 'You shall not steal.' 'You shall not bear false witness' was observed by Judah, as it is written, 'Judah recognized [them, and said, "She is more in the right than I"]' (Gen. 38:26). 'You shall not covet' was observed by Abraham, as it is written, 'I will not take so much as a thread or a sandal strap, [or anything that is yours]' (Gen. 14:23)." Then they concluded in unison, "Our ancestors observed the Torah; shall we not observe it?" —PESIKTA HADETA

I have heard the following attributed to Rabbi Yizhak Me'ir of Gur: Why did they say, "We will do and we will hear," in the plural? Each could have spoken for himself, in which case it would have been "I shall do and I shall hear." But because of the savor ('arevut) and sweetness of the Torah, so dear to them, they all undertook to be responsible ('arev) for each other's (observance of it). —SIAH SARFEI KODESH

"All the people answered as one, saying, 'All that the Lord has spoken we will do!' "—yet later on in the section beginning "Come up to the Lord," they say, "We will do and we will hear" (Exod. 24:7). [The reason for the difference is] that when the Lord spoke to them, His words would sink in of their own accord, so that they did not need to say "we will hear"; but when Moses spoke to them, they said, "We will do and we will hear," meaning, we will hear in order to try to understand. —YALKUT DAVID

---

*This is clearly the commandment meant. The text actually cited, however, is "Slaughter and prepare an animal" (Gen. 43:16).

Here it says, "All the people answered as one, saying, 'All that the Lord has spoken we will do!' "; but further along, in the section beginning "Then He said to Moses," it says, "They said, 'All that the Lord has spoken we will do and we will hear' " (Exod. 24:7). [How to account for this discrepancy?] The whole people, each according to his understanding, answered, "All that the Lord has spoken we will do," and those capable of a deeper understanding answered, "We will do and we will hear"*—each according to his understanding. —HA'AMEK DAVAR

THE SECRET OF THE MATTER

"And all the people answered with one voice. . . . 'All that the Lord has spoken we will do and we will hear' "—Here one must ask how they could "do" before they had "heard" [what was to be done]? Furthermore, what sense did it make to say "all that the Lord has spoken," in the past tense? He had yet to speak and give them the Torah! Rather, they should have said, "All that He will speak."

An answer could be given from the plain sense of the text, that, as our Sages—may their memory be a blessing—said, [the laws of] the Sabbath and civil laws had been given at Marah, and it was to these that they were referring when they said "all that the Lord has spoken we will do." Why "all"? Because both laws (ḥok) and ordinances (mishpat) were included.† Hence "all," meaning both.

But the hidden meaning is that the Israelites of that generation were on the level of Yovel.‡ The Torah had been written on high, and their souls had heard it even before coming into the world. Thus, "all that the Lord has spoken"—to our souls, before we came into the world—"we will do." In addition, we will now hear [God's word] again, in this world, in order to subject our bodies to it as well. Thus, each individual Jew could say, "All that the Lord has spoken"—to our souls, before we came into this world. It is as our Sages, may their memory be a blessing, said: [The unborn fetus] is taught the entire Torah, and his seed are even sworn to observe it. A similar comment is made by the holy Zohar on the verse, "If a person incurs guilt: When he has

*The root shm' can mean "understand," as well as "hear" and "obey."

†Cf. Exod. 15:25, where God is said to have given the people ḥok umishpat, understood by some medieval authorities as referring to nonrational and rational commandments respectively.

‡In the kabbalistic scheme, a very high spiritual level equivalent to the sefirah of Understanding.

heard a public imprecation. . . ." (Lev. 5:1). "We shall do [and we shall hear]" thus means, we shall also listen to and study the words of the Torah in this world, so as to subject our bodies [to it] as well. —MAGGID MEISHARIM

Rabbi Tanhuma bar Abba began his discourse as follows: "You plucked up a vine from Egypt" (Ps. 80:9)—Why is Israel compared to a vine? Because when the owners of a vine want it to flourish, what do they do? They transplant it to a different location. In the same way, when the Holy One, blessed be He, wanted to make [the people] Israel known in the world, what did He do? He uprooted them from Egypt and brought them to the wilderness, where they began to flourish. They began to receive the Torah, and they said, "All that the Lord has spoken we will do and we will hear." And they made a name for themselves in the world, as it is written, "Your beauty won you a name among the nations, [for it was perfected through the splendor which I set upon you—declares the Lord God]" (Ezek. 16:14). —EXODUS RABBAH 44:I

Rabbi Yannai said: The Torah need only have begun with "This month shall mark for you [the beginning of the months]" (Exod. 12:2).* Why did the Holy One, blessed be He, reveal to Israel what happened on the first day, the second day, and so on until the sixth day? Because they said, "All that the Lord has spoken we will do and we will hear." When they said this, He immediately revealed [the rest] to them. —SONG OF SONGS RABBAH I

Rabbi Yehoshu'a ben Levi said: Great is peace, for when Israel stood and said, "All that the Lord has spoken we will do and we will hear," the Holy One, blessed be He, rejoiced in them and gave them His Torah and blessed them with peace, as it is written, "May the Lord grant strength to His people; may the Lord bless His people with peace" (Ps. 29:11) —DEREKH EREZ

What is the difference between "We will do and we will hear," which is always interpreted as reflecting favorably [on Israel], and "We will hear and we will do" (Deut. 5:24), which appears in Deuteronomy among the Warnings? Said Rabbi Me'ir Shalom of Porisev: In the case of "We will do and we will hear," their reason had been suspended under the impact of the revelation; in the case of "We will hear and we will do," they were speaking rationally. —DEREKH ZADDIKIM

*It is here that the commandments addressed to Israel begin.

Rabbi Yose bar Rabbi Yehudah said: Israel saw the glorious majesty of their King face to face, and none of them was blind, lame, limbless, or deaf. Blind we know from the verse, "All the people saw" (Exod. 20:15); lame from the verse, "They stood at the foot of the mountain" (Exod. 19:17); limbless and deaf from the verse, "We will do and we will hear." Concerning the Time to Come, [too,] it says, "Then the lame shall leap like a deer, and the tongue of the dumb shall shout aloud" (Isa. 35:6). —ZOHAR, Exodus 82b

"The wise shall obtain honor" (Prov. 3:35)—This refers to Israel. . . . When did Israel obtain honor? When they accepted the Torah. Rabbi Yohanan said: Six hundred thousand ministering angels descended upon Mount Sinai together with the Holy One, blessed be He, as it is written, "God's chariots are myriads upon myriads, thousands upon thousands; [the Lord is among them as in Sinai in holiness]" (Ps. 68:18); and each of them placed a crown on the head of one of the Israelites. Said Rabbi Abba bar Kahana: When Israel stood at Mount Sinai and said, "All that the Lord has spoken we will do and we will hear," the Holy One, blessed be He, immediately felt a fondness for them and sent each of them two angels, one to gird a sword upon him and the other to place a crown on his head. Rabbi Simon said: He dressed them in royal robes, as it is written, "I clothed you with embroidered garments" (Ezek. 16:10). . . . Rabbi Shim'on ben Yohai said: On every sword that He girded upon them was engraved the Tetragrammaton. Hence, "The wise shall obtain honor." —TANHUMA, Tezaveh

Ponder the matter of the two crowns given to everyone at the Giving of the Torah, the crown of Torah and the crown of kingship, the one attached to the other. At the time of the Redemption, the [double] crown shall be restored— the Holy One, blessed be He, will return it to us—and everlasting joy shall be upon [our] heads [cf. Isa. 35:10, 51:11]. —OZAR HAKAVOD

THE INNOCENCE OF THE UPRIGHT

A gentile saw Rava studying the law with his fingers tucked under his feet, and [in the intensity of his concentration] he chafed his fingers so much that they bled. He said to Rava, "You rash people, who gave precedence to your mouths over your ears, you are as rash as ever! You should have listened first, and if you saw that you were capable [of fulfilling the commandments], accepted [the Torah]; if not, you should not have accepted it." He replied, "Concerning us who walk with Him in innocence it is written, 'The innocence of the upright guides them' (Prov. 11:3); and concerning those who spread libel [against us] it is written, 'The deviousness of the treacherous leads them to ruin' (Prov. 11:3)." —SHABBAT 88a

"All the people answered as one"—"The remnant of Jacob shall be, [in the midst of the many peoples,] like dew [from the Lord, like droplets on grass— which do not look to any man nor place their hope in mortals]" (Mic. 5:6). This is what is meant by the verse, "My roots reaching water, [and dew lying on my branches]" (Job 29:19). Said Israel: Because our children devote them- selves to the study of Torah, which is compared to water—as it is written, "Ho, all who are thirsty, come for water" (Isa. 55:1)—because of this, we were blessed, as it is written, "My roots reaching water." When? When the Holy One, blessed be He, went about to all the inhabitants of the world seeking to give them the Torah—as it is written, "The Lord came from Sinai" (Deut. 33:2)—and they refused it; but when He came to Israel, they immediately took it upon themselves, as it is written, "All the people answered as one, [saying, 'All that the Lord has spoken we will do!']." Said He to them, "If so, take these blessings [as well], as it is written, 'May [God] give you [of the dew of heaven and the fat of the earth, abundance of new grain and wine]' (Gen. 27:28)." Hence, "My roots reaching water," and thus also, "dew lying on my branches" and "The remnant of Jacob shall be, [in the midst of the many peoples, like dew from the Lord]." —AGGADAT BERESHIT

IN ORDER TO HEAR AND DO

"My son, if you have stood surety for your friend" (Prov. 6:1)—This refers to Israel, who are guarantors to the Holy One, blessed be He. It is a sign that [the people] Israel are beloved that they are *called* friends, as it is written, "For the sake of my kin and friends, [I pray for your well-being]" (Ps. 122:8). And how did they become guarantors? When the Holy One, blessed be He, was trying to give the Torah [to the nations of the world], none was willing to take it except Israel. This is like the case of a king who had a field that he wanted to lease to tenant farmers. He summoned one man and said, "Will you take this field?" He said, "I don't have the strength [to work it]; it would be too hard for me." The same thing happened with a second, a third, and a fourth: they would not take it from him. He summoned a fifth man and said, "Will you take this field?" He said, "Yes, I will." "To till?" "Yes," he said. But once he had taken it, he let it lie fallow. Now, with whom should the king be exacting, those who said they could not take the field or the one who took it but then let it lie fallow? Should it not be the latter? Thus, when the Holy One, blessed be He, revealed Himself on Mount Sinai, there was not a people whom He did not entreat to accept [the Torah] and not one that agreed to observe it, until He came to Israel, who said, "All that the Lord has spoken we will do and we will hear." Therefore it is only right that you do, in fact, "hear." Hence, "Hear the word of the Lord, O House of Jacob" (Jer. 2:4). And if you do not, you will have to pay the penalty [for one another] as guarantors. Hence, "My son, if you have stood surety for your friend." —EXODUS RABBAH 27:8

"All that the Lord has spoken we will do"—but further on it says, "We will do and we will hear." Rabbi Simḥah Bunem of Przysucha asked: Why did Israel say, "*We* will do and *we* will hear"? Should each of them not have said, "*I* will do and *I* will hear"? It is like the case of people tied up in prison on a hot day, who thirst for water but are given none. Suddenly someone comes and asks them if they'd like a drink, and they all say, "We would!" For each of them knows that all the others are thirsty and wish to drink. Thus it was at the receiving of the Torah: each person yearned for it [and knew that the others did as well], and so each of them said, "We will do and we will hear."

But if indeed they all yearned for the Torah and responded "We will do and we will hear" [when offered it], why did the Holy One, blessed be He, have to threaten them by holding the mountain over them like a barrel?* Said Rabbi Yisha'yah of Praga: The Israelites were at that moment in an exalted spiritual state as a result of the abstinence Moses, may he rest in peace, had imposed on them. They were truly uplifted above this world, to the extent that they had no capacity for physical acts. Thus, later on, when they were told, "Return to your tents," it was only the direct command that induced them to carry out the Lord's order, so rarefied was their state of mind, tantamount to that of angels. What they expected from the Holy One, blessed be He, in the Giving of the Torah was the disclosure of its sublime mysteries, so they quickly replied, "We will do and we will hear." The Holy One, blessed be He, knew that if what they heard from Him was "You shall not steal," "You shall not commit adultery," "You shall not murder," they would not accept it, heaven forbid, for they were far removed from such matters. Therefore He lifted the mountain over their heads like a barrel to compel them to accept this Torah. —ZEKHUTA DE-AVRAHAM

*A reference to the well-known midrash in Shabbat 88a: "The Holy One, blessed be He, held the mountain over them like a barrel and said, 'If you accept the Torah, well and good, but if not, this shall be your burial place.' "

When Israel gave precedence to "We will do" over "We will hear," the Holy One, blessed be He, said, "Who revealed this secret to My children, a secret hitherto used only by the ministering angels, as it is written, 'Bless the Lord, O His angels, mighty creatures who do His bidding, ever ready to hear His bidding' (Ps. 103:20)?" Indeed, I say, the main thing is the 613 commandments, which represent His will, may He be blessed: the 248 positive commandments, representing the things we must do to comply with His will, may He be blessed; and the 365 negative commandments, representing the things we must avoid doing in order not to violate His will, may He be blessed.

Observe that the Lord gives His vital energy and beneficence to all things, even material things in the workaday world, in order to enable man to cleave to Him, may He be blessed, in this world. But this only applies when man believes with perfect faith that "the whole world is filled with His glory," as it is written, "[You alone are the Lord. You made the heavens, the highest heavens, and all their host, the earth and everything upon it, the seas and everything in them]. You keep them all alive, [and the host of heaven prostrate themselves before You]" (Neh. 9:6). [When he has such faith,] he accepts the yoke of the rule of heaven, undertaking not to violate the will of his Master, who gives him vital energy and beneficence, but to do His will, may He be blessed. Thus the main purpose of the texts of the Torah and the liturgy is to know His will, may He be blessed. As for the angels, who have no evil inclination, their main purpose is to do His holy will. For them it is easy to give precedence to doing over hearing. But for human beings, who have free choice, it is not so easy. It is only [possible for] the Israelites, who have a heritage of faith and of hearing about all the miracles and wonders the Lord performed for Moses and Israel, from which their perfect faith derives. —BEIT YISRA'EL, citing Rabbi Abraham Ya'akov of Sadgora

BLESS THE LORD, O HIS ANGELS

Rabbi Hiyya began his discourse as follows: "Bless the Lord, O His angels, mighty creatures who do His bidding" (Ps. 103:20)—[the people] Israel are privileged above the other nations of the world in that the Holy One, blessed be He, chose them from among the nations and made them His own portion and inheritance. And He gave them the holy Torah because at Mount Sinai they were unanimous in giving precedence to doing over hearing. Because they did this, the Holy One, blessed be He, summoned His court and said to them, "Until now you were unique to Me in all the world, but henceforth My children on earth shall share everything with you. You may not sanctify My Name until Israel joins you below and all of you sanctify My name as one fellowship. For they have given precedence to doing over hearing, just as the highest angels do in heaven, as it is written, "Bless the Lord, O His angels, mighty creatures who do His bidding, ever ready to hear His bidding"—doing His bidding first, and only then hearing [seeking to understand] it. —ZOHAR, Genesis 90a

"Bless the Lord, O my soul; O Lord, my God, You are very great; You are clothed in glory and majesty" (Ps. 104:1)—The same idea is conveyed in the verse, "Yours, Lord, are greatness, might, [splendor, triumph, and majesty—yes, all that is in heaven and on earth; to You, Lord, belong kingship] and pre-eminence above all" (1 Chron. 29:11). Said Rav Huna: What is meant by "pre-eminence above all"? We see that all praise the Holy One, blessed be He, for it is written, "From east to west the name of the Lord is praised" (Ps. 113:3). But there is no greater praise for the Holy One, blessed be He, than that of Israel, "the people I formed for Myself that they might declare My praise" (Isa. 43:21).

You can be sure this is the case, for it is written in the previous psalm, "Bless the Lord, O His angels, mighty creatures who do His bidding, ever ready to hear His bidding" (Ps. 103:20). Should it not have said "[who *hear* His bidding,] ever ready to *do* His bidding"? After all, one does what one has heard! Why is it written this way? Because it is referring to Israel, who stood at Sinai and gave precedence to doing over hearing, as it is written, "All that the Lord has spoken we will do and we will hear." [Therefore] when Israel praise [Him], the angels follow suit, as we find written in the next verse: "Bless the Lord, all His hosts" (Ps. 103:21)—"hosts" referring to angels, as it is written, "The Lord will punish the host of heaven in heaven" (Isa. 24:21).

This then, is what is meant by pre-eminence above all *(lerosh)."* *Rosh* can only refer to Israel, as it is written, "When you take a census *(tissa et rosh)* of the Israelite people" (Exod. 30:12). Nor is any [people] referred to as "holy" except Israel, as it is written, "Israel was holy to the Lord" (Jer. 2:3). —MIDRASH ON PSALMS 104

ALL THAT THE LORD HAS SPOKEN

First they said "We will do" and only then "We will hear," because deeds are greater than learning. —HIDDUSHEI HATORAH

"All the people answered as one, saying, 'All that the Lord has spoken we will do!' "—Some of the commandments apply only to the priests, some only to the Levites, some only to the high priest or the king or the Sanhedrin; and there

are commandments that apply only to one who owns land. But the fulfillment
of the Torah in its entirety is the responsibility of the whole people of Israel,
all [the people of] Israel are responsible for one another, and for the fulfillment
of the Torah all are rewarded. This is what the prophet meant when he said,
"For you, My flock, flock that I tend, are *adam* [one person]" (Ezek. 34:31)—
the whole Jewish people is one person. There are those who serve as the heart,
as our Sages said, "The righteous are the heart of Israel"; those who serve as
the head, as it is written, "the family heads of the community" (Num. 31:26);
and those who serve as the eyes, the eyes of the community. And each person
must fulfill the commandments that pertain to him, so that all together they
form a complete person. As for a commandment that does not pertain to you,
you are nevertheless obliged to study it, for whoever engages in [the study of]
the sin offering, [for example,] is as though he offered it. Alternatively, you
must support those who study the Torah. Therefore, further on in Parashat
Mishpatim [Exod. 24:7], they answered, "All that the Lord has spoken we will
do and we will hear"—those we can fulfill "we will do," and those that we
cannot fulfill [because they do not pertain to us] "we will hear"—that is, we
will study and try to understand their laws and ordinances. But here [in Exod.
19:8], "all the people answered as one, saying, 'All that the Lord has spoken we
will do!' "—meaning that the whole people would do together everything the
Lord had commanded, while each person would do what was incumbent upon
him specifically. —MESHEKH ḤOKHMAH

THE PRACTICAL AND THE INTELLECTUAL

"We will do and we will hear"—Rabbi Yosef Ibn-Kaspi wrote: The Earlier
Authorities all had difficulty with this verse, for the logic of the language
requires that hearing precede doing. How then could they reverse the order?
What is meant, in fact, is that they answered "we will do" in regard to the
commandments that entail action and "we will hear" in regard to the commandments of the heart. —MISHNEH KESEF, Ve-eleh Hamishpatim

You must know, first of all, that the ancients related all the powers in the world
to the seven planets. They also related the seven parts of the inhabited world
to them, one part to each planet, and in some cases the days of the week as well.
And seeing that the sun was greater than all of them, followed by the moon and
then the stars—seeing how exalted the sun was over this lowly world, they
believed it to be the highest god. Each of the nations freely chose [one of the
planets to be its guiding star], and all their sages, observing that nature renewed

itself according to the movements of the seven spheres, worshiped them and prayed to them. This was the intention of Balaam the magician in building seven altars and offering upon them seven steers and seven rams.

But they did not understand what they were seeing; they imagined that the spheres move of their own accord and have the power to effect change, but it is not so. The latter behave according to the natural laws ordained for them by their Creator. They have no power to innovate or alter but act only according to the will of Him who set them in motion. Therefore, whoever worships them is wasting his efforts and angering the Lord of All.

Now there is a possibility that some Jewish sages, too, will err in this matter. They will see that the number seven occurs over and over again in the Torah in relation to the unending cycles of days and years. It also appears in relation to the festivals. In the circling of Jericho, there are seven priests with seven trumpets, and after seven days they circle it seven times. They will see that the seven spheres have forty-nine motions, while in the prophecy of Zechariah [4:2] each of the seven lamps has seven pipes, making forty-nine in all. It is also written in the Book of Isaiah, "And the light of the sun shall become sevenfold, like the light of the seven days" (Isa. 30:26).

Thus our Torah, in its perfection, had to rule out false beliefs and illuminate the true path for us, teaching us that all domains are under the greater, prior domain of God, may His Name be blessed, that He alone is sovereign and "pre-eminent above all" [1 Chron. 29:11], and that they are all His servants, who do His will, as it is written, "[You alone are the Lord. You made the heavens, the highest heavens, and all their host. . . .] You keep them all alive, [and the host of heaven prostrate themselves before You]" (Neh. 9:6). Thus the Torah warned the Israelites against the error of thinking that, because the Holy One, blessed be He, gave the other nations over to the rule of the host of heaven, He did the same with Israel. So the Torah says explicitly, "[When you look up to the sky and behold the sun and the moon and the stars, the whole heavenly host, you must not be lured into bowing down to them or serving them.] These the Lord your God allotted to the other peoples" (Deut. 4:19); and the prophet says, "Thus said the Lord: [Do not learn to go the way of the nations,] and do not be dismayed by the portents in the sky; [let the nations be dismayed by them!]" (Jer. 10:2). "Let the nations be dismayed" and not "Let Israel be dismayed," to teach us that as long as [the people] Israel do the will of the Omnipresent they shall not fall under the influence of the stars or the planets, nor will the movements of the latter harm them, nor will they be abandoned to chance, nor will any nation or people rule over them.

And so, to erase the false belief from the Israelites' hearts and fix firmly in them the right belief that only the blessed Lord rules over them, the Torah commands, in regard to days and years, that, following the number 49, the number 50 be made holy. This is to teach Israel that God is above all, that He is the Mover and is not moved. This is the reason He commands us to sanctify, among the years, the fiftieth, as the time when chattel and land are to be freed; and, among the days, the fiftieth of the counting of the Omer. The first day [of the Omer] was the day when the Israelites' bodies were freed [from bondage in Egypt], but the fiftieth day is holy because it was the day of the Giving of the Torah, which was the liberation of Israel's souls, which had been enslaved to their bodies as long as they did not have the Torah.

It is to this that [the Sages] were alluding when they commented on the verse "[The tablets were God's work, and the writing was God's writing,] incised upon the tablets" (Exod. 32:16) as follows: "Read it not as 'incised' (harut) but as 'freedom' (herut)." The Sages were also alluding to this idea when they said that at the time of the Giving of the Torah the Holy One, blessed be He, split open the seven heavens and the seven parts of the earth and said to them, "Take heed above and take heed below, and know that there is no God beside Me." [Israel] replied forthwith, giving precedence to "We will do" over "We will hear." This teaches us that all motion in the world comes, not from those seven spheres, but from Him, and there is no domain except that of His power and His word.

Accordingly, [Israel] realized that the true, eternal, unceasing good lay in accepting the Torah, with its practical virtues under the heading of "We will do" and its intellectual virtues under the heading of "We will hear." Israel gave precedence to "We will do" over "We will hear" because the right way is to begin by reforming one's behavior and only then to enter the realm of thought, meditating on the Torah, which contains all wisdom, knowledge, and morality. For the Torah's commandments are divided into two overall categories: those called the practical commandments, which perpetuate human life, foster right conduct, avert harm, and achieve useful ends; and those called the intellectual commandments, which foster faith in the blessed Creator and the mind's adherence to the path of truth. —MENORAT HAMA'OR 3

THE PEOPLE'S WORDS

Beit Naftali, commenting on Parashat Devarim (Deut. 1:1–3:22), reports an anecdote related by the venerable Rabbi Aharon of Ujhely, may his memory be a blessing: He happened to be visiting the holy preacher of Koznitz when a woman came to him in tears, complaining that the husband of her youth had come to hate her and had told her he was disgusted with her. The preacher said to her, "Might you not in fact be disgusting [to him]?" The woman cried bitterly, "Woe is me! When we got married he thought I was beautiful. Why am I now ugly to him?" When the preacher heard her crying, he said, "Master of the Universe, when Israel said 'We will do and we will hear,' and You bound them to You in marriage, they were beautiful [in Your eyes], and You chose them from among all the nations; but now, heaven forfend, You have come to despise us. 'O Rock of Israel, arise to the aid of Israel!' (Siddur)."

"And Moses brought back the people's words to the Lord" (Exod. 19:8)—this refers to the third day [after their arrival]. Another interpretation of "Moses brought back the people's words to the Lord": scripture is teaching you etiquette; for even though one may have heard another person's request, he should still repeat it back to him. —MEKHILTA DE-RABBI SHIM'ON BAR YOHAI

It is taught in a baraita: "Moses brought back the people's words to the Lord" (Exod. 19:8)—but [immediately afterwards] it is written [again], "Moses reported the people's words to the Lord" (Exod. 19:9). What [in the meantime] did the Holy One, blessed be He, say to Moses, and what did Moses say to Israel, and what did Israel say to Moses, and what did Moses reply to the All-Powerful? It was [all in regard to] the commandment to set boundaries (Exod. 19:12). So says Rabbi Yose bar Yehudah.

Rabbi [Yehudah Hanasi] said: Moses began by explaining the punishment [for violating this commandment], for it is written, "Moses brought back (vayashev)," implying words that chasten (meshavevin) the mind; then he explained the reward, for it is written, "Moses reported (vayagged)," implying words that appeal to the heart, in the way that a story (aggadah) does.

But then there are some who say that first he explained the reward, for it is written, "Moses brought back (vayashev)," implying words that ease (meshivin) the mind; and afterward he explained the punishment, for it is written, "Moses reported (vayagged)," implying words that are as distasteful as wormwood (giddin) to hear. —SHABBAT 87a

"Moses brought back the people's words to the Lord"—He returned to Him on the mountain with the people's reply. But surely all is known to Him, and He did not have to ask him, "What did this people answer you?" Surely it is as in the verse, "The Lord heard your plea as you spoke to me" (Deut. 5:25). [What is meant, however, is this:] When [Moses] came before Him, the blessed Lord said, "I will come to you in a thick cloud, in order that the people may

hear when I speak with you and so trust you thereafter" (Exod. 19:9). Then he reported [the people's words], saying, "Master of the Universe, Your children [already] trust [me] and will take upon themselves whatever You tell them."
—NACHMANIDES

"Moses brought back the people's words"—He went back to the Holy One, blessèd be He, to relay to Him what the people had said, but he was afraid to open his mouth in front of the King until the Holy One, blessed be He, spoke first. For it is not appropriate for a student to speak to his teacher until the teacher speaks to him, as our Sages, may their memory be a blessing, said: "He who greets his teacher is a boor." So the Holy One, blessed be He, initiated the conversation, saying, "I will come to you . . . [so that they believe you are in fact My messenger]"; and only then did Moses report the people's words, saying, "They already believe." Thus the Torah first says, "Moses brought back," and only then "[he] reported." —TOSFOT HAROSH

"He who greets his teacher is a boor"—See Palestinian Talmud, Berakhot, chapter 2: "Rabbi El'azar saw Rabbi Yohanan and hid, because it was their custom that a young person does not greet an older one, in fulfillment of the verse, 'Young men saw me and hid, [elders rose and stood]' (Job 29:8)." See also *Shulhan Arukh,* Yoreh De'ah, Laws of Respect for One's Teacher 242:16, and commentaries ad. loc.
    "Moses brought back the people's words to the Lord"—because Moses had not yet divined their true intention in saying "All that the Lord has spoken we will do." He could not gauge what they really meant, only that they had said they would accept everything He told them. Hence it does not say "Moses reported" at first, because "reporting" *(haggadah)* implies interpretation of what is meant, but rather "[he] brought back," implying that he simply relayed the [people's] words without getting into their meaning.
    True, when the Lord, be He exalted, said, "I will come to you in a thick cloud, in order that the people may hear when I speak with you and so trust you thereafter," [Moses] understood that it was for good reason that He had said this, that He had foreseen they would want to hear His words directly. But then he took a closer look at their true intention and divined that when they said, "All that the Lord has spoken we will do," what they meant was, we will do whatever we can be convinced the Lord has said, as scripture says, "If you will hear [i.e., understand] My voice" (Exod. 19:5). This is why scripture again says, "Moses reported the people's words to the Lord"—that is, now I know

what they really meant when they said, "All that the Lord has spoken we will do," what is really acceptable to them. Until this point he could only relay without understanding; now he could report the deeper truth.

This is what [the Sages], may their memory be a blessing, meant when they said in the Mekhilta that the response Moses relayed to God was, "We wish to see our King." In other words, concerning what You have told them up till now, their response certainly is, "[Yes, yes, but] we wish to see our King." And, indeed, they were quite sincere in this. It is as scripture says elsewhere concerning this verse, "Oh, give me of the kisses of your mouth, for your love is more delightful than wine" (Song 1:2).* So [Moses] was told, "Go to the people and warn them to stay pure today and tomorrow. Let them wash their clothes." Without doing this they would not have been able to hear [God] in the way they wanted. —'AKEDAT YIZHAK

"Moses brought back"—This was on the third day. He went [back to God then], bearing a reply. But before he had a chance to say anything, the Omnipresent said to him, "I will come to you" (Exod. 19:9). Then "Moses reported" (Exod. 19:9). He had to report, even though [God] knows all. The same was true of all the prophets, as we see further on in the scripture: "When Samuel heard all that the people said, he reported it to the Lord" (1 Sam. 8:21); "Now consider carefully what reply I shall take back to Him who sent me" (2 Sam. 24:13). It is true even for angels, as we see in the verse, "Then the man clothed in linen . . . brought back word, saying, ['I have done as You commanded me']" (Ezek. 9:11). The point is to teach us etiquette. As for "[I will] come to you," the meaning is, I do not want to speak to them through an intermediary but directly. —RABBI MEYUHAS BEN ELIYAHU

"Moses brought back the people's words"—He relayed to Him their unanimous consent to "do." His intention was not to inform [God], who, may He be exalted, knows all hidden things, not to mention things that are not hidden; rather, he meant to laud and exalt the Israelite people, as it is written, "And who is like your people Israel, a unique nation on earth" (2 Sam. 7:23). —OR HAHAYYIM

"Moses brought back the people's words to the Lord"—Moses reflected on Israel's response, the fact that they gave precedence to doing over hearing. It was something wondrous that human beings could not do without Divine

*Cf. Song of Songs Rabbah 1:3.

help, as the Midrash says: " 'Who revealed to My children this secret, which the angels use, as it is written, "Bless the Lord, O His angels, mighty creatures who do His bidding, hearing [His words]" (Ps. 103:20)'—first doing, then hearing." And now Israel below had done what the ministering angels do on high! Moses understood that this could only be the spirit of the Lord speaking through them, His words on their lips [cf. 2 Sam. 23:2], that the Shekhinah itself was saying from the throat of each and every Jew, "We will do and we will hear." Hence scripture says, "Moses brought back the people's words to the Lord"—that is, he brought back to the Lord the same words [He Himself had spoken]. [Moses] had attributed these words to the blessed Lord, assumed that He Himself had given this answer, that it had been, as it were, His will, be He blessed, that they give precedence to doing over hearing. —KEDUSHAT LEVI

"Moses brought back the people's words to the Lord"—Moses our Teacher, may he rest in peace, had told them what the blessed Lord had commanded him to tell: "You shall be to Me a kingdom of priests and a holy nation" (Exod. 19:6)—that is, [you shall enjoy] high station. And they had answered, "All that the Lord has spoken we will do"—meaning, We do not wish to serve the blessed Lord in order to achieve high station, but rather because "the Lord has spoken," only because He commanded it, be He blessed. Moses liked their reply, so he "brought back the people's words"—that is, he replied to the blessed Lord in like fashion, saying, I too would like to serve You because You commanded it and not in order to achieve high station. —OR YESHARIM, quoting Rabbi Moshe Kubrin

"[The people] Israel, because they stood at Mount Sinai, lost the taint of sin" (Shabbat 146a)—and [so] they readily understood the Torah. This is what the author of the Haggadah meant when he wrote, "Had He brought us to Mount Sinai and not given us the Torah, it would have been enough for us!" Because they had lost the taint of sin, they were able to grasp the Torah of their own accord. This is what they meant by, "We will do and we will hear"—"We will do," for we already know what to do, and "We will hear," so that when we do it, it will be in response to being commanded. —AVNEI ELIYAHU

Until Israel arrived at Sinai to receive the Torah, the mouth of the world was stopped up. When the Torah was given, it was opened and the world's speech restored. —MIDRASH HANE'ELAM on Song of Songs 61a

EXODUS 19:9
And the Lord said to Moses,
"I will come to you in a thick cloud,
in order that the people may hear when I
speak with you, and so trust you thereafter."
Then Moses reported the people's words to the Lord.

IN A THICK CLOUD

"I will come to you in a thick cloud"—This is to tell us that before and after this, the Shekhinah appeared to him as though through a clear glass, a sight that Moses alone could withstand seeing. But here at Sinai, He came "in a thick cloud"—that is, veiled in darkness, so that the whole people could look upon Him. "When I speak with you" refers to [the first two of the Ten Commandments:] "I [the Lord am your God]. . . . You shall have no [other gods beside Me]"—when I say these words to you they, too, will be able to hear, so that they will believe the rest of what you tell them ever after. —SEFER HAMIZVOT HAGADOL, Introduction

"And the Lord said to Moses, 'I will come to you in a thick cloud' "—Although all Moses' prophecies from the Giving of the Torah on came to him as though through a clear glass—as it is written, "He beholds the likeness of the Lord" (Num. 12:8)—on this one occasion his prophecy came to him in a thick cloud. —SFORNO

"I will come to you in a thick cloud"—It is this that is referred to in the verse, "Moses approached the thick cloud" (Exod. 20:18). —ME'OR HA'AFELAH

"And the Lord said to Moses, 'I will come to you in a thick cloud *('av he'anan)*' "—'*Anan* means a heavy fog, as in the verse, "A dense cloud *('anan kaved)* upon the mountain" (Exod. 19:16).

Rabbi Yose the Galilean said: Moses sanctified himself in the cloud for seven days, as it is written, "[The Presence of the Lord abode on Mount Sinai,] and the cloud hid him for six days. On the seventh day He called to Moses from the midst of the cloud" (Exod. 24:16). [All this] followed the giving of the Ten Commandments, which was the start of the forty days [Moses was on the mountain]. Rabbi 'Akiva said: "The cloud hid him for six days"—[God] had called upon Moses to purify himself beginning with the new moon [i.e., six days before the giving of the Ten Commandments]. Then, "on the seventh day [of the month, the day the Ten Commandments were given], He called to Moses," [immediately] after the giving of the Ten Commandments; and then began the forty days. —MEKHILTA DE-RABBI SHIM'ON BAR YOHAI; [cf. YOMA 4a–b]

"[He] makes the clouds His chariot]" (Ps. 104:3)—The Holy One, blessed be He, came to Israel in a cloud twice. The first time was in Egypt, as it is written, "Mounted on a swift cloud, the Lord will come to Egypt" (Isa. 19:1). The second time was at Sinai, as it is written, "I will come to you in a thick cloud." —MIDRASH ON PSALMS

IN ORDER THAT THE PEOPLE MAY HEAR

"In order that the people may hear when I speak with you"—Rabbi Yehudah said: The Holy One, blessed be He, said to Moses, "I will say something to you, you will answer Me, then I will acknowledge your answer." Rabbi [Yehudah Hanasi] said: It was not merely out of respect for Moses that the Omnipresent acknowledged what he had said; rather, He was saying to him, "I am going to repeat for you here the commandments that I gave you at Marah." It does not say "that the Lord had commanded" but "that the Lord had commanded *him*" (Exod. 19:7), implying that hearing the commandments from Moses would be like hearing them directly from the Holy One; and not only from him but from the elders who would come after him and from the prophets. That is why it says, "And so trust you thereafter." —MEKHILTA DE-RABBI SHIM'ON BAR YOHAI

"I will come to you in a thick cloud, in order that the people may hear"—My grandfather Rabbi David, may the memory of the righteous be a blessing, told me that the book Ruah Hen cites the following [interpretation]: Human beings have four senses—sight, hearing, etc. When one of the senses is blocked, another becomes doubly acute. Since His intention, be He blessed, was to sharpen the sense of hearing, so that they would hear [Him], He blocked their vision and came to them in a thick cloud. Thus, when the Torah says, "I will come to you in a thick cloud," it means, to block their vision "in order that the people may hear"—My whole intention is that the people hear when I speak to you. —HELKEI AVANIM

WHEN I SPEAK WITH YOU

"In order that the people may hear"—that they may hear Me speaking with you with their own ears and so recognize that you are a true prophet and that all the things you say are straight from My mouth. "And so [they will] trust you thereafter"—not only in regard to commandments that apply at the moment but also in regard to commandments that will apply throughout the generations. —RABBI MEYUHAS BEN ELIYAHU

AND SO TRUST YOU THEREAFTER

"And so trust you thereafter"—This is what is meant by the verse at the beginning of his prophecy: "It shall be your sign that it was I who sent you. [And when you have freed the people from Egypt,] you shall worship God at this mountain" (Exod. 3:12). Moses knew that those who trusted him on the basis of the signs [God would give in Egypt] would not be firm in their faith. He therefore held back from going until the Blessed One told him that these signs would only be to get them out of Egypt, and once they were out and stood at the mountain they would be purged of their doubts. When they heard the voice speaking with Moses and saying to him, "Go tell them such and such," they themselves, to whom he was being sent, would be his witnesses. Thus they would come to have unqualified trust in him. —ME'OR HA'AFELAH; see also Maimonides, YESODEI TORAH 8:2

"And so trust you thereafter"—Not only you but also the prophets who are to arise after you. —MEKHILTA

"Thereafter (le'olam)"—The letter vav* is missing from all instances of the word le'olam in the scripture except two: "And so trust you thereafter (le'olam)," which comes to teach us that the whole world ('olam) may pass away but that not a word of Torah will ever do so; and "You shall never undertake anything for the welfare or benefit [of the Ammonites and Moabites] as long as you live (le'olam)" (Deut. 23:7), [where the inclusion of the vav] is to tell us that even if they convert, there will still be hatred in their hearts. —MIDRASH HASER VEYATER

*One of several letters indicating vowel sounds that may be omitted from Hebrew words without any change of meaning.

MOSES REPORTED

"Then Moses reported the people's words to the Lord"—Rabbi Eli'ezer ben Parta said: What did the Omnipresent tell Moses to say to Israel, and what did Israel tell Moses to say to the Omnipresent? This refers to the verse, "Moses went and repeated to the people [all the commands of the Lord . . . and all the people answered with one voice, saying, 'All the things that the Lord has commanded we will do!']" (Exod. 24:3). What he said to them was, If you accept the penalties joyfully, you shall be rewarded, but if not, you shall be punished. So they accepted the penalties joyfully. —MEKHILTA

"Then Moses reported the people's words"—What did he report? That they had said, "All that the Lord has spoken we will do!" Now you may object that it is already stated in the verse above, "Moses brought back [the people's words to the Lord]." But note that it says "brought back *(vayashev),*" not "reported." This teaches that [in the first instance] Moses came bearing a reply *(lehashiv teshuvah),* namely, what the people had said, and before he had begun to speak, the Holy One, blessed be He, said to him, "I will come to you in a thick cloud." Then, when [God] had finished speaking, it says, "Moses reported"— he said exactly what he had been about to say earlier. —MIDRASH LEKAH TOV

THE PEOPLE'S WORDS

"Moses reported the people's words to the Lord"—They said, "We wish to see our King." For hearing is not the same as seeing. The Omnipresent said, "Give them what they wish": "On the third day the Lord will come down, in the sight of all the people, on Mount Sinai." —MEKHILTA

"Moses reported the people's words to the Lord"—What he said was, "They already trust [me], saying, 'All that the Lord has spoken we will do!' " Then the Holy One, blessed be He, said, "Since they have already agreed to carry out [the commandments], go and sanctify them. Let them know they have been summoned to hear My words and receive them." —BEKHOR SHOR

"All the people answered as one, saying, 'All that the Lord has spoken we will do!' And Moses brought back the people's words to the Lord. And the Lord said to Moses, 'I will come to you in a thick cloud, in order that the people may hear when I speak with you and so trust you thereafter' " (Exod. 19:8–9)—The verses should be explained in their own terms. "All that the Lord has spoken we will do!" can be interpreted in two different ways.

One is that they believed in [Moses'] word and that it was to the Lord that they were speaking when they said, "All that the Lord has spoken"—according to [Moses'] word—[we will do!]"

Alternatively, "All that the *Lord* has spoken we will do"—that is, "whatever we know to have been spoken by Him, be He blessed, but not what you, Moses, have spoken." Now, Moses our Teacher did not like this second interpretation, and he prayed that there not be a recurrence of what happened when God sent him on his mission to Egypt and took him to task for saying, "What if they do not believe me . . . ?" What did [Moses] do? "[He] brought back the people's words," as if to say, "I am merely relaying these words back to Your glorious throne for You to interpret as You see fit." That is the significance of the words "brought back."

What, then, did the Holy One, blessed be He, do, knowing that the true interpretation of what was in their hearts was the second one? He said, "I will come [to you in a thick cloud]"—that is, "I know that what they are thinking is according to the second interpretation, that they do not trust you; and I want them to trust you. Therefore I will have to speak to you and them at the same time. Then they will trust you, for they will 'hear when I speak with you.' But how shall I do it? If I speak to you as though appearing through a clear glass, they will not be able to hear, for they are not prepared for this." After all, when the Divine word came to Moses, even Aaron, who was with him, could not bear to hear it; how much less would Israel be able to do so. Hence the Holy One, blessed be He, said to Moses, " 'I will come to you in a thick cloud'—the Divine word will come to you in a thick cloud, that is," as Rashi explains, "fog, which is thicker than an ordinary cloud, but not so thick as to block your prophetic perception, which can see even in near-darkness—'in order that the people may hear when I speak with you'—so that they will be drawn to Me—'and so trust you thereafter.' " This is hinted at by the cantillation sign *zarka* on the word *elekha* ("to you"): there is an upward lilt when He says, "to you in a thick cloud," meaning, "You are on a higher plane, but do not be dismayed, because it is only in order that the people may hear."

This then is the meaning of "Moses reported the people's words," namely, "Until now I was afraid to report, because the second interpretation of what they said [might have been correct]. All I could do was 'bring back.' But now that the Holy One, blessed be He, has provided a way to make them trust me, I can 'report'—that is, explicate—'the people's words to the Lord.' "
—ALSHEKH

"Moses reported the people's words"—Rabbi Yoḥanan explained this verse as referring to Israel when they came up to Mount Sinai. It may be compared to the case of a king who wanted to marry a highborn woman. He sent a messenger to speak with her. She said, "[I consent, although] I am not worthy to be his servant; nevertheless, I would like to hear [the proposal] from his own lips." When the messenger came back to the king, he was looking cheerful but his speech was inaudible. Being an intelligent man, the king said to himself, "From the fact that he looks cheerful I assume she consented; from the fact that his speech is inaudible I assume she wants to hear the proposal directly from me." Israel is like the highborn woman; Moses is like the messenger; the Holy One, blessed be He, is like the king. And it was at just such a moment that "Moses brought back the people's words to the Lord" [without as yet spelling out audibly what they had said]. —SONG OF SONGS RABBAH 1:14

"Moses reported the people's words to the Lord"—What reporting did he do? Earlier, scripture says, "We will do and we will hear," using the plural, when it should have said, "I will do and I will hear," for each one spoke for himself. The reason for this is that, in fact, each of them accepted the Torah as a member of the people of Israel as whole. Thus, when the Holy One, blessed be He, said to Moses, "I will come to you in a thick cloud, in order that the people may . . . trust you thereafter," Moses inferred that he was being treated as though he were on a much higher level than the rest of Israel. "Now Moses was a very humble man" (Num. 12:3), and so he simply "reported the people's words." That is, just as the people had said, "We will do and we will hear," each including himself in the generality of Israel without singling himself out, so Moses our Teacher, may he rest in peace, did not seek to aggrandize himself but rather included himself together with all of Israel. —SIAH SARFEI KODESH, quoting Rabbi Yizḥak Me'ir of Gur

AS A REWARD FOR "WE WILL DO AND WE WILL HEAR"

"Why, you are less than nothing, your effect is less than nullity" (Isa. 41:24)—Said Rabbi Levi: All the good things the Holy One, blessed be He, will ever do for Israel, all the consolations He will bring them, are merely a reward for their roar to Him at Sinai, "All that the Lord has spoken we will do and we will hear!" (Exod. 24:7). —PESIKTA DE-RAV KAHANA, passage beginning "When an ox or a sheep" (Lev. 22:27ff.)

We have concluded the section on
"We will do and we will hear."
May it be His will that
we do and hear.

ABSTINENCE AND BOUNDS

EXODUS 19:10
The Lord said to Moses,
"Go to the people and warn them
to stay pure today and tomorrow.
Let them wash their clothes."

"The Lord said to Moses, 'Go to the people and warn them to stay pure today' "—the fourth [of Sivan]—" 'and tomorrow' "—the fifth. " 'Let them be ready for the third day' "—the sixth of the month, the day on which the Torah was given. And what did Moses do on the fifth? He arose early and built an altar, as it is written, "Early in the morning, he set up an altar at the foot of the mountain, with twelve pillars for the twelve tribes of Israel" (Exod. 24:4). So says Rabbi Yehudah. But the Sages say he built twelve pillars for each tribe.

After building the altar, he sacrificed on it a burnt offering and a peace offering. He put blood from the burnt offering in two cups, one for the Omnipresent and one for the people; then he put blood from the peace offering in two cups, one for the Omnipresent and one for the people, as it is written, "Moses took half the blood"—the part for the Omnipresent—"[and put it in basins, and] the other half of the blood"—the part for the people—"he dashed against the altar" (Exod. 24:6).

"Then he took the record of the covenant and read it aloud to the people" (Exod. 24:7)—but it does not tell us from where he read to the people. Rabbi Yose be-Rabbi Assi said: from the beginning of Genesis up to this point. Rabbi [Yehudah Hanasi] said: the commandments given to Adam, to the sons of Noah, in Egypt, and at Marah, and all the other commandments. Rabbi Yishma'el said: He began by saying, "The land shall observe a sabbath of the Lord. Six years you may sow your field" (Lev. 25:2–3), and then he spoke about the sabbatical years and the jubilee years [Lev. 25], the blessings and the curses [Lev. 26]. And with what did he conclude? "These are the laws, norms, and directions" (Lev. 27:46). The people said, "We take these things upon our-selves." When he saw that they had taken these things upon themselves, he took the blood and dashed it upon the people, as it is written, "Moses took the blood and dashed it on the people" (Exod. 24:8); and he said to them, "You are hereby bound, tied, and obligated. Come back tomorrow and take upon yourselves all the [other] commandments." Rabbi Yose be-Rabbi Yehudah said: All these things were done on the same day. —MEKHILTA

"Warn them to stay pure"—As our forefathers stood at Mount Sinai to receive the Torah, the Holy One, blessed be He, said to Moses, "Go to the people and warn them to stay pure." Moses then came and said to them, "Be ready for the third day: do not go near a woman" (Exod. 19:15). But was it only from women that he told them to abstain? Rather, what he told them was, "Keep away from iniquity, theft, and ugly deeds, so that all of you may be pure when you stand at Mount Sinai." It is as Joshua came and told them, "Purify yourselves, for tomorrow the Lord will perform wonders in your midst" (Josh. 3:5), and as he was to tell them further, "Get provisions ready, [for in three days' time you are to cross the Jordan]" (Josh. 1:11)—in other words, repent, so that you may enter the land. —SEDER ELIYAHU RABBAH 18

EXODUS 19:11
Let them be ready for the third day;
for on the third day the Lord will come down,
in the sight of all the people, on Mount Sinai.

"Let them be ready for the third day"—that was the sixth [of Sivan], the day on which the Torah was given, as it is written, "For on the third day the Lord will come down, in the sight of all the people, on Mount Sinai." This is one of ten instances recorded in the Torah in which [the Lord] came down.

"In the sight of all the people"—this teaches us that none among them was blind.

Another interpretation of "In the sight of all the people"—We learn from this that at that moment they were able to see things that Ezekiel and Isaiah did not, as it is written, "[For I granted many visions,] and spoke in parables [rather than directly] through the prophets" (Hos. 12:11).

Another interpretation of "In the sight of all the people"—This teaches that if even one of them had not been present as a witness they would not have merited receiving the Torah. Rabbi Yose said: Had only twenty-two thousand of them been there, they would still have merited receiving it, as it is written, "When [the Ark] halted, he would say: Return, O Lord, unto the ten thousands of the families of Israel!" (Num. 10:36). —MEKHILTA

"Let them be ready for the third day"—This teaches that they established a fixed place of study.

"For on the third day the Lord will come down, in the sight of all the people"—This teaches that none of them was blind.

Rabbi Shim'on ben Yehudah of Kfar Ikkus said: How do we know that if even one of those who had gone out of Egypt had absented himself, the Torah would not have been given to them? Because the Torah says, "On the the third day the Lord will come down, in the sight of all the people." From this we also learn that there had never been, nor would there ever be, a generation as worthy as that one of receiving the Torah. Concerning them scripture says, "He reserves ability for the upright and is a shield for those who live blamelessly" (Prov. 2:7). —MEKHILTA DE-RABBI SHIM'ON BAR YOHAI

"For on the third day"—Why on the third day? Because it was on the third day that the trees and grasses had been created, as it is written, "And God said, 'Let the earth sprout [vegetation]' " (Gen. 1:11). Said the Holy One, blessed be He, "On the third day I created that which sustains life, and the Torah too is called a tree of life, as it is written, 'She is a tree of life to those who grasp her' (Prov. 3:18); it [too] I gave on the third day." —MIDRASH HADASH AL HATORAH, cited in TORAH SHELEMAH

"Let them be ready"—Let them prepare themselves to see and hear wondrous things, so that they are not driven mad by the sudden sight and sound of marvels. In the same way, let them prepare for solitary contemplation, each as best he can. Such preparation knows no measure. Thus, further on, we find the Holy One, blessed be He, saying to Moses, "Be ready by morning" (Exod. 34:2). Now, no one was ever as ready for prophecy as he was; but because the Holy One, blessed be He, wanted to show him the wondrous sight of the Divine glory, He warned him to prepare himself even more than usual. How much more did ordinary people [need to prepare themselves], each as best he could. —HA'AMEK DAVAR

"Let them be ready"—even though they really did not know what to prepare
for, for "no man can set a value on it" (Job 28:13), nor was it something they
could even grasp. The main point of the preparation, however, was to empty
themselves out, so as to stand ready for whatever the Lord would command.
—HASHAVAH LETOVAH, citing Rabbi Hanokh Hakohen of Alexander

"Let them be ready for the third day"—but it does not say what they were to
prepare for. Rabbi Avraham of Sochaczew said: The preparation alone was half
the act of receiving the Torah; it was itself Torah. This is the meaning of [the
words of the Haggadah]: "Had he brought us to Mount Sinai and not given us
the Torah, it would have been enough for us." —SIAH SARFEI KODESH

"For on the third day the Lord will come down, in the sight of all the
people"—even if they are not ready. —ABRABANEL

"For on the third day the Lord will come down"—In the Time to Come, too,
Israel is destined to see the Shekhinah face to face, as it is written, "For every
eye shall behold [the Lord's return to Zion]" (Isa. 52:8), and it is written, "[In
that day they shall say:] This is our God; we trusted in Him" (Isa. 25:9). Amen,
and may it be His will. —VEHIZHIR

EXODUS 19:12
You shall set bounds for the people round about, saying,
"Beware of going up the mountain or touching
the border of it. Whoever touches the
mountain shall be put to death."

"You shall set bounds"—Fix boundaries for them, to demarcate the point
where they may not draw any nearer. In other words, the boundary will
indicate, "Beware of going up any further," and you should warn them about
this. —RASHI

"You shall set bounds for the people"—Lay out a clearly marked boundary at
the foot of the mountain, and tell the people they may only go up that far. Both
the people and the mountain will thereby be circumscribed. This is what is
meant in the later verse, "[You warned us, saying:] Set bounds about the
mountain" (Exod. 19:23). —MISHNEH KESEF

"You shall set bounds for the people round about"—It does not say, "You shall set bounds about the mountain," as indeed it does in verse 23 below. This is a separate matter: boundaries for the people as they stood around the mountain, with Aaron in front, then the priests, according to rank, behind him, the leaders of Israel behind them, then ordinary men, then women and children.

[The effect was] to tell the people, "Be careful," an added warning against violating the prohibition, for which all of them would be equally subject to the death penalty. But as regards keeping their distance from the mountain itself, although there was no actual prohibition, [there too] the people were set bounds, as we see further on in verses 21 and 22. ["The Lord said to Moses, 'Go down, warn the people not to break through to the Lord to gaze, lest many of them perish. The priests also, who come near the Lord, must purify themselves, lest the Lord break out against them.' "] —HA'AMEK DAVAR

Since at the time of the Giving of the Torah Israel had a powerful love [for God] but had not yet been given many commandments to [express it], the Holy One, blessed be He, commanded them concerning boundaries and abstinence. These commandments provided vessels to contain the love and awe they already felt. —KEDUSHAT LEVI

"You shall set bounds for the people round about, saying . . ."—Moses was inspired by the holiness of Mount Sinai to purify the surrounding wilderness, which was inhabited by poisonous snakes and scorpions, to diminish the power of impurity there. And the guardian angel of the wilderness went before him in chains. Had that generation been worthy of entering the Land of Israel, the air of the entire world would have been purified by the holiness of this wilderness, which is called the Wilderness of the Nations, because many nations border upon it. But in committing the sin of the Golden Calf, they polluted the air of the wilderness with the two *klippot* of Shor and Ḥamor,* so that Israel met its downfall there, and good became mixed with evil. And since we did not merit this fault being remedied [for us] miraculously in the wilderness itself, we must remedy it [ourselves] through our sufferings in exile. This is what is meant by the verse, "So He raised His hand in oath [to make them fall in the wilderness], to disperse their offspring among the nations and scatter them through the lands" (Ps. 106:26)—until such time as our Maker takes pity on us.

For all this, there will in the future be [another] period of forty years in the desert, when Moses will once again be revealed to [us] and bring down

*In kabbalistic doctrine, forces of evil.

manna. Then the Messiah will conquer the whole world and purify the air. Then the world will be renewed, and even Gehinnom [hell] will be hallowed and added to the area of the Garden of Eden. It is there that the Dance of the Righteous will take place [see Ta'anit 31]. —'EMEK HAMELEKH

"Beware of going up the mountain or touching the border of it. Whoever touches the mountain shall be put to death"—Make a fence about the Torah [cf. Avot 3:13], and do not touch the edge of it, for "whoever touches the mountain shall be put to death." —MELEKHET MAḤSHEVET

"Beware of going up the mountain or touching the border of it"—Said Rabbi Menahem of Kotzk (may the memory of the righteous be a blessing): One who ascends on high should not content himself with touching the edge but should go all the way to the top. At the same time, "beware of going up the mountain" all at once, only touching the edge [i.e., in a superficial manner], rather than gradually [and more thoroughly]. —'AMUD HA'EMET

EXODUS 19:13

No hand shall touch him, but he shall be
either stoned or pierced through;
beast or man, he shall not live.
When the ram's horn sounds a long blast
They shall come up unto the mountain.

"No hand shall touch him, but he shall be either stoned or pierced through"— We find references to the hand of the Lord, in connection with prophecy, at those times when the prophet is not prepared to prophesy. For example, in reference to Elijah, [scripture says,] "[He lay down] and fell asleep [under a broom bush. Suddenly an angel] touched him [and said to him, 'Arise and eat']" (1 Kings 19:5). Similarly, when Ezekiel sees the glory of the Lord outside the Land, in a place unfit for prophecy, he speaks of "the hand of the Lord" [being upon him] [Ezek. 3:14, 33:22]. Here too, at the moment when the glory of the Lord is to be revealed to the masses of the House of Israel, one might think the [Divine] spirit would rest even upon those not ready for prophecy, as soon as they touched the mountain. Hence scripture says, "No hand shall touch him," meaning that the spirit of prophecy will not rest upon him who ascends the mountain, but rather "he shall be . . . stoned." —MESHEKH HOKHMAH

"No hand shall touch him, but he shall be . . . stoned"—There is a certain mountain with water on top of it. Whoever touches the water and speaks a word shall die on the spot. That is what is meant by the verse, "He touches the mountains and they smoke" (Ps. 104:32). Thus He commanded concerning Mount Sinai that "no hand shall touch it,*" for that place was intended for the angels. —SEFER ḤASIDIM

"Beast or man, he shall not live"—He who is at times like a beast, lacking intelligence, and at times a man, having intelligence, shall not live. His life is no life, for he is a mixture of good and evil,† now leaning toward evil, now dipping into holiness. One should always cling to holiness, as it is written, "But you, who held fast to the Lord your God, are all alive today" (Deut. 4:4). —'ATERET YESHU'AH

"When the ram's horn sounds a long blast—when the blast of the horn ceases—they shall come up unto the mountain." Similarly, scripture says, "When a long blast is sounded on the horn—as soon as you hear that sound of the horn[— all the people shall give a mighty shout. Thereupon the city wall will collapse,] and the people shall advance" (Josh. 6:5). —MEKHILTA DE-RABBI SHIM'ON BAR YOHAI

"They shall come up unto the mountain"—Rabbi Yose said: This is the basis of the saying, "It is not the place that honors the man, but the man who honors the place." As long as the Shekhinah rested upon the mountain, "whoever touches [it] shall be put to death." When the Shekhinah departed, all were allowed to climb the mountain. —MEKHILTA

EXODUS 19:14

Moses came down from the mountain to the people
and warned the people to stay pure,
and they washed their clothes.

---

*The word *bo* can be understood as "it" (i.e., the mountain) or "him" (i.e., the one who trespasses).

†*Klippat nogah,* lit. "husk of brightness," a Hasidic term denoting a morally ambiguous entity with a potential for sanctification.

FROM THE MOUNTAIN TO THE PEOPLE

"Moses came down from the mountain to the people"—This teaches that Moses did not turn to his own affairs or go down to his house but went straight "from the mountain to the people." One might have thought it happened only after this one revelation; how do we know it happened after the others? Because the Torah says, "The Lord came down upon Mount Sinai. . . . [And Moses went down to the people and spoke to them]" (Exod. 19:20,25).* So it is clearly stated.

Why did the Torah have to tell us, "Moses came down from the mountain to the people"? To teach us that Moses did not turn to his own affairs or go down to his house but went straight "from the mountain to the people." Now one might have thought it happened only after the Sinai revelations; how do we know it happened with the revelations at the Tent of Meeting as well? Because the Torah says, "Moses went out [of the Tent of Meeting] and reported . . . to the people" (Num. 11:24). —MEKHILTA

"Moses came down from the mountain to the people and warned the people to stay pure"—Moses cleaved as completely to the Creator, be He blessed, as anyone can, so that when he had to purify the people, he was compelled to lower himself to do so. This is what is meant by, "Moses came down from the mountain [to the people]." —NETA' SHA'ASHU'IM

"Moses came down from the mountain to the people"—"This teaches that Moses did not turn to his own affairs . . . but went directly from the mountain to the people" and back. What affairs could Moses have had in the wilderness? Every Jew was preparing himself for the Divine revelation of the receiving of the Torah, each according to his [spiritual] level. Obviously, Moses, the leading figure of his generation, in his great holiness, had more preparation to do than any other Jew. In spite of this, he paid no heed to himself and did not turn to his own affairs—affairs of Torah—but rather exerted all his efforts for the good of Israel [as a whole]. —NIFLA'OT HATIF'ERET SHLOMO

"Moses came down from the mountain to the people"—"This teaches that Moses did not turn to his own affairs . . . but went directly from the mountain to the people." But this interpretation poses a difficulty: What affairs could

---

*Eifat Zedek, [a commentary on the Mekhilta,] in referring to this passage, omits v. 20 and cites only v. 25.—S.Y.A.

Moses have had in the wilderness? With his exalted standing, Moses our Teacher, peace be to him, could easily have petitioned on high for lofty things for himself, things the rest of Israel did not merit. That is why [it is stressed that Moses] "went directly from the mountain to the people." In other words, Moses did not try to distinguish himself from the rest of Israel in regard to lofty things but rather sought to be equal to the others. —GEDULAT MORDEKHAI; GEDULAT HAZADDIKIM

"Moses came down from the mountain to the people"—The commentators write that only when Moses had come down were the Ten Commandments spoken, so that no one could say, "If Moses our Teacher can go there, so can I," and so dare to go up himself. Therefore Moses came down to the people, to be with them. —MA'AGELEI ZEDEK

"Moses came down from the mountain to the people"—to be included with all the rest of Israel in accepting the Torah. —KOL DODI

"[Moses] warned the people to stay pure"—He ordered [the men] to abstain from relations with women. For the Torah is called holy, as it is written, "Knowledge of holy things is understanding" (Prov. 9:10), and thus man must hallow himself in order that it may attach itself to him. Now it can be argued *a fortiori* that if Moses our Teacher hallowed himself by abstaining from bread and water, which the body needs to live, for forty days before being given the Torah, how much more must an ordinary person rid his body of every impurity.

Thus scripture says, "The fear of the Lord is pure" (Ps. 19:10). When is it pure? When a person rids himself of all impurity. Thus the Torah is compared to oil, to teach you that just as one can defraud by adding [water] to every liquid except oil, so too is it impossible to defraud [by adding to] the words of the Torah. How do we know that the words of the Torah are compared to oil? From the verse, "Rightly has God, your God, chosen to anoint you with oil of gladness over all your peers" (Ps. 45:8).

Another interpretation: When is [the fear of the Lord] pure? When one purges himself of the tendency to make use of it [for his own ends], when he stops saying to himself, "Since I am so wise, other people should serve me, should provide for me." Hillel would say: "He who uses the crown [of Torah for his own aggrandizement] will soon pass away" [Avot 1:13], meaning, one who makes use of the words of the Torah has forfeited his share in this world. If Belshazzar was cast out of this world for making use of the vessels of the

Temple, how much more likely is this to happen to one who makes use of the very instrument by which the world was created.

Another interpretation: When is [the fear of the Lord] pure? When man purges himself of his pride. Rabbi Yose, son of Rabbi Yehudah said: What causes scholars to die young? Not adultery or robbery, but self-satisfaction.

Another interpretation of "The fear of the Lord is pure": When is it pure? When one purges himself of the love of silver and gold. Thus the prophet says, "Even if you give me half your wealth, I will not go in with you" (1 Kings 13:8). Similarly, Elisha says, "As the Lord lives, whom I serve, I will not accept anything" (2 Kings 5:16). And Daniel says, "You may keep your gifts for yourself, and give your presents to others" (Dan. 5:17). Said Rabbi Yose, the son of Rabbi Halafta: Once while walking along a road I met someone who greeted me. "Where are you coming from?" he asked. "From visiting residents of a great city of sages and scribes." He said to me, "If you could see fit to live with me, I would support you and give you silver and gold." "Even if you were to give me all the wealth in world," I said, "I would not live with you." "So you refuse?" he said to me. I replied, "All living things that you see in this world revert to dust, and man has nothing to hold onto at the hour of his death but the words of the Torah. Indeed, it was only because of neglect of the Torah that Jerusalem was destroyed, as it is written, 'All this is for the transgression of Jacob' (Mic. 1:5)." So he said to me, "Blessed be the Omnipresent, who has given you words of Torah to which you can devote and entrust yourselves, so that you can put aside all the trivialities of this world." I said to him, "May it be His will that others not become envious of us, nor we of them." And thus I parted with him.

Another interpretation: When is [the fear of the Lord] pure? When one rids himself of sin, for the words of the Torah require purity and holiness. Hence it is written, "[Moses] warned the people to stay pure." —MEKHILTA DE-RABBI SHIM'ON BAR YOḤAI

URGING UPON URGING

EXODUS 19:15

And he said to the people,
"Be ready for the third day:
do not go near a woman."

"Be ready for the third day"—that is, for the third day following this warning, namely, the sixth of Sivan.

"Be ready"—so that not only the soul but also the body is pure and ready for prophecy. —SFORNO

"Do not go near a woman"—He did not need to warn them about food and drink, because none of them was a wine swiller or a meat glutton. Their whole diet consisted of manna and cold water. What may well have been included in the preparation and purification was the avoidance of labor during those days and an effort to dwell upon the wonders He had performed for them and to listen to the wisdom and correction being taught by their elders and sages. —ABRABANEL

"Do not go near a woman"—The Targum has it, "next to a woman." When one is in one place, he cannot be in another; and when one is alongside one person, he cannot be alongside another. —'AMUD HA'EMET, citing Rabbi Menahem of Kotzk, may the memory of the righteous be a blessing.

We hereby conclude the section
concerning bounds.
Let us now contemplate
what happened on Sinai.

THUNDER AND LIGHTNING

EXODUS 19:16

On the third day, as morning dawned,
there was thunder, and lightning,
and a dense cloud upon the mountain,
and a very loud blast of the horn,
and all the people who were in the camp trembled.

"On the third day"—The Holy One, blessed be He, does not leave the righteous in the lurch for more than three days. Thus it is written, "In two days He will make us whole again; on the third day He will raise us up, and we shall be whole by His favor" (Hos. 6:2). Why the third day? The Sages say, By virtue of the "third day" on which the Torah was given: "On the third day, as morning dawned." —GENESIS RABBAH 56

"On the third day, as morning dawned"—This teaches that the Omnipresent consented to [Moses' request to add a third day],* fulfilling the verse, "While the king was on his couch, my nard gave forth its fragrance" (Song 1:12). "There was thunder"—great claps of sound of all kinds. "And lightning"— great flashes of light of all kinds. "And a dense cloud upon the mountain"—a thick fog, as referred to in the verse, "Moses approached the thick fog" (Exod. 20:18). "And a very loud blast of the horn"—usually, the longer [the sounding of a horn is] drawn out, the softer it becomes, but here the longer it was drawn out the louder it became. Why [was it soft at first]? So as to begin within normal hearing range [and gradually build up]. "And all the people who were in the camp trembled"—This teaches that they were shaken. —MEKHILTA

"On the third day, as morning dawned"—just when he was told it would happen. This teaches that certain times and certain actions are right for each other, for it was then that life was given to all the inhabitants of the world. Lest

*Another version reads: "This teaches that the Omnipresent was there before him."

we think the Torah was given at night, scripture says, "On the . . . day"; lest we think it was given in silence, scripture says, "There was thunder* and lightning"—great claps of sound, great flashes of light, sounds of all kinds, light of all kinds. Similarly, scripture says, "The voice of the Lord is over the waters; the God of glory thunders, the Lord, over the mighty waters. The voice of the Lord is power; the voice of the Lord is majesty; the voice of the Lord breaks cedars. . . . The voice of the Lord kindles flames of fire; the voice of the Lord convulses the wilderness; . . . the voice of the Lord causes hinds to calve and strips forests bare, while in His temple all say 'Glory!' " (Ps. 29:3–9). Scripture tells us that on the day of the giving of the Torah there were clouds and lightning and rain. Thus it is written, "O Lord, when You came forth from Seir, advanced from the country of Edom, the earth trembled; the heavens dripped, yea, the clouds dripped water" (Judg. 5:4). And it is written, "Your thunder rumbled like wheels; lightning lit up the world" (Ps. 77:19). Something like the sound of a horn filled the air—as it is written, "a very loud blast of the horn"—to the point where the whole world shook.

All the nations of the world gathered around Balaam, son of Beor, and said to him, "The Omnipresent seems to be destroying His world with water, as in the verse, 'The Lord sat enthroned at the Flood' (Ps. 29:10)." He replied, "What fools there are in the world! Did He not swear He would not bring [another] flood upon the world, as it is written, 'For this to Me is like the waters of Noah: As I swore that the waters of Noah nevermore would flood the earth, [so I swear that I will not be angry with you or rebuke you]' (Isa. 54:9)?" They said to him, "He will certainly not flood the earth with water, but He might engulf it with fire!" He said to them, "He is bringing neither a flood nor a firestorm." "What then is this sound?" they said. He replied, "He is giving the Torah to His people, as it is written, 'May the Lord grant strength (*'oz*) to His people' (Ps. 29:11), and *'oz* means Torah, as it is written, 'With Him are strength (*'oz*) and resourcefulness' (Job 12:16)." They said, "If so, 'May the Lord bestow on His people well-being!' (Ps. 29:11)."

"And all the people who were in the camp trembled"—They were shaken. Now it can be argued *a fortiori* that if [the people] Israel, who were long destined to stand at Mount Sinai, were shaken, how much more so were the other nations of the world. Thus scripture says, "In heaven You pronounced sentence; the earth was numbed with fright" (Ps. 76:9). —MEKHILTA DE-RABBI SHIM'ON BAR YOHAI

Kolot may be understood as "sounds," "voices," or "thunder." The translation here varies according to the sense assumed by each midrash or comment.

"There were voices, and lightning, and a dense cloud upon the mountain"—
The voices were those of the angels who praise the Holy One, blessed be He,
each morning, as it is written, "When the morning stars sang together and all
the Divine beings shouted for joy" (Job 38:7). The lightning, too, was made
by angels, as it is written, "He makes the winds His messengers, fiery flames His
servants" (Ps. 104:4), and it is written, "[Such then was the appearance of the
creatures. With them was something that looked like burning coals of fire.] The
fire had a radiance, and lightning issued from the fire" (Ezek. 1:13). "And a
dense cloud"—to separate Israel from the angels, for had Israel seen them their
vision would have been disrupted. Similarly, Ezekiel writes, "[I looked, and lo,
a stormy wind came sweeping out of the north—]a huge cloud and flashing fire,
[surrounded by a radiance; and in the center of it, in the center of the fire, a
gleam as of amber]. In the center of it were also the figures of four creatures"
(Ezek. 1:4–5). Thus Rabbenu Hanan'el. —RABBENU BAHYA

"Thunder (kolot) and lightning"—a roar like that of the Chariot in motion (in
Ezek. 1), or as in the subsequent verse, "A roar (vekolo) like the roar of mighty
waters [was the Presence of the God of Israel]" (Ezek. 43:2). Similar to this was
the sound of the horn coming from heaven. "And all the people . . . trembled"—When they heard these sounds, they emerged from their tents trembling. —RABBI MEYUHAS BEN ELIYAHU

One verse says, "There was thunder and lightning," but another says, "[And after
the fire], a still, small voice [demamah]" (1 Kings 19:12). How can both verses be
true? When the Holy One, blessed be He, speaks, all are silent, as it is written, "Be
silent [domu], you coastland dwellers, you traders of Sidon! You were filled with
men who crossed the sea" (Isa. 23:2), and it is also written, "[Then Moses said to
Aaron, 'This is what the Lord meant when He said: Through those near to Me I
show Myself holy, and assert My authority before all the people.'] And Aaron was
silent [vayidom]" (Lev. 10:3). Thus Rabbi Yoshiah.
     Rabbi Yohanan said: One verse says, "[The Lord spoke those words]—
those and no more" (Deut. 5:19), while another says, "And after the fire, a still,
small voice [demamah]." How can both verses be true? When the Holy One
speaks, He speaks in a loud voice and the ministering angels [reply] softly, as
it is written, "[Upon your walls, O Jerusalem, I have set watchmen,] who shall
never be silent [by day or by night]. O you, the Lord's remembrancers, be not
silent [domi]" (Isa. 62:6), and it says further, "Be not silent [domi] before Him,
until He establish Jerusalem and make her renowned on earth" (Isa. 62:7).
—SIFREI, Naso

ALL THE PEOPLE . . . TREMBLED

"All the people . . . trembled *(vayeherad)"*—This is not a term of fear but of agitation and commotion, as in the verse, "The outposts and the raiders were [also] agitated *(hardu)"* (1 Sam. 14:15), and "The rest of the people bestirred themselves *(hardu)* to follow him" (1 Sam. 13:7). The meaning is, they heard the thunder while still in bed, and, realizing that the Shekhinah was waiting for them on the mountain, they bestirred themselves and got up. —HIZKUNI

"All the people who were in the camp trembled"—Surely this was not mere creaturely fear, for at this moment Israel was in a state of exaltation, high above [worldly concerns]. Rather, it is as in the comment of Rashi, may his memory be a blessing, on the verse, "I bore you on eagles' wings": "Like the eagle, which has no fear of any other bird, being above them all." For Israel had become tied to the Root of All. What then does "trembled" mean? They feared the Lord, be He blessed, as it is written, "To such a one I look: [to the poor and broken-hearted,] who fears *(vehared)* for My word" (Isa. 66:2). Likewise, it means love [of God], as our Sages, may their memory be a blessing, said: "With each word that issued forth from the mouth of the Holy One, blessed be He, they fainted away"*—"They fainted away" with the desire and longing they felt for the [Divine] holiness.

And all this was by way of preparation for receiving the Torah, to give them wings with which, in love and awe, they might fly upward, as the Zohar says. It is concerning this that scripture states, "I bore you on eagles' wings," for it is by bringing together the two wings of love and awe [that the soul takes flight]. This is the meaning of the verse, "All the people answered with one voice, [saying, 'All the things that the Lord has commanded we will do!']" (Exod. 24:3): their one voice was formed by a joining together of fire, water, and air *(ruah);* and it was the spirit *(ruah)* that joined them together, the way eagles' wings [are brought together by the air]. It was by a joining together of awe and love that they were united and bound heart and soul to the Root of All. —TORAT EMET

*The Hebrew phrase *parhah nishmatam* (lit., "their souls took flight") suggests actual death (from fear); but in this context a temporary state is meant, as is made clear subsequently.

THE SINAI EVENT

EXODUS 19:17
Moses led the people toward God, out of the camp,
and they took their places beneath the mountain.

MOSES LED THE PEOPLE . . . OUT

"Moses led the people toward God"—Rabbi Yehudah ben Pazi said in the name of Rabbi [Yehudah Hanasi]: How can we read [the following] without feeling ashamed?

For a good purpose, "everyone whose heart so moves him [shall bring them—gifts for the Lord]" (Exod. 35:5); but for an evil purpose, "all the people took off the gold rings that were in their ears [and brought them to Aaron]" (Exod. 32:3).

For a good purpose, "Moses led the people"; but for an evil purpose, "all of you came to me [and said, 'Let us send men ahead']" (Deut. 1:22).

For a good purpose, "Moses and the Israelites sang [this song to the Lord]" (Exod. 15:1); but for an evil purpose, "the whole community broke into loud cries" (Num. 14:1). —PALESTINIAN TALMUD, Shekalim 1:1

The meaning of this passage is: How can we read these verses without embarrassment?

When Israel had to gather donations for a worthy purpose, it says, "Everyone whose heart so moves him," meaning only the generous made donations. But when it was for an evil purpose, the making of the Golden Calf, it says, "all the people took off [the gold rings]," even those who were not generous.

When it was for a good purpose, [the receiving] of the Torah, which is the highest good of all, it says that "Moses led the people," for he had to lead them up. [But when it was for an evil purpose, scouting out the Land, it says, "All of you came to me and said, 'Let us send men ahead.' "]*

When it was for a good purpose, it says, "Moses and the Israelites sang," but there he had to spur them on by starting the singing himself. But when it was for an evil purpose, it says, "The whole community broke into loud cries"—they cried of their own accord.

TOWARD GOD

"They took their places beneath the mountain"—They huddled together. From this we learn that they were frightened by the flashes and booms, the thunder and lightning.

"Beneath the mountain"—This teaches us that the mountain was uprooted, and they came and stood under it, as it is written, "You came forward and stood beneath the mountain" (Deut. 4:11). Of this, tradition says, "O my dove, in the cranny of the rocks, hidden by the cliff, let me see your face, let me hear your voice; for your voice is sweet and your face is comely" (Song 2:14). "Let me see your face"—This refers to the twelve pillars [set up] for the twelve tribes of Israel. "Let me hear your voice"—This refers to [their response to] the Ten Commandments. "For your voice is sweet"—[in responding to] the Ten Commandments. "And your face is comely"—when "the whole community came forward and stood before the Lord" (Lev. 9:5).

Rabbi Eli'ezer said: [The verse in the Song of Songs] refers, rather, to what happened at the Reed Sea. "Let me see your face"—when you "stand by, and witness the deliverance which the Lord [will work for you today]" (Exod. 14:13). "Let me hear your voice"—and so, "Greatly frightened, the Israelites cried out to the Lord" (Exod. 14:10). "For your voice is sweet"—when "their cry for help rose up [to God]" (Exod. 2:23). "And your face is comely"—when "[Aaron] performed the signs in the sight of the people, and the people were convinced" (Exod. 4:30–31).

Another interpretation: "For your voice is sweet" [refers to their singing] at the sea, "I will sing to the Lord, for He has triumphed gloriously" (Exod. 15:1). "And your face is comely"—when "from the mouths of infants and sucklings You have founded strength on account of Your foes, to put an end to enemy and avenger" (Ps. 8:3). —MEKHILTA

*Likely reconstruction of a sentence missing from the Hebrew.

["Let me see your face"]—This refers to the twelve pillars [set up] for the twelve tribes of Israel. For it is written there, "They saw the God of Israel" (Exod. 24:10). —ZEH YENAHAMENU

"Let me hear your voice"—in response to the Ten Commandments; ["For your voice is sweet," when] they assented to both the negative and the positive injunctions. —ZAYIT RA'ANAN

" 'For your voice is sweet' was said before the Ten Commandments"—So reads the version [of the Midrash] cited by [the commentary] *Eifat Zedek*. The meaning is, [Israel's voice is sweet to Me] for having said, "We wish to see our King." "Your face *(mar'ekh)* is comely" is then understood to mean "your seeing *(re'iyatekh)* is comely"—that is, the fact that you took note of the wonders I did and trusted Me. —BEIRUREI HAMIDDOT

"O my dove, in the cranny of the rocks, hidden by the cliff"—The Israelites were hidden behind Mount Sinai. "Let me see your face"—as it is written, "All the people witnessed the thunder" (Exod. 20:15). "Let me hear your voice"— referring to what they said before the Ten Commandments were given, as it is written, "All that the Lord has spoken we will do and we will hear" (Exod. 24:7). "For your voice is sweet"—referring to what they said after the Ten Commandments were given, as it is written, "The Lord heard your plea as you spoke to me, and the Lord said to me, 'I have heard the plea that this people made to you; they did well [to speak thus']" (Deut. 5:25). —SONG OF SONGS RABBAH

"Moses led the people toward God"—Rabbi Yose said: According to Yudan, "The Lord came from Sinai" (Deut. 33:2) means He was revealed on Sinai; but I say it means He came down from Sinai to greet His children joyfully. This can be understood by way of a parable: What does the matter resemble? It resembles the case of a bridegroom who went out to greet his bride. From the station of the one who goes out to greet, one can infer the station of the one who is greeted. That is why it says, "Moses led the people toward God."

"And they took their places beneath the mountain"—huddled to-gether. Concerning this, tradition says, "O my dove, in the cranny of the rocks, hidden by the cliff." Rabbi El'azar says this verse refers to [what happened] at the sea. "Let me see your face *(mar'ekh),*" as in the verse, "Stand by, and witness *(ure'u)* the deliverance which the Lord [will work for you today]" (Exod. 14:13). "Let me hear your voice," as in the verse, "As Pharaoh drew near, . . . the Israelites cried out to the Lord" (Exod. 14:10). "For your voice is sweet" [refers to the verse] "Their cry . . . rose up to God" (Exod. 2:23). "And your face is comely" refers to the verse, "The people were convinced. [When they heard that the Lord had taken note of the Israelites . . . they bowed low in homage]" (Exod. 4:31).

Rabbi 'Akiva said: The passage refers, rather, to what happened at Mount Sinai. "Let me see your face" refers to the verse, "Early in the morning, he set up an altar at the foot of the mountain" (Exod. 24:4). "Let me hear your voice" refers to the verses, "All the people answered with one voice, saying, . . . All that the Lord has spoken we will do and we will hear!" (Exod. 24:3, 7). "For your voice is sweet" refers to the verse, "[The Lord said to me, 'I have heard the plea that this people made to you;] they did well to speak thus' " (Deut. 5:25). "And your face is comely"—at the Tent of Meeting, [as it is written,] "[They brought to the front of the Tent of Meeting the things that Moses had commanded,] and the whole community came forward and stood before the Lord" (Lev. 9:5).

Others say the passage refers to future generations. "O my dove, in the cranny (ḥagvei) of the rocks" refers to the verse, "[It is He who is enthroned] above the vault (ḥug) of the earth" (Isa. 40:22). "Hidden by the cliff" refers to [the people] Israel, who must live with the sufferings inflicted upon them by their foreign rulers until their time comes.

"Let me see your face" refers to deeds. "Let me hear your voice" refers to study. "For your voice is sweet and your face is comely"—This tells you how superior study is to deeds. [When the academy met in the upper story of the Aris home, they took a vote as to which was greater, study or deeds. Said Rabbi Tarfon: Study is greater. Said Rabbi 'Akiva: Deeds are greater. All the others replied: Study is greater, for it leads to deeds, but deeds do not lead to study.

Another interpretation of "They took their places beneath the mountain"—This teaches that the Holy One, blessed be He, held the mountain over their heads like a barrel, saying, "If you take the Torah upon yourselves, it will go well [with you], but if not, this shall be your burial place" (Shabbat 88a). Thereupon they all burst out crying and poured out their hearts in penitence, saying, "All that the Lord has spoken, we will do and we will hear!"

Said the Holy One, blessed be He, "I need guarantors." They said, "Let the heaven and the earth be our guarantors." He said to them, "They are too busy." They said, "Let our children be our guarantors." He said, "They will make fine guarantors, for it is written, 'From the mouths of infants and suck-lings You have founded strength' (Ps. 8:3), and it says further, 'Because you have spurned the teaching of your God, I, in turn, will spurn your children' (Hos. 4:6)." —MEKHILTA DE-RABBI SHIM'ON BAR YOHAI

"Toward God, out of the camp"—The verse is inverted. What it means is, Moses led the people out of the camp toward God. —RABBI MEYUHAS BEN ELIYAHU

"Moses led the people toward God out of the camp"—Pirkei Rabbi Eli'ezer cites the view that the Israelites were sleeping and that Moses our Teacher, peace be to him, awakened them in order to receive the Torah. The holy sage Rabbi Levi Yizhak, may his memory be a blessing, said: Far be it from us to imagine that the holy people fell into slothful slumber on that great day. After all, they knew that the Holy One, blessed be He, would be giving them the Torah [on that day]. In fact, however, their intentions were entirely for the sake of heaven: since the second of Sivan they had been preparing to receive the Torah, working as hard as they could, their holy thoughts [concentrated on the task], until they were overcome with weariness. Fearing that when it came time to receive the Torah their minds would not be as clear as they should be, they went to sleep in order to refresh their minds and recover their strength for receiving the holy Torah. —'AVODAT YISRA'EL; KEDUSHAT LEVI

"Toward God"—meaning, toward the camp of God, which consisted of the ministering angels who had come down there. Our Rabbis, may their memory be a blessing, taught that six hundred thousand ministering angels came down there, corresponding to the six hundred thousand Israelites. Jacob hinted at this: "[He said, 'This is God's camp.'] So he named that place Mahanaim (two camps)" (Gen. 32:2)—because there were two camps opposite each other. Solomon, peace be to him, also referred to this: "['Turn, turn, O maid of Shulem! Turn, turn, that we may gaze upon you.' Why will you gaze at the Shulammite] like the Mahanaim dance?" (Song 7:1). And since [the people] Israel have been subject to four [foreign] kingdoms, each of which has told them to turn to its faith and embrace it, the verse says "turn" four times. We today are subject to the fourth kingdom [Rome], which says to us, "Turn, that we may gaze (venehezeh) upon you." What they mean is, [if you agree] we shall make you rulers and give you all kinds of authority, the word [venehezeh] being used here as in the verse, "You shall also seek out (tehezeh) from among all the people [capable men who fear God . . . and set these over them as chiefs]" (Exod. 18:21).

Our Rabbis, may their memory be a blessing, taught that "the Shulammite" is a people upon which the well-being *(shelom)* of all the worlds depends. She replies, "Why will you gaze *(tehezu)* at the Shulammite?"—What authority or status or honor could you give the Shulammite that would equal the joy of standing before God at Sinai? This is the meaning of "like the Mahanaim dance": two camps coming toward each other, the joy of what they attain on this occasion being compared to that of a dance. Concerning this our Rabbis, may their memory be a blessing, taught: "In the Time to Come, the Holy One, blessed be He, will make a dance for the righteous, and He will sit among them in the Garden of Eden" (Ta'anit 31a). Therefore, [says Israel], I shall not turn to your faith, for I remember that dance, namely, the Sinai Event. —RABBENU BAHYA

WHEN THE HOLY ONE, BLESSED BE HE, WAS REVEALED ON MOUNT SINAI

Said Rabbi Yizhak: When the Holy One, blessed be He, was revealed on Mount Sinai the mountain shook, and when that mountain shook all the other mountains in the world shook up and down, until the Holy One, blessed be He, laid His hand on them and they subsided. Then a voice proclaimed, "What alarmed you, O sea, that you fled, Jordan, that you ran backward, mountains, that you skipped like rams . . . ?" (Ps. 114:5, 6); and they answered, "Tremble, O earth, at the presence of the Lord, at the presence of the God of Jacob" (Ps. 114:7). —ZOHAR, Exodus 84a

"Why so contentious *(terazedun)*, O hunchbacked mountains, [toward the mountain God desired as His dwelling? The Lord shall abide there forever]" (Ps. 68:17). Rabbi Yose the Galileean and Rabbi 'Akiva [discussed this]. Rabbi Yose the Galileean explained the verse in terms of actual mountains: When the Holy One, blessed be He, came to Sinai to give the Torah, the other mountains ran around *(razim)* arguing *(umedayenim)* with one another. One said, "It is on me that the Torah is to be given," while another said, "[No,] on me." Tabor came from Beit Elim and Carmel from Aspamea, as we learn from the verse, "As I live—declares the King, whose name is Lord [of Hosts]—as surely as Tabor is among the mountains [and Carmel is by the sea, so shall this come to pass]" (Jer. 46:18). One said, "It is I who was called," while another said, "[No,] it was I." Said the Holy One, blessed be He, " 'Why so contentious, O hunchbacked mountains?' Do you think you are mountains? You are merely hunchbacks!"—as in the verse, "[No one at all who has a defect shall be qualified]. . . . who is a hunchback, or a dwarf" (Lev. 21:18, 20)—"You have all had idolatry performed on top of you, but Sinai, which has not, is 'the mountain God desired as His dwelling.' " Hence, "The Lord will come down . . . on Mount Sinai" (Exod. 19:11). Nevertheless, "The Lord shall abide there [on Mount Moriah, rather than on Mount Sinai,] forever"—in the Eternal House. —GENESIS RABBAH 99

"Hunchbacked"—that is, deformed. "Nevertheless"—even though [Sinai was the mountain] "God desired as His dwelling," His Shekhinah dwells forever "in the Eternal House."

"O godly mountain, Mount Bashan; [O hunchbacked mountain, Mount Bashan]" (Ps. 68:16)—When the Holy One, blessed be He, was about to give the Torah to Israel, Mount Carmel came from Aspamea and Mount Tabor from Beit Elim [to plead for consideration]. Of this, scripture says, "As I live—declares the King, whose name is Lord of Hosts—as surely as Tabor is among the mountains and Carmel is by the sea, so shall this come to pass" (Jer. 46:18). The one says, "I am called Mount Tabor. It would be fitting for the Shekhinah to dwell upon me, for I am the highest of the mountains, and the waters of the Flood did not cover me." The other says, "I am called Mount Carmel. It would be fitting for the Shekhinah to dwell upon me, because I spread myself out [over the Reed Sea], enabling [Israel] to cross [it]."

Said the Holy One, blessed be He, "I have already ruled you both out because of your haughtiness. I have ruled you all out." They replied, "Do You show favoritism? Or are You withholding our just reward?" The Holy One, blessed be He, answered, "Since you have gone to some trouble on account of My honor, I shall reward you. To Mount Tabor I give [the privilege of] saving Israel in the time of Deborah, as it is written, 'Go, march up to Mount Tabor' (Judg. 4:6); and to Mount Carmel I give [the privilege of] saving Elijah, as it is written, '[Ahab] . . . gathered the prophets at Mount Carmel' (1 Kings 18:20)." All the mountains began to rumble and break apart, as it is written, "The mountains quaked—before the Lord" (Judg. 5:5). Said the Holy One, blessed be He, " 'Why so contentious (terazedun)?' Why do you wish to contend (tirzu ladun) with Mount Sinai? You are all hunchbacked, and it says, '[No one at all who has a defect shall be qualified]. . . . who is a hunchback, or a dwarf.' [Sinai is] 'the mountain God desired as His dwelling'—I desire only Sinai, for it is the humblest of you all, as it is written, 'I dwell on high, in holiness; yet with the contrite and the lowly in spirit' (Isa. 57:15); and it is written, 'High though the Lord is, He sees the lowly; lofty, He perceives from afar' (Ps. 138:6)."

Lest we think, however, that He intended to dwell there throughout the generations, the Torah says, "The Lord shall abide in eternity" (Ps. 68:17)—meaning, His Shekhinah returned to dwell on high.

As for Sinai, whence did it come? Rabbi Yose said: It was detached from Mount Moriah, like a piece of dough, from the place where Isaac our Father was bound. Said the Holy One, blessed be He, "Since Isaac your Father was bound upon [that mountain], it is fitting that his children receive the Torah upon it." And how do we know that [Mount Sinai] will return to its place? Because it is written, "[In the days to come,] the Mount of the Lord's House shall stand firm above the mountains" (Isa. 2:2)—referring to Tabor, Carmel, Sinai, and Zion alike. "The mountains (heharim)" means five (he) mountains (harim)—that is, the same number as the books of the Pentateuch. —MIDRASH ON PSALMS 68

THE HOLY MOUNTAINS

"A psalm. A song. [The Lord loves the gates of Zion,] His foundation on the holy mountains" (Ps. 87:1–2)—Jerusalem is the foundation of the world, by virtue of the two holy mountains, Sinai [which was taken from Jerusalem] and Moriah. Rabbi Pinhas said in the name of Rabbi Re'uven: There will come a time when the Holy One, blessed be He, will bring Sinai, Tabor, and Carmel together and place Jerusalem on top of them, as it is written, "In the days to come, the Mount of the Lord's House shall stand firm above the mountains" (Isa. 2:2). Rabbi Hanina said: What is more, [God] will sing, and the others will respond with songs and hymns, as it is written, "Also Chenaniah, officer of the Levites in song; he was in charge of the song"* (1 Chron. 15:22). —MIDRASH ON PSALMS 87

Rav Huna said: Enough, you go too far! Say rather that the Temple [not God] will sing and the mountains respond. What basis can we find for this in the verses? It is written, "[In the days to come, the Mount of the Lord's House shall stand firm above the mountains] and be lifted (venisa) above the hills" (Isa. 2:2), and the verb "to be lifted" (ns') is associated with song. Thus

*Apparently reading the name as konan yah, "God will establish it," and "he" as referring to God.

scripture says, "Also Chenaniah, officer of the Levites in song *(bemasa)*; he was in charge of the song *(bamasa)*" (1 Chron. 15:22). —YALKUT SHIM'ONI on Isaiah, section 391

"Also Chenaniah, officer of the Levites [in song]"—Here it says "Chenaniah," and there [in Isaiah 2:2], it says, "The Mount of the Lord's House shall stand firm *(nakhon)*," [thus reinforcing the connection between song and the Temple Mount]. —MIDRASH ON PSALMS 36

"In song *(bemasa)*"—What was he in charge of? *Bamasa,* the lifting up *(nesi'ut)* of voices in song.

"He was in charge *(yasor)* of the song"—He would reprove *(meyaser)* and correct [the Levites] on their rendition of the melodies, be it to raise or lower their voices. —[PSEUDO-]RASHI

"How welcome on the mountain are the footsteps of the herald announcing happiness, heralding good fortune, announcing victory, telling Zion, 'Your God is King!' " (Isa. 52:7)—This comes to teach you that in the Time to Come the Holy One, blessed be He, will lower the rebuilt Jerusalem from heaven and set it on the tops of the four mountains, Sinai, Tabor, Hermon, and Carmel. Then, resting on the mountaintops, it shall announce Israel's final redemption. Why on the mountaintops? Because He said: I will announce it from the very place where they received the Torah and then violated it. —Midrash cited in BINEFUZOT YEHUDAH 52

THE PASSAGE CONCERNING THE MOUNTAIN

"[Who is she that comes up from the desert, leaning on her beloved?] Under the apple tree I roused you" (Song 8:5)—Paltion the Roman interpreted this as follows: Mount Sinai was uprooted and set on high, and the Israelites found themselves underneath it, as it is written, "You came forward and stood beneath the mountain" (Deut. 4:11). —SONG OF SONGS RABBAH 8

"God, You are my God; I search for You" (Ps. 63:2). "You are my God"—at the Sea, where I recognized You and said, "This is my God and I will enshrine Him" (Exod. 15:2). [There] I searched you out and [saw You, yet] was not harmed. "My soul thirsts for You" (Ps. 63:2)—thirsts to see You, in the wilderness. "I shall behold You in the sanctuary *(bakodesh)*" (Ps. 63:3)—Just as I saw You at the sea, so did I see You at Sinai. *(Kodesh* means Sinai, as it is written, "The Lord is among them as in Sinai in holiness [*kodesh*]" [Ps. 68:18].) And I was not harmed, as it is written, "Yet He did not raise His hand against the leaders of the Israelites; they beheld God" (Exod. 24:11). —YALKUT SHIM'ONI 785

This mountain has three names [in the scripture]: the Mountain of God, Mount Horeb, and Mount Sinai. Why is it called the Mountain of God? Because it was there that the Holy One, blessed be He, made known His divinity. Why was it called Sinai? Because [God demonstrated there that] He hated *(sana)* the high and mighty and loved the lowly. Why was it called Horeb? Because there was given the Torah, which is called *herev** (a sword), as in the verse, "With paeans to God in their throats and two-edged swords *(veherev)* in their hands" (Ps. 149:6). —EXODUS RABBAH 51

"He hated the high and mighty"—who were desirous of being given the Torah. But rather than give it to them, He gave it to Israel. [The mountain] has five names: Mount Sinai, Mount Horeb, the King's Mountain, the Mountain of God, and Mount Bashan. —PIRKA DE-RABBENU HAKADOSH

The biblical name *Sin* refers to Sinai; after the Ten Commandments were given there, it was called Sinai [the additional letter in Hebrew having the numerical value of ten]. —HIZKUNI

There are ten wildernesses: Sin, Sinai, Rephidim, Beersheba, Shur, Zin, Tekoa, Zif, Ma'on, and 'Ein Gedi. Yet of all of them He chose Sinai. This is the meaning of the verse, "He stood and took the measure of the earth" (Hab. 3:6). He took the measure of all the generations and found only the Generation of the Wilderness worthy of receiving the Torah. He took the measure of all the wildernesses and chose Sinai through which to lead the redeemed. He took the measure of all the mountains and [chose] to bring the Torah down upon [Mount Sinai], upon which no idolatry had ever been performed, as it is written, "The mountain God desired as His dwelling" (Ps. 68:17). —HEMDAT YAMIM on the Torah

---

*The Hebrew spelling is identical to that of Horeb.

One of the Sages asked Rav Kahana, "Do you know what the name Mount Sinai means?" He said, "The mountain on which miracles *(nissim)* were done for Israel." "If so, it should have been called Nisai!" "Then it means the mountain on which a good omen *(siman)* appeared for Israel." "If so, it should have been called Mount Siman!" He said to him, "You ought to have sat at the feet of Rav Papa and Rav Huna, son of Rav Yehoshu'a, when they were studying the aggadah of Rav Ḥisda and Rabbah, son of Rav Huna. The latter two taught: 'What does the name Mount Sinai mean? The mountain where hatred *(sin'ah)* of the other nations came down.' "

This corresponds to what Rabbi Yose, son of Rabbi Ḥanina, said: [The Wilderness of Sinai] has five names: the Wilderness of Zin, for Israel was commanded *(niztavu)* there; the Wilderness of Kadesh, for Israel was hallowed *(nitkadeshu)* there; the Wilderness of Kedemot, for a pre-eminence *(kedumah)* was given there; the Wilderness of Paran, for Israel was fruitful *(paru)* and multiplied there; and the Wilderness of Sinai, for hatred *(sin'ah)* of the other nations came down there.

And what is its [real] name? Horeb. This is in disagreement with Rabbi Abahu, who taught: Mount Sinai is its [real] name. Why then was it called Horeb? Because the destruction *(hurvah)* of the other nations came down there. —SHABBAT 89a

---

Kedumah (pre-eminence) refers to the Torah, which existed before the world was created.

"Hatred of the other nations"—for not accepting the Torah. —RASHI

Why was it called Sinai? Because there came down from it hatred *(sin'ah)* for idolaters, who envy Israel its Torah. —LEKAḤ TOV

Know that this is the truth: at the time of the Giving of the Torah, higher meanings came to be united with the Ten Commandments. Then the destruction and hatred of the other nations came down, along with peace, tranquillity, and security for Israel. And had it not been for our sins, these would have lasted forever.

As you know, our Rabbis, may their memory be a blessing, compared the day the Torah was given to Israel with the day heaven and earth were created.

Thus they taught in regard to this passage that the Holy One, blessed be He, stipulated with the rest of creation, saying, "If Israel accepts the Torah, it will be well, but if not, I shall cause you to revert to chaos." Ponder that.

In the End of Days, when the Time for Love arrives [cf. Ezek. 16:8], and the pure Divine Will resolves to restore all things to their original state, the King shall return to His garden dwelling, Israel shall be restored, and the Matron too shall go back to her Husband in the palace. But this is a secret that should only be told to those who are chaste and pure. Ponder it. —OZAR HAKAVOD

HE DID NOT DO SO FOR ANY OTHER NATION

We have explained above that it was called Sinai because it was from there that hatred of idolaters, who envy Israel its Torah, came down. In fact, the Holy One, blessed be He, first tried to persuade all the other nations to accept the Torah, but they refused. He then forced Israel to accept it by holding the mountain over them like a barrel; and "He did not do so for any other nation" (Ps. 147:20).

The nations of the world ask why He did not hold a mountain over them like a barrel as well, forcing them to accept the Torah the way He did with Israel. They do not realize that the mountain was held over Israel because the existence of the world depended on Israel's acceptance. For Israel's soul emanated from the Torah itself; indeed, it is its very essence. This is not the case with the other nations; even if they had accepted the Torah, it would not have been enough to sustain the world.

As for the fact that the Holy One, blessed be He, tried to persuade all the other nations, His purpose was not necessarily that they accept it directly; they could come to it in a roundabout way, as indeed they will in the future. For it is written, "[And strangers shall join them] and shall cleave (nispehu) to the House of Jacob" (Isa. 14:1), and this term connotes roundaboutness, as in the verse, 'Please, assign me (sap-heni) to one of the priestly duties, [that I may have a morsel of bread to eat']" (1 Sam. 2:36).

The Torah could not have been upheld by them alone, for they do not partake of its essence. Hence the stipulation rests on Israel's acceptance—Israel's and no other's. And in holding the mountain over them like a barrel He was simply telling them the truth. This is what is meant by the saying, "If you accept it, it will be well"—you and not the other nations. For this was said to Israel alone. —YISMAH MOSHE

The Sages taught: "A stairway was set on the ground" (Gen. 28:12)—referring to the Eternal House*—"and its top reached to the sky" (Gen. 28:12)—as scripture says, "[You will bring them and plant them in Your own mountain,] the place You made Your abode, O Lord, [the sanctuary, O Lord, which Your hands established]" (Exod. 15:17). What is its top? It is Zion, where are to be found the Shekhinah, the Cherubim, and the Holy of Holies. Rabbi Abba said: "A stairway" refers to Sinai, where the Torah was given and the chariots of the Holy One, blessed be He, were revealed. —MIDRASH HANE'ELAM

"[He had a dream;] a stairway" (Gen. 28:12)—referring to Sinai.
    "Set (muzav) on the ground" (Gen. 28:12)—[referring to the verse], "They took their places (vayityazvu) at the foot of the mountain" (Exod. 19:17).
    "And its top reached to the sky"—[referring to the verse], "The mountain was ablaze with flames to the very skies" (Deut. 4:11).
    Another interpretation of "a stairway": This refers to Sinai, the two words [for stairway and Sinai] having the same numerical value. —GENESIS RABBAH 68

"A stairway (sulam) was set on the ground and its top reached to the sky"—Sulam and Sinai have the same value in gematria,† for what God showed Jacob was the Sinai Event. —BA'AL HATURIM

Be it known that there is testimony concerning Mount Sinai that drawn upon its stones is the image of the Burning Bush (sneh). Hence, this mountain is called Sinai, after the bush, from within which the Lord revealed Himself to Moses. One of the worthies of Barcelona, a son of Ben Hasdai, brought back one of these stones and showed it to me, and I saw a very definite representation of a bush on it. It is a Divine representation. When I broke the stone in half, the image of the bush appeared on each half. I then broke each of the parts, in turn, in half, and the image of the bush appeared all the way through. And so on, a number of times, until the fragments were the size of peanuts; and yet the bush still appeared on them. And I marveled at this. —NARBONI

*The Holy Temple, in Jerusalem.
†See glossary.

Thus wrote Rabbi [Profiat Duran] in his commentary on the *Guide of the Perplexed:* I saw one of the stones from that mountain, and there was a figure of a bush on it, definitely a miraculous figure, whose color changed into the color of the rock. —MA'ASEH EFOD 1:66

Rabbah bar Bar-Hannah related: We were once traveling in the desert and were joined by an Arab sage. [He] . . . said, "Come, I will show you Mount Sinai." I went with him, and [when we got there] I saw that it was surrounded by scorpions, which stood like white asses. I heard a celestial voice saying, "Woe is Me that I have taken a vow, and now that I have done so, who will release Me from it?" When I came to the Sages, [I asked them about what I had heard, and] they said to me, "Every Abba is an ass, and every bar Bar-Hannah a fool! You should have said, 'You are released from Your vow.' " [Rabbah had not said this because] he thought it was the vow after the Flood, [a vow beneficial to mankind,] from which [God sought release]. The Sages, [for their part, thought,] If [He was referring to that vow,] why did He say "Woe is Me"? —BABA BATRA 74a

---

"I have taken a vow"—that I will not redeem Israel prematurely.

"Every Abba is an ass"—Rabbah bar Bar-Hannah's name was Abba, [Rabbah being a contraction of Rabbi Abba].

"He"—Rabbah bar Bar-Hannah—"thought it was the vow after the Flood to which [God sought release]"—"I swore that the waters of Noah [nevermore would flood the earth]" (Isa. 54:9)—that it was this vow that [God] wished to annul, thereby leading to the destruction of the world by flood [once again]. Hence [Rabbah] did not want to annul it. But the Sages, who called him an ass, said, "If [He was referring to that vow,] why did He say, 'Woe is Me'?" It was because He feels all [Israel's] sufferings as His own.

HOREB AND SINAI ARE ONE AND THE SAME

Nachmanides wrote: Horeb is the area surrounding Mount Sinai where Israel lived during that year. For the wilderness is large, and the mountain is there, and so the whole wilderness is called Sinai, meaning "the wilderness of Mount Sinai." It is also possible that both the wilderness and the mountain were called Sinai, for the shrubs called *sneh* grow there in abundance. There is also a place or settlement called Horeb near the mountain, and it is there that they stood then. The verse "[Moses] came to Horeb, the mountain of God" (Exod. 3:1) means he came to Horeb, where the mountain of God is located. The bush was on the mountain, and Moses was in Horeb, the place at the foot [of the mountain] where Israel had its camp for a year. Hence scripture says, "I must turn aside to look [at this marvelous sight; why is the bush not burnt?]" (Exod. 3:3), meaning he would turn from Horeb to the mountain. Sometimes scripture calls the mountain Horeb, as it is written, "The Israelites remained stripped of their finery from Mount Horeb on" (Exod. 33:6), meaning from the mountain that is in Horeb, within its boundaries or in front of it. Or [it could be] that the whole area was called Horeb, including the mountain. Rabbi Avraham [Ibn Ezra, on the other hand,] explains that Horeb *is* Mount Sinai, the shrubs growing there because of the dryness *(horev)*, and it is called by the two names interchangeably. —TUR ON DEUTERONOMY

WITH BOTH THE FATHERS AND THE SONS

Rabbi Ḥiyya taught: When Israel came to Mount Sinai, the Holy One, blessed be He, gathered together all Israel's seed. He examined them all and found all holy and truthful, none unfit. The Holy One, blessed be He, then said to Moses, "Now I am determined to give the Torah to Israel. Draw them closer with the love of the Patriarchs, with My love for them, and with the signs I have performed for them. Be My messenger, and tell them these things." Said Rabbi Yosef, in the name of Rabbi Yehudah: What the Holy One, blessed be He, said to Moses was, "In this matter you must be My faithful messenger: to draw Israel after Me." —ZOHAR, Exodus 78b

"The Lord our God made a covenant with us at Horeb" (Deut. 5:2)—This teaches that the covenant was made with both the fathers and the sons. Thus the Torah says, "It was not with our fathers that the Lord made this covenant, [but with us, the living, every one of us who is here today]" (Deut. 5:3). Hence it is said of one who throws off the yoke of Torah that his ancestors certainly did not stand at Mount Sinai.

"Face to face the Lord spoke to you" (Deut. 5:4)—Since they heard "I [the Lord am your God. . . .]" and "You shall have no other [gods beside me]" (Exod. 20:2–3) directly from God and not through Moses, this commandment is described by scripture as having been given "face to face." We find the same in relation to Moses: Since he heard the commandments directly and not through any angel—as it is written, "He would hear the Voice addressing him"

(Num. 7:89)—therefore it is said of him, "[Never again did there arise in Israel a prophet like Moses,] whom the Lord singled out, face to face" (Deut. 34:10). —MIDRASH HAGADOL on Deuteronomy (Yallon MS)

ABOVE AND NOT BELOW

Israel alone stood upon Mount Sinai, while the Mixed Multitude [of gentile camp-followers] stood below the mountain. For it is written, "Moses led the people out of the camp toward God, and they took their places beneath the mountain" (Exod. 19:17), and in the view of the Torah commentary Siftei Kohen on Parashat Yitro, "people" [here] means the Mixed Multitude, which stood apart beneath the mountain. But of Israel it is written, "You will always be at the top and never at the bottom—[if only you obey and faithfully observe the commandments of the Lord your God]" (Deut. 28:13). It was here [below] that "He held the mountain over them like a barrel"—over the Mixed Multitude, not over Israel. —HIDDUSHEI HATORAH

Rabbi Mendele of Kotzk would say: Each person should try to imagine the Sinai Event. —EMET VE-EMUNAH

In the seventh homily of the volume *Binat Ya'akov,* it is stated: I heard Rabbi Naftali of Ropshits cite Rabbi Elimelekh of Lyzhansk as saying: Not only do I remember the Sinai Event, but I remember who was standing next to me. —TA'AMEI HAMINHAGIM

BENEATH THE MOUNTAIN

"They took their places beneath the mountain"—Rabbi Avdimi bar Hama bar Hasa said: This teaches that the Holy One, blessed be He, held the mountain over them like a barrel and said to them, "If you accept the Torah, it will be well, but if not, there shall be your grave" (Shabbat 88a). [God did this] because the world could not endure without the Torah: "Were it not for My covenant day and night, I would not uphold the laws of heaven and earth" (Jer. 33:25). Clearly, then, if Israel refused to accept the Torah, all living things would be buried beneath the ruins of the world, not only those standing at Mount Sinai—it is not written "here shall be your grave" but "there," wherever you are. But if Israel did accept the Torah, the entire world would endure. —HAFEZ HAYYIM on the Torah

"He held the mountain over them like a barrel"—In holding the mountain [over them], He was showing them the reward and the punishment. If they did not uphold the Torah, they would be exiled among the nations, as it is written, "[Our pursuers were swifter than the eagles in the sky;] they chased us in the mountains" (Lam. 4:19), and further, "[Because of this our hearts are sick . . . ,] because of Mount Zion, which lies desolate" (Lam. 5:18). But if they accepted the Torah, they would be redeemed by the redeemer known as "mountain," as it is written, "Whoever you are, O great mountain in the path of Zerubbabel, turn into level ground! [For he shall produce that excellent stone; it shall be greeted with shouts of 'Beautiful! Beautiful!']" (Zech. 4:7), and further, "In the days to come, the Mount of the Lord's House shall stand firm above the mountains" (Isa. 2:2). —IR GIBBORIM

Rabbi Ya'akov, author of the *Tur*, writes in his commentary on the Torah that they only consented to [accept] the Written Torah and not the Oral, for it is written, "all that the Lord has spoken" (Exod. 24:7), and not, "all that [the Lord] will speak."

Rabbi Yosef Kimḥi's interpretation was that by the time He held the mountain over them they had already consented and said, "We will do and we will hear." [He did this] to show His love for them, saying, "It is a good thing you have consented, because if you had refused I would not have given up on you the way I did with the other nations." —TUR

Rabbi 'Ovadiah of Bertinoro writes that when they said, "All that the Lord has spoken we will do," they meant only the commandments that have no death penalty attached to them. For the name "Lord" *(YHVH)* refers to His merciful aspect, and they did not say, "All that God *(Elohim)* has spoken," which would have referred to His judgmental aspect. Thus, in order to get them to agree to the warnings and the punishments, He held the mountain over them. —'AMAR NEKE

But a contradiction is posed by *Midrash Shoḥar Tov* on Psalm 1: " 'I am a rose of Sharon' (Song 2:1)—I am she, and I am beloved; for I was hidden at Sinai when He held the mountain over me like a barrel, as it is written, 'They took their places beneath the mountain,' but I quickly softened like a rose and said, 'All that the Lord has spoken we will do and we will hear!' " From these words of our Sages it would seem that first He held the mountain over them like a barrel, and only then did they say, "We will do and we will hear." —'EINEI KOL ḤAI

The same point is made by Rabbi Ya'akov Knozel in his book, *Perushim le-Rashi Zazal.*

Since they said, "We will do and we will hear," why did He hold the mountain over them like a barrel? He did it [to get them to accept] the Oral Torah. When they said "We will do and we will hear," it was only in regard to the Written Torah. —TOSAFOT

[He held the mountain over them] on account of the Oral Torah, which contains warnings, punishments, and many hedges and fences [around the law]. But as for the Written Torah, they had all accepted it wholeheartedly and with great joy and did not need to be forced. —Rabbenu Baḥya, VAYISHMA YITRO

THE WRITTEN TORAH AND THE ORAL TORAH

"The heaven and the earth were finished, and all their array" (Gen. 2:1)—The making of things above and below, of heaven and earth, was completed. "The heaven and the earth"—above and below. Rabbi Shim'on said: This refers to the overall construction of the Written Torah and the overall construction of the Oral Torah. "And all their array" refers to the details of the Torah, the facets of the Torah—for the Torah has seventy facets. "Were finished *(vaye-khulu)*" means the two Torahs reinforced and complemented *(venishtakhlelu)* each other.

Or "the heaven and the earth" could refer to details and general rules, while "all their array" could refer to the hidden meanings of the Torah, the laws of purity and impurity in the Torah, [etc.].

"And with the seventh day God finished" (Gen. 2:2) refers to the Oral Torah, which is called the seventh day. It completes the world and undergirds the existence of all things. "The work which He had been doing"—but not all of it, for the Written Torah was to produce the totality, through the power of the written word, which, in turn, issued from Wisdom.*

*Ḥokhmah, one of the ten *sefirot,* and also a synonym for Torah.

The phrase "on the seventh day" occurs three times here: "on the seventh day God finished," "He ceased on the seventh day," and "God blessed the seventh day" (Gen. 2:3)—three times in all. "On the seventh day God finished" refers to the Oral Torah, for with the seventh day the world was completed, as we have said. —ZOHAR, Genesis 47b

THE ORAL TORAH

"God said, 'Let there be light'; and there was light" (Gen. 1:3)—Rabbi Yohanan said: There were two great lights, as it is written, "And there was light," [repeating the word "light"]. And concerning both of them it says "how good [it] was." The Holy One, blessed be He, took one of them and hid it away for the righteous for the Time to Come. This is what scripture means when it says, "How abundant is the good that You have in store for those who fear You" (Ps. 31:20). This teaches that the first light is hidden away, and no mortal creature can look upon it, as it is written, "God saw how good the light was" (Gen. 1:4), and it is written, "God saw all that He had made, and found it very good" (Gen. 1:31).

The Holy One, blessed be He, saw all that He had made, and He saw a brilliant, shining goodness (tov). He took (lakah) a part of that goodness, incorporated into it the thirty-two paths of wisdom, and gave it to this world. It is to this that scripture refers when it says, "For I give you good instruction (lekah tov)" (Prov. 4:2), meaning, this is the treasure of the [Oral] Torah. And the Holy One, blessed be He, said, "If in this world they keep this Torah, the Oral Torah, which is intended to serve as a vessel in this world, it shall earn them the World to Come, which is the goodness that has been hidden away."

And what is the strength of the Holy One, blessed be He? As scripture says, "It is a brilliant light" (Hab. 3:4). The brilliance taken from the first light, [says God,] will itself become a light, if [My] children keep the Torah and the commandments that I have written to instruct them, as it is written, "My son, heed the discipline of your father, and do not forsake the instruction of your mother" (Prov. 1:8), and it is written, "[It] gives off rays on every side—and therein is the hiding place of His strength" (Hab. 3:4). What is "the hiding place of His strength"? It is the light that He hid away, as it is written, "[How abundant is the good] that You have in store for those who fear You" (Ps. 31:20). And that which was left over "You made . . . for those who take refuge in You" (Ps. 31:20) in this world, those who keep Your Torah and fulfill Your commandments and sanctify Your name and proclaim [Your] unity in private and public, as it is written, "in the full view of men" (Ps. 31:20).

Said Rabbi Rehumai: We learn here that [the Torah] is the light of Israel, that its lamp gives light. But is it not written, "For the commandment is a lamp, the Torah is a light" (Prov. 6:23), [which we understand to mean:] the "lamp" is "the commandment," and "the commandment" is the Oral Torah, while the "light" is the Written Torah [i.e., the two Torahs are described by different metaphors]? The explanation is: Since the light is sustained by the oil in the lamp, the lamp itself is called light. It is like a small room hidden away in the recesses of a house: though it is daytime and very bright outside, one cannot see anything in that room without lamplight. Such is the Written Torah. [Even though it is called "light,"] it is in fact like a "lamp," in that it needs the Oral Torah to explain its difficult points and clarify its secrets. —SEFER HABAHIR

IN THE ACADEMY ON HIGH AND THE ACADEMY BELOW

Know that there is no academy below without a corresponding academy on high, and each member of the [earthly] academy has his own counterpart on high. Even if there were a thousand academies below there would be a thousand on high. What is studied below is studied on high, for they have the same Torah. And all of them—the Tannaim and Amoraim, their students and their students' students—were at Mount Sinai, standing together with the rest of Israel. Before the Giving of the Torah they were all on high, and they recited the entire Torah many times. —YALKUT RE'UVENI, citing SEFER HAPELI'AH

IN PRAISE OF THE ORAL TORAH

May the Name of the King, the King of Kings, the Holy One, blessed be He, be blessed. He chose Israel from among the seventy nations, as it is written, "The Lord's portion is His people, Jacob His own allotment" (Deut. 32:9). He gave us the Written Torah, filled with allusions, hidden things and obscurities, and He explained these in the Oral Torah, which He revealed to Israel. Furthermore, the Written Torah contains general rules and the Oral Torah specifics. The Oral Torah is voluminous, while the Written is brief. Concerning the Oral Torah it is written, "Its measure is longer than the earth and broader than the sea" (Job 11:9).

It is also written, "[No man can set a value on it;] it cannot be found in the land of the living" (Job 28:13). What is meant by "it cannot be found in the land of the living"? Shall it be found in the land of the dead? What is meant, rather, is that the Oral Torah is not to be found among those who seek worldly pleasures, sensual gratification, honor, or greatness in this world but among those who are willing to mortify their flesh for it, as it is written, "This is the Torah: when a person dies in a tent" (Num. 19:14). "And such is the way of Torah: You eat bread with salt, drink water in scant measure, sleep on the ground, and live a life of hardship while you labor at the Torah" [Avot 6:4].

The covenant the Holy One, blessed be He, made with Israel was only for the Oral Torah. For it is written, "In accordance with these commandments I make a covenant with you" (Exod. 34:27), and our Sages, may their memory be a blessing, pointed out that in the Torah the Holy One, blessed be He, did not write "for the sake of these commandments" or "on account of these commandments" or "because of these commandments" but "in accordance with (*'al pi*) these commandments"—meaning the Oral (*shebe'al peh*) Torah.

[The Oral Torah] is difficult to learn and fraught with anguish. It is compared to darkness, as it is written, "The people that walked in darkness have seen a brilliant light" (Isa. 9:1). It is the scholars of the Oral Torah who "have seen a brilliant light," for the Holy One, blessed be He, illuminates for them what is permitted and forbidden, pure and impure. And in the Time to Come, "His friends [shall] be as the sun rising in might!" (Judg. 5:31).

But Israel did not accept the Torah until the Holy One, blessed be He, held the mountain over them like a barrel, as it is written, "They took their places beneath the mountain" (Exod. 19:17), and Rav Dimi bar Ḥama said: The Holy One, blessed be He, said to Israel, "If you accept the Torah, it will be well, but if not, [here] will be your grave" [cf. Shabbat 88a]. Now you might think that it was in regard to the Written Torah that He held the mountain over them; but [earlier,] when He asked them, "Do you accept the Torah?" they had all answered, "We will do and we will hear," [without the threat of the mountain,] because [then He was referring to the Written Torah, which] is not onerous or troublesome, and it is brief. Here what He was referring to was the Oral Torah, which contains the fine points of the commandments, both major and minor. [This Torah] is "fierce as death" and its "passion is difficult as Sheol" [cf. Song 8:6], for one cannot learn it without loving the Holy One, blessed be He, with all one's heart, all one's soul, and all one's might, as it is written, "You must love the Lord your God with all your heart and with all your soul and with all your might" (Deut. 6:5). How do we know this means love for the study of the Oral Torah? From what follows: "Take to heart these words with which I charge you this day" (Deut. 6:6). What words? Those of the Oral Torah, which must be engraved in one's heart. In other words, "Repeat them to your children" (Deut. 6:7) [also] refers to the study of the Oral Torah, which requires repetition.

Thus we learn that this first paragraph of the *Shema'** does not deal with this-worldly reward, which we find only in the second paragraph: "If, then, you obey [the commandments that I enjoin upon you this day . . .], I will grant the rain for your land" (Deut. 11:13–14). What is meant in the latter passage is reward for the fulfillment of the commandments† without engaging in the study of the Oral Torah. This paragraph says, "loving the Lord your God and serving Him with all your heart and soul" (Deut. 11:13–14), but not "with all your might," teaching us that whoever loves wealth and pleasure cannot study the Oral Torah, for it entails trouble and lack of sleep, and one can wear oneself out doing it. Thus its reward is only in the World to Come, as it is written, "The people that walked in darkness have seen a brilliant light" (Isa. 9:1)—a light that was created on the First Day and that the Holy One, blessed be He, hid away for those who labor day and night over the Oral Torah. It is through their merit that the world endures, as it is written, "Thus said the Lord: Were it not for My covenant day and night, I would not uphold the laws of heaven and earth" (Jer. 33:25). What covenant must be attended to day and night? That of the Oral Torah. Thus scripture says, "Thus said the Lord: If you could break My covenant with the day and My covenant with the night, only then could My covenant with My servant David be broken" (Jer. 33:20, 21); and it says, "The teaching of the Lord is his delight, and he studies that teaching day and night" (Ps. 1:2).

The Holy One, blessed be He, Himself made a covenant with Israel that the Oral Torah not depart from their lips or the lips of their children to the end of time, as it is written, "And this shall be my covenant with them, said the Lord: My spirit which is upon you, and the words which I have placed in your mouth shall not be absent [from your mouth, nor from the mouth of your children, nor from the mouth of your children's children—said the Lord—from now on, for all time]" (Isa. 59:21). It does not say "[not] from you" [alone] but "[not . . .] from your mouth, nor from the mouth of your children, nor from the mouth of your children's children."

Hence the Holy One, blessed be He, established two academies for Israel [in Babylonia, those of Sura and Pumbedita, and ordained that] they should gather there from far and wide twice a year, in the months of Adar and Elul, to ponder the Torah day and night, to debate the Torah and struggle over it, bringing proof from scripture, Mishnah, and Gemara, until matters are clarified

*A group of scriptural passages—Deut. 6:4–9, Deut. 11:13–21, and Num. 15:37–41—read in daily worship, which constitute the central affirmation of Jewish faith.
†Another version: "reward for engaging in the study of the Written Torah."

and the halakah established, so that Israel does not stumble over the words of the Torah, as it is written, "Those who love Your teaching enjoy well-being; they encounter no stumbling block" (Ps. 119:165). "May the Lord grant strength to His people; may the Lord bestow on His people well-being" (Ps. 29:11).

Those two academies were never taken captive or forced into apostasy or despoiled, nor did Greece or Rome ever rule them. The Holy One, blessed be He, had rescued them [and brought them to Babylonia] twelve years before Jerusalem was destroyed, with their Torah and learning intact. Thus scripture says, "He exiled all of Jerusalem: all the commanders and all the war heroes—ten thousand exiles—as well as all the craftsmen and smiths; only the poorest people in the land were left" (2 Kings 24:14); and what heroism can there be among people taken into exile? The heroism of the Torah, of which it is written, "Therefore the Book of the Wars of the Lord speaks" (Num. 21:14). And among them were "the craftsmen and smiths"—craftsmen (harash), because when one of [the scholars of the academies] speaks, all are dumbfounded (keḥirshim); smiths (masger), because when one of them gives a definitive ruling (soger) on a question of purity and impurity or things forbidden and permitted, no one in the whole world can overturn it, pronouncing pure or permitted [what has been declared the opposite]. Thus is fulfilled the verse, "I will place the keys of David's palace on his shoulders; and what he unlocks none may shut, and what he locks none may open" (Isa. 22:22).

[As for the verse,] "He carried away the nobles of the land" (Ezek. 17:13), that refers to the princes of Judah and Benjamin, of whom it is written, "Thus said the Lord . . . : As with these good figs, so will I single out for good the Judean exiles whom I have driven out from this place to the land of the Chaldeans" (Jer. 24:5); and it is written, "Hence the Lord was intent upon bringing calamity upon us, for the Lord our God is in the right [in all that He has done, but we have not obeyed Him]" (Dan. 9:14). Is it in fact that "the Lord our God is in the right" in that He "was intent upon bringing calamity upon us"? Rather, the Holy One, blessed be He, treated Israel righteously in bringing the exile of Jeconiah before that of Zedekiah.* This prevented the Oral Torah from being forgotten and made it possible for them to sit and study it in Babylonia from that time until now.

Neither Rome nor Greece ever ruled over [the Jews of Babylonia], nor

*King Jeconiah [Jehoiachin] surrendered Jerusalem to Nebuchadnezzar in 597 B.C.E. and was exiled to Babylonia together with the elite of Judea, including the prophet Ezekiel. This group was treated relatively well, unlike those led by his successor Zedekiah, who rebelled against the Babylonians and was exiled some years later.

were they ever forced to apostasize. And when the Messianic Age arrives, [the Babylonian Jews] will not have to witness the Birthpangs of the Messiah. Thus it is written, "Away, escape, O Zion, [you who dwell in Fair Babylon!]" (Zech. 2:11)—from Rome and Greece and their decrees. And it is written, "Writhe and scream, fair Zion, like a woman in travail! For now you must leave the city and dwell in the country" (Mic. 4:10)—"dwell *(veshakhanta)* in the country," because even though [you] are exiled to the country, My Shekhinah shall not abandon you. "And you will reach Babylon. There you shall be saved, there the Lord will redeem you from the hands of your foes" (Mic. 4:10)—"there," to teach you that it is from there that the redemption is to begin, from there that the [exiles] are to go up to Jerusalem, as it is written, "For liberators shall march up on Mount Zion [to wreak judgment on Mount Esau]" (Obad. 1:21). It is then that "dominion shall be the Lord's" (Obad. 1:21)—and so may it be His will. —MIDRASH TANHUMA, Noah

The Gemara [Shabbat 88a] says we learn from this passage that He held the mountain over them like a barrel, but Tosafot asks: Had they not already said, "We will do and we will hear"? Replied Rabbi Yizhak Me'ir of Gur: He held the mountain over them in order to compel them [to agree] to study [the Torah]. For even when one studies only out of a sense of obligation it is considered [legitimate] Torah study. —SIAH SARFEI KODESH

I heard from my master [the Ba'al Shem Tov], may he be remembered for life in the Next World, that the Holy One, blessed be He, held the mountain over Israel like a barrel to teach us that even one who feels no desire for the study of Torah and the service of the Lord is not free to desist from them but must force himself to do them as if he were acting under duress. Thus even when a Jew is dispirited, it is better that he not be lax in study or the service of the blessed Lord, however little desire he may have for them, for his actions carry weight even when he does them under compulsion. —BEN PORAT YOSEF

One should begin by studying Torah, even though he may not feel drawn to it; for it was in order to get us to force ourselves to study, as if someone else were compelling us to do so, that the mountain was held over Israel like a barrel at the time of the Giving of the Torah. —BEN PORAT YOSEF

Our master Rabbi Yisra'el Ba'al Shem explained that [God] held [the mountain] over them to teach us that even when we are dispirited and the Torah seems like a heavy burden, we must accept the yoke of the Torah, like an ox

that is yoked in order to benefit the world. —NETIV MIZVOT, The Path of Torah
1:25

HUMILITY FROM SINAI

Rav Yosef said: One should always learn from his Lord. Thus the Holy One,
blessed be He, bypassed all the other mountains and hills in order to bestow His
Shekhinah on Mount Sinai, and He bypassed all the beautiful trees in order to
bestow His Shekhinah on the [Burning] Bush. —SOTAH 5a

"He measured all the mountains and did not find any worthy of having the
Torah given upon it except Mount Sinai" (Leviticus Rabbah 13). Let us learn
humility from Sinai, and let those who study Torah learn humility from it; for
the Holy One, blessed be He, bypassed all the other mountains and bestowed
His Shekhinah on Mount Sinai, even though it is relatively low. —PENEI DAVID

"The Lord came from Sinai" (Deut. 33:2)—The giving of the holy Torah
exemplifies the virtue of humility, this being the message of Sinai, the lowest
of the mountains. By [rewarding] this humility, God graciously teaches us how
to live. —MAHAZEH AVRAHAM

"Had He brought us to Mount Sinai and not given us the Torah, it would have
been enough for us!" (Haggadah). What point would there have been in
bringing us to stand at Sinai if not in order to give us the Torah? Our Rabbis,
may their memory be a blessing, said: Abraham fulfilled the entire Torah even
before it was given; his mind was so highly refined that he could divine the
Torah and the purpose of the commandments on his own. Thus they taught:
"From the secretions of his innards he learned Torah and wisdom" (Genesis
Rabbah 61). Similarly, by the time Israel stood at Sinai, that knowing generation was so thoroughly purified that [it could have divined the Torah] even if
He had not given it to them. —ZIKKARON LARISHONIM

Furthermore, the humility they learned from Mount Sinai led them to shed
their worldly concerns and to purify themselves to such a degree that they
grasped the entire Torah even before it was given to them. This is what the
author of the Haggadah means by the words, "Had He brought us to Mount
Sinai and not given us the Torah, it would have been enough for us!"—for they
had grasped the Torah on their own. As for the fact that the Holy One, blessed
be He, did give Israel the Torah, it was out of love for them, so that they might

act correctly in order to fulfill the commandments; for "one who acts correctly in order to fulfill a [Divine] commandment is more virtuous than one who does so without having been commanded" (Kiddushin 31a). —HANOTEN IMREI SHEFER; see also BINYAN SHLOMO

"His cheeks are like beds of spices, producing perfume; his lips are like lilies; they drip flowing myrrh" (Song 5:13)—You can see that when the Holy One, blessed be He, revealed Himself on Mount Sinai the world was filled with perfume, for it is written, "Producing perfume; his lips are like lilies; they drip flowing myrrh." Where did it flow? The Holy One, blessed be He, hid it away for the righteous in the Garden of Eden.

"Ah, you are fair, my darling" (Song 4:1)—This is what scripture means by, "Truly, Ephraim is a dear son to Me" (Jer. 31:20). Said the Holy One, blessed be He, to Israel, "Since the day I spoke to you at Sinai I remember that event. Hence scripture says, "Since the time I spoke with him I surely still remember him" (Jer. 31:20) —MIDRASH ON THE SONG OF SONGS

Father in heaven, may Your great name be blessed to all eternity, and may You take delight in Israel Your servants, wherever they may dwell. For You have not nursed a grudge or desire for retribution or turned Your back on them or denied them words of Torah because of all the ugly and unseemly things they have done in Your sight. You have remembered the good rather than the bad, the good deeds they have done before You rather than the bad ones. You have said to them what Your lips once uttered: "The former things shall not be remembered, they shall never come to mind" (Isa. 65:17).

And when our forefathers stood at Mount Sinai, willingly to take upon themselves the rule of heaven, He too descended from the highest heaven, from the place of His glory and greatness and splendor and holiness, and He willingly allowed His great Name to dwell among them, as it is written, "But the generous has generous intentions [and is constant in generous acts]" (Isa. 32:8). —SEDER ELIYAHU RABBAH 16

Rabbi Yehoshu'a ben Levi said: Each day a heavenly voice issues forth from Mount Horeb and proclaims, "Woe to mortals because of offense to the Torah." For whoever does not engage in [the study of] Torah is reprehensible. —AVOT 6:2

"Reprehensible"—subject to rebuke by the Holy One, blessed be He. —MIDRASH TANHUMA, Ki Tissa

"Mount Horeb"—one of Mount Sinai's five names (see Shabbat 89b). Why is it called Horeb? Because at the time of the Giving of the Torah the destruction *(hurvah)* of the nations of the world came down there, for their refusal to accept it. That is why the term Mount Horeb is used here.

Now in our own time many have abandoned the Torah, claiming [its observance] makes it difficult to earn a living. In fact, this was the very claim made by the idolaters at the time of the Giving of the Torah; they refused it because [they said] it would interfere with their livelihoods. Thus, when Israel answered and said in one voice, "We will do and we will hear," they meant even if it did interfere with their livelihoods.

That is why [the mountain] is called Horeb here. —RUAH HAYYIM

The Sages said: Whenever people neglect the study of Torah, the Holy One, blessed be He, seeks to destroy the world. —SEDER ELIYAHU RABBAH 2

The commentators ask: Why does it say "[The Israelites remained stripped of their finery] from Mount Horeb on" (Exod. 33:6) instead of "from Mount Sinai on"? Because whenever Israel does not engage in [the study of] Torah, Mount Sinai becomes Mount Horeb, in the sense of *hurvah* (destruction). —MIDRASH SHMU'EL

"Each day a heavenly voice issues forth from Mount Horeb and proclaims, 'Woe to mortals because of offense to the Torah' " [Avot 6:2]. The Ba'al Shem Tov, may his memory be a blessing, said: Either way there is a difficulty—if the proclamation can be heard, why does no one listen to it; and if it cannot be heard, why is it made? In fact, however, what is on high is the world of thoughts—"There is no utterance, there are no words" (Ps. 19:4)—and the proclamation consists of virtuous thoughts and aspirations [that enter our hearts from on high]. Thus there is not even a wicked person who does not have some virtuous thoughts each day because of the proclamation. But when he has these good thoughts, he puts them out of his mind and makes his mind blank. —TOLDOT YA'AKOV YOSEF

You are familiar with the saying of the Zohar, "Each day a heavenly voice issues forth, proclaiming, 'Return, O wayward children' [cf. Hagigah 15a], and another heavenly voice issues forth, proclaiming, 'Woe to mortals because of offense to the Torah!' [cf. Avot 6:2]." But this presents a difficulty: To whom are the voices speaking? Surely no one hears a thing! In fact, however, it is just as our Rabbis, may their memory be a blessing, taught: although one does not himself hear, his spirit hears (Megillah 3a). Thus it is written, "Your work is wonderful *(nifla'im)*" (Ps. 139:14)—in the sense of obscure, as in the verse, "If a case is too baffling *(yipale)* for you to decide" (Deut. 17:8)—nevertheless, "I know it very well" (Ps. 139:14). Thus there are times when the voice calling to the ear of one's soul awakens in him a pure spirit. That is what is meant by the verse, "If you will heed [the Lord your God] diligently *(im shamo'a tishma').*" That is, if you listen *(tishma')* with your bodily ear, you will be given to hear with the ear of your soul. —SEFER HAREDIM, Conclusion

EXODUS 19:18

Now Mount Sinai was all in smoke,
for the Lord had come down upon it in fire;
the smoke rose like the smoke of a kiln,
and the whole mountain trembled violently.

"Now Mount Sinai was all in smoke"—One might have thought [there was smoke] only in the spot where the Divine glory rested; hence scripture says "all."

"For the Lord had come down upon it in fire"—This teaches that the Torah is fire, was given out of fire, is comparable to fire. And just as in the case of fire one is burned if he gets too close and chilled if he gets too far away, [so it is with the Torah]: what one should do is warm himself by its light.

"The smoke rose like the smoke of a kiln"—One might have thought it was ordinary smoke; thus scripture says, "[the smoke] of a kiln." If it had said only this, one might have thought an ordinary kiln was meant; thus scripture says, "The mountain was ablaze with flames" (Deut. 4:11, 5:20, 9:15). Why then does the Torah say "kiln"? To soothe the ear with what it is capable of hearing. Similarly, it is written, "A lion has roared, who can but fear? [My Lord God has spoken, who can but prophesy?]" (Amos 3:8). Who gave the lion its power? Was it not He [i.e., is it not God that is meant]? But we describe Him [with this metaphor] in order to soothe the ear. Similarly, it is written, "And there, coming from the east [with a roar like the roar of mighty waters,] was the Presence of the God of Israel, [and the earth was lit up by His Presence]" (Ezek. 43:2). Who gave the waters their power? Was it not He? But we describe Him [with metaphors] drawn from His creatures in order to soothe the ear.

"And the whole mountain trembled violently"—In fact, it was like all the other mountains. After all, it is written, "The mountains quaked before the Lord, even Sinai" (Judg. 5:5), and it is written, "Why so hostile, O hunch-backed mountains, [toward the mountain God desired as His dwelling]?" (Ps. 68:17), meaning, He said to them, "You are all hunchbacks [including Sinai], hunchbacks as in the verse, '[No man . . . shall be qualified . . .] who is a hunchback, or a dwarf' (Lev. 21:17, 20)."

And why did the Holy Spirit rest [eventually] on the portion of Benjamin [i.e., on Mount Moriah]? Because all the other tribes took part in the selling of Joseph, but not Benjamin. Furthermore, all the other tribes had been born abroad, but Benjamin was born in the Land of Israel. Nevertheless, [Sinai was] "the mountain God desired as His dwelling." —MEKHILTA

"All in smoke *('ashan)"*—[Read the word *'ashan,* not as a noun, but as] a singular, intransitive, past-tense verb ["smoked"] like *'amad* (stood) or *yashav* (sat); or as a transitive verb like *'ibbed* (lost) or *ahav* (loved). What is meant is, the whole [mountain] was smoking, and thus only the smoke could be seen, not the mountain itself, "for the Lord had come down upon it." —Rabbi Ya'akov Knozel, COMMENTARY ON RASHI

"Now Mount Sinai was all in smoke, for the Lord had come down upon it in fire"—It was not as is usual in nature, where smoke rises into the sky above fire. Here it was the opposite: "the Lord . . . in fire" on top of the mountain and the rest of the mountain in smoke; the fire above, the smoke below. —MELE-KHET MAHSHEVET

"Now Mount Sinai was all in smoke"—The mountain was in smoke, but not the fire, for the fire before the glory of the Lord has no smoke. And as for the phrase "like the smoke of a kiln," we know that a simile does not [entirely] resemble its referent, but because we are physical beings we can only imagine spiritual things by means of the physical objects that surround us. On such matters our Rabbis, may their memory be a blessing, said, "The Torah speaks in human language" (Berakhot 31b). —RABBENU BAHYA

"Now Mount Sinai was all in smoke"—The smoke was intended to frighten them. For [the Sages] said, "Five things were reported about the heavenly fire [on the altar in the Temple]: it stretched out [serenely] like a lion, it was as clear as sunlight, it had substance, it consumed wet [wood] as well as dry, and it gave off no smoke" (Yoma 21b). —PENEI DAVID

Rabbi Abba said: When the smoke of Sinai appeared, the fire arose, enveloped in the cloud, like a cluster [of grapes surrounded by leaves], and it flared up and down. And the smoke, appearing, by turns, white *(lavan)*, red, and black, gave rise to all the aromas and fragrances of the Garden of Eden. That is what is meant by the verse, "In clouds of myrrh and frankincense *(levonah)*, of all the powders of the merchant" (Song 3:6).

Who was this smoke? Said Rabbi Yizhak: The Shekhinah, who revealed Herself there, as scripture says, "Who is she that comes up from the desert like columns of smoke?" (Song 3:6).

Rabbi Yehudah said: Why do you need all this [interpretation]? The text speaks for itself! For it is written, "Now Mount Sinai was all in smoke, for the Lord had come down upon it in fire; the smoke rose like the smoke of a kiln." Happy are the people who witnessed this and know about it! —ZOHAR, Exodus 84

"Now Mount Sinai was all in smoke, for the Lord had come down upon it in fire"—There is a tradition beginning with the Prophets that the day of the Sinai Event was a day of clouds, smoke, and fire, and He brought down lightning and rain, as it is written, "O Lord, when You came forth from Seir, . . . [the earth trembled; the heavens dripped, yea, the clouds dripped water]" (Judg. 5:4). The Torah itself alludes to this by saying, "The whole mountain trembled violently." Now, in every instance where the Lord is said to have descended, a disembodied Divine command* is dispatched from the spiritual to the material world, either to perfect some general or specific thing or to direct the affairs of the world through the flow of Divine energy, which is like a burning fire. —ME'OR HA'AFELAH

"Now Mount Sinai was all in smoke"—The smoke came to blind the eyes of the nations, to prevent them from casting the evil eye on Israel out of envy and hatred and to deprive them of a basis for calumny. The smoke also blinded the evil eye of the wicked Balaam. —HIDDUSHEI HARIM; GUR ARYEH

"Now Mount Sinai was all in smoke"—The word *'ashan* (smoke) is an acronym for *'olam-shannah-nefesh*. Just as the world *('olam)* is a whole unit, so is the year *(shannah)*, and so is the soul *(nefesh)*. The world is a vessel [in space], the year [a vessel] in time, the soul [a vessel] in the human being. At the time

*A free-floating utterance, akin to the notion of *logos*.

of the receiving of the Torah, all three came together. That is what is meant by "Mount Sinai was all in smoke"; as soon as they came to Mount Sinai, it was "all in smoke," for [the three] joined together, and thus [Israel] could receive the Torah. —BEIT AHARON

"For the Lord had come down upon it in fire"—in the fiery passion of Israel. According to the heat of man's preparation for the service of the blessed Lord, so does the blessed Lord come down to him. —BEIT AHARON

"Now Mount Sinai was all in smoke, for the Lord had come down upon it in fire"—This does not seem plausible as a reason. On the contrary, as a fire grows the smoke diminishes. But [the Sages] explain in the Gemara [Sota 5a], in relation to the verse "Why so hostile, O hunchbacked mountains" (Ps. 68:17), that Mount Sinai was chosen as the site for the receiving of the Torah mainly because of its humility. Moses our Teacher, too, was found worthy of being the one to receive the Torah because of his humility. Hence [the Sages] said: "Moses received the Torah from Sinai" (Avot 1). And it is to this [humility] that the holy Torah is alluding here. The fact that "the Lord had come down upon it in fire" would lead us to assume that the flames greatly increased, owing to the fire of the Lord that had descended on [the mountain]; yet Sinai, in its humility, did not go up in flames; rather, "Mount Sinai was all in smoke." —AHAVAT SHALOM

"[Moses received the Torah] from Sinai"—because of the same merit that entitled [Sinai] to be the place where the Torah was given.

EXODUS 19:19

The blare of the horn grew very much louder.
Moses spoke, and God answered him with a voice.

"The blare of the horn"—a good omen in scripture: wherever the horn *(shofar)* is mentioned it augurs well for Israel. Thus scripture says, "God ascends midst acclamation; the Lord, to the blasts of the horn" (Ps. 47:6); and it says, "On that day, a great horn shall be sounded" (Isa. 27:13); and it says, "[The Lord will manifest Himself to them . . .]; my Lord God shall sound the horn and advance in a stormy tempest" (Zech. 9:14).

"Very much louder"—ordinarily, the longer [a horn] sounds the softer it becomes, but here the longer it sounded the louder it became. Why was it soft at the beginning? To soothe the ear with what it is capable of hearing.

"Moses spoke, and God answered him with a voice"—Rabbi Eli'ezer said: How do we know that the Holy One, blessed be He, only spoke when Moses said [to Him], "Speak, for Your children have already accepted"? Because it is written, "Moses spoke, and God answered him with a voice." Rabbi 'Akiva said to him: Undoubtedly you are right [about God and Moses], but we must still explain the words "Moses spoke [and God answered him *with a voice*]." [What this comes to tell us is:] the Holy One, blessed be He, gave Moses strength and bolstered his voice (bekolo), so that when he spoke to Israel he would speak with the same sound he had heard [from God]. Hence it says, "Moses spoke, and God answered him with a voice (bekol)." —MEKHILTA

"God ascends midst acclamation (bako'ah)" (Ps. 47:6)—At the time of the Giving of the Torah, He lowered His voice according to Israel's ability (kohan) to hear, as it is written, "God answered him with a voice"—with Moses' own voice. —RASHI

"The blare of the horn grew very much louder"—Unlike other horns, the sound of which grows softer as the blower's breath is exhausted, this one sounded as loudly at the end as at the beginning.

"Moses spoke"—*when* Moses spoke, for example, when he said that the people would not be able to ascend [the mountain]—"God answered him with a voice"—so that the people could hear the Holy One, blessed be He, speaking to him, as scripture says, "In order that the people may hear when I speak with you" (Exod. 19:9). —BEKHOR SHOR

"The blare of the horn grew very much louder"—All material things are limited and finite. Not so the disembodied Divine command,* which must be imagined as all-powerful and infinite in relation to those who receive it, considering their weaknesses and limitations. —ME'OR HA'AFELAH

*See note above, p. 175.

"The blare of the horn grew very much louder"—The horn was the left horn of Isaac's ram.* Its right horn is being held in readiness for the time of the Messiah.

"Grew very much louder"—What it actually says is not that it grew but that it continues to grow [louder].

"Louder (vehazek)"—It grew stronger (hazek) itself and also strengthened (mehazek) others.

"Very much (me'od)"—Me'od has the same letters as adam (man) [viz., aleph, dalet, and mem]. For nothing that is reported in the scripture concerning the sounds and the flashes of lightning [at Sinai] was new from the point of view of the Holy One, blessed be He; it was, rather, intended to instruct humankind eternally. For the receiving of the Torah takes place over and over again, throughout the generations. —BEIT AHARON

"Moses spoke, and God answered him with a voice"—Here is how the voice reached Israel: each according to his capacity [to hear]. The elderly heard according to their capacity, the young men according to their capacity, the adolescents according to their capacity, the children according to their capacity, the infants according to their capacity, and the women according to their capacity. Moses, too, heard according to his capacity, as it is written, "Moses spoke, and God answered him with a voice"—meaning with a voice that Moses could stand hearing. Similarly, scripture says, "The voice of the Lord is power" (Ps. 29:4)—not His power, but "power," for each according to his powers. The pregnant women, too, heard according to their capacity. In other words, each of them heard according to his capacity to hear. —TANHUMA, Exodus 21

"Moses spoke, and God answered him with a voice"—Rabbi Luliani said, quoting Rabbi Yishma'el: It is customary for a teacher to speak and his pupil to answer, but with the Holy One, blessed be He, it is different: "Moses spoke, and God answered him with a voice." What does "with a voice" mean? With Moses' own voice. This is the meaning of the verse, "Your response has made me great" (Ps. 18:36). —MIDRASH ON PSALMS 18

See how great is the humility of the Holy One, blessed be He. The Torah says, "Moses spoke, and God answered him with a voice." What it should have said is, "God spoke, and Moses answered him with a voice"! This is the meaning of the verse, "Your humility has made me great" (2 Sam. 22:36). —YALKUT SHOFTIM

*The ram that came to take Isaac's place at the sacrifice on Mount Moriah (Gen. 22).

"Moses spoke, and God answered him with a voice"—The great sage Rabbi Yizhak of Volozhyn explained: When Moses spoke he merely whispered, yet the Holy One, blessed be He, can hear us even when we whisper. But when the Holy One, blessed be He, answered, He answered in a loud voice, for Moses, being a man and not God, could not have heard things said in a whisper. —MILIN YEKIRIN

"God answered him with a voice"—He amplified [Moses'] voice so that all Israel could hear it. —HA'AMEK DAVAR

MOSES SPOKE

"Moses spoke, and God answered him with a voice"—"Rabbi Shim'on ben Pazi said: How do we know that the translator [of the public reading of the Torah] may not speak more loudly than the reader? From the verse, 'Moses spoke, and God answered him with a voice.' What does the Torah mean by adding 'with a voice'? With a voice [no louder than that] of Moses" (Berakhot 45a).

One could interpret it that the Holy One, blessed be He, was the translator. Every word the Holy One, blessed be He, said Himself came out in seventy languages, so that all the nations could understand it, but Moses spoke to Israel in a language the nations could not understand, and the Holy One, blessed be He, had to translate [for them]. But in no case did He speak more loudly than Moses.

One could also offer an interpretation closer to the plain meaning of the text: that Moses was the translator. Scripture teaches us that the voice of the Holy One, blessed be He, was no louder than that of Moses; and if the reader did not speak more loudly than the translator, the translator certainly could not speak more loudly than the reader, who enjoys a higher standing. (Even a child can serve as a translator.) The main point the scripture is making, then, is that the two voices, that of the Holy One, blessed be He, and that of Moses, were of equal volume. —SEFER ESHKOL, beginning of Laws of the Priestly Blessings

Rabbi Alfas (in the edition of the Vilna Gaon: Rabbi Eli'ezer, one of the Tosafists) interpreted ["God answered him with a voice"] as meaning, with Moses' own voice: "Moses naturally had to respond as loudly as he could to enable the people to hear him, but the Holy One, blessed be He, would not have had to raise His voice, for He was only speaking to Moses. Nonetheless, He did raise His voice, so that the voice of Moses the translator would not be louder than that of the Holy One, blessed be He, the reader" [Tosafot on Berakhot 45a, "With a voice"]. The same point is intended by the Maharsha [Shmuel Edels], in his commentary on the Aggadah. —NAHAL ESHKOL

"Moses spoke"—meaning Moses was speaking, for he spoke continuously. "And God answered him with a voice"—for speech is something delimited, whereas the voice is infinitely expansive. This, then, is the meaning of "God answered him with a voice": Moses was capable of speech but lacked a voice, and God helped him with this. —BEIT AHARON

"Moses spoke"—though the future-tense form of the verb is used, the sense of it is the past continuous ["would speak"]. The same is the case with "answered him." Similarly, "Miriam answered them" (Exod. 15:21), [where the future-tense form of the verb conveys past-continuous action]. The Omnipresent, blessed be He, would read to Moses, and Moses would speak to Israel, as when Jews listen to one another read the Torah. This is what is meant in the earlier verse by the words, "In order that the people may hear" (Exod. 19:9). Similarly, it is written further along, "I stood between the Lord [and you at that time to convey the Lord's words to you]" (Deut. 5:5). —RABBI MEYUHAS BEN ELIYAHU

"O my dove, in the cranny of the rocks" (Song 2:14)—This refers to our standing at Mount Sinai. "Let me hear your voice" (Song 2:14)—Israel said, "We will do and we will hear." Another interpretation of "Let me hear your voice": God amplified Moses' voice so that when he recited and interpreted the Torah the whole people would be able to hear him from as far away as twelve miles.* This is what scripture means by "God answered him with a voice." —Rabbi Avigdor Kohen-Zedek, COMMENTARY ON THE SONG OF SONGS

GOD ANSWERED HIM WITH A VOICE

It is written, "Moses spoke, and God answered him with a voice." Here there are sublime things being said. We have learned that when it says, "God answered him with a voice," it means Moses' own voice, the voice that Moses [customarily] relied upon. We must look into this further, for it was in fact just the opposite. It is written, "God spoke [all these words]" (Exod. 20:1), yet here it is written, "Moses spoke." This [apparent contradiction] may be explained

*Traditionally, the extent of the Israelite camp. Cf. note, p. 24.

on the basis of the verse, " 'You speak to us,' they said to Moses, 'and we will obey; but let not God speak to us' " (Exod. 20:16); therefore "Moses spoke and God answered him with a voice" [i.e., with an additional voice, not his own].

Indeed, there is not a single word in the Torah said by Moses alone. As for what we have learned about the curses in Deuteronomy, that "Moses said them with his own mouth," note that it says "with his own mouth" and not "of his own accord." While those curses [that appear in Lev. 26:14–43] were uttered by God Himself, those [in Deut. 27:15–28:68] were uttered by Moses, [not of his own accord but] "with his own mouth"—that is, by the voice lent to him, which is referred to in this way. This clears up the difficulty nicely.

Now, in the Book of Aggadah of the School of Rav it is said that, whereas the entire Torah was dictated by God Himself, it is also said to have been spoken by Moses "with his own mouth." To what does this refer? To the curses in Deuteronomy, for example, which were then confirmed by the All-Powerful Himself. Hence it is written, "Moses spoke and God answered him with a voice"—"Moses spoke" refers to Moses' voice, while "God answered him with a voice" refers to God's voice, which was confirming that of Moses. Hence, "God answered him with a voice"—answered Moses' voice.
—ZOHAR, Leviticus 6a

"Moses spoke"—Not the past but the future tense is used, for he was to speak with each person in each subsequent generation. Whoever wished to purify himself and take upon himself the yoke of Torah would be addressed by Moses. "And God answered him with a voice"—giving voice to his words and uniting voice with words and thoughts. —BEIT AHARON, Yitro

Rabbi Yehoshu'a ben Karḥa said: The horn was created solely to benefit Israel, for it was with the horn that the Torah was given to Israel, as it is written, "The blare of the horn grew louder and louder" (Exod. 19:19). And it was by means of the horn that the walls of Jericho were brought down, as it is written, "When the people heard the sound of the horns, the people raised a mighty shout and the wall collapsed" (Josh. 6:20). And the Holy One, blessed be He, is destined to blow the horn when the Son of David, our righteous one, appears, as it is written, "[The Lord will manifest Himself to them . . . ;] my Lord God shall sound the ram's horn" (Zech. 9:14). And the Holy One, blessed be He, is destined to blow the horn when He restores the exiles of Israel to their rightful place, as it is written, "In that day, a great ram's horn shall be sounded; and the strayed who are in the land of Assyria and the expelled who are in the land of

Egypt shall come and worship the Lord on the holy mount, in Jerusalem" (Isa. 27:13). Thus it is written, "Cry with full throat, without restraint; raise your voice like a ram's horn!" (Isa. 58:1). —TANNA DEVEI ELIYAHU ZUTA 22 (Sadilkov edition)

THE APPEARANCE OF
THE SHEKHINAH

EXODUS 19:20

The Lord came down upon Mount Sinai,
on the top of the mountain,
and the Lord called Moses to the top
of the mountain and Moses went up.

THE LORD CAME DOWN UPON
MOUNT SINAI

"The Lord came down"—a repetition of what has already been stated [two verses previously], following a digression describing for us the power of the manifestations of the Divine and the sounds. —RABBI MEYUḤAS BEN ELIYAHU

Rabbi Shmuel bar Nahman said: When the Holy One, blessed be He, created the world, He wished to have a dwelling-place below as He had above. He created man and charged him, "Of every tree of the garden [you are free to eat;] but as for the tree of knowledge of good and bad, you must not eat of it" (Gen. 2:16–17). But man transgressed His commandment. Said He to him, "I so much wished to have a dwelling-place below, but the one thing I commanded you you did not keep." The Holy One, blessed be He, thereupon removed His Shekhinah to the First Heaven. Then came Cain and killed Abel, and God removed His Shekhinah to the Second Heaven. Then came the generation of Enoch and worshiped idols, as it is written, "It was then that men began to invoke the Lord by name" (Gen. 4:26); so He removed His Shekhinah to the Third Heaven. Then came the Generation of the Flood, of whom it is written, "They say to God, 'Leave us alone, we do not want to learn Your ways' " (Job 21:14); so He removed His Shekhinah to the Fourth Heaven. Then came the Generation of the Parting and they said, "Come, let us build us a city, [and a tower with its top in the sky]" (Gen. 11:4). What did He do? He scattered them far and wide and removed His Shekhinah to the Fifth Heaven. Came the

Sodomites, of whom it is written, "The inhabitants of Sodom were very wicked sinners against the Lord" (Gen. 13:13), and He removed His Shekhinah to the Sixth Heaven. Then came Amraphel and his cohorts and angered Him, and He removed His Shekhinah to the Seventh Heaven, saying, "Who will take my part against evil men? Who will stand up for me against wrongdoers?" (Ps. 94:16).

What did the Holy One, blessed be He, do then? He set aside all the previous generations and established Abraham, who distinguished himself by his deeds. Thereupon He descended from the Seventh Heaven to the Sixth. Then came Isaac and stretched out his neck on the altar, so He descended from the Sixth Heaven to the Fifth. Then came Jacob, and He descended from the Fifth to the Fourth. Then came the tribe of Levi, and He descended from the Fourth to the Third. Then came Kehath, and He descended from the Third to the Second. Then came Amram, and he descended from the Second to the First. Then came Moses, and He came down to earth, as it is written, "The Lord came down upon Mount Sinai." This is what is meant by the verse, "I have come to my garden, my own, my bride" (Song 5:1).
—TANHUMA, Naso

ON TOP OF THE MOUNTAIN

"The Lord came down upon Mount Sinai"—One might have thought He came down over the whole mountain, so scripture says, "on the top of the mountain." One might have thought the Divine Glory actually came down and rested upon Mount Sinai, so scripture says, "I spoke to you from the very heavens" (Exod. 20:19). This teaches us that the Holy One, blessed be He, brought the lowest heavens and the highest heavens down to the top of the mountain, and His Glory descended [onto them]. He spread [the heavens] over Mount Sinai as one lays a pillow at the head of a bed and as one who speaks with his head on the pillow, as it is written, "[If You would but tear open the heavens and come down, so that mountains would quake before You]—as when fire kindles brushwood, and fire makes water boil—to make Your name known" (Isa. 63:19–64:1); and it is also written, "When You did wonders we dared not hope for, You came down and mountains quaked before You" (Isa. 64:2).

Rabbi Yose said: "The heavens belong to the Lord, [but the earth He gave over to man]" (Ps. 115:16)—Neither Moses nor Elijah went on high, nor did the Divine Glory come all the way down; rather, scripture teaches us that the Omnipresent said to Moses, "I shall call you from the top of the mountain, and you will come up, as it is written, 'The Lord called Moses [to the top of the mountain].' " —MEKHILTA

"The Lord came down"—Know that the human soul is noble and exalted. It belongs to the middle realm, whereas the body belongs to the lower realm. Other than the human being, there is no creature in the lower realm that speaks. The human being also listens, so as to understand what is in the heart of whoever speaks to him. The most learned person cannot invent language but only make use of what already exists and is known. And all languages are based upon the human pattern, which is a composite of the incorporeal soul and the body. The latter, in turn, is derived from four sources.

When one person speaks to another about human matters and in a language they share, the latter will understand him without the use of special imagery. But if he wishes to speak about levels of creation lower than the human, he will have to describe them in human terms if he is to be understood. Thus one speaks of the earth having a head—"head of the world's clay" (Prov. 8:26)—and a mouth—"The earth opened its mouth" (Num. 16:32)—and a thigh (yerekh)—"[A great nation is roused] from the remotest parts (yarketei) of the earth" (Jer. 6:23). Moreover, it is written, "at the hand of the Jordan" (Num. 13:29) and "in the heart of the sea" (Exod. 15:8), and there are many similar instances. All these are metaphors, for the sea does not have a heart. Moreover, parts of the body are sometimes made to represent the whole, for example, in the verse, "Death and life are in the power of the tongue" (Prov. 18:21) and in many similar instances.

By the same token, when a person wishes to speak of things higher than himself, things belonging to the upper realm, he must bring them down to the human level, speaking of them in human terms. Thus, in order that the human listener might understand, scripture speaks of "the man Gabriel" (Dan. 9:21) and "His arms and legs [had the color of burnished bronze] and the sound of his speech was like the noise of a multitude" (Dan. 10:6).

Similarly, we employ this method in regard to the celestial realm. Thus it is written, "A helmet of triumph on His head" (Isa. 59:17); "The mouth of the Lord has spoken" (Isa. 58:14); "The eyes of the Lord are on the righteous, His ears attentive to their cry. The face of the Lord is set against evildoers" (Ps. 34:16, 17); and "Under His feet [there was the likeness of a pavement of sapphire" (Exod. 24:10). In the same way, it says, "The Lord came down" (Exod. 19:20) and "God went up [from Abraham]" (Gen. 17:22). —IBN 'EZRA

"The Lord came down upon Mount Sinai." "The Lord came down"—meaning when He began to lower His Shekhinah. At this point, the mountain shook and rose to meet Him, as a servant runs to greet his master. This is the plain sense of the scriptural words "The Lord came down." Scripture has not yet revealed at what exact spot on the mountain He descended; it has only informed us of the activity of the mountain: though inanimate, it came alive. Only afterwards does scripture tell us where He descended on the mountain: "on the top of the mountain." From this we may conclude that the mountain rose even before the Shekhinah reached down to its top. —OR HAHAYYIM

Rabbi Yehudah said: How fortunate Moses was, for it is written concerning him, "The Lord came down upon Mount Sinai . . . and the Lord called Moses." Fortunate, too, was the generation of whom it is written, "The Lord will come down, in the sight of all the people, on Mount Sinai" (Exod. 19:11). —ZOHAR, Exodus 82a

Rabbi Yohanan said: When the Holy One, blessed be He, came to Sinai, He gave life to the idols, and they bowed down to Him. Said Rabbi Tahlifa: Scripture supports Rabbi Yohanan's view, for it is written, "All Divine beings bowed down to Him" (Ps. 97:7)—not "shall bow down to Him" but "bowed down to Him," for they had already done so. —YALKUT SHIM'ONI, Psalms 714

It should be read as "bowed," the past tense, rather than "bow," the imperative, [the Hebrew hishtahavu lending itself readily to either interpretation]. —RADAK

"The Lord came down upon Mount Sinai"—Wherever scripture speaks of the Holy One, blessed be He, "descending," it has to do [not with physical movement but] with His revealing or disclosing Himself to rational understanding. For example, "The Lord appeared to him" (Gen. 18:1), which refers to Abraham, is translated by the Targum as "He revealed Himself." But scripture prefers to speak of "descent," for when the Shekhinah reveals Herself to the lower world, it represents a descent from the level of the Most High. Here, the words "The Lord came down" can be explained to mean that the Unique Name* was perceived by the whole people; for it says, above, that "on the third day the Lord will come down, in the sight of all the people" (Exod. 19:11). [In

---

*The Tetragrammaton, generally translated here as "Lord" and commonly employed, using the euphemism "the Name," as synonymous with God Himself.

fact, what is meant is that,] having seen the Divine Glory as a consuming fire at the top of the mountain, they realized that the Unique Name was there. This is what is meant by "The Lord came down," not that they actually saw the Unique Name, for it is written, "Man may not see Me and live" (Exod. 33:20).

Similarly, in the case of Abraham it is written, "The Lord appeared to him" (Gen. 18:1), and one might have thought this meant that the Unique Name itself appeared to Abraham; but it is well known that this name was not known to the Patriarchs, that He only revealed Himself to them as El-Shaddai, which is [merely] the gate to the Lord. Thus scripture had to add, "He was sitting at the entrance of the tent" (Gen. 18:1), which explains "The Lord appeared to him"; scripture is hereby teaching us that God's appearance to Abraham was only through the entrance of a tent [i.e., veiled], so that we do not get the idea that he actually saw the Unique Name. Here, "The Lord came down" has the same force, for the appearance of the Unique Name to all the people was only from within the Divine glory, which they saw as a consuming fire. —RABBENU BAHYA

"The Lord came down upon Mount Sinai"—The *Targum of Onkelos* renders it, "The Lord was revealed." Maimonides, then, in the *Guide of the Perplexed,* explains that the *Targum*'s purpose is to avoid any association of the Holy One, blessed be He, with physicality. The Maharal of Prague, in *Tif'eret Yisra'el,* expresses surprise at this: "The Torah was not concerned about this; why then should we be?" (See Nachmanides, Vayiggash 46:1.) And indeed, there is no cause for concern, for the holy tongue [Hebrew] is suited only to discussing spiritual matters, and when it employs physical terms it is only a kind of borrowing. What the Torah in fact means by "came down" is something spiritual, without the slightest physical connotation. The language of the *Targum* [Aramaic], on the other hand, is appropriate to physical matters as well; thus it had to render the verb "was revealed" so as to avoid attributing physicality to the Most High.

And just as one may not attribute physicality to the Most High, one may also not attribute it to the Torah. The Torah did not take on physical form when it came down but rather was revealed in all its power, glory, and splendor just as it had been on high. —MEI MAROM

MOSES WENT UP

"The Lord came down upon Mount Sinai"—yet it is also written, "Moses went inside the cloud and ascended the mountain" (Exod. 24:18). Now the

Holy One, blessed be He, was on Mount Sinai, as it is written, "The Presence of the Lord [appeared in the sight of the Israelites] as a consuming fire on top of the mountain" (Exod. 24:17); how, then, could Moses ascend to Him? It says, "Moses went inside the cloud and ascended the mountain"—he went inside the cloud like one putting on a garment, and having put on the cloud, having entered it, he was able to draw near to the fire. —ZOHAR, Exodus 197a

"Moses went inside the cloud and ascended the mountain"—What was this cloud? There is a reference to this in the verse, "I have set My bow in the clouds" (Gen. 9:13). We have learned that that same rainbow took off its garments [i.e., the clouds] and gave them to Moses, and it was in those garments that Moses went up Mount Sinai and saw what he saw and took delight in it all. —ZOHAR, Exodus 99a

SEPARATE PLACES

EXODUS 19:21

The Lord said to Moses, "Go down, warn the people
not to break through to the Lord to gaze,
lest many of them perish."

"The Lord said to Moses, 'Go down, warn the people' . . . But Moses said to
the Lord, 'The people cannot come up to Mount Sinai, for You warned us
[saying, "Set bounds about the mountain and sanctify it"]' " (Exod. 19:21,
23)—Now you may ask, What is the meaning of Moses' reply? Is it fitting for
a servant to answer his master in this way? Surely the Holy One, blessed be He,
would not have given Moses this command if there had been no need to do
so. The answer is that Moses' reply was only a request to know where his own
bounds were to be. What he was saying was, "Master of the Universe, there
is no need to warn Israel since 'You warned us,' me and my brother Aaron,
'saying, "Set bounds about the mountain and sanctify it" '; and if, God forbid,
the people 'break through to come up,' we shall [be there to] warn them, for
we shall be within the bounds set for them." Then the Holy One, blessed be
He, revealed His word to Moses, saying, " 'Go down, and come back . . . with
Aaron' (Exod. 19:24) your brother; you will not stay within the bounds set for
the people."

"But let not the priests or the people break through to come up to the
Lord" (Exod. 19:24)—They all had their separate places. —TOSFOT HAROSH

"The Lord said to Moses, 'Go down, warn the people [not to break through
to the Lord to gaze]' "—Whoever went up was urged not to look, and whoever
did not go up was urged not to go up.

"Not to break through to the Lord to gaze"—They must not violate the
bounds, "lest many *(rav)* of them perish *(venafal)*." *Rav* means a multitude, the
idea being that even if only one of them falls [*venafal* being the singular form]
to the ground, he will be considered by God to be like a multitude.

Another interpretation of "lest many *(rav)* of them perish": lest those few fall who by their distinction influence the majority *(rubo)*. —MEKHILTA DĒ-RABBI SHIM'ON BAR YOḤAI

"The Lord said to Moses, 'Go down, warn the people' "—warn them publicly—" 'not to break through to the Lord' "—lest they press forward to see.

"Lest many *(rav)* of them perish"—This tells us that the angels were given permission to wreak destruction. Another interpretation: Even if only one distinguished person *(rav)* out of their number falls, to Me it will be as if all of them had fallen. This teaches that even a single individual can cause harm to an entire group. Another interpretation: Every one of them who is eliminated will be worth all of creation to Me, as it is written, "For a man's eye will be to the Lord—like all the tribes of Israel" (Zech. 9:1). —MEKHILTA

The fact that it says "perish" in the singular and not the plural means that even a single individual is considered "many," for, as it says above, if even one of them had been absent the Shekhinah would not have come. Thus, even one person who harms the group is considered as if he were many.

"Worth all of creation"—for if even one of them had been absent they would not have gotten the Torah, and all of creation was conditional on Israel receiving the Torah, as the Midrash says concerning the sixth day, and as it is written, "Were it not for My covenant day and night—[the laws of heaven and earth]" (Jer. 33:25).* Consequently the absence of even one of them would have caused creation itself to be nullified.

"For a man's eye will be to the Lord—like all the tribes of Israel" (Zech. 9:1)—even a single eye is as important to Him as all the tribes of Israel. —ZEH YENAHAMENU

SIX HUNDRED THOUSAND

Our Rabbis, the authors of the Aggadah, said: Had only one of them been absent the Torah would not have been given. Rabbi Aharon Halevi, may his memory be a blessing, wrote: It is for this reason that the Torah was given to

*Cf. above, p. 15ff.

six hundred thousand people. It was the will of the Holy One, blessed be He, that the Torah be accepted by all factions, and the six hundred thousand included all factions and opinions. —PEKUDAT HALEVI'IM

"Go down, warn the people"—He commanded Moses to guide the people, referring to the act of exerting leadership over them as "going down," just as the pouring of the glorious Divine bounty into the physical world is referred to as "going down." —ME'OR HA'AFELAH

"Not to break through"—for they were standing in a single row along the boundary, forming a kind of fence. Thus scripture uses the term "break through," as in the verse, "Its stone fence was broken through" (Prov. 24:31). —BEKHOR SHOR

"Not to break through *(yehersu)* to the Lord to gaze"—Destruction *(harisah)* is the undoing of construction. When one presses on in his thinking beyond the point that his nature permits him to attain, the foundations of his faith are undermined, and not only does he become confused about that which he aspired to understand, but the understanding he has already attained is confused and destroyed. —ME'OR HA'AFELAH

"[Warn the people] not to break through to the Lord to gaze, lest many of them perish"—Let them not agree to their own destruction provided they can see the Lord, thinking that such a death would be life-giving, as in the verse, "Truly Your faithfulness is better than life" (Ps. 63:4).

"Lest many of them perish"—Not only would they die, but they would die a thousand deaths.

Another interpretation of "not to break through to the Lord to gaze": His light, may He be blessed, was all-pervasive. Thus, if they came up to see, He would, as it were, have to remove the light to prevent them from looking at it. This is the meaning of "not to break through to the Lord to see"—to see His light. The implication is that they would not be given to see His light.

"Lest [many of them] perish"—Not only will they not see anything; they will be harmed as well.

"Many *(rav)* of them"—even the greatest *(rav)* of them, lest it be said that I am only strict with the masses of the people but not with the leaders, who are worthy of direct contact with the Shekhinah. Hence the Torah says, "lest the greatest of them perish." —OR HAḤAYYIM

EXODUS 19:22

The priests also, who come near
the Lord, must purify themselves,
lest the Lord break out against them.

"The priests also"—that is, even those who are blameless, if they wish to delve into Divine matters, must remain in their places and refrain from forcing their way into things which they are not capable of understanding. "Lest the Lord break out against them"—as happened to Nadab and Abihu and the seventy elders, who incurred death by breaking into the Divine presence. —ME'OR HA'AFELAH

"The priests also, who come near the Lord"—Although they are closest [to sanctity], they are nevertheless warned to sanctify themselves, indeed to purify their thoughts even more—"lest the Lord break out against them"—lest the power of the appearance of the Shekhinah harm them. If they were not properly prepared, the light of the countenance of the Living King would be destructive for them. That would not be true for the rest of Israel, who could not reach as far and therefore were not as susceptible to harm for want of proper preparation. —HA'AMEK DAVAR

"Lest the Lord break out (*yifroz*) against them"—lest He make a breach (*pirzah*) in their ranks. Another interpretation: Lest they break out (*yifrozu*). —MEK-HILTA DE-RABBI SHIM'ON BAR YOHAI

EXODUS 19:23

But Moses said to the Lord,
"The people cannot come up to Mount Sinai,
for You warned us saying, 'Set bounds
about the mountain and sanctify it.' "

"But Moses said . . . 'The people cannot come up to Mount Sinai, for You warned us. . . . ' "—This reply of Moses to the Holy One, blessed be He, poses a difficulty: Are there not a number of other commandments to which two warnings are attached? Furthermore, what is the meaning of His answer to Moses: "Go down, and come back together with Aaron"? All this can be explained as follows: Because Moses had not warned Israel concerning the commandment to set bounds but only concerning abstinence (as we have previously explained in connection with this verse), the Holy One, blessed be He, said to him, "Go down, warn the people," meaning, it is more important for you to warn them about the commandment to set bounds, which carries a penalty of death, than concerning any of the other commandments you warned them about. To this he replied, "The people cannot come up . . . for You warned us," my brother Aaron and me, against going up; and since we will be with them, we will warn them not to go up [when the time comes]. To this the Holy One, blessed be He, replied, "Go down," and warn them now, then "come back together with Aaron," for, [being with Me,] you will not be there to warn them when the time comes. Forthwith, "Moses went down to the people and spoke to them"—concerning the commandment of setting bounds. —TOSFOT HAROSH

"But Moses said . . . , 'The people cannot come up' "—[Sa'adyah] Gaon said he had pondered this verse for many years and could not explain it, until he read in a Persian royal-protocol manual that a messenger may not tell the king he has done his bidding until he is sent on another errand; then he can tell him.

But in my opinion, since the Lord had told Moses, "[Warn the people] not to break through to the Lord to gaze" (Exod. 19:21), he did not know whether to warn them [separately] against *looking,* for he had already warned them against crossing the boundary. Hence the Lord said to him, "Go down" as I have commanded you and warn them publicly; for Israel needed a second warning. —IBN EZRA

"[The people cannot] come up to Mount Sinai, [for You warned us saying, 'Set bounds about the mountain']"—This warning, [thought Moses,] was essentially against going up the mountain and not just against crossing the boundary [which was at some remove from the mountain]. This was clear from the Lord's expression "not to break through [to the Lord to gaze]," which only forbids actually ascending the mountain. But doing so was, [Moses assumed,] already out of the question. After all, [he said,] "You warned us, [saying, 'Set bounds about the mountain']"—that is, Aaron and I have already been warned to set bounds about the mountain so that we ourselves do not ascend it; how then can the people break through and go past us? —HA'AMEK DAVAR

"The people cannot come up to Mount Sinai, for You warned us"—Rabbi Menahem of Kotzk explained this as follows: Moses did not understand how it could occur to any Jew to transgress the word of the Lord and ascend on high: "[The people] cannot [come up . . .], for You warned [us]." The Holy One, blessed be He, then answered him, "Go down"—climb down from your exalted perch, for others are not like you; they need another warning. —'AMUD HA'EMET

"The people cannot come up"—Why did they need so many warnings? When they were found worthy of receiving the holy Torah they undoubtedly had all forty-eight virtues with which the Torah is acquired [cf. Avot 6:5], one of which is knowing one's place. In fact, they were all in their proper places, but in order to prevent them from taking pride in having imposed this restriction on themselves—the Holy One, blessed be He, cannot abide pride—they were warned for their own good, so that they would stay where they were because they had been commanded to do so and not of their own accord. —SIFTEI ZADDIKIM

EXODUS 19:24

So the Lord said to him, "Go down,
and come back together with Aaron;
but let not the priests or the people
break through to come up to the Lord,
lest He break out against them."

"Go down"—and warn them publicly a second time. For one should exhort a person before he does something and then again when it comes time to do it. —RASHI

Ibn 'Ezra writes: " 'Go down'—quickly." In other words, having already said, "Go down, warn the people" (Exod. 19:21), what point was there in telling him once again, "Go down"? This time it was to order him to go down quickly. —MEKOR HAYYIM

"So the Lord said to him, 'Go down, and come back' "—Lest we think they all came back with him, the Torah says, "Come back together with Aaron," but without the priests. And lest we think Aaron was allowed to enter the same area [as Moses], the Torah says, "Only Moses shall come near the Lord" (Exod. 24:2), from which we can conclude that Moses had his place and Aaron his. —MEKHILTA DE-RABBI SHIM'ON BAR YOḤAI

"Go down, and come back"—Moses gave a double warning to the people. [The first one,] "not to break through" (Exod. 19:21), was so that they would understand that the Lord loved them and was keeping them away so that none of them would be hurt. It was also to teach them the great holiness of the mountain at the time that the Lord descended upon it. —Rabbi Ya'akov Knozel, SUPERCOMMENTARY ON RASHI

"Go down, warn the people not to break through . . . to come up"—Rabbi Menaḥem of Kotzk said: Had He not already told them, "[Whoever touches the mountain shall be put to death:] no hand shall touch him, but he shall be stoned" (Exod. 19:13)? What He meant on that occasion, however, was simply that it would be dangerous, but there might well be some who would brave the danger and go up, forfeiting their lives for the sanctification of the Name. Thus He warned them a second time "not to break through . . . to come up," this time using terms of prohibition, which were sure to keep them away. —'AMUD HA'EMET

EXODUS 19:25
And Moses went down to the people and spoke to them.

"And spoke to them"—He spoke to them immediately, without delay.
    Another interpretation of "and spoke to them": He said to them, "Be ready to accept the rule of heaven with joy."
    Another interpretation of "and spoke to them": "You must respond negatively to the negative commandments and affirmatively to the positive ones." —MEKHILTA

"Moses went down to the people and spoke to them"—This teaches us that he did not go home or turn to other affairs. But from here we only know that he did not go home or turn to other affairs after receiving the commandments on Mount Sinai; how do we know the same was true after he received the commandments in the Tent of Meeting? Because the Torah says, "He came out [of the Tent] and told the Israelites what he had been commanded" (Exod. 34:34).

Only when Moses came down to call Aaron did the Holy One, blessed be He, make His voice heard, so that the Israelites would not say, "It is Moses speaking to us from heaven!"

With the first Divine utterance, heaven and earth rumbled, mountains and hills collapsed, seas and rivers fled, all the trees bent low, the dead of Israel came to life and stood up, and the Israelites recoiled twelve miles,* their hearts in their mouths. It was in this one utterance that they heard the words, "I [the Lord am your God]" and "You shall have [no other gods beside Me]" (Exod. 20:2–3). Thus scripture says, "One thing God has spoken; two things have I heard" (Ps. 62:12).

At that moment they said to Moses, "You go closer and hear all that the Lord our God says; then you tell us" (Deut. 5:24). The Holy One, blessed be He, heard what they said, and it pleased Him. He sent Michael and Gabriel to take Moses' hands against his will and bring him into the cloud. For it is written, "Moses approached *(niggash)* the thick cloud" (Exod. 20:18), using [the less active form] *niggash,* meaning unwillingly, rather than [the more active form] *gash.* Then Moses uttered the rest of the Ten Commandments to Israel. It is said of him, "Like the coldness of snow at harvest time is a trusty messenger to those who send him; he lifts his master's spirits" (Prov. 25:13). —MEKHILTA DE-RABBI SHIM'ON BAR YOHAI

"And Moses went down to the people"—It has been said (in the *Guide of the Perplexed,* Part 2, chap. 33) that as far as the first two commandments were concerned, the people assembled before Mount Sinai had the same level of understanding as Moses did; for wonders are grasped equally well by those who witness them as by prophets. Know that the Sinai Event was a supernatural happening, a miracle, for it cannot happen naturally that an entire people are given the gift of prophecy at one and the same time, concerning the same matter. It only happened on this one occasion. —ME'OR HA'AFELAH

"The Lord came down upon Mount Sinai" (Exod. 19:20)—On the sixth of Sivan the Holy One, blessed be He, revealed Himself to Israel at Mount Sinai. Mount Sinai was uprooted, the heavens opened, the top of the mountain went

*See note, p. 24.

up into heaven, and the mountain as a whole was shrouded in thick cloud. The Holy One, blessed be He, sat on His throne with His feet on the cloud, as it is written, "He bent the sky and came down, thick cloud beneath His feet" (2 Sam. 22:10; Ps. 18:10).

Rabbi Tarfon said: The Holy One, blessed be He, shone forth from Mount Seir, as it is written, "He said: The Lord came from Sinai; He shone upon them from Seir" (Deut. 33:2). From there He revealed Himself to Ishmael, as it is written, "He appeared from Mount Paran" (Deut. 33:2). From there He sent word to the other nations, saying, "Will you accept the Torah?" They replied, "We cannot abandon the ways of our fathers, so we do not want the Torah. Give it, rather, to Your own people, as it is written, 'May the Lord grant strength to His people; may the Lord bestow on His people well-being' " (Ps. 29:11).

From there He again revealed Himself to the Israelites, as it is written, "[He] approached from Rivevot-kodesh (lit., the sacred myriads)" (Deut. 33:2), and it is written, "And when it halted, he would say: Return, O Lord, to Israel's myriads *(rivevot)* of thousands!" (Num. 10:36). And He had with Him "myriads upon myriads of chariots, thousands upon thousands"—the holy angels. His right hand was holding the Torah, as it is written, "Lightning flashing at them from His right" (Deut. 33:2), from which we learn that the words of the Torah are like live coals. He gave it to them affectionately, as it is written, "His left hand was under my head" (Song 2:6). And He gave it in the language of an oath, as it is written, "The Lord has sworn by His right hand, by His mighty arm" (Isa. 62:8), the right hand connoting an oath, as it is written, "The Lord has sworn by His right hand" (Isa. 62:8).

Rabbi Eli'ezer said: Ever since they had left Egypt, the Israelites had been journeying and camping in a state of division—as it is written, "[They] journeyed . . . and they encamped" (Exod. 13:20, 17:1, 19:2) [using the plural form of "encamped"]—until they all arrived at Mount Sinai and encamped in front of the mountain, as it is written, "Israel encamped there in front of the mountain" (Exod. 19:2) [using the singular form]. God said to them, "Will you accept the Torah?" They replied in unison, "Without having heard the Torah, we already keep and observe all the commandments that are written there!" as it is written, "They said, 'All that the Lord has spoken we will do and we will hear' " (Exod. 24:7).

Rabbi Eli'ezer Hamoda'i said: Ever since the creation of heaven and earth, the mountain had been called Horeb. When the Holy One, blessed be He, revealed Himself to Moses there from within the bush, it was named for the bush *(sneh)*. Sinai is the same as Horeb. And how do we know that they took the Torah upon themselves at Mount Horeb? From the verse, "The day you stood before the Lord your God at Horeb" (Deut. 4:10).

Rabbi Pinhas said: On sabbath eve Israel stood at Mount Sinai, the men and the women in separate formations. Said the Holy One, blessed be He, to Moses, "Go ask the daughters of Israel if they will accept the Torah"; for men generally follow the views of their wives, as it is written, "Thus shall you say to the house of Jacob" (Exod. 19:3)—the women—"and declare to the sons of Israel" (Exod. 19:3)—the men. They all answered in unison, "All that the Lord has spoken we will do and we will hear" (Exod. 24:7). And it is written further, "Singers and dancers* alike [will say]: 'All my roots are in You' " (Ps. 87:7).

Rabbi Hakhinai said: In the third month [Sivan], there is twice as much daylight as darkness, and Israel slept [that morning] until the second hour of daylight, the daytime hours being longer at the time of Shavu'ot† and the nightime hours shorter. ["Sleep on Shavu'ot is sweet, the night being short."— Rabbi David Luria]. Moses went out into the camp of Israel to awaken them. He said to them, "Rouse yourselves! The bridegroom has already come asking for the bride, and He is waiting to lead her under the bridal canopy." God was waiting to give them the Torah, and His best man came to get the bride just the way a best man always does for his friend, as it is written, "Moses led the people . . . toward God" (Exod. 19:17). Then the bridegroom came out to meet the bride—to give them the Torah, as it is written, "O God, when You went out before Your people" (Ps. 68:8).

Rabbi Yehoshu'a ben Korha said: Moses stood with his feet on the mountain and the rest of his body in heaven, the way people sit on a couch inside a tent with only their feet protruding. He gazed at all there was to see in heaven, and the Holy One, blessed be He, spoke with him as one person speaks to another, as it is written, "The Lord would speak to Moses face to face" (Exod. 33:11).

The Holy One, blessed be He, said to him, "Go and sanctify Israel for the space of two days," as it is written, "And the Lord said to Moses, 'Go to the people and warn them to stay pure today and tomorrow' " (Exod. 19:10). In what did the [further] sanctification of Israel in the wilderness consist? [Already] they had been purged of callousness; they had received manna from

---

*I.e., the men and the women, respectively.

†The festival, observed on the sixth of Sivan, which commemorates the Giving of the Torah. The date falls in late spring.

heaven; they had drunk water from the Well;* and clouds of Divine Glory surrounded them. What it refers to, however, is abstinence from relations with their wives. Moses weighed the matter in his mind; "If a man goes to be with his wife," he said to himself, "they will delay receiving the Torah." What did he do? He added a day of his own, so that if a man went to be with his wife [beforehand], they would still be pure for two days [afterwards]. That is the reason he added a day of his own. Said the Holy One, blessed be He, to him, "Moses, you have done well"; the Holy One, blessed be He, deferred to him, as it is written, "Let them be ready for the third day" (Exod. 19:11).

Said the Holy One, blessed be He, "Let Moses first go down into the camp, and then I will proclaim My Torah to Israel, so that no one says, 'It was Moses who was speaking to us from the cloud!' " Moses said to Him, "I have already warned the people." He replied, "Call Aaron." When Moses went down into the camp to look for Aaron, the Holy One, blessed be He, proclaimed His Torah to Israel, as it is written, "The Lord said to him, 'Go down [and come back together with Aaron]' " (Exod. 19:24).

"And Moses went down to the people and spoke to them" (Exod. 19:25)—What is written next? "God spoke all these words, saying: I the Lord am your God who brought you out. . . . " (Exod. 20:1–2). With this first utterance, the heavens and the earth rumbled, the seas and the rivers fled, the mountains and hills collapsed, and all the trees bent low. The dead in the netherworld came back to life and stood up, as it is written, "With those who are standing here with us this day" (Deut. 29:14); and all those destined to be created thenceforth to the end of time stood together with them there at Mount Sinai, as it is written, "With those who are not with us here this day" (Deut. 29:14). Jews who were living at that moment fell down and died; but there came a second utterance, and they came back to life and stood up and said to Moses, "O Moses, our teacher, we cannot bear to hear the voice of the Holy One, blessed be He; we shall die again, as we just did!" as it is written, "My soul left me because of what he said" (Song 5:6), and it is written, " 'You speak to us,' they said to Moses, 'and we will hear' " (Exod. 20:16). The Holy One, blessed be He, heard what Israel was saying, and it pleased Him, so He sent Michael and Gabriel to take Moses' hands, against his will, and lead him into the thick cloud, as it is written, "[The people remained at a distance,] while Moses approached (niggash) the thick cloud [where God was]" (Exod. 20:18)—

*A miraculous well, created at the onset of the first sabbath, which will, in the End of Days, provide water to Jerusalem.

using [the less active form] *niggash* rather than [the more active form] *nogesh*. Then He uttered the rest of the [Ten] Commandments to Moses [alone, who then relayed them to the people]. Concerning this, scripture says, "Like the coldness of snow at harvest time is a trusty messenger to those who send him" (Prov. 25:13).

"When you heard the voice out of the darkness, [while the mountain was ablaze with fire, you came up to me]" (Deut. 5:20)—Why did the Holy One, blessed be He, speak out of fire and darkness rather than out of light? To what may this be compared? To a king who had an astrologer. When the king's son got married, [the king] adorned his son's wedding canopy with black curtains instead of white. His courtiers said to him, "Your majesty, it is customary to adorn one's son's wedding canopy with white curtains." He replied, "I know that my son will only be faithful to his bride for forty days, and I do not want people to say, 'The king's astrologer did not know what would happen with his son.' " What the king did is like what the Holy One, blessed be He, did; the king's son is Israel, and the bride is the Torah. The Holy One, blessed be He, knew that Israel would only wait for the commandments forty days [before building the Golden Calf], so He spoke to them out of fire and darkness [instead of out of light].

Rabbi Yehudah said: When one person speaks to another, he is visible, but his voice is not. Israel, however, not only heard the voice of the Holy One, blessed be He, but also saw it issue forth from the Divine, from the lightning and thunder, as it is written, "All the people witnessed the thunder [lit., saw the voices] and lightning" (Exod. 20:15).

The sum of the commandments in the Torah is 613; that is why it is called "Torah." How so? The numerical value of the word *torah* is 611, and the commandments spoken [directly] by the Lord [to Israel] were twofold, as it is written, "One thing God has spoken; two things have I heard" (Ps. 62:12), thus making 613.

Rabbi Pinḥas said: That entire generation, which was found worthy of hearing the voice of the Holy One, blessed be He, at Mount Sinai, was also found worthy of being like the ministering angels: when they died, their bodies did not succumb to worms and decay. Happy was their lot in this world, and happy was their lot in the next. Concerning them, scripture says, "Happy is the people who have it so" (Ps. 144:15). —PIRKEI DE-RABBI ELI'EZER 41

THE GIVING OF THE TORAH

EXODUS 20:1
God spoke all these words, saying.

"God spoke all these words, saying"—The Holy One, blessed be He, treated Israel with royal ceremony, as it is written, "From Lebanon [come with me; from Lebanon,] my bride, with me!" (Song 4:8). Why? Because they said, "We will do and we will hear" (Exod. 24:7).

"Moses brought back the people's words to the Lord" (Exod. 19:8). At that moment, the Holy One, blessed be He, wanted to give them the Torah and speak to them [forthwith], but Moses was standing there. Said the Holy One, blessed be He, "What shall I do about Moses?" Rabbi Levi said: It is like the case of a king who wanted to enact a particular law without consulting the district governor. He said to the governor, "Go do such and such." The governor replied, "It has already been done." He said, "Go get Councillor So-and-So and bring him back with you." While he was gone, the king did what he had wanted to do.

In the same way, the Holy One, blessed be He, wanted to give Israel the Ten Commandments, but Moses was standing next to Him. Said the Holy One, blessed be He, "When I reveal the heavens to them and say, 'I the Lord am your God,' they will ask, 'Who said that, the Holy One, blessed be He, or Moses?' It will be better if Moses goes down and then I say it." So the Holy One, blessed be He, said to Moses, "Go to the people and warn them to stay pure today and tomorrow. Let them wash their clothes" (Exod. 19:10). He said to Him, "I have already purified them, as it is written, 'You warned us, saying [set bounds]'!" (Exod. 19:23). He said to him, "Go down, and come back together with Aaron" (Exod. 19:24). When Moses went down the mountain, the Holy One, blessed be He, revealed Himself [to the people], for it is written, "Moses went down to the people" (Exod. 19:25), and right afterward, "God spoke" (Exod. 20:1). —EXODUS RABBAH 25

"God spoke"—The name God *(Elohim)* refers to the Judge, who punishes and faithfully rewards.*

"All"—all at once, something that mortals cannot do, as it is written, "God spoke all these words, saying," [i.e., saying them all at once]. Why then does scripture say, "I am the Lord am your God. . . . You shall have no [other gods beside Me] etc." [i.e., spelling out each commandment]? This is to teach us that, although God uttered the Ten Commandments all at once, He went back and explained each one separately. One might think the other commandments in the Torah were likewise uttered all at once. Hence scripture says, "all these words"—meaning, these words, [the Ten Commandments,] were uttered all at once, but the other [603] commandments were uttered one at a time.

"Saying"—the people saying yes to the positive commandments and no to the negative ones, according to Rabbi Yishma'el. According to Rabbi 'Akiva, they said yes to both the positive and the negative commandments.

Another interpretation of "saying": "Go tell them these things and bring Me their reaction." How do we know Moses brought the people's response back to the All-Powerful? From the verse, "Moses brought back the people's words to the Lord" (Exod. 19:8). What then was their response? "All that the Lord has spoken we will do and we will hear" (Exod. 24:7). And how do we know the Omnipresent approved of their response? From the verse, "The Lord said to me, ['I have heard the plea that this people made to you;] they did well to speak thus' " (Deut. 5:25). —MEKHILTA

"God spoke all these words, saying"—"Saying" teaches us that they answered yes to the positive commandments and no to the negative ones. In other words, we are not to understand [the seemingly redundant word] "saying" as "saying to Israel," for [we already know that] He was speaking to Israel. (We heard "I the Lord am your God. . . . You shall have no [other gods beside Me]" directly from the All-Powerful.) Nor should we understand "saying" as "telling them the Oral Torah," for this was told to Moses, not to Israel. Rather, we must interpret the word as meaning that Israel answered the Holy One, blessed be He, yes to the positive commandments and no to the negative ones. —'AMAR NEKE

*See note, p. 103.

ALL THESE WORDS

"God spoke all these words, saying"—He said to them, "I shall pass judgment as between you and these words. Had you not taken it upon yourselves to uphold them, I would not punish you for violating them." He who assumes an obligation is not like a person who refuses one. Rabbi Yehudah Hanasi made the following analogy: A man marries a prominent woman, and people then say to her, "Now that you have given your hand to him, you will have to card his wool." [God says,] "So it is with you, O Israel. Now that you have drawn close to Me and are indentured to Me, you must be prepared to do My bidding."

Another interpretation of "God spoke [all these words]": It teaches us that the words spoken here [in Exodus] have the same import as those spoken later [in Deuteronomy, where the Ten Commandments are repeated]; both deal with the same matters, things that the mortal tongue cannot say nor the mortal ear hear. Here it says, "God spoke all these words," and further on it says, "One thing God has spoken; two things have I heard" (Ps. 62:12). It also says, "Behold, my word is like fire—declares the Lord—[and like a hammer that shatters rock!]" (Jer. 23:29)—Just as fire scatters in the form of many sparks, so does one Divine utterance yield many scriptural texts.

Another interpretation of "God spoke [all these words]": [God was saying, "I hereby serve notice that] I will exact punishment and provide reward in the following ways." Similarly, scripture says [by way of introducing the second listing of the Ten Commandments], "Face to face the Lord spoke to you" (Deut. 5:4), [i.e., very clearly].

Another interpretation of "God spoke [all these words]": It teaches us that He spoke of first things first and last things last.

Another interpretation of "God spoke all these words": One might have thought they would be expected to give their consent only after the last of the Ten Commandments was uttered. Therefore, scripture says, "I the Lord am your God" [as a distinct commandment]: though implied in a general law, it is also specified.* Just as this commandment, [though part of the single, simultaneous utterance of the Ten Commandments,] was given separately and had to be accepted separately, each of the other Ten Commandments was given separately and had to be accepted separately. Why is the word "saying" added? To indicate that He asked them concerning each of the commandments separately whether they would say yes (in the case of the positive commandments)

---

*Thereby shedding light on all other provisions of the general law, according to the Thirteen Principles of talmudic reasoning.

or no (in the case of the negative ones). —MEKHILTA DE-RABBI SHIM'ON BAR YOHAI

AN EXPLANATION

"I shall pass judgment as between you [and these words]"—the name *Elohim* (God) [in Exod. 20:1] indicates the Divine Attribute of Judgment.

"You will have to card his wool"—do his chores.

"It is only right"—fitting and proper under the circumstances.

"This teaches us that He spoke of first things first and last things last"— that He pronounced the commandments in order, [one at a time] and not two at once.

"Those spoken later"—in Deuteronomy.

"Here it says, 'God *(Elohim)* spoke all these words,' and further on it says, 'One thing God *(Elohim)* has spoken; two things have I heard.' It also says, 'Behold, my word is like fire—declares the Lord—[and like a hammer that shatters rock!]' "—The name [*Elohim*], which refers to the Divine Attribute of Judgment, implies reward and punishment. When He was showing them the punishment of the wicked, He would do so with an angry countenance; when He was showing them the reward of the righteous, He would do so with a cheerful countenance.

" 'I the Lord am your God,' though . . . implied in a general law, . . . is also specified."—The commandment "I the Lord am your God," which [obliges us to recognize] God's existence, is an integral part of the larger body of the commandments, for unless one believes in the existence of God, none of the rest will be considered commandments at all.

"Just as this commandment was given separately. . . . "—First one must accept God's divinity and only then the rest of the commandments. —RABBI DAVID ZVI HOFFMANN

"All these words, saying"—He does everything simultaneously: causes to die and brings to life; wounds and heals. He heeds all at once the cries of women giving birth, sailors, wayfarers in the desert, and prisoners, east, west, north, and south. Thus scripture says, "I form light and create darkness, [I make weal and create woe—I the Lord do all these things]" (Isa. 45:7). Man is formed from dust, then returns to dust, as it is written, "[He] who turns deep darkness into dawn [and darkens day into night, . . . His name is the Lord!]" (Amos 5:8). What is meant here by "dawn"? The way it was at first. At first, it is said, "All the water in the Nile was turned into blood" (Exod. 7:20); then the blood was turned back into water. Living flesh turns to dead flesh, dead flesh to living. The staff is turned into a serpent, then back into a staff again. The sea becomes dry land, then the dry land turns to sea, as it is written, "[He] who summons the waters of the sea [and pours them out upon the earth—His name is the Lord!]" (Amos 5:8). There is the commandment, "Remember the sabbath day and keep it holy [by performing no work]" (Exod. 20:8), but also, "On the sabbath day [you shall bring as sacrifice] two yearling lambs" (Num. 28:9). There is the commandment, "Do not uncover the nakedness of your brother's wife" (Lev. 18:16), but also, "When brothers dwell together [and one of them dies and leaves no son, the wife of the deceased shall not be married to a stranger . . . Her husband's brother shall unite with her]" (Deut. 25:5). All these commandments God uttered at once. Hence, "God spoke all these words, saying."

Observe how the attributes of the Holy One, blessed be He, differ from those of mortals. A mortal king cannot simultaneously wage war and be a scribe and teach little children, but the Holy One, blessed be He, can. Yesterday He was waging war, as it is written, "The Lord, the Warrior—[Lord is His name!]" (Exod. 15:3), and it is written, "By His power He stilled the sea" (Job 26:12). Today, at the Giving of the Torah, He came down to teach Torah to His children, as it is written, "See, God is beyond reach in His power; who instructs like Him?" (Job 36:22). Hence, "God spoke all these words, saying."
—EXODUS RABBAH 28

EVERYTHING THE PROPHETS WERE TO PROPHESY

"God spoke all these words, saying"—Rabbi Yizhak said: Everything the prophets throughout the generations were to prophesy they received at Mount Sinai. Thus Moses tells Israel, "[I make this covenant] . . . both with those who are standing here with us this day . . . and with those who are not with us here this day" (Deut. 29:14). It does not say "[not] standing with us here this day," only "[not] *with us* here this day," referring to the souls yet to be created [as physical beings], which had no substance and thus could not have been said to stand: even though at that time they did not yet have [physical] existence, nevertheless each of them received his portion [of the revelation].

Thus scripture says, "A pronouncement: The word of the Lord to Israel in the hands of Malachi" (Mal. 1:1); and it does not say "in the days *(bimei)* of Malachi" but "in the hands of *(bidei)* Malachi," for he had had the prophecy in his hands ever since Sinai but had not been allowed to proclaim it. Similarly, Isaiah says, "[From the beginning I did not speak in secret;] From the time anything existed, I was there" (Isa. 48:16), meaning, I was there on the day the Torah was given at Sinai, and there I received this prophecy, but only "now the Lord God has sent me, endowed with His spirit" (Isa. 48:16)—only now was [I] allowed to prophesy.

And it was not only that the prophets received their prophecy at Sinai; the sages, too, who were to arise in every generation all received their [teachings] there. Thus scripture says, "The Lord spoke those words—those and no more—to your whole congregation [at the mountain,] with a mighty voice" (Deut. 5:19).

Rabbi Yohanan said: One voice split into seven, and these in turn split into the seventy languages [of man]. Rabbi Shim'on ben Lakish said: [It was from the echoes of this voice] that all the prophets who were ever to arise derived their prophecy. But the Sages said: It had no echo [down through the ages but rather was heard by them all at Sinai].

Rabbi Shmu'el bar Nahmani said in the name of Rabbi Yohanan: What is meant by the verse, "The voice of the Lord is with power" (Ps. 29:4)? Could it have been [that He spoke with the full power of His voice]? Do we not know that no mortal can withstand the sound of the voice even of a single angel, as it is written, "[The angel's] body was like beryl . . . and the sound of his speech was like the noise of a multitude" (Dan. 10:6)? As for the Holy One, blessed be He, of whom it is written, "I fill both heaven and earth" (Jer. 23:24), did He really need to speak "with power"? What is meant by "The voice of the Lord is with power," rather, is that He spoke with the power of all [subsequent] voices. And Rabbi Yohanan's view is supported by the following verse: "The Lord gives a command; those who bring the news are a great host" (Ps. 68:12).
—EXODUS RABBAH 28:4

"But both with those who are standing here with us this day [before the Lord our God] and with those who are not with us here this day" (Deut. 29:14)— "Those who are standing here with us this day" refers to the souls who stood at Mount Sinai. "Those who are not with us here this day" refers to their bodies, which were yet to be created, created for those same souls.

"By the hand of Malachi" (Mal. 1:1)—Because he was the last of the prophets, scripture hints that [even] his prophecies had come to [his soul] at Mount Sinai but that he was not allowed to proclaim them until later. Until the proper time came, the prophets forgot [what they had heard at Sinai], and only then did their prophecy come back to them.

"[The Lord spoke those words]—those and no more—[to your whole congregation at the mountain,] with a mighty voice" (Deut. 5:19)—The Holy One, blessed be He, did not give any new prophecy to the prophets [in later times], only what He had already given them at Sinai.

"It had no echo"—the way a human voice does. Rather, because the Lord is pure oneness, His utterances, too, are pure sounds without reverberations. —YEFEH TO'AR

When a human being speaks, he can imagine [from the echo] that there is someone else, a second voice, calling out to him. [In this instance there was no echo] so that no one could claim there were two divinities, God forbid. —YEDEI MOSHE

Rabbi Shim'on ben Lakish said: What is meant by "those and no more"? When a person calls out to someone, his voice has an echo, but the voice of the Holy One, blessed be He, had none. Should you wonder at this, [recall that] Elijah, when he came to Mount Carmel, gathered all the pagan priests there and said to them, "Shout louder! After all, he is a god" (1 Kings 18:27). What did the Holy One, blessed be He, do? He silenced the whole world, both heaven and earth, and the world was utterly desolate, as though there were no living thing around, as it is written, "There was no sound, and none who responded or heeded" (1 Kings 18:29). For if anything had made a sound, they would have said, "Baal has answered us!" All the more so was the Holy One, blessed be He, concerned to silence the whole world when He spoke on Mount Sinai, so that all human beings would know that there was none beside Him. —EXODUS RABBAH 29 (end)

"The Lord gives a command; those who bring the news are a great host" (Ps. 68:12)—With one utterance and one voice, God proclaims and speaks to a great host, to many nations, each in its own tongue. —MATNOT KEHUNAH

"[One voice] split into seven"—The voice was not spent at Mount Sinai but carried to all corners of the world, in all the languages. —Maharzu, COMMENTARY

"God spoke all these words, saying"—As our Sages, may their memory be a blessing, said: When the Holy One, blessed be He, told Moses to "go down, and come back [together with Aaron]," it was so that Moses would not be on the mountain when He Himself, may He be blessed, pronounced the Ten Commandments. Thus "God spoke all these words" refers to what He said to

Moses: "Go down . . . "; and "saying" (lit., "to say") means, so that the Blessed One might say, "I the Lord. . . . "—that is, the Ten Commandments—alone, without Moses being there. —ZEKAN AHARON

"God spoke all these words, saying"—In *gematria,* this clause is the numerical equivalent of the phrase "all that is in the Oral and the Written [Torot]." —Ya'akov of Vienna, PA'NEAH RAZA: EXPLICATIONS OF THE PLAIN AND HIDDEN MEANING OF THE SCRIPTURES

"All these words, saying"—In *gematria,* the numerical equivalent of this phrase is 613.* —KETORET HASAMIM

Rabbi Shim'on said: It is written, "God spoke all these words. . . . "—"spoke" by way of proclaiming the commandments. For we have learned that when the Holy One, blessed be He, revealed Himself and began to speak, both heavenly and earthly creatures were shaken, and Israel fainted away. And we have learned that that [first] commandment flew up and down, borne aloft and back to earth by the four winds. As it ascended, it was filled with the pure [fragrance of the] persimmon mountains and with heavenly dew, which, bathing Israel, revived them. The commandment then etched itself into the tablets of stone, in its appointed place. The same thing happened with the other commandments.
    Rabbi Shim'on said: Each of the commandments was filled with explanations and decrees, rewards and punishments, secrets and mysteries, like a treasure trove that contains all things. When the commandment issued forth, it appeared to be one thing, but once it was engraved [in stone] there appeared to grow out of it seventy branches, with forty-nine crowns on each side, as though a hammer were striking the mountain, as it is written, "like a hammer that shatters rock!" (Jer. 23:29). All Israel saw this with their own eyes and rejoiced. And all subsequent generations were brought there, and all of them received the Torah at Mount Sinai, as it is written, "Both with those who are standing here with us this day . . . and with those who are not with us here this day" (Deut. 29:14). Each received it according to his capacity, and all of them saw and accepted the commandments. —ZOHAR 83b

"God spoke all these words"—You should know that these Ten Commandments encompass all the commandments in the Torah. Thus God intended to have Israel hear them [directly] and not through Moses, so that they would

---

*The number of the commandments in the Torah.

believe in them and not harbor any doubts about their being from the Lord, may He be exalted. —GERSONIDES

JUDGMENT AND MERCY

"God spoke all these words"—The reason the name God is used in connection with the Giving of the Torah is that the latter was done out of the Divine Attribute of Judgment as well as the Divine Attribute of Mercy. The Attribute of Judgment we see in the verse, "God spoke . . . "; the Attribute of Mercy we see in the verse, "I the Lord. . . . "* We learn further that the secret of the name *Lord* is the name *God,* for it was God who said "I the Lord." Thus we lovingly affirm His unity each day, eternally, with the words, "Hear, O Israel! The Lord our God, the Lord is one" (Deut. 6:4).

"All these words"—everything, implying that He is only pleased with one who takes upon himself the entire Torah, and he who takes on all except one commandment does not have the Torah at all. —OR HAHAYYIM

A gentile who presents himself as willing to take on the entire Torah except for one thing is rejected [for conversion]. —BEKHOROT 30b

"God spoke [all these words, saying]"—This is why it says, "Then He saw it and gauged it; He measured it and probed it" (Job 28:27), and only then, "He said to man" (Job 28:28). Scripture is here teaching you that if you wish to be a person of Torah you should not be so coarse as to teach something in public without having gone over the matter two or three times by yourself. Once Rabbi 'Akiva was called up in public by the cantor to read from the Torah, and he refused. His students asked him, "Master, did you not teach us that 'thereby you shall have life and shall long endure' (Deut. 30:20)? Why then did you not go up to read?" He replied, "I swear I only refrained from reading because I had not previously gone over that passage two or three times; for one may not speak words of Torah in public until he has first gone over their meaning two or three times by himself." Thus although it is the Holy One, blessed be He, who gives human beings the power of speech, and although the Torah is crystal clear to Him, we find that when He comes to give the Torah to Israel, it is written of Him that "He saw it and gauged it; He measured it and probed it" and only then that "He said to man." Likewise, it is written, "God spoke all these words"—to Himself, and only then—"saying." —TANHUMA, Yitro

*See note, p. 103.

Rabbi El'azar said: Although the Torah was given at Sinai, Israel did not become subject to punishment for violating it until it was interpreted for them at the Tent of Meeting. It is like an edict that is written, sealed, and delivered to a particular location [where it is to apply] but to which the local residents do not become subject until it is explained to them. Thus it was not until the Torah was interpreted for Israel at the Tent of Meeting that Israel became subject to punishment for violating it. This is the meaning of the verse, "[I would not let him go] till I brought him to my mother's house"—that is, Mount Sinai—"to the chamber of her who conceived me" (Song 3:4)—that is, the Tent of Meeting, where the Teaching first became incumbent upon Israel. —SONG OF SONGS RABBAH 2

THE COUNSEL OF THE LORD

"God spoke all these words, saying"—Rabbi Yehudah began his discussion of this passage with the verse, "Who can tell the mighty acts of the Lord, proclaim all His praises?" (Ps. 106:2). In how many ways does the Torah warn a person not to sin against his Master! In how many ways does it counsel him not to depart from His ways, neither to the right nor to the left! In how many ways does it advise him how to return to his Master! As we have learned, the Torah gives a person 613 kinds of advice [i.e., the commandments] about how to be at one with his Master. For his Master wishes to deal benevolently with him both in this world and in the next. Thus we have learned that whatever benevolence a person merits receiving from the Holy One, blessed be He, he only receives it fully in the World to Come. Why? Because the World to Come belongs to the Holy One, blessed be He. —ZOHAR, Exodus 82b

"God spoke all these words, saying"—It is also written, "God said, 'Let there be light' " (Gen. 1:3). This teaches us that the day of the Giving of the Torah was like the day the world was created, for the world, too, was created by a mere utterance, as it is written, "By the word of the Lord [the heavens were made]" (Ps. 33:6). —MIDRASH ḤADASH, cited in TORAH SHLEMAH

CONCERNING EACH COMMANDMENT

Rabbi Yehoshu'a ben Levi said: What is meant by the verse, "His cheeks are like beds of spices" (Song 5:13)? Each utterance of the Holy One, blessed be He, filled the world with fragrance. And since the first utterance had already filled it, what happened with the second? The Holy One, blessed be He, took the wind from His storehouses and with it caused the fragrance of each utterance in turn to be wafted away, as it is written, "His lips are like lilies; they drip flowing myrrh" (Song 5:13). Read it not as "lilies" *(shoshanim)"* but "those who study" *(sheshonim).*

Rabbi Yehoshu'a ben Levi also said: With each utterance of the Holy One, blessed be He, Israel fainted away, as it is written, "I was faint because of what he said" (Song 5:6). But if they had fainted from His first utterance, how could they receive the second? He rained down dew, that which one day will resurrect the dead, and revived them, as it is written, "You released a bountiful rain, O God; when Your own land languished, You sustained it" (Ps. 68:10).

Rabbi Yehoshu'a ben Levi said further: With each utterance of the Holy One, blessed be He, Israel recoiled twelve miles,* but the ministering angels led them back, as it is written, "The angels† of the hosts are in headlong flight" (Ps. 68:13). Read it not as *yidodun* (are in headlong flight) but as *yedaddun* (lead them). —SHABBAT 88b

Our Sages, may their memory be a blessing, said: When Israel heard the words "I [the Lord. . . .]" and "You shall have [no other gods. . . .]," they recoiled twelve miles, but the ministering angels brought them back, as it is written, "The angels of the hosts lead them" (Ps. 68:13). Our teacher Rabbi Yizhak the Bachelor raised the following difficulty: What this verse actually says is "kings" *(malkhei),* not "angels" *(mal'akhei)!* How then can they say that angels led them? The explanation, according to the Midrash, is that Michael and Gabriel were "kings of the angels" *(malkhei hamal'akhim)*—that is, the greatest and most important of the angels—and it was they who brought Israel back. —PA'NEAḤ RAZA, Yitro

"With every utterance Israel recoiled twelve miles"—But was the Torah not given on the sabbath, and if so, how could they have walked beyond the sabbath boundary [the limit placed on how far one may walk on the sabbath]? Some say the cloud carried them, and some say they were surrounded by clouds, so that it was as if they remained in a closed residential courtyard [where any amount of walking would be permitted]. —LEKET YOSEF; MAHARAN, Beiurim; PA'NEAḤ RAZA

*See note, p. 24.
†Reading *mal'akhei* (angels) instead of *malkhei* (kings).

"O God, when You went at the head of Your army" (Ps. 68:8)—as it is written, "The Lord went before them [in a pillar of cloud] by day" (Exod. 13:21). "When You marched through the desert, *selah*" (Ps. 68:8)—on the day of the Giving of the Torah. —MIDRASH ON PSALMS

THE TIME OF THE GIVING OF THE TORAH

The day of the Giving of the Torah was the fiftieth day after the Exodus from Egypt. Thus it is written, "[Who is she that comes up from the desert, leaning upon her beloved?] Under the apple tree I roused you" (Song 8:5); and it is written, "Like an apple tree among trees of the forest, [so is my beloved among the youths]" (Song 2:3)—Just as an apple tree bears fruit fifty days after it flowers, so the Torah was given fifty days after the redemption of Israel. Furthermore, the Torah was given after seven generations—Abraham, Isaac, Jacob, Levi, Kehath, Amram, and Moses—seven weeks after their redemption, on the holy seventh day, "on which God ceased from all the work [of creation which He had done]" (Gen. 2:3). —MIDRASH LEKAH TOV, Yitro

The year of the Exodus from Egypt came 2,448 years after the creation of humankind—that is, during the 2,449th year since the creation of humankind, which was the 2,450th year since the creation of the world.* According to the Sages, it took place on the sixth day of Sivan, but Rabbi Yose [in Yoma 4a–b] holds that it was on the seventh. All agree, however, that it was on a sabbath, and that the [Ten Commandments] were given in the morning and the laws [that follow in Exodus 21–23] in the evening. —Rabbi Avraham Aryeh 'Akaviah, SIDREI HAZEMANIM

They journeyed from Rephidim and came to the Wilderness of Sinai and found it covered with clouds of glory. Each day for five days, Moses would go up to the top of the mountain and come down again and tell them what the Omnipresent had said, then go back up bearing their reply to the Omnipresent. In the third month, on the sixth of the month, they were given the Ten Commandments, and it was on the sabbath. —SEDER 'OLAM 5

*According to one view, in Leviticus Rabbah 29:1, humankind was created on the New Year, so that Creation, which began five days earlier, dates to the previous year.

"Go up . . . come down . . . tell"—That is, he would come down immediately; he went up at daybreak and came down at daybreak.

"The sixth of the month"—This is from a *baraita,* not according to Rabbi Yose but according to the Sages. —BEI'UR VEHAGAHOT HAGRA

The sixth of Sivan is the festival of Shavu'ot (Weeks), as it is written, "On the day of the first fruits, your Feast of Weeks, when you bring an offering of new grain to the Lord, you shall observe a sacred occasion" (Num. 28:26); and it is written, "From the day after the sabbath, the day that you bring the sheaf of wave offering, you shall keep count [until] seven full weeks have elapsed: you shall count fifty days, until the day after the seventh week; then you shall bring an offering of new grain to the Lord" (Lev. 23:16). Having begun the Counting [of the 'Omer]* on the sixteenth of Nisan, one reaches the end of seven weeks, or forty-nine days, on the fifth of Sivan, so that the sixth of Sivan is the fiftieth day, and it is this day that was designated as Shavu'ot.

A midrash aggadah asks: Why was it that scripture made the festival of Shavu'ot, unlike all the other holy days, dependent on the Counting of the 'Omer? Because when it was proclaimed that Israel would leave Egypt, it was also proclaimed that they would receive the Torah on the fiftieth day after their departure. For it is written, "When you have freed the people from Egypt, you shall worship *(ta'avdun)* God at this mountain" (Exod. 3:12), and the letter *nun* in *ta'avdun,* the numerical value of which is fifty, is [apparently] superfluous; [it is there] to indicate that it is at the end of fifty days that you are to worship God by accepting the Torah. Out of love, Israel began counting the days, saying: "The first day has passed," "The second day has passed," etc. So great was their devotion in this matter that the time seemed to pass slowly. Thus the Counting became established as a practice throughout the generations.

I have also found it written in the *Ta'amim* of Rabbi Yehudah Hehasid, may the memory of the righteous be a blessing, that because the days of the Counting are days of work in the fields and there is no one there to inform people as to whether the month of Iyar [which precedes Sivan] has twenty-nine or thirty days† [in a given year], scripture tells us to count fifty days and then "you shall observe a sacred occasion." —SHIBBOLEI HALEKET

*The ritual marking of the days between the second day of Passover and Shavu'ot.
†The months of the Jewish calendar have either twenty-nine or thirty days.

The Exodus from Egypt is mentioned fifty times in the Torah. Fifty days passed [from then] until the receiving of the Torah. Slaves are freed after fifty years. —ZOHAR, Exodus 85b

"Fifty days passed until the receiving of the Torah"—from Passover to Shavu'ot.

Our Rabbis said that "On the third day" (Exod. 19:16) refers to the sixth of Sivan, and that it was a sabbath day [see Shabbat 86b ff.]. But the scriptural texts themselves do not prove this [directly]. What they show is that, since the twenty-second [of Iyar, the preceding month] was a sabbath (as we have written in connection with the manna), the thirtieth of Iyar would have been a Sunday. And since Iyar did have thirty days that year,* we must conclude that the first of Sivan fell on a Monday, and the sixth, when the Torah was given to Israel, was a Sabbath. —Rabbi Meyuḥas ben Eliyahu, COMMENTARY

"On the day of the first fruits, [your Feast of Weeks,] . . . you shall present a burnt offering *('olah)* [. . . to the Lord]" (Num. 28:26–27)—Each time the Torah speaks of an *'olah* in connection with one of the festivals, the vowel-letter *vav* is omitted, except here in the case of the Shavu'ot burnt offering, where the letter appears. This is a hint that it was on the sixth of Sivan [six being the numerical value of the letter] that the Torah was given. —BA'AL HATURIM

THE DAY OF THE GIVING OF THE TORAH

The day of the Giving of the Torah was a cloudy day, with thunder—like ordinary thunder—and lightning and some rain. This is what is meant by the verse, "The earth trembled; the heavens dripped, yea the clouds dripped water" (Judg. 5:4). First came the clouds, then the lightning, then the thunder. The last mentioned in the scripture came first; for normally one sees lightning before hearing thunder. The fact that scripture seems to reverse the order can be explained, in my view, as a way of exalting the sound of the ram's horn. Had the events been mentioned in the order in which they occurred, the sounding of the ram's horn would have come right after the mention of the thunder, and it would have seemed as though they were

*Since, according to tradition, the manna began to fall on the sixteenth of Iyar and fell for two full weeks until the end of Iyar, the month must have had thirty days that year.

equivalent or at least close in magnitude. Thus scripture mentions the thunder earlier, to separate it from the sounding of the ram's horn and to make clear that they were very far apart, as far apart as physical and mental things are. —Rabbenu Bahya, Vayishma' Yitro

The day of the Giving of the Torah was called the festival of Shavu'ot. Aside from the simple explanation for this [viz., that the festival marks the enumeration of "weeks," shavu'ot], the name also alludes to the matter of the verse, "An oath (shevu'at) before the Lord shall decide between the two of them" (Exod. 22:10)—that is, between the blessed Lord and the people of Israel. He is our God, and we are His people, sworn since Sinai to serve Him alone. Even if all the nations of the world were to seek, God forbid, to drive us from our faith in the Blessed One, we would prove the most resilient of peoples. For "strong as death" (Song 8:6) is our love for the blessed Lord and the love of the Blessed One for His people Israel.

The Giving of the Torah was like a nuptial ceremony, where bride and groom swear that their love will last forever, unless "he finds something obnoxious about her, and he writes her a bill of divorcement" (Deut. 24:1). And concerning the people of Israel it is written, "[Thus said the Lord:] Where is the bill of divorce of your mother . . . ?" (Isa. 50:1). At the time of the Giving of the Torah He held the mountain over us like a barrel,* putting us in the position of one who is [sexually] forced; and concerning a woman who has been forced it is written, "He can never have the right to divorce her" (Deut. 22:29). Thus, "the Lord will not forsake His people; He will not abandon His very own" (Ps. 94:14). The Lord will yet return and have mercy on Zion; "He shall gather in the exiles of Israel" (Ps. 147:2) and "renew our days as of old" (Lam. 5:21), with doubled and redoubled portions of good. —MAHAZEH AVRAHAM

Why does the Torah not tell us the reason for the festival of Shavu'ot, as it does for the other festivals? (In the liturgy of the day, it is referred to as "the Occasion of the Giving of our Torah.") A likely explanation is that the Lord said to Himself, "If I tell them, 'In the third month, on the sixth day of the month, I gave you the Torah; it shall be festival to the Lord,' they will say, 'How can we rejoice and celebrate the Lord's festival? "While the king was on his couch, [my nard gave forth its fragrance]" (Song 1:12)—[i.e., while God was still on

*See note, p. 114.

Mount Sinai, a bad odor had issued forth from below:] our rejoicing had been turned to mourning by the sin of the Golden Calf, and all the punishments we receive [at God's hand] are due in part to that sin.' "

Hence, the Torah does not refer to it as the Day of the Giving of the Torah but says, rather, "On that same day *(be'ezem hayom hazeh)* you shall hold a celebration; it shall be a sacred occasion [for you]" (Lev. 23:21)—the day has substance *('ezem)* and will last forever. This is as our Rabbis, may their memory be a blessing, said concerning the verse, "There was evening and there was morning, the sixth day" (Gen. 1:31): Why "*the* sixth day" [when in regard to the other days it says "a"]? To tell us that all of creation depends on the sixth day, on which the Torah was given. This day endures forever, just as all days on which we carry out the commandments endure forever. It is fitting, then, that this day should have been made into a festival. And if you did not rejoice on the day when the Giving of the Torah was concluded [but sinned instead], it was not "the Lord's doing" (Ps. 118:23), for the Lord had done much to prepare you, so that you would not sin. —ALSHEKH

Shavu'ot is called the Occasion of the Giving of the Torah and not the Occasion of the Receiving of the Torah, for the receiving of it was also a gift from heaven, as it is written, "For I give you good instruction (lit., taking)" (Prov. 4:2). And the Holy One, blessed be He, tells us, "Do not forsake My Torah" (Prov. 4:2)—one must be aware that it is His Torah. —SIAH SARFEI KODESH, quoting Rabbi Yizhak Meir of Gur

Why is it called the Occasion of the Giving of Our Torah and not the Occasion of the Receiving of Our Torah? Said Rabbi Menahem of Kotzk, in the name of Rabbi Simhah Bunem of Przysucha: The Giving of the Torah took place in the month of Sivan, but the receiving of the Torah takes place every day. Rabbi Menahem of Kotzk said further: the Giving of the Torah was the same for everyone, but the receiving is different for each person according to his ability to understand. —EMET VE'EMUNAH

In the Great Hallel [Ps. 136, incorporated into the liturgy], we do not praise God for the Giving of the Torah, because "the commandments were not given for pleasure" ('Eruvin 31a), but rather, as Rashi, may his memory be a blessing, explains, they were given as a yoke, and we only give thanks for that which gives us pleasure. And while there may be pleasure and joy in the fulfillment of a commandment, the pleasure and the joy are themselves commanded. —HIDDUSHEI HARIM; GUR ARYEH

One Shavu'ot I was visiting the sainted Rabbi of Lęczna. At the evening meal the rabbi began his talk by saying, in the name of Rabbi [Ya'akov Yizhak of Przysucha, known as the Holy] Jew, that one does not speak of Torah on the night of Shavu'ot, for etiquette preceded the Torah, and since the Torah was only received on the following day it is not good etiquette to speak of it as yet. "What then do we do on the night of Shavu'ot?" the Rabbi of Lęczna concluded by asking. "We prepare ourselves to receive the Torah, in fear and dread and trembling." As he was speaking, he himself was seized with fear and trembling, and his whole body began to shake, until his bones began to knock together. He took hold of the table, but it did not help. Those gathered around grew afraid; they picked him up and carried him from the table to his room, where they stretched him out on his bed. He lay there until he recovered from his fear, then returned and sat down at the table. Sitting, as I was, right next to him, I saw all this with my own eyes. —Rabbi Shmuel of Sieniawa, RAMATAYIM ZOFIM

BY VIRTUE OF THE GIVING OF THE TORAH

The sage, author of *Kol Aryeh,* made it his custom to visit his master in Sanz each year at Shavu'ot. Early one Shavu'ot morning, he entered the synagogue and took out a volume of Talmud to study. A rich man came in and, seeing him studying, began to dance and sing with great joy. The sage asked him, "Why so joyful?" He replied, "I was thinking about myself, about the sort of state I would be in today had the Holy One, blessed be He, not given us the Torah. You, sir, being so intelligent, would probably have been appointed a governor or cabinet minister or the like, but I, a simple man, what would I have amounted to? Probably a farmer or a woodchopper. But seeing that I am a Jew, how can I not rejoice?" When the sage heard this, he closed his book, stood up, took the man's hand, and began to dance with him. As the worshipers came in, one by one, and saw the prince of Torah and the millionaire rejoicing together in the joy of the Torah, they too began to dance, until the whole synagogue was filled with dancing. Nor did they leave off dancing until the Sanzer Rebbe arrived. "Why are you dancing?" he asked them, and they told him. He nodded and said, "Fine, fine." —TOLDOT KOL ARYEH

"Shavu'ot is the day on which the Torah was given" (Pesahim 68b). Israel should rejoice on that day, for [on it] the Holy One, blessed be He, forgives their sins. In the Palestinian Talmud, at the end of Tractate Rosh Hashanah, it is written: Rabbi Mesharshia said in the name of Rabbi Aha: The sin offering is mentioned in connection with all the sacrifices except that of Shavu'ot. [In effect,] the Holy One, blessed be He, was saying to Israel, "Since you took upon yourselves the yoke of the Torah [on this day] I shall consider it as though you had never sinned in your lives," [and therefore no sin offering is needed on this day].

Thus, in the description of the festival observances in Parashat Emor (Lev. 23) there is no mention of [an offering by fire of] a pleasing aroma except in the case of the 'Omer festival and Shavu'ot. In the case of the 'Omer, which marks the barley [harvest], I might think barley was not acceptable for the making of a pleasing aroma; hence the phrase must be mentioned explicitly. In the case of Shavu'ot, [the idea is that] he who makes do with "meager bread and scant water" (Isa. 30:20) in order to study Torah and fulfill the commandments produces an aroma more pleasing [to God] than that of myrrh and frankincense. —HAROKEAH

Mar, the son of Ravina, used to fast on any day of the year except for Shavu'ot, Purim, and the eve of the Day of Atonement. Shavu'ot is the day the Torah was given, [and so Israel must rejoice then]. . . .

On the day of Shavu'ot, Rav Yosef would order a three-year-old [i.e., particularly choice] calf prepared, saying, were it not for this day [on which the Torah, the source of my calling, was given], I would be just another Yosef. —PESAHIM 68b

"Were it not for this day"—because of which I learned Torah and thus came to be elevated. After all, there are many people named Yosef; what would there have been to distinguish me from them? —RASHI

I once heard a woman in Medzibezh say in Russian, "We made the right choice in choosing our God, even as the blessed Lord made the right choice in choosing Israel. It is no surprise that the blessed Lord chose us, for He has all wisdom and knowledge and knew Israel's superiority over the other nations. But it took special wisdom and talent for Israel to know the virtues of the blessed Lord and His Torah. —TOLDOT YA'AKOV YOSEF

THE TEN COMMANDMENTS

IN WHAT FORM WERE THE TEN COMMANDMENTS GIVEN?

In what form were the Ten Commandments given? [In effect,] the Lord's name was on each tablet: "I the Lord am your God" on the one, "You shall not murder" on the other. Thus scripture teaches us that whoever spills blood is considered to have diminished the image of the King. It can be compared to a mortal king who assumed control of a new province and had portraits painted, statues built, and coins minted [bearing his image]. Later, his portraits were ripped down, his statues smashed, and his coins defaced. The image of the king was thus diminished. In the same way, whoever spills human blood is considered to have diminished the image of the King, as it is written, "Whoever sheds the blood of man, [by man shall his blood be shed; for in the image of God was man created]" (Gen. 9:6).

[On one tablet] was written, "You shall have no [other gods beside Me]" (Exod. 20:3), while opposite it [on the other] was written, "You shall not commit adultery" (Exod. 20:13). Scripture thus teaches us that whoever worships false gods is regarded as having committed adultery against the Omnipresent. For it is written, "[You were like] the adulterous wife who welcomes strangers instead of her husband" (Ezek. 16:32); and it is also written, "The Lord said to me further, 'Go, befriend a woman who, while befriended by a companion, consorts with others, [just as the Lord befriends the Israelites, but they turn to other gods and love the cups of the grape]' " (Hos. 3:1).

[On one tablet] was written, "You shall not swear falsely by the name of the Lord your God" (Exod. 20:7), while opposite it [on the other] was written, "You shall not steal" (Exod. 20:13). This teaches us that whoever steals will end up swearing falsely as well. For it is written, "Will you steal and murder and commit adultery [and swear falsely]?" (Jer. 7:9); and it is written, "[False] swearing, dishonesty, and murder, and theft and adultery [are rife; crime follows upon crime!]" (Hos. 4:2).

[On one tablet] was written, "Remember the sabbath day and keep it holy" (Exod. 20:8), while opposite it [on the other] was written, "You shall not bear [false witness against your neighbor]" (Exod. 20:13). Scripture thus teaches us that whoever violates the sabbath is testifying that He-Who-Spoke-and-the-World-Came-Into-Being did not, in fact, create His world in six days or rest on the seventh, while whoever observes the sabbath is testifying that He-Who-Spoke-and-the-World-Came-Into-Being did create His world in six days and did rest on the seventh. For it is written, "You are My witnesses—declares the Lord" (Isa. 43:10).

[On one tablet] was written, "Honor your father and your mother" (Exod. 20:12), while opposite it [on the other] was written, "You shall not covet" (Exod. 20:14). Scripture thus teaches us that whoever covets ends up begetting a child who curses his own father and mother and honors one who is not his father. —MEKHILTA

It might have been thought that one would not be held culpable until he had violated all of the commandments. This is why the Torah [presents each commandment as a distinct sentence]: "You shall not murder. You shall not commit adultery. You shall not steal. You shall not bear [false witness against your neighbor.] You shall not covet. . . ." (Exod. 20:13–14)—indicating that one is culpable for violating each of the commandments. Why then does it [present them all in one sentence] further on: "You shall not murder, and you shall not commit adultery, and you shall not steal, and you shall not bear [false witness], and you shall not covet. . . ." (Deut. 5:17–18)? This is to teach us that they are all interconnected; if a person violates one of them, he will end up violating them all.

How do we know that if one commits murder he will end up commiting adultery as well? Because it is written, "My son, if sinners entice you, do not yield; if they say, 'Come with us, let us set an ambush to shed blood, let us lie in wait for the innocent (without cause!).' . . . Throw in your lot with us; we shall all have a common purse" (Prov. 1:10, 14). And how do we know that if one commits adultery he will end up stealing? Because it is written, "When you see a thief, you fall in with him, and throw in your lot with adulterers" (Ps. 50:18). How do we know that if one steals he will end up swearing falsely? Because it is written, "He who shares with a thief is his own enemy; he hears the imprecation and does not tell" (Prov. 29:24). —MEKHILTA DE-RABBI SHIM'ON BAR YOHAI

For this reason the Ten Commandments were arranged five on one tablet and five on the other, according to Rabbi Ḥanina ben Gamliel. But the Sages say: All ten were on one tablet and all ten on the other, as it is written, "The Lord spoke those words. . . . He inscribed them on two tablets of stone" (Deut. 5:19); and it is written, "Your breasts are like two fawns, twins of a gazelle" (Song 4:5); and it is written, "His hands* are rods of gold, studded with beryl" (Song 5:14). —MEKHILTA

Our Rabbis, may their memory be blessing, had a tradition that five of the Ten Commandments were on one tablet and five on the other. It was to this that Solomon was referring in the verse, "His hands are rods of gold" (Song 5:14). Five of them deal with the honor of the Lord and five with the honor of our fellow human beings, which is juxtaposed with the honor of the Lord. —YEHO-SHU'A IBN SHUAIB, Homilies

The first five of the Ten Commandments are spiritual in nature, while the last five are, as it were, material. That is why they are joined together, like body and soul, soul and body. That is also why it is said they are juxtaposed to one another. —ZEROR HAMOR

ONE CORRESPONDING TO THE OTHER

The Ten Commandments correspond to the Ten Utterances by which the world was created.

"I the Lord [am your God]" corresponds to "God said, 'Let there be light' " (Gen. 1:3), according to the verse, "For the Lord shall be your light everlasting" (Isa. 60:19).

"You shall have no [other gods]" corresponds to "God said, 'Let there be an expanse [in the midst of the water,] that it may separate water from water' " (Gen. 1:6). Said the Holy One, blessed be He, "You shall distinguish between [serving] Me and the worship of idols, which are called stagnant water, as in the verse, '[For My people . . .] have forsaken Me, the Fount of living waters, and hewed them out cisterns, broken cisterns' " (Jer. 2:6).

"You shall not [swear falsely]" corresponds to "God said, 'Let the water below the sky be gathered [into one area, that the dry land may appear']" (Gen. 1:9). Said the Holy One, blessed be He, "The water honored Me by making way, but you do not honor Me, for you swear falsely by My name."

"Remember [the sabbath day]" corresponds to "God said, 'Let the earth sprout [vegetation]' " (Gen. 1:11). Said the Holy One, blessed be He, "You

*Two hands, each having five fingers. Another possible connection: the word *yad* (hand) can also be read as *yod,* the letter of the alphabet with the numerical value of ten.

must appreciate what you eat on the Sabbath, for the world was created on the assumption that you would not sin but rather live forever and enjoy the fruits of the land."

"Honor [your father and your mother]" corresponds to "God said, 'Let there be lights in the expanse of the sky' " (Gen. 1:14). Said the Holy One, blessed be He, "See, I have created two lights for you, your father and your mother; honor them scrupulously."

"You shall not murder" corresponds to "God said, 'Let the waters bring forth swarms [of living creatures]' " (Gen. 1:20). Said the Holy One, blessed be He, "Be not like the fish, of which the large ones swallow the small ones, as it is written, 'You have made mankind like the fish of the sea, [like creeping things that have no ruler]' " (Hab. 1:14).

"You shall not commit adultery" corresponds to "God said, 'Let the earth bring forth [every kind of living creature]' " (Gen. 1:24). Said the Holy One, blessed be He, "See, I have created a mate for you. Each of you must cleave to your mate."

"You shall not steal" corresponds to "God said, 'See, I give you every seed-bearing plant' " (Gen. 1:29). Said the Holy One, blessed be He, "None of you may stretch forth your hand to steal another's money but only to take what is free for the taking, like these plants." Rabbi Hiyya taught: Whatever is tended in a garden may not be taken, for that would be theft; but whatever in a garden remains untended may be taken without violating the prohibition against theft.

"You shall not bear [false witness]" corresponds to "God said, 'I will make man in My image, after My likeness' " (Gen. 1:26). Said the Holy One, blessed be He, "See, I have made your fellow human beings in My image [as well]; do not bear false witness against them."

"You shall not covet" corresponds to "God said, 'It is not good for man to be alone; [I will make a fitting helper for him']" (Gen. 2:18). Said the Holy One, blessed be He, "See, I have made a mate for you; let each of you cleave to your own mate and not covet your neighbor's." —PESIKTA RABBATI

The Ten Commandments correspond to ten utterances with which the Holy One, blessed be He, blessed Adam: "Be fertile and increase, fill the earth and master it; and rule the fish of the sea, the birds of the sky, and all the living things that creep on earth. . . . See, I give you every seed-bearing plant that is upon all the earth, and every tree that has seed-bearing fruit; [they shall be yours for food]" (Gen. 1:28–29).

Correspondingly, Abraham endured ten trials. Correspondingly, there are ten references to the covenant in the passage describing [Abraham's] circumcision (Gen. 17:1–14]. Correspondingly, Isaac gave Jacob ten benedictions: "May God give you of the dew of heaven and the fat of the earth, abundance of new grain and wine. Let peoples serve you, and nations bow to you; be master over your brothers, and let your mother's sons bow to you. Cursed be they who curse you, blessed they who bless you" (Gen. 27:28–29). Correspondingly, the Egyptians were struck with ten plagues. Correspondingly, ten animals are mentioned as permitted to be eaten: the ox, the sheep, the goat, the gazelle, the deer, the roebuck, the ibex, the antelope, the buffalo, and the mountain goat. —MIDRASH TADSHE

The Ten Commandments correspond to the Ten Plagues the Holy One, blessed be He, visited on the Egyptians in Egypt.

"I [the Lord am your God]" corresponds to the plague of the blood: "He turned their rivers into blood." Do not say, as Pharaoh did, "My Nile is my own; I made it for myself" (Ezek. 29:3)—do not say, I created myself.

"You shall have no [other gods beside Me]" corresponds to the plague of the frogs, which leaped up [even] into the hot ovens. Said the Holy One, blessed be He, "The frogs honored Me [by sacrificing their lives to do My bidding], but you do not."

"You shall not swear [falsely]" corresponds to the plague of the lice, whom the Holy One, blessed be He, adjured to swarm forth.

"Remember [the sabbath day]" corresponds to the plague of the swarms of insects *('arov)*. Said the Holy One, blessed be He, "Do not mix *(ta'arov)* sabbath with weekday, regarding them as one."

"Honor [your father and your mother]" corresponds to the plague of the pestilence [which shortened their lives], as it is written, "that you may long endure."

"You shall not murder" corresponds to the plague of the boils. Said the Holy One, blessed be He, "Do not murder, for the blood of the victim shall be [visible] upon your body."*

"You shall not commit adultery" corresponds to the plague of the hail: "The hail was [very heavy]—fire flashing in the midst of the hail" (Exod. 9:24); and it is written, "Can a man rake embers into his bosom [without burning his clothes? . . .] It is the same with one who sleeps with his fellow's wife" (Prov. 6:27–29).

"You shall not steal" corresponds to the plague of the locusts. It is written, "They enter like thieves by way of the windows" (Joel 2:9).

*Apparently a reference to Cain, who, according to tradition, was marked by boils.

"You shall not bear [false witness]" corresponds to the plague of the darkness. Said the Holy One, blessed be He, "If your testimony is not clear as day to you, do not testify."

"You shall not covet. . . ." corresponds to the plague against the first-born, for the Egyptians wallowed in fornication, so that all of them were first-born.* —PESIKTA RABBATI

There are ten kinds of affliction, corresponding to the Ten Commandments. If Israel fulfills the commandments, the Holy One, blessed be He, will spare them the afflictions. Six of the afflictions affect a person's body and four a person's property. There is a kind of affliction that erupts from the bones "onto the skin" [Lev. 13:2ff.], a kind that has within it "quick raw flesh" [Lev. 13:10], a kind that erupts "from the scar of an inflammation" [Lev. 13:23], a kind that is caused by "a burn by fire" [Lev. 13:24], an affliction "on the head or on the beard" [Lev. 13:29], and an affliction of "the bald part in the front or at the back of the head" [Lev. 13:42]—six bodily afflictions in all.

Then there is an affliction that appears "in a cloth of wool or linen fabric" [Lev. 13:47], one that appears "in the warp or the woof [of woven cloth]" [Lev. 13:48], an affliction "in a skin or anything made of skin" [Lev. 13:48], and one that appears "in the walls of the house" [Lev. 14:37]—all together, four afflictions of property. —MIDRASH TADSHE

"[Solomon] made ten bronze lavers for washing" (2 Chron. 4:6)—in order to bring on more rain; for the lavers were filled with water. The ten lavers corresponded to the Ten Commandments. Why then had only one laver been made in the wilderness? Because in the wilderness Israel did not need rain, having wells and the manna that came down. Solomon made ten lavers in order to bring on more rain, for the land was settled and they needed a great deal of rain, as it is written, "[The land you are about to cross into and occupy,] a land of hills and valleys, [soaks up its water from the rains of heaven]" (Deut. 11:11).

"[Then he made ten bronze lavers . . .] each laver containing forty baths" (1 Kings 7:38)—corresponding to the forty days in which the Torah was given, one [laver] for each of the Ten Commandments. This is why Solomon made each laver four cubits [wide], as it is written, "each laver measuring four cubits" (1 Kings 7:38).

"One laver on each of the ten laver stands" (1 Kings 7:38)—correspond-

*The first fruit of the union between a particular woman and a particular man.

ing to the Ten Utterances [by which the world was created], one utterance for each stand, one commandment for each laver.

"And the tank he placed on the right side of the House, at the southeast [corner]" (1 Kings 7:39)—Why east? Because it is from there that the constellations and planets and great lights come out over the world, from there that the world itself derives, from there that the ancestors of humankind came, and there that the world became sensate. —MIDRASH TADSHE

"Became sensate"—by being filled with the Divine.

The Holy One, blessed be He, said to Jeremiah, "I am calling [Israel] to account concerning [the fulfillment of] My word.

"I told them, 'I the Lord am your God,' but they did not act accordingly. Rather, 'they said to wood, "You are my father" ' (Jer. 2:27).

"I told them, 'You shall have no other gods,' but they did not act accordingly. Rather, '[they] bow down on the roofs [to the host of heaven]' (Zeph. 1:5).

"I told them, 'You shall not swear falsely by the name of the Lord your God,' but they did not act accordingly. Rather, 'they are sure to be swearing falsely' (Jer. 5:2).

"I told them, 'Remember the sabbath day and keep it holy,' but they did not act accordingly. Rather, '[You have . . .] profaned My sabbaths' (Ezek. 22:8).

"I told them, 'Honor your father and your mother,' but they did not act accordingly. Rather, 'fathers and mothers have been humiliated within you' (Ezek. 22:7).

"I told them, 'You shall not murder,' 'You shall not commit adultery,' 'You shall not steal,' but they did not act accordingly. Rather, 'you steal and murder and commit adultery' (Jer. 7:9).

"I told them, 'You shall not bear false witness against your neighbor,' but they did not act accordingly. Rather, 'they bend their tongues like bows; [they are valorous in the land for treachery, not for honesty]' (Jer. 9:2).

"I told them, 'You shall not covet,' but they did not act accordingly. Rather, 'they covet fields, and seize them; houses, [and take them away]' (Mic. 2:2)." —PESIKTA DE-RAV KAHANA, The Words of Jeremiah

YOU OVERPOWERED ME AND YOU PREVAILED

"You enticed me, O Lord, and I was enticed; You overpowered me and You prevailed" (Jer. 20:7)—The Assembly of Israel said to the Holy One, blessed be He, "Master of the Universe, you enticed me into accepting the Torah, and You placed the yoke of the commandments around my neck; then I was punished for violating them. Had I not accepted the Torah I would have been like any other nation, without reward or punishment."

Said the Assembly of Israel to the Holy One, blessed be He, "Master of the Universe, You exhorted me at Sinai, saying, 'I the Lord am your God,' and I thought You would let up. But then 'You overpowered me and You prevailed,' adding, 'I the Lord your God am an impassioned God' (Exod. 20:5).

"You exhorted me at Sinai, saying, 'You shall have no other gods,' and I thought You would let up. But then 'You overpowered me and You prevailed' by saying, 'Whoever sacrifices to a god [other than the Lord alone] shall be proscribed' (Exod. 22:19).

"You exhorted me at Sinai, saying, 'You shall not swear [falsely],' and I thought You would let up. But then 'You overpowered me' by saying, 'The Lord will not clear [one who swears falsely by His name]' (Exod. 20:7).

"You exhorted me at Sinai, saying, 'Remember the sabbath day,' and I thought You would let up. But then 'You overpowered me' by saying, 'He who profanes it shall be put to death' (Exod. 31:14).

"You exhorted me at Sinai, saying, 'Honor your father and your mother.' Then 'You overpowered me' by saying, 'He who repudiates his father or his mother shall be put to death' (Exod. 21:17).

"You exhorted me at Sinai, saying, 'You shall not murder.' Then 'You overpowered me' by saying, 'Whoever sheds the blood of man, by man shall his blood be shed' (Gen. 9:6).

"You exhorted me at Sinai, saying, 'You shall not commit adultery.' Then 'You overpowered me' by saying, 'The adulterer and the adulteress shall be put to death' (Lev. 20:10).

"You exhorted me at Sinai, saying, 'You shall not steal.' Then 'You overpowered me' by saying, 'He who kidnaps [lit., steals] a man . . . shall be put to death" (Exod. 21:16).

"You exhorted me at Sinai, saying, 'You shall not bear [false witness].' Then 'You overpowered me' by saying, 'You shall do to him as he schemed to do to his fellow' (Deut. 19:19).

"You exhorted me at Sinai, saying, 'You shall not covet,' and I thought

You would let up. Then 'You overpowered me' by saying, 'Do not lust for her beauty . . . It is the same with one who sleeps with his fellow's wife: none who touches her will go unpunished' (Prov. 6:25, 29)." —PESIKTA RABBATI, The Ten Commandments

WHO MAY SOJOURN IN YOUR TENT

Rabbi Yizhak began with the passage,

> A psalm of David. Lord, who may sojourn in Your tent, who may dwell on Your holy mountain? He who lives without questioning, who does what is right, and in his heart acknowledges the truth; [whose tongue is not given to evil; who has never done harm to his fellow or borne reproach for (his acts toward) his neighbor; for whom a contemptible man is abhorrent, but who honors those who fear the Lord; who stands by his oath even to his hurt; who has never lent money at interest or accepted a bribe against the innocent. The man who acts thus shall never be shaken] (Ps. 15).

Rabbi Yehudah bar Rabbi Yose said: There are ten [virtues] here, corresponding to the Ten Commandments Jacob's children would one day fulfill in this place. But there are eleven! said Rabbi Yose. He replied: "Whose tongue is not given to evil; who has never done harm to his fellow"—these are one and the same thing, for whoever slanders his fellow has already done him harm, but if he does not slander him he has done him no harm.

How do we know that they correspond to the Ten Commandments? Rabbi [Yehudah Hanasi] said: All the Ten Commandments are implied in them:

"Who lives without questioning" corresponds to "I the Lord am your God." This teaches us that a person must assume the dread yoke of the rule of heaven and may not question the things he does not understand. We know this because, on the one hand, it is written simply, "I the Lord am your God," and on the other hand, [in this psalm,] it says, "Who lives without questioning," [but the two verses are linked to each other by a third verse,] "You must be unquestioning with the Lord your God" (Deut. 18:13)—meaning, you may not question that which is forbidden to you to question.

"Who does what is right" corresponds to "You shall have no other gods beside Me. . . . You shall not bow down to them or serve them." From here Rabbi Yehudah derives his dictum that nothing outweighs the prohibition against profaning the Divine name. How do we know this? From the case of the corrupter, where it is written, "Let your hand be the first against him to put him to death" (Deut. 13:10). Why? "For he sought to make you stray from the Lord your God" (Deut. 13:11). He who kills him is called righteous, zealous, and one who does what is right. Hence, "who does what is right."

"In his heart acknowledges the truth" corresponds to "You shall not swear falsely by the name of the Lord your God." (Rabbi Yehudah said: They are not in the same order, but we can disregard this.)

"Whose tongue is not given to evil; who has never done harm to his fellow" corresponds to "You shall not bear false witness against your neighbor."

"Or borne reproach for [his acts toward] his neighbor" refers to public desecration of the sabbath. Rabbi Yose says it corresponds to "You shall not steal."

"For whom a contemptible man is abhorrent" corresponds to "You shall not murder." One who is lowly in his own eyes does not provoke others to the point of killing or being killed.

"Who honors those who fear the Lord" corresponds to "Honor your father and your mother." Rabbi Yose asked: Must you honor your father and mother no matter what? Not if they order you to violate the teachings of the Torah or to engage in idolatry. That is why it says [specifically], "Who honors those who fear the Lord."

"Who stands by his oath even to his hurt" corresponds to "You shall not commit adultery." For if a person's evil inclination threatens to get the better of him, he must take an oath against it, like Boaz, who said, "[If he does not want to act as a redeemer for you, I will do so myself,] as the Lord lives! [Lie down until morning]" (Ruth 3:13).

"Who has never lent money at interest" corresponds to "You shall not steal." For if a person does not take interest on a loan he will certainly not steal outright.

"Or accepted a bribe against the innocent" corresponds to "You shall not covet." —MIDRASH HANE'ELAM, Vayeze

---

"They are not in the same order"—The virtues in the psalm are not listed in the same order as the Ten Commandments—"but we can disregard this"— that is, it is of no consequence.

GOD SAID ALL IN A WORD

"Speak to the whole Israelite community and say to them: You shall be holy, [for I, the Lord your God, am holy]" (Lev. 19:2)—Why does God open this *parashah* with the inclusive expression "the whole Israelite community," rather than simply saying, as He does elsewhere, "Speak to the Israelite people"? Because the [Ten] Commandments are all included in this *parashah*. How so?

In the Ten Commandments it is written, "I the Lord am your God," and here too it is written, "I the Lord am your God" (Lev. 19:4).

In the Ten Commandments it is written, "You shall have no [other gods beside Me]," and here it is written, "Do not turn to idols" (Lev. 19:4).

In the Ten Commandments it is written, "You shall not swear [falsely by the name of the Lord]," and here it is written "You shall not swear falsely by My name" (Lev. 19:12).

In the Ten Commandments it is written, "Remember the sabbath day," and here it is written, "Keep My sabbaths" (Lev. 19:3).

In the Ten Commandments it is written, "Honor your father and your mother," and here it is written, "You shall each revere your mother and father" (Lev. 19:3).

In the Ten Commandments it is written, "You shall not murder," and here it is written, "Do not stand upon the blood of your neighbor" (Lev. 19:16).

[In the Ten Commandments it is written, "You shall not commit adultery," and here it is written, "You shall be holy" (Lev. 19:2).]

In the Ten Commandments it is written, "You shall not steal," and here it is written, "You shall not steal" (Lev. 19:11).

In the Ten Commandments it is written, "You shall not bear [false witness against your neighbor]," and here it is written, "Do not go about as a talebearer among your fellows" (Lev. 19:16).

In the Ten Commandments it is written, "You shall not covet," and here it is written, "You shall not coerce your neighbor. You shall not commit robbery" (Lev. 19:13).

Thus we see why the Holy One, blessed be He, opens this *parashah* with the inclusive expression, "Speak to the whole Israelite community," for it includes all of the Ten Commandments. —TANHUMA HAYASHAN, Kedoshim

THE *SHEMA'*

Why do we recite the two passages [from Deuteronomy and Numbers] every day? Rabbi Levi said: Because they include the Ten Commandments:

"I the Lord am your God" [is implied in] "Hear, O Israel! The Lord is our God" (Deut. 6:4).

"You shall have no other gods beside Me" [is implied in] "the Lord alone" (Deut. 6:4).

"You shall not swear falsely by the name of the Lord your God" [is implied in] "You must love the Lord your God" (Deut. 6:5). Whoever truly loves the King does not swear falsely by His Name.

"Remember the sabbath day and keep it holy" [is implied in] "Thus you shall be reminded" (Num. 15:40). Rabbi [Yehudah Hanasi] said: This verse refers to the commandment of the sabbath, which outweighs all the other commandments in the Torah put together, as it is written, "You made known to them Your holy sabbath, and You ordained for them laws, commandments and Torah" (Neh. 9:14), implying that the sabbath outweighs all the other commandments in the Torah.

"Honor your father and your mother" [is implied in] "to the end that you and your children may endure" (Deut. 11:21).

"You shall not murder" [is implied in] "you will soon perish" (Deut. 11:17), for he who kills is killed.

"You shall not commit adultery" [is implied in] "so that you do not follow your heart and eyes" (Num. 15:39). Rabbi Levi said: The heart and the eyes are the two agents of sin. Thus it is written, "Give your heart to me, my son; let your eyes watch my ways" (Prov. 23:26). Said the Holy One, blessed be He, "If you give Me your heart and your eyes, I will know that you are Mine."

"You shall not steal" [is implied in] "you shall gather in your new grain" (Deut. 11:14)—meaning, you shall not gather in your neighbor's.

"You shall not bear false witness against your neighbor" [is implied in] "I the Lord am your God" (Num. 15:41). For it is also written, "The Lord is truly God" (Jer. 10:10). What is meant by "truly"? Rabbi Abbin said: He is the living God and King of the World. Rabbi Levi said: the Holy One, blessed be He, says, "If you bear false witness against your neighbor, I shall judge you as if you had testified that I did not create heaven and earth."

*See note, p. 167.

"You shall not covet your neighbor's house" [is implied in] "Inscribe them on the doorposts of your house" (Deut. 6:9)—your house, and not your neighbor's house. —PALESTINIAN TALMUD, Berakhot 1

"Two passages"—but the *Shema'* has three passages! [We are told explicitly why the third], dealing with the fringes, must be recited every day: because it mentions the Exodus from Egypt, as it is written, "So that you may remember the day of your departure from the land of Egypt as long as you live" (Deut. 16:3).

Rabbi Ḥiyya bar Abba said: Whoever fulfills the precept of reciting the *Shema'* is as if he had fulfilled the Ten Commandments, for it was at the hour prescribed for the recitation of the *Shema'* [in the morning] that the Ten Commandments were given. —PESIKTA ḤADETA, Beit Hamidrash 6

BY ALL RIGHTS THE TEN COMMANDMENTS SHOULD BE RECITED DAILY

In the Temple, the Ten Commandments were recited every day. —TAMID 5:1

Rav Yehudah said in the name of Shmuel: They would have liked to recite them outside the Temple as well, but the practice was stopped because of the insinuations of the *minim*.* Rabbah bar bar Ḥannah proposed instituting this practice in Sura, but Rav Ḥisda said to him: It has been stopped because of the insinuations of the *minim*. Ameimar proposed instituting the practice in Nehardea,† but Rav Ashi said to him: It has been stopped because of the insinuations of the *minim*. —BERAKHOT 12a

Recite the Ten Commandments daily, for they are the main principles and the beginning of religion. It is said [in Tractate Berakhot of the Babylonian Talmud]: "They would have liked to recite them outside the Temple as well, but the practice was stopped because of the insinuations of the *minim*." This is clarified at the beginning of Tractate Berakhot in the Palestinian Talmud as follows: "By all rights the Ten Commandments should be recited daily. Why

*In this instance, probably a reference to the Jewish Christians. See Maimonides, below.

†Sura and Nehardea were the sites of two of the major Babylonian Jewish academies during the talmudic period.

then are they not recited? Because of the *minim,* who would then claim that these commandments alone were given to Moses at Sinai."* —Maimonides, COMMENTARY ON THE MISHNAH

BY VIRTUE OF THE TEN COMMANDMENTS

These are the promises—I will keep them without fail" (Isa. 42:16). What promises are meant? The good tidings and consolations and assurances given by the Holy One, blessed be He, as to what He would do for the righteous in the Time to Come. By virtue of what will He fulfill His promises to you of consolation? By virtue of your having fulfilled the Ten Commandments, of which it is written, "The Lord spoke those words . . . to your whole congregation" (Deut. 5:19). How so?

[Said the Holy One, blessed be He: If you fulfill the verse, "I (the Lord am your God)," I shall fulfill for you the verse, "I, I am He who comforts you!" (Isa. 51:12).]

Said the Holy One, blessed be He: If you fulfill the verse, "You shall have no [other gods beside Me]," I shall fulfill for you the verse, "I will be your God" (Exod. 6:7).

If You fulfill "You shall not swear falsely [by the name of the Lord]," I shall fulfill for you "The Lord has sworn by His right hand, by His mighty arm: [Nevermore will I give your new grain to your enemies for food, nor shall foreigners drink the new wine for which you have labored]" (Isa. 62:8).

If you fulfill "Remember [the sabbath day]" and "Observe [the sabbath day]" (Deut. 5:12), I shall fulfill for you "Thus they shall remain in the land which I gave to My servant Jacob" (Ezek. 37:25).

If you fulfill "Honor [your father and your mother]," I shall fulfill for you "You shall be called 'Priests of the Lord,' and termed 'Servants of our God.' You shall enjoy the wealth of nations and revel in their riches" (Isa. 61:6).

If you fulfill "You shall not murder," I shall fulfill for you "No sword shall cross your land" (Lev. 26:6).

If you fulfill "You shall not commit adultery," I shall fulfill "Then shall maidens dance gaily, young men and old alike" (Jer. 31:13).

If you fulfill, "You shall not steal," I will fulfill for you "You shall enjoy the wealth of nations" (Isa. 61:6).

*The appearance of the Ten Commandments as a distinct text in the Jewish liturgy could be held up by the *minim* as proof of their claim that only these commandments, and not the other 603, enjoyed Sinaitic authority, for it would seem to indicate that the Jews themselves regarded these commandments as having special status.

If you fulfill "You shall not bear [false witness against your neighbor]," I shall fulfill for you "You are My witnesses—declares the Lord—and I am God" (Isa. 43:12).

If you fulfill "You shall not covet," I shall fulfill for you "No one will covet your land" (Exod. 34:24).

When will the Holy One, blessed be He, fulfill all these promises to you? When you fulfill all these commandments. In the verse "The Lord spoke those words . . . to your whole congregation," "those words" refers to the Ten Commandments. The Israelites heard the first two commandments, "I [the Lord am your God]" and "You shall have no [other gods]," directly from the mouth of the All-Powerful, all in one sound, a sound such as [mortal] mouth cannot make nor [mortal] ears hear, the sound of "a mighty voice which cannot be exceeded" (Deut. 5:19). It is concerning this that scripture says, "One thing God has spoken; two things have I heard" (Ps. 62:12). —MIDRASH HAGADOL (Yalon MS), Deuteronomy

Said the Holy One, blessed be He, to Israel: If you fulfill "I the Lord am your God," I shall fulfill "I the Lord am your God, [who freed you from the burdens of the Egyptians]" (Exod. 6:7). But if you do not, I shall fulfill against you "I the Lord your God am an impassioned God, [visiting the guilt of the fathers upon the children]" (Exod. 20:5).

If you fulfill "You shall have no [other gods beside Me]," I shall fulfill for you "I will be your God" (Exod. 6:7). But if you do not, I shall fulfill against you "Dismiss them from My presence, and let them go forth" (Jer. 15:1).

If You fulfill "You shall not swear falsely [by the name of the Lord]," I shall fulfill for you "The Lord has sworn by His right hand, by His mighty arm: [Nevermore will I give your new grain to your enemies for food, nor shall foreigners drink the new wine for which you have labored]" (Isa. 62:8). But if you do not, I shall fulfill against you "He was angry. He vowed: Not one of these men, [this evil generation,] shall see [the good land that I swore to give to your fathers]" (Deut. 1:34–35).

If you fulfill "Remember [the sabbath day]," I shall fulfill [for you] "that you may be remembered before the Lord your God and be delivered [from your enemies]" (Num. 10:9). But if you do not, I shall fulfill against you "They shall see all your nakedness" (Ezek. 16:37).

If you fulfill "Honor [your father and your mother," I shall fulfill [for you] "that you may long endure" (Exod. 20:12). But if you do not, I shall fulfill against you "Fathers and mothers have been humiliated within you" (Ezek. 22:7).

If you fulfill "You shall not murder," I shall fulfill for you "No sword shall cross your land" (Lev. 26:6). But if you do not, I shall fulfill against you "I will bring a sword against you" (Lev. 26:25).

If you fulfill "You shall not commit adultery," I shall fulfill for you "Then shall maidens dance gaily" (Jer. 31:13). But if you do not, I shall fulfill [against you] "They have ravished women in Zion" (Lam. 5:11).

If you fulfill "You shall not steal," I will fulfill for you "Share the spoil of your enemies" (Josh. 22:8). But if you do not, [I shall fulfill against you] "King Shishak of Egypt marched [against Jerusalem. He took away the treasures of the House of the Lord and the treasures of the royal palace; he took away everything; he took away the golden shields that Solomon had made]" (2 Chron. 12:8–9).

If you fulfill "You shall not bear [false witness against your neighbor]," I shall fulfill for you "My witnesses are you—declares the Lord" (Isa. 43:10). But if you do not, [I shall fulfill against you] "I am He who knows and bears witness—[declares the Lord]" (Jer. 29:23).

If you fulfill "You shall not covet," I shall fulfill for you "No one will covet your land" (Exod. 34:24). But if you do not, [I shall fulfill against you] "All that was dear to us is ruined" (Isa. 64:10). —PESIKTA HADETA

"I the Lord am your God"—If you fulfill it, "you are Divine beings, sons of the Most High, all of you" (Ps. 82:6); but if you violate it, "you shall die as men do, fall like any prince" (Ps. 82:7).

"You shall have no [other gods beside Me]—If you fulfill it, "I will look with favor upon you, and make you fertile" (Lev. 26:9); but if you violate it, "I will set My face against you" (Lev. 26:17).

"You shall not swear [falsely by the name of the Lord your God]"—If you fulfill it, "the Lord has sworn by His right hand, by His mighty arm: [Nevermore will I give your new grain to your enemies for food]" (Isa. 62:8); but if you violate it, "thereupon the Lord was incensed and He swore, 'None . . . shall see the land that I promised on oath to Abraham, Isaac, and Jacob, [for they did not remain loyal to Me]' " (Num. 32:10, 11).

"Remember [the sabbath day]"—If you fulfill it, "then you can seek the favor of the Lord" (Isa. 58:14); but if you violate it, "then shall the land make up for its sabbath years [throughout the time that it is desolate and you are in the land of your enemies]" (Lev. 26:34).

"Honor [your father and your mother]"—If you fulfill it, "nations shall see your victory, and every king your majesty" (Isa. 62:2); but if you violate it, "assuredly, parents shall eat their children in your midst, and children shall eat their parents" (Ezek. 5:10).

"You shall not murder"—If you fulfill it, "no sword shall cross your land" (Lev. 26:6); but if you violate it, "I will bring a sword against you" (Lev. 26:25).

"You shall not commit adultery"—If you fulfill it, "then shall maidens dance gaily" (Jer. 31:13); but if you violate it, "I will not punish their daughters for fornicating [nor their daughters-in-law for committing adultery; for they themselves turn aside with whores and sacrifice with prostitutes, and a people without sense must stumble]" (Hos. 4:14).

"You shall not steal"—If you fulfill it, "You shall destroy all the peoples [that the Lord your God delivers to you]" (Deut. 7:16); but if you violate it, "Nebuchadrezzar . . . devoured me and discomfited me" (Jer. 51:34).

"You shall not bear [false witness against your neighbor]"—If you fulfill it, "My witnesses are you—declares the Lord . . . and I am God" (Isa. 43:10, 12); but if you violate it, "what can I take as witness or liken to you, [O Fair Jerusalem? What can I match with you to console you, O Fair Maiden Zion? For your ruin is vast as the sea: Who can heal you?]" (Lam. 2:13).

"You shall not covet [your neighbor's house]"—If you fulfill it, "no one will covet your land" (Exod. 34:24); but if you violate it, "they covet fields, and seize them; houses, and take them away" (Mic. 2:2). —SEDER ELIYAHU RABBAH 24

TEN SANCTUARY SHEKELS

"If his offering is a sacrifice of well-being" (Lev. 3:1)—Rabbi Shim'on said: "[This was the dedication offering for the altar. . . . :] Ten (lit., ten ten) sanctuary shekels per ladle" (Num. 7:86)—Why "ten ten"? Ten for Creation and ten for the Giving of the Torah. There were ten utterances at the time of Creation and ten utterances at the time of the Giving of the Torah. What do we learn from this? That the world was only created for the sake of the Torah. As long as Israel devotes itself to the Torah the world will endure, but as soon as Israel ceases to devote itself to the Torah, what is written? "Were it not for My covenant day and night, I would not maintain the laws of heaven and earth" (Jer. 33:25–26).

Come and see: there were ten utterances at the time of Creation, as we have learned, "The world was created with ten utterances" (Avot 5). The ten utterances at the time of the Giving of the Torah are likened to the Ten Commandments.

It is written, "I the Lord am your God," and it is written concerning Creation, " 'Let there be light'; and there was light" (Gen. 1:3). This refers to the faithfulness* of the Holy One, blessed be He, which is called light, as it is written, "The Lord is my light and my help; [whom should I fear?]" (Ps. 27:1).

It is written, "You shall have no other gods beside Me," and it is written concerning Creation, " 'Let there be an expanse in the midst of the water, [that it may separate water from water.' . . . God called the expanse Heaven]" (Gen. 1:6). This refers to [the people] Israel, who are the portion of the Holy One, blessed be He, and who are united in the place called Heaven.† This is the secret about which Rabbi Yisa Saba asked Rabbi Ila'i, saying, "The Holy One, blessed be He, appointed guardian angels to rule over the other nations. Where did He place those of Israel?" He answered, " 'God set [the two great lights] in the expanse of Heaven' (Gen. 1:17)." And this was a good reply. "In the midst of the water"—among words of Torah. "That it may separate water from water"—that it may separate the Holy One, blessed be He, who is called a well of living waters, from idolatry, which is called "broken cisterns, [which cannot even hold water]" (Jer. 2:13)—[cisterns of] bitter, muddy, stagnant, foul-smelling, polluted water. Hence the holy people of Israel separate water from water.

It is written, "You shall not swear falsely by the name of the Lord your God," and it is written concerning Creation, "Let the water below heaven be gathered into one area" (Gen. 1:9). Come and see: if one swears falsely by the name of the Holy One, it is as if he were separating the Mother [the sefirah of Sovereignty] from her place on high and keeping the Holy Crowns [the sefirot] from their rightful places. Thus it is written, "A querulous one alienates his friend" (Prov. 16:28), and "friend" means the Holy One, blessed be He. The verse "Let the water below heaven be gathered into one area" means, Do not cause a separation by swearing falsely. "Into one area"—the place of truth, not the place of falsehood. And what is falsehood? When the water flows to a place where it does not belong [i.e., to the realm of evil].

It is written, "Remember the sabbath day and keep it holy," and it is written concerning Creation, "Let the earth sprout vegetation: seed-bearing plants" (Gen. 1:11). When was the Holy Land made great and crowned with its crowns? We learn here that it was on the sabbath, when the Bride [the sefirah of Sovereignty] and the King [Ze'ir Anpin] were joined to produce plants and blessings for the world.

---

*A reference to the sefirah of Sovereignty (Malkhut).
†A reference to Ze'ir Anpin, the lower seven of the sefirot.

It is written, "Honor your father and your mother," and it is written concerning Creation, "Let there be lights in the expanse of the sky" (Gen. 1:14). What does this come to teach us? That the two lights are your father and your mother. Your father is the sun [*Ze'ir Anpin*], your mother the moon. The sun can only be the Holy One, blessed be He, as it is written, "The Lord God is sun and shield" (Ps. 84:12); and the moon can only be the Assembly of Israel [the *sefirah* of Sovereignty], as it is written, "Your moon no more withdraw" (Isa. 60:20). Thus all is as one.

It is written, "You shall not murder," and it is written concerning Creation, "Let the waters bring forth swarms of living creatures" (Gen. 1:20). Do not then murder human beings, who are called [living creatures], as it is written, "man became a living creature" (Gen. 2:7); and do not behave like the fish, the larger of which swallow the smaller.

It is written, "You shall not commit adultery," and it is written concerning Creation, "Let the earth bring forth every kind of living creature" (Gen. 1:24). This teaches us that a man should not behave treacherously with a woman who is not his wife. It is regarding this that scripture says, "Let the earth bring forth every kind of living creature": a woman should not give birth except to her own kind. And what is her own kind? Her husband['s progeny].

It is written, "You shall not steal," and it is written concerning Creation, "God said, 'See, I give you every seed-bearing plant' " (Gen. 1:29). What I have given you and entrusted to you shall be yours; do not steal what belongs to others.

It is written, "You shall not bear false witness against your neighbor," and it is written concerning Creation, "God said, 'I will make man in My image' " (Gen. 1:26). You must not bear false witness against one who is made in the image of the King, and if one gives false testimony against another, it is as if he had given false testimony against the One above.

It is written, "You shall not covet . . . your neighbor's wife," and it is written concerning Creation, "It is not good for man to be alone; [I will make a fitting helper for him]" (Gen. 2:18). Your wife is fitting for you; therefore, do not covet your friend's wife.

Here we have the ten utterances connected with Creation and the ten connected with the Giving of the Torah. Thus it is written, "Ten [ten ten] sanctuary shekels per ladle." [The two sets of utterances] had the same weight (*nishkelu*). It is because of this [balance between the two] that the world endures in peace. Moreover, [the balance] atones for [the violation] of both the positive and the negative commandments, so as to bring general peace. —ZOHAR, Leviticus 11–12

INTERTWINED

"I the Lord am your God [who brought you out of the land of Egypt]"—This is the first of the Ten Commandments. "I command you to take me as your master and judge, because 'I took you out of the land of Egypt,' and it is better for you to serve Me than to serve those slaves." The Holy One, blessed be He, could have said, "I made you" or "I created you"; "I poured you out like milk, congealed you like cheese, clothed you with skin and flesh and wove you of bones and sinews, bestowed on you life and care" [cf. Job 10:10–12]; "I made you secure at your mother's breast" [cf. Ps. 22:10]; "I hold the power of life and death to recompense those who hate and love Me, and I sustain and nourish you without limit." In other words, the Holy One, blessed be He, could have called us to account concerning our obligation to keep His commandments and serve Him wholeheartedly and willingly. But had He done so, the Israelites could have responded, "You have treated all human beings and all nations the same way; why then impose the work of your Torah upon us in particular?" Therefore He only mentioned what He had done for them in Egypt and the extra affection He had shown them, over and above all the other nations, whom He also loved. "[Has any god ventured to go and] take for himself one nation from the midst of another by prodigious acts, by signs and portents, by war, by a mighty hand and outstretched arm [and awesome power, as the Lord your God did for you in Egypt before your very eyes?]" (Deut. 4:34). This is something He has not done for any other nation. Hence it is written, "who brought you out," and thus He has a right to demand of [the people] Israel that they, more than the other nations, recognize His uniqueness and divinity.

"You shall have no other gods [beside Me]"—so that no one says, "I shall be Your servant, as You commanded me," but then goes and serves other gods as well, recognizing many masters and sources of help. Therefore, it is written, "You shall have no [other gods]," for you do not need anyone but Him. The other gods are but emptiness and vanity, and their help is but emptiness and vanity.

"You shall not make for yourself a sculptured image or any likeness"— Do not say, "I shall not worship other gods, but since You are a hidden, invisible god—'man may not see me and live' (Exod. 33:20)—I will make myself statues and pictures [of You], and I will bow down to them and serve them in Your honor, and when I do so I will remember You, as the *minim* said." Therefore it is written, "You shall not make for yourself. . . ." And if others make them, "you shall not bow down to them or serve them." Elsewhere the Torah gives the reason for this: "Since you saw no shape when the Lord your God spoke to you [at Horeb out of the fire]" (Deut. 4:15), why, then, make an image [now]? Thus it is also written, "To whom, then, can you liken God?" (Isa. 40:18). "So I am warning you not to make 'any likeness of what is in the heavens' "—meaning the inhabitants of the highest heavens, such as the sacred beasts and *ofanim* and ministering angels, as our Rabbis taught— "or on the earth below"—such as people, animals, birds, fish, the sun, the moon, the stars, and all the other things we see from the earth—"or in the waters under the earth"—everything in the deep. "For I the Lord your God am a jealous *(kana)* God"—as in the verse, "A fit of jealousy *(kin'ah)* comes over him" (Num. 5:14). "I love you so much that I do not want you to serve anyone but Me; and in return for this I shall honor and love you. Those other gods are so despicable that whoever serves them becomes despicable to Me, so that when he comes into My presence I immediately grow angry.

"And do not imagine that I shall forget this iniquity, for I '[visit] the guilt of the fathers upon the children, [upon the third and upon the fourth generations of those who reject Me].' This does not mean that I punish the child for the father's sins, for 'a person shall be put to death only for his own crime' (Deut. 24:16)." The child shall not be put to death for the sin of the father; that is not the way of the Divine. If a person sins, the Holy One, blessed be He, waits for him to repent, or to see if his child turns out to be righteous, so that he need not be punished. And if the child turns out wicked, the Holy One, blessed be He, waits for him, too, to repent or to have a good child, and the same in the third generation. But if the fourth-generation child is wicked, He wipes him from the face of the earth on account of his own iniquities. For though his forebears did not cause him to sin, they did establish themselves as evildoers, and so the Holy One, blessed be He, does not wait for him [as He did with the others]. In any event, the Holy One, blessed be He, only punishes him for the sins he himself has committed. That is what is meant by "visiting the guilt of the fathers"; had his forebears not sinned, he himself would not be punished. "But showing kindness to the thousandth generation [of those who love Me and keep My commandments]"—To those thousands [of generations] whose children are righteous and serve the Holy One, blessed be He, generation after generation to the end of time, He extends extra love; but the line of the wicked does not last more than four generations. That is why He does not say "upon the fifth and the sixth generations," for these never come into the world. Thus we find that in the case of Jehu, when he behaved wickedly, the Holy One, blessed be He, said to him, "Four generations of your descendants shall occupy the throne of Israel" (2 Kings 10:30); and further, "They shall return here in the fourth generation, for the iniquity of the Amorites will not be fulfilled until then" (Gen. 15:16).

"You shall not swear [falsely by the name of the Lord your God]; for the Lord will not clear one who swears falsely by His name]"—You may say, "Since the Holy One, blessed be He, forbids us to have any other Lord, so that I cannot swear by the name of any other god, I shall swear by His name, whether truly or falsely." Therefore it is written, "You shall not swear [falsely by the name of the Lord your God]." For the Holy One, blessed be He, is true, and thus one may not swear by Him except in truth. But if one swears in truth, one may swear by Him, for it is written, "Swear by His name" (Deut. 6:13). "Falsely *(lashav)*" means affirming something impossible—for example, that a stone column is actually gold. A lie *(sheker),* on the other hand, is the affirmation of something that could be but is not. The Torah warns us against this else-where: "You shall not swear falsely *(lashaker)* by My name" (Lev. 19:12).

"For [the Lord] will not clear [one who swears falsely by His name]"— One speaks of "clearing" in connection with oaths, as in, "Thus only shall you be cleared of my adjuration" (Gen. 24:41), and, "We shall likewise be cleared of the oath which you made us take" (Josh. 2:20). It is written, "The Lord] will not clear," for one who robs and despoils can clear himself by restoring what he has taken, but one who swears falsely cannot clear himself. Hence it is written, "You shall not steal; you shall not deal deceitfully. . . . You shall not swear falsely by My name" (Lev. 19:11–12). For stealing and lying lead to taking false oaths, which cannot be undone. Thus our Rabbis said, "People will desist from taking an oath in regard to a doubtful claim, while they will not desist from appropriating money their right to which is doubtful" (Baba Mezi'a 6a); for one can be returned, but the other cannot. Thus it is written in regard to an oath, "[The Lord] will not clear."

"Remember the sabbath day [and keep it holy]"—Be careful to remem-ber the sabbath day, counting watchfully the days of the week, so that you do not mistake the sabbath for another day. For now, this is unnecessary, because the coming of the [extra portion of] manna lets you know that the sabbath day is approaching, but when you get to the Land you will have to be careful about this, for the manna will not be there to remind you. He had said, "You shall have no other gods [beside Me]," meaning, "You must not honor any mere mortal but only the Holy One, blessed be He; yet you must honor the sabbath, which is tantamount to honoring Me, for in doing so you testify that I created the world and rested on the sabbath," as is explained anon. "Six days you shall labor and do all your work, but the seventh day is a sabbath of the Lord your God"—to honor the Lord your God.

"[You shall not do any work—you . . . or] your cattle"—In the second version of the Ten Commandments, the reason for letting one's cattle rest is given: "So that your male or female slave may rest as you do" (Deut. 5:14). If it were allowed to work one's cattle, one's slaves would be prompted to lead them out to work. It is written, "For in six days the Lord made heaven and earth," and by [letting our slaves rest] we testify that He did so. It is for this reason, too, that the Holy One, blessed be He, blessed the sabbath day and hallowed it. In the second version of the Ten Commandments it is written, "Remember that you were a slave in the land of Egypt and the Lord your God freed you from there" (Deut. 5:15). When you rest on the sabbath, recall your enslavement in Egypt, when you could not rest; now that you are resting on the sabbath, know that you are free of the labor [of servitude], and remember the kindness shown you by the Holy One, blessed be He. In this first version of the Ten Commandments it says, "Remember," for it refers to Creation. (It is customary to speak of "remembering" things [long] past, as in the verse, "Do not recall what happened of old" [Isa. 43:18], or the verse, "Do not remember our former iniquities against us" [Ps. 79:8].) But in the second version of the Ten Commandments, which speaks about the Exodus from Egypt, then a recent event, it is not appropriate to say "remember [the sabbath day]," but rather "Observe [the sabbath day]" (Deut. 5:12). Thus, in the sabbath Kiddush [benediction], when we speak of Creation, we use the word "remember," as in the first version of the Ten Commandments, and when we speak of the Exodus from Egypt, we use the word "observe," as in the second version of the Ten Commandments.

"Honor your father and your mother, [that you may long endure on the land which the Lord your God is giving you]"—"Although I instructed you not to honor or serve anyone but Me, you must honor your father and mother and not forget all that they have done for you. For it was they who brought you into the world and bestowed all manner of kindness upon you until you reached adulthood. It was for your sake that they fretted and labored. If you honor them and repay them for their kindness, I know that you will honor Me as well for all the kindness I did you in bringing you into this world and [that I will do] in bringing you into the next." "That you may long endure"—"For doing this I will reward you with long life. Furthermore, if you adhere to the commandments, your children will honor you and support you in your old age, and you will not die before your time."

"You shall not murder"—You might say, "Seeing that the Holy One, blessed be He, only commanded me to honor Him, the sabbath, and my father and mother, I am free to strike a mortal blow at anyone else who provokes me." Hence it is written, "You shall not murder"—"for I only commanded you to honor Me in contradistinction to other gods, [not in contradistinction to other human beings,] and murder is a grave iniquity." Murder is wrongful death, and the term only applies when it is wrongful. "Death" and "killing" can be used whether the act is wrongful or not. Thus it is written concerning capital punishment ordered by a court, "Take his life" (Deut. 13:10), and "He shall be put to death. . . . His bloodguilt is upon him" (Lev. 20:9). Therefore no other interpretation is needed here; the term "murder" makes clear that the warning is only concerning wrongful death.

"You shall not commit adultery"—Since He said "You shall not murder," meaning that it is forbidden to diminish humankind, one might have thought that increasing humankind [by any means] was permitted and thus that a man could take any woman he came upon, be she married to another man or not, in order to propagate the species. Hence it is written, "You shall not commit adultery." For adultery means illicit intercourse, such as when a man takes a married woman or commits some other kind of fornication.

"You shall not steal"—You might say, "I have been warned against murder, and I have been warned against adultery lest I father a bastard and be compelled to give all the fruits of my labor to support an illegitimate child who is not my own; but kidnapping someone or stealing from him for the sake of monetary gain is permitted." Therefore it is written, "You shall not steal." Elsewhere we are told, "You shall not rob," but here the warning is concerning stealing, which is more common. Robbery is less common because the robber risks being beaten and reported to the authorities. "You shall not steal" seems to refer also to kidnapping, which carries the death penalty like murder and adultery. Similarly, "You shall not bear [false witness]" is a warning [specifically] against those who bear false witness in capital cases.

"You shall not bear [false witness against your neighbor]"—You may not even cause his death or his financial loss [indirectly]. Then "You shall not covet"—you shall not trick him into giving you what is his, either *gratis* or for payment. For one who pays for something [in order to take possession of it] against its owner's wishes is a *hamsan*,* and it is covetousness that leads a person to do such things. —BEKHOR SHOR

*In the Talmud, one who commits such an act, in violation of the law.

WHY ARE THEY IN THE SINGULAR?

Why are the Ten Commandments addressed in the singular? Because [the people] Israel had become one heart and one soul, as it is written, "Israel encamped [sing.] there [in front of the mountain]" (Exod. 19:2). And being of one heart and one soul, they were worthy to receive the Torah, which is one, from the Lord, who is one. —VARIOUS SOURCES

Why are the Ten Commandments addressed in the singular? Because each person received them according to his powers and the strength of his soul. —VARIOUS SOURCES

Why are the Ten Commandments addressed in the singular? To give Moses an opportunity to come to the [people's] defense in the matter of the Golden Calf. This is the meaning of the verse, "Let not your anger, O Lord, blaze forth against your people" (Exod. 32:11)—"It is not them you commanded 'You shall have no other gods' but only me!" —RASHI

Why are the Ten Commandments addressed in the singular? So that each person would think he alone, in the whole world, was responsible for studying, performing, and upholding all the words of the Torah. —VARIOUS SOURCES

Why are the Ten Commandments addressed in the singular? To teach us that every Jew should say, "It was for me that the Ten Commandments were given, and I am obligated to fulfill them," rather than that he should say, "The Torah can just as well be fulfilled by other people." —LEKAH TOV

Why are the Ten Commandments addressed in the singular? The sage Rabbi David Deutsch said: So that no one should think, "What difference does it make if I am not among the servants of the Lord? He has so many angels, so many righteous people serving Him; what need has He of me?" Therefore the Holy One, blessed be He, said to each of us, "I the Lord am your God"— "Imagine that I am only your God, that I have no other servants but you and thus the whole responsibility for My service falls upon your shoulders." —TA'AMEI HAMINHAGIM

Why are the Ten Commandments in the singular? Because they were violated by individuals: "I [the Lord am your God]" was violated by Micah. "You shall have no [other gods beside Me]" was violated by Jeroboam. "You shall not

swear [falsely by the name of the Lord your God]" was violated by the blasphemer [in Lev. 24]. "Remember [the sabbath day]" was violated by the one who gathered wood [in Num. 15]. "Honor [your father and your mother]" was violated by Absalom. "You shall not murder" was violated by Joab. "You shall not commit adultery" was violated by Zimri [in 1 Kings 16]. "You shall not steal" was violated by Achan [in Josh. 7]. "You shall not bear [false witness] was violated by Ziba [in 2 Sam. 9]. "You shall not covet" was violated by Ahab: "Would you murder and take possession?" (1 Kings 21:19).
—PESIKTA RABBATI

Why are the Ten Commandments addressed in the singular? To teach us that even when they are violated by individuals it is as if we all violated them, for all Israel are responsible for one another. —HEMDAT YAMIM on the Torah; MIDRASH HAGADOL

Rabbi Ḥiyya said: In the first instance [where the Ten Commandments are mentioned, the language is,] "I the Lord am your God," "Remember the sabbath day," "You shall not swear [falsely]," "You shall not murder," "You shall not commit adultery," and "You shall not steal"—all in the singular; but here [in Lev. 19, where a set of commandments analogous to the Ten appears, the language is,] "I the Lord am your God," "You shall each revere his mother and his father, and keep My sabbaths," and "Do not turn to idols"—all in the plural. Come see the reason: Since they first came into the world, [the people] Israel had never been so united in purpose and whole-hearted before the Holy One, blessed be He, as they were on the day they stood at Mount Sinai. Thus the [Ten Commandments] are in the singular. But later the plural is used, for by that time they were no longer so united in purpose. —ZOHAR, Leviticus 84b

Rabbi El'azar taught: In these Ten Commandments were engraved all the Torah's commandments, the decrees and penalties, the laws of purity and impurity, the branches and the roots, the trees and the plants, the heavens and the earth, the seas and the abysses. For the Torah [in its entirety] is a name of the Holy One, blessed be He. Just as the Name of the Holy One, blessed be He, was engraved in the Ten Commandments, so too was the Torah engraved in the Ten Commandments. The Ten Commandments are a name of the Holy One, blessed be He, and the Torah is all one name, the name of the Holy One, blessed be He, Himself. Fortunate is he who is deemed worthy of the Torah, for he who is deemed worthy of it is also deemed worthy of the Holy Name. Rabbi Yose said: He is deemed worthy of the Holy One, blessed be He,

Himself, for He and His Name are one and the same. Blessed be His Name for ever and ever, amen. —ZOHAR, Exodus 90b

FIVE CORRESPONDING TO FIVE

The last five commandments correspond to the first five.

"You shall not murder" corresponds to "I [the Lord am your God]." Said the Holy One, blessed be He, "If you commit murder, I shall regard it as though you diminished My image."

"You shall not commit adultery" corresponds to "You shall have no [other gods beside Me]." Said the Holy One, blessed be He, "If you commit adultery, I shall regard it as though you had worshiped idols."

"You shall not steal" corresponds to "You shall not swear [falsely by the name of the Lord your God]." Rabbi Hiyya taught: "You shall not steal; you shall not deal deceitfully or falsely with one another. You shall not swear falsely by My name" (Lev. 19:11–12)—for if you steal you will end up denying it, you will end up lying, you will end up swearing falsely by My name.

"You shall not bear [false witness against your neighbor]" corresponds to "Remember [the sabbath day]." Said the Holy One, blessed be He, "If you bear false witness against your neighbor, I shall regard it as though you had testified against Me that I did not create the world in six days and rest on the seventh."

"You shall not covet" corresponds to "Honor [your father and your mother]." Gaius of Gadara and Lucius of Susitha* would steal off with each other's wives. Eventually they fell to quarreling. One of them killed his own father, not knowing who he was. —PESIKTA RABBATI

"Gaius of Gadara and Lucius of Susitha"—two Roman legions, one stationed at Gadara, the other at Susitha.

MY NAME IS IN HIM

God's Name appears in the first five of the Ten Commandments but not in the last five. It is like a king who entrusts his seal to others. To whom? To those who are loyal to him. Thus God's Name appears in the first five of the Ten

*Gaius and Lucius were typical Roman names. See following paragraph.

Commandments, because they speak only of piety and awe. But the last five speak of murderers and adulterers and thieves and those who bear false witness and covet. Said the Holy One, blessed be He, "My Name shall not be in their custody." —TANḤUMA HAYASHAN, Introduction

"My Name is in it" (Exod. 23:21)—This refers to the Ten Commandments written on the tablets. In five instances, the words "the Lord your God" appear: ["I the Lord am your God,"] "For I the Lord your God," "the name of the Lord your God," "a sabbath of the Lord your God," and "which the Lord your God." But in the other five the words "the Lord your God" do not appear. "Lord" refers to the Divine Attribute of Mercy; "God" refers to the Divine Attribute of Strict Judgment.* The name "Lord" appears five times, corresponding to the five positive injunctions—recognizing God, abolishing idolatry, swearing by His name, remembering the Sabbath, and honoring parents. The name "God" appears five times, corresponding to the five negative injunctions: "You shall not murder," "You shall not commit adultery," "You shall not steal," "You shall not bear false witness," and "You shall not covet." Hence it is written, "My Name is in it." —LEKAḤ TOV

Hadrian, may his bones crumble, posed the following question to Rabbi Yehoshu'a ben Ḥananyah: "The Holy One, blessed be He, honored the nations of the world greatly, did He not, by including His Name in the first five commandments, which He gave Israel. That is, if Israel sins [by violating them], He will prosecute them. But His Name does not appear in the last five commandments, which He gave to the nations of the world, meaning that if they sin [by violating them] He will not prosecute them."

He replied, "Come with me on a tour of the districts." In each place to which they came, Hadrian saw statues of himself set up. Said Rabbi Yehoshu'a to him, "What are these?" He answered, "Statues of me." Finally he brought him to an outhouse. He said, "Your highness, I see that you reign over this whole district, for everywhere there are statues of you set up, but in this place there is none!" He said, "You are the elder of the Jews. Do you really think it befits the honor of a king to have his statue set up in a place of scorn and filth and pollution?" He said, "Listen to yourself! Does it then befit the dignity of the Holy One, blessed be He, to have His name mixed up with murderers, adulterers, and thieves?" With that he sent [Hadrian] on his way.

After he had left, Rabbi Yehoshu'a's students asked him, "Master, you

*See note, p. 103.

have managed to put him off [with the answer you gave him], but what answer will you give us?" He said to them, "It was [simply] God's intention [to put it this way]!" —PESIKTA RABBATI, The Ten Commandments

Nachmanides writes: Of the Ten Commandments, five are to the glory of the blessed Creator and five for the good of human beings. The honor of your father is also the honor of God, so that it is for the sake of the honor of the Creator that He commands us to honor our fathers, who are partners in creation. This leaves five commandments that are [purely] for human benefit.

Now in some of the Ten there is mention of reward and punishment, while in others there is none. In the second commandment it says, "I the Lord your God am an impassioned God, [visiting the guilt of the fathers upon the children]"; in the third it says, "the Lord will not clear one"; and in the fifth it says, "that you may long endure." But there is no mention of reward or punishment in the others. For the last five commandments are for man's sake, and they carry their own reward, which comes in the performance of them. But concerning idolatry, a warning of punishment is needed in order to stress the severity of the offense, which is against the honor of the blessed Creator.

He would appear to be saying, "[I . . . am] an impassioned God" concerning "You shall have no [other gods]," and "showing kindness" concerning "I am the Lord your God [who brought you out of the land of Egypt]," for punishment is [usually] attached to negative injunctions and reward to positive ones. He does not immediately indicate the reward [for fulfilling the positive injunction] because the acceptance of the yoke of the kingship of heaven and the warning against idolatry are in fact one thing. Thus He completes this [first] commandment, [which includes both, by indicating the reward] and then goes on to the injunction against swearing falsely, the punishment for which is "[the Lord] will not clear."

In regard to the sabbath, He does not indicate the reward for observing it or the punishment for desecrating it, because the sabbath is essentially part of the first two commandments [the reward and punishment for which have already been indicated]. For he who observes the sabbath is testifying to Creation and acknowledging "I [am the Lord]," while he who desecrates it is denying Creation and affirming the pre-existence of the world, thereby denying "I [am the Lord]." Thus [the commandment of the sabbath, too,] is subject to the promises of "[I . . . am an] impassioned [God]" and "visiting [the guilt of the fathers upon the children]," as well as "showing kindness." Regarding the fifth commandment, concerning [honoring] one's father, on the other hand, He does mention a reward, because it is a positive injunction.

There were five commandments on one tablet, corresponding to five on the other:

"I [the Lord am your God]" on the first tablet corresponds to "You shall not murder" on the second, for one who commits murder diminishes the [Divine] image.

"You shall have no [other gods beside Me]" on the first tablet corresponds to "You shall not commit adultery" on the second, for he who goes whoring after idols will end up commiting fornication. That is the way of "the adulterous wife who welcomes strangers instead of her husband" (Ezek. 16:32).

"You shall not swear [falsely by the name of the Lord]" on the first tablet corresponds to "You shall not steal" on the second, for one who steals will eventually swear falsely.

"Remember [the sabbath day]" on the first tablet corresponds to "You shall not bear [false witness]" on the second, for he who desecrates the sabbath is bearing false witness against the Creator, saying that He did not rest at the time of Creation.

"Honor [your father and your mother]" on the first tablet corresponds to "You shall not covet" on the second, for he who covets will eventually beget a child who disdains him and honors someone else who is not his father. —TUR, Commentary on Yitro

In a debate between Rabbi Yehoshu'a ben Levi and the Sages, Rabbi Yehoshu'a ben Levi said: Israel heard two of the [Ten] Commandments directly from the Holy One, blessed be He: "I [the Lord am your God]" and "You shall have no [other gods beside Me]." This is the meaning of the verse, "Oh, give me of the kisses of your mouth" (Song 1:2)—meaning, not all your kisses. But the Sages said: Israel heard all the [Ten] Commandments directly from the Holy One, blessed be He.

Rabbi Yehoshu'a of Sikhnin said in the name of Rabbi Levi: The Sages base their argument on [the fact that they only said to Moses after all the Ten Commandments had been given], "You speak to us . . . and we will obey" (Exod. 20:16). What does Rabbi Yehoshu'a ben Levi do with this verse? He disagrees, saying there is neither before nor after in the Torah. Even so, might Israel not have said, "You speak to us . . . and we will obey" after two or three of the commandments instead?

Rabbi 'Azaryah and Rabbi Yehudah bar Simon took the approach of Rabbi Yehoshu'a ben Levi, saying: It is written, "Moses charged us with the Torah as the heritage [of the congregation of Jacob]" (Deut. 33:4). There are 613 commandments altogether in the Torah, but the numerical value of the word *Torah* is only 611. These are the commandments that Moses gave us; and we heard [the other two,] "I [the Lord am your God]" and "You shall have no [other gods beside Me]," not from Moses but from the Holy One, blessed be He, Himself. —SONG OF SONGS RABBAH 1:2

They heard, "I [the Lord am your God]" and "You shall have no [other gods beside Me]" directly from the All-Powerful and the rest of the Ten Commandments from Moses. Rabbi Yosef Kara, may his memory be a blessing, explained that the verses themselves prove this, for "I [the Lord am your God]" and "You shall have no [other gods beside Me]" speak in the first person, while beginning with "You shall not swear" [the third commandment], the speaker seems to be an intermediary [who speaks of God in the third person]. Thus it says "the Lord will not clear," rather than "I will not clear"; "in six days the Lord made," rather than "I made"; and "which the Lord your God is giving you," rather than "which I am giving you." —PLEITAT SOFRIM, citing Rabbi Yosef Bekhor Shor

Rabbi Yehoshu'a of Tomashov, the sainted son of martyrs, relates:

> I once spent Shavu'ot with Rabbi Shalom of Belz. At the noonday meal, the Zaddik told us to sing the line [from one of the sabbath table hymns], "They all entered the covenant together;/With one voice they said, 'We will do and we will hear;'/Then they burst out in response, 'The Lord is one!'" We sang these lines over and over several times. Then he told us to stop and said, "At the Giving of the Torah, Israel said 'yes' to each positive commandment and 'no' to each negative one. But since 'I [the Lord am your God]' and 'You shall have no [other gods beside Me]' were a single utterance, they did not know how to respond. If they said 'yes', it might have been mistaken, God forbid, for an affirmative response to 'You shall have no [other gods beside Me]'; and if they said 'no', it might have been mistaken, God forbid, for a negative response to 'I [the Lord am your God].' They thought the matter over and replied, 'The Lord is one!'— which applies equally well to both commandments." As the Zaddik said the words, "They burst out in response, 'The Lord is one!'" he roared like a lion. A great fear came over those who stood round his holy table, and they literally fainted with dread. Rabbi Yehoshu'a himself, in telling the story, collapsed from [the memory of] the fear he had felt when he heard the Zaddik say, "They burst out in response, 'The Lord is one!'"
>
> —DOVER SHALOM

THE FOUNDATION OF FAITH

The Ten Commandments are the foundation of our faith, and they include all the 613 commandments in the Torah. To those who heard Him utter them, the Holy One, blessed be He, gave the mental fortitude to believe thenceforth in the prophecy of Moses our Teacher, peace be to him, as it is written, "[The Lord said to Moses, 'I will come to you in a thick cloud,] in order that the people may hear when I speak [with you and so trust you thereafter]' " (Exod. 19:9).

Moreover, [in giving them the commandments] He elevated Israel above all other peoples and tongues, as it is written, "Has any people heard the voice of a god speaking [from out of a fire, as you have, and survived?]" (Deut. 4:33). At the same time he lifted from Israel the stain of iniquity of the primordial serpent, as we learn in Shabbat, chapter 22, page 146, and 'Avodah Zarah, chapter 2 (q.v.). Clearly, there is no other people beside Israel that is fit to receive the Torah: the children of Abraham, who loved God; they who were sealed into the covenant of circumcision and who were schooled in servitude.

For whoever wishes to take upon himself the yoke of the Torah must keep away from luxury and pride, so as not to forget and spurn his Creator. Thus it is written, "[Beware lest] your heart grow haughty and you forget [the Lord your God]" (Deut. 8:14); and it is written, "Jeshurun grew fat and kicked . . . ; [he spurned the Rock of his support]" (Deut. 32:15). This being the way of Torah, how can any nation bear the yoke of the Torah if it is accustomed to luxury and drunkenness and unable to humble its spirit and mortify its flesh in order to fulfill the Torah and its commandments? The Torah exhausts *(mateshet)* human powers. That is why it is called "wisdom" *(tushiah)* [in Prov. 8:14]. Hence, only [the people] Israel were fit [to receive the Torah], for they [alone] were prepared to exhaust themselves in their devotion to it. And the Holy One, blessed be He, gives them the strength to bear up under it. —MENORAT HAMA'OR 3

Be aware that these Ten Commandments came to Moses in a prophetic vision. And as he was receiving them, the voice proclaiming them renewed itself from within the fire, saying the same things to Israel. Thus it is written, "God answered him with a voice" (Exod. 19:19). For what God said to him came to him in an audible voice, which was renewed. Thus it says in Deuteronomy, "The Lord spoke those words . . . to your whole congregation at the mountain, with a mighty voice out of the fire" (Deut. 5:19). —GERSONIDES

A SUMMATION OF ALL THE
COMMANDMENTS IN THE TORAH

These Ten Commandments are a summation of all the commandments in the Torah, of what is above and below, of the Ten Utterances of Creation. The commandments were inscribed on stone tablets, and all the treasures they contained were made visible to everyone, so that they could know and contemplate the secret of the 613 commandments of the Torah included in them. Everything was in plain sight. In their entirety, they were expressed with such wisdom as to be intelligible and illuminating to every Jew.

At that hour, all the secrets of the Torah and all the secrets of heaven and earth were made plain to them, for they could see with their own eyes the Glory of their Lord. What happened on that day at Mount Sinai had never happened since the creation of the world: the Holy One, blessed be He, revealed Himself. Now we have learned that the humblest maidservant saw more at the Reed Sea than the prophet Ezekiel [in his visions]; might the same not apply to the day Israel stood at Mount Sinai? No, [here they saw even more,] for on this day God removed the taint of sin from them, and all their bodies were scrubbed clean like the cleanliness of the angels on high when they put on their best clothes to do their Lord's bidding. In such spotless raiment one may step into fire without fear, like the angel who appeared to Manoah, then entered a pillar of flame and went up to heaven, as it is written, "[As the flames leaped up from the altar toward the sky,] the angel of the Lord ascended in the flames of the altar" (Judg. 13:20). When the taint of sin was removed from them, [the people] Israel were left pure in body, without the slightest contamination, and their souls shone like the splendor of the heavens [in readiness] to receive the light.

Such were [the people] Israel as they gazed upon the Glory of their Lord. This had not been the case at the sea, where the taint [of sin] had not yet been removed from them. Here at Sinai, where the taint had been taken from their bodies, even fetuses in their mothers' bellies could gaze upon the Glory of their Lord. Each received according to the measure that suited him.

And the joy that day before the Holy One, blessed be He, was greater than it had been on the day the world was created, for on the day [of Creation] the existence of the world had not yet been ensured by Israel's acceptance of the Torah, as it is written, "Were it not for My covenant day and night, I would not uphold the laws of heaven and earth" (Jer. 33:25). Once Israel had accepted the Torah at Mount Sinai, the world's foundations were secured, and heaven and earth were firmly established. The Holy One, blessed be He, was then known throughout heaven and earth, and He ascended in His glory over all. Of this day it is written, "The Lord is king, He is robed in grandeur; the Lord is robed, He is girded with strength. [The world stands firm; it cannot be shaken]" (Ps. 93:1). Now "strength" can only refer to the Torah, as it is written, "May the Lord grant strength to His people; may the Lord bestow on His people well-being" (Ps. 29:11). —ZOHAR, Exodus 83b–84a

Know that all the commandments are woven from these ten, and that a commandment hangs from each letter. It is as Rashi, may his memory be a blessing, wrote on Parashat Yitro [Exod. 18:1–20:23], that Rabbi Sa'adyah [Gaon] was able to derive from here an ordering of all the commandments, showing how each commandment hangs from a single letter of the Ten Commandments. —TORAT HA'OLAH 3

I heard from my teacher [the Ba'al Shem Tov] that the Ten Commandments include the entire Torah, as our teacher Sa'adyah Gaon explained. And just as the entire Torah is included in the Ten Commandments, the entire Torah is also included in a single word. —BEN PORAT YOSEF

How can the entire Torah be included in a single word? The book *Degel Mahaneh Efrayim* cites the following explanation: Parashat Tezaveh [Exod. 27:20–30:10] says, "Inside the breastpiece of decision you shall place the Urim and Tummim" (Exod. 28:30). Herein lies a deep secret, which I shall reveal to you only in part. It is well known that there were twenty-two letters* squeezed into the Urim and Tummim (see Yoma 73b). How did they obtain an augury when two or three letters [in the answer] were the same,† such as "Shall I go to Babylonia (בבל)?" Herein lies a deep secret, and this, too, I shall explain to you only in part. I received a tradition from my grandfather [the Ba'al Shem Tov], may his memory be a blessing, that each of the twenty-two letters, [because its name was spelled out, and the names of these letters were, in turn, spelled out, etc.],‡ contained all twenty-two, except for the letter *mem*, which, though its name, too, was spelled out, yielded only more *mem*s. When the priest who wore the Urim and Tummim posed a question, since the Lord had commanded that they contain all twenty-two letters and the spelling out of the

---

*The number of letters in the Hebrew alphabet.
†The answer would be given by a simultaneous glowing of the letters making it up.
‡For example, the name of the letter *alef* is spelled *alef lamed fe;* the names of these letters, in turn, are spelled *alef lamed fe lamed mem dalet fe alef,* etc., etc., *ad infinitum.*

names of the letters yielded [all the other letters], the answer would be given
by a glowing of the appropriate letters. That is what is meant by, "Inside the
breastpiece of decision you shall place the Urim"—referring to the light (or) of
the holy spirit in which the priest wrapped himself—"and the Tummim"—
for the answer was completed (mittamem) by the spelled-out letters that lit
up for the priest. —MEKOR MAYIM HAYYIM

Rabbi Simlai gave the following exposition: Six hundred thirteen commandments were given to Moses, 365 negative ones, corresponding to the days of
the solar year, and 248 positive ones, corresponding to the parts of the human
body. Rav Himnuna said: What is the scriptural basis for this? "When Moses
charged us with the Torah as the heritage of the congregation of Jacob" (Deut.
33:4). The numerical equivalent of the word Torah is 611, and we heard, "I [the
Lord am your God]" and "You shall have no [other gods]" directly from the
All-Powerful. —MAKKOT 23b

"Two hundred forty-eight positive ones"—for each part of the body reminds
us to carry out commandments. "Three hundred sixty-five negative ones"—
for each day we are warned not to transgress. "We heard . . . directly from the
All-Powerful"—as it is written, "One thing God has spoken; two things have
I heard" (Ps. 62:12). —RASHI

Regarding each part of the body, the Holy One, blessed be He, instructed us
what not to do and what to do. As for what not to do, the heart and the eyes
were told, "Do not follow your heart and eyes [in your lustful urge]" (Num.
15:39). The ears were told, "You must not carry false rumors [lit., false hear-
ing]" (Exod. 23:1). The mouth was told, "You shall not eat anything abhorrent" (Deut. 14:3). The tongue was told, "You shall not swear falsely by the
name of the Lord your God"—you shall not swear, and you shall not lie—and
"You shall not bear false witness against your neighbor." The hands were told,
"Do not join hands with the guilty" (Exod. 23:1). The genitals were told, "You
shall not commit adultery" and "[Let the land] not fall into harlotry" (Lev.
19:29). The feet were told, "Do not walk after other gods" (Deut. 6:14). These
are the negative commandments. And thus said Solomon: "A scoundrel, [an
evil man, lives by crooked speech,] winking his eyes, [shuffling his feet, pointing his finger]. Duplicity is in his heart; [he plots evil all the time; he incites
quarrels]. . . . Six things the Lord hates; [seven are an abomination to Him]"
(Prov. 6:12–14, 16).
    What about the positive commandments? The heart was told, "Therefore

impress these My words upon your very heart" (Deut. 11:18). The eyes were told, "Do not forget the things that you saw with your own eyes" (Deut. 4:9). The ears were told, "Hear, O Israel!" (Deut. 6:4). The tongue was told, "Impress [these words upon your children]" (Deut. 6:7). The hands were told, "You must open your hand [and lend him sufficient for whatever he needs]" (Deut. 15:8). The genitals were told, "Be fertile and increase" (Gen. 1:28); and it is also written, "Take wives and beget sons and daughters" (Jer. 29:6). The feet were told, "Walk only in the path that the Lord your God has enjoined upon you" (Deut. 5:30). Just as the Holy One, blessed be He, decreed how mortals and other creatures should act, He did the same for the parts of the human body. —MIDRASH TADSHE

"If, [along the road,] you chance upon a bird's nest, . . . do not take the mother together with her young. Let the mother go" (Deut. 22:6). This is what is meant by the verse, "More than all that you guard, guard your heart, for it is the source of life" (Prov. 4:23). Rabbi Ada said: The Torah contains 248 positive commandments, corresponding to the parts of the human body. Every day they exhort man, saying, "Perform us, that you may enjoy life and length of days on our account!" The Torah also contains 365 negative command-ments, corresponding to the days of the solar year. Every day, from the time it rises to the time it sets, the sun exhorts man, "I adjure you, by Him who kept you alive until this day, that you not commit this transgression while I shine, that you not incriminate yourself and the world as a whole." Altogether, 613 commandments.

The reward for performing each commandment is also referred to, [though sometimes only implicitly]. For example, for honoring one's father and mother and sending the mother bird away from the nest, scripture speaks of length of days. For performing other commandments, the reward is progeny, such as in the case of Sarah, who showed hospitality, and the Shunamite who hosted Elisha. There are transgressions that carry the punishment of stoning, burning, beheading, or strangling. There is no easier commandment to fulfill than the injunction to send the mother bird away from the nest, yet what is its reward? "That you may fare well and have a long life." To what may this be compared? To the case of a king who sent workers into his fields to sow without telling them how they would be compensated. At the end of the day, one who had planted a tree was given a gold coin. The others all wondered at this, saying, "If he gives one gold coin to the person who planted but a single tree, how much more will he give us, who planted far more!" Thus, if the reward for sending the mother bird away from the nest is length of days, how much greater is the reward for performing commandments that entail sacrifice and effort and diligence!

Hence the Holy One, blessed be He, did not [always] spell out the reward for performing the commandments in the Torah; rather, He left it to Israel [to infer it and] to fulfill the commandments for the sake of that [inferred,] even greater reward. Thus we have learned, "Be not like servants who serve their master in order to receive a [specified] reward, but rather like those who serve their master for [an unspecified] reward" (Avot 1). Hence it is written, "More than all that you guard, guard your heart." —TANḤUMA, Ki Teze

Why did the Holy One, blessed be He, give us 613 commandments? One can earn a place in the World to Come by performing even one commandment! But there are many commandments that not everyone can fulfill. For example, a poor man cannot fulfill the commandment to give charity; a sick man cannot fulfill the command to build a sukkah*; in the absence of priests, the sacrifices cannot be offered. Therefore the Holy One, blessed be He, gave us many commandments, so that if one person could not get credit for carrying out a particular commandment, someone else could. Thus it is said: The Holy One, blessed be He, wanted to give credit to Israel, so He gave them much Torah and many commandments. —YALKUT DAVID

It has been taught: Rabbi Shim'on ben El'azar said: Those commandments, such as the ones concerning idolatry and circumcision, for which Israel has submitted to martyrdom in times of persecution, are still firmly upheld, while those commandments, such as the one concerning phylacteries, for which they have not martyred themselves, are not firmly upheld. —SHABBAT 130a

Rabbi Eli'ezer ben Ya'akov said: He who fulfills a commandment acquires a defender, and he who violates a commandment acquires a prosecutor. Repentance and good deeds serve as a bulwark against Divine punishment. —AVOT 4:11

"In order that the teachings of the Lord may be in your mouth" (Exod. 13:9)—I once observed a person who was so fastidious in his piety that he had written all 613 commandments in a notebook, and every day he would go over

---

*The open-air ritual hut used during the festival of Sukkot (Tabernacles).

and over them until he had them all memorized. He knew that a particular commandment was number 40 or 50 or 20 or whatever. Whoever feels moved by the love of the Torah could well do likewise. —SHNEI LUḤOT HABRIT, Shavu'ot 185

The Ten Commandments, which were engraved on the stone tablets, were made of sapphires, and the handwriting was that of God. They were made up of 613 letters, corresponding to the 613 commandments [in all] given to us by Moses our Teacher. For it is written, "Moses charged us with the Torah" (Deut. 33:4), the word *Torah* having the numerical value 611; and [the first two of the Ten Commandments], "I [the Lord am your God]" and "You shall have no [other gods]" we heard directly from the All-Powerful, [making a total of 613].

It is also written, "For Your dew is like the dew on fresh growth *(orot)*" (Isa. 26:19), where the word *orot* has the numerical value 613. But the letters [of the Ten Commandments] add up to 621! [How to reach this figure?] Take 613, the number of the commandments, [and add eight for] the 600,000 [adult male Jews who came out of Egypt]—the children of the three patriarchs and the twelve tribes—who had been circumcised at the age of eight days. The total then is 621. (Eight is for the days between birth and circumcision, [which is unique to Israel,] as it is written, "He did not do so for any other nation; [of such rules they know nothing. Hallelujah]" [Ps. 147:20].)

The Ten Commandments mention the Divine name thirteen times, corresponding to the number of the tribes of Israel, counting the tribe of Ephraim the son of Joseph [separately], Manasseh [Joseph's other son] being counted together with the tribe of Joseph, as it is written, "From the tribe of Joseph, from the tribe of Manasseh" (Num. 13:11). —MIDRASH LEKAḤ TOV, Yitro

"You came forward and stood at the foot of the mountain" (Deut. 4:11)— They stood in separate rows and separate groups, each group seeing what it deserved to see.

Said Rabbi Shim'on: The leaders of the people, the leaders of the tribes, and the women all stood separately, five ranks to the right and five to the left. That is the meaning of the verse, "You stand this day, all of you, before the Lord your God—your tribes, your heads, your elders, and your officials, all the men of Israel" (Deut. 29:9). That makes five ranks to the right. Who made up the five to the left? Those mentioned in the verse, "Your children, your wives, even the stranger within your camp, from woodchopper to waterdrawer"

(Deut. 29:10)—five all together. All the ranks were arrayed according to the celestial pattern. Corresponding to them, Israel received as an eternal inheritance the Ten Commandments, the source of all the other commandments, all the privileges, all of the heritage that is Israel's goodly portion. —ZOHAR, Exodus 82a

The Ten Commandments begin with "I the Lord am your God" and end with "anything that is your neighbor's," for everything depends on these two things. "I the Lord am your God" encompasses what is between man and God, and "anything that is your neighbor's" encompasses what is between man and man.* Hence our Sages said concerning the verse "Love your neighbor as yourself: [I am the Lord]" (Lev. 19:18), "That is the great principle of the Torah." For the Ten Commandments encompass the entire Torah. They contain 620 letters,† corresponding to the 613 commandments in the Torah and the seven rabbinical commandments, which between them comprise all the commandments pertaining to what is between man and man and between man and God. —MEGALEH 'AMUKOT, Kedoshim

TRULY GOOD TO ISRAEL

The Ten Commandments begin with *alef* and end with *khaf*. This is a reference to the verse, "[God is] truly *(akh)* good to Israel" (Ps. 73:1). The Ten Commandments have 620 letters, corresponding to the 613 commandments [in the Torah as a whole] and the Seven Noahide Commandments, and symbolized by the words *Keter Torah* (the Crown of the Torah).‡ —BA'AL HATURIM

The Ten Commandments begin with *alef* and end with *khaf,* symbolizing the verse, "[God is] truly *(akh)* good to Israel" (Ps. 73:1). *Akh* is numerically equivalent to *Ehyeh* ("I am"),§ for He is good to Israel and full of mercy. "[God *(Elohim)* is] good . . . to those whose heart is pure" (Ps. 73:1)—to those who have no fear of the Divine Attribute of Strict Judgment. [That is, Divine judgment is good to those who are pure of heart.—S.Y.A.]‖

From this number, one can also understand the saying of the Sages, may

*The Commandments are traditionally divided into these two categories.
†The different tallies may be owing to variations in spelling.
‡The numerical value of the word *keter* being 620.
§Understood from Exod. 3:14 to be one of the Divine names.
‖The name *Elohim* is taken to refer to God as judge. (See note, p. 103).

their memory be a blessing, "Things having to do with holiness are never less than ten in number" (Berakhot 21b). For the secret of holiness is in the arrangement of the ten *sefirot* with respect to one another. The tractate Kelim [1:6] lists ten holy places in the Land of Israel, one higher than the next. There are also ten [Divine] names that may not be erased, an allusion to this weighty matter.

One may well ask, why of all the 613 commandments were these ten singled out? And why do they comprise three positive commandments and seven negative ones? The first question can be answered simply: these ten include all 613, as our teacher Sa'adyah Ga'on, may his memory be a blessing, wrote in his commentary on *Sefer Yezirah (The Book of Creation)*. Now we learn from the mystical tradition that these ten commandments allude to the Ten Utterances [by which the world was created]. Hence they comprise three positive commandments and seven negative ones, as I have hinted to you concerning the secret of the seven days of Creation.

(The latter were seven in number and not ten, because the first three [of the ten *sefirot*] could not be described in terms of days. Corresponding to [these three *sefirot*] were the three Utterances: "When God began to create" [Gen. 1:1]; "God said, 'Let there be light' " [Gen. 1:3]; and "God said, 'Let the water . . . be gathered' " [Gen. 1:9].)

The three positive commandments [of the Ten]—"I [the Lord am your God]," "Remember [the sabbath day]," and "Honor [your father and your mother]"—include all aspects of being and their inner unity. "I [the Lord am your God]" corresponds to the brain, which is the source of everything; hence it came first. "Remember [the sabbath day]" corresponds to the heart, and you must know that the heart and brain are the dominant features of the Higher Man,* to which the secret of the phylacteries alludes.† "Honor [your father and your mother]" alludes to the unification of all things. Therefore, these three were chosen as the positive commandments.

The other seven, the negative commandments, were selected out of all the negative commandments [in the Torah] because they, in particular, do damage to the supernal image. "You shall have no [other gods beside Me]" [forbids idolatry, which] is the opposite of unification. "You shall not swear [falsely by the name of the Lord]" contains the same principle as "A querulous

---

*In the Kabbalah, the ten sefirot are visualized as the parts of a microcosmic human body, referred to as "the Higher Man."

†The phylacteries are bound on the head and on the left arm, next to the heart, as a sign of consecrating intellect and emotion (as well as physical strength) to God's service.

one alienates his friend" (Prov. 16:28), as it is written, "I have sent it forth—declares the Lord of Hosts—and [the curse] shall enter the house of the thief and the house of the one who swears falsely by My name" (Zech. 5:4). The third is "You shall not murder"—one who murders defaces with his own hands, the hands of Esau, the image of the King. The fourth is "You shall not commit adultery," corresponding to the verse, "[Who forsakes the companion of her youth] and disregards the covenant of her God" (Prov. 2:17). The fifth is "You shall not steal," as I have already indicated. The sixth is "You shall not bear [false witness against your neighbor]," and the seventh is "You shall not covet." I have already hinted at the hidden meaning of these two. —RECANATI

Our teacher, the author of Levushim, interprets the verse "[The curse] shall enter the house of the thief" as follows: He who swears falsely by the Name of the Lord is like a thief who steals and cuts the plantings.* —EVEN YEKARAH

The Ten Utterances of Creation, the Ten Commandments, the ten holy places in the Land of Israel—all are one. It is this with which we are concerned on the Ten Days of Penitence, when we seek to uncover the secrets of the Torah in order to draw Divine grace upon ourselves, the grace by which the world was created and established in the Ten Utterances. We seek then to reveal the holiness of the Ten Commandments, which was originally concealed in the Ten Utterances and through which we shall merit reaching all ten holy places in the Land of Israel. It was for this purpose that the High Priest, on the Day of Atonement, entered the Holy of Holies, the place where the Ark containing the Tablets stood on the Foundation Stone, the holiest of the ten holy places in the Land of Israel. —LIKKUTEI 'EZOT ḤADASH

"You shall be to Me a kingdom of priests" (Exod. 19:6)—You shall crown the angels on high. This interpretation is in accord with the following idea: [God said,] "Who caused Me to serve idols? You [Israel] did!" How so? When Israel worshiped idols in Babylonia, they attracted the heavenly Chariot, that which Ezekiel saw, to that place. For Israel controlled the vital force of all the worlds, and the Lord would be drawn into whatever they did. If they had served the Lord, they would have brought all the worlds under His rule. All this [power] they merited because they would [one day] accept the Torah. They went down

*I.e., mutilates the Divine image. An apparent reference to the passage in Ḥagigah 14b, where the heretic Aḥer (Elisha ben Avuyah) is said, figuratively, to have "entered the Garden [of mystical knowledge]" and "cut the plantings."

to Egypt in order to sift from the dross the Ten Utterances by which the world was created. The word "utterance" (ma'amar) is [used because it] connotes softness, for, pending [Israel's] acceptance of the Torah, [the world] had not yet become solidified. But when He gave them the Ten Commandments (dibrot), the world become solidified. The word "commandment" (dibbur) [is used because it] connotes hardness, for all the worlds were then solidified. —OR TORAH

IN A SINGLE UTTERANCE

Mortals cannot say two things at once. But the Holy One, blessed be He, spoke the Ten Commandments twice in a single utterance. That is something the mortal mouth cannot utter nor the mortal ear hear. —MISHNAT RABBI ELI'EZER

"God spoke all these words, saying" (Exod. 20:1)—"One thing God has spoken; two things have I heard" (Ps. 62:12)—Know that Maimonides, may his memory be a blessing, in his *Guide of the Perplexed,* part 2, chapter 33, expresses the view that Israel heard the tremendous voice [of God] without distinct phonemes, that they heard it only once, and that they only heard it speak the first two of the Ten Commandments. Of this the Torah says, "[The Lord spoke those words]—those and no more—[to your whole congregation at the mountain,] with a mighty voice" (Deut. 5:19). It is also written, "You heard the sound of the words [but perceived no shape—nothing but a voice]" (Deut. 4:12)—the sound of words, but without words. This is what is meant by the verse, "That the people may hear when I speak with you" (Exod. 19:9)—i.e., the people will hear the voice, but the words will be addressed to you. Similarly, our Sages, may their memory be a blessing, said: "We heard [the first two of the Ten Commandments,] 'I [the Lord am your God]' and 'You shall have no [other gods],' directly from the All-Powerful."

This, then, was the difference between Moses and Israel: Israel heard sounds, but Moses heard the words themselves. Moses then had to articulate the words for them, which we see in the verse, "I stood between the Lord and you at that time to convey the Lord's words to you" (Deut. 5:5)—namely, those first two commandments that you heard from Him, but without distinct phonemes. This is why Onkelos translates both "The Lord spoke to Moses saying" (Exod. 6:10 *inter alia*) and "God spoke all these words" as "God articulated," meaning that Israel could then understand. "Let not God speak to us" (Exod. 20:16) he translates as "Let the Lord not speak (yitmalel) to us." He does not say "articulate" *(yemalel),* for they had not heard His speech as distinct phonemes, only as the sound of a voice.

Then, having heard this voice uttering the first two of the Ten Commandments, Israel fainted away, as in the verse, "I was faint because of what he said" (Song 5:6). Thinking they might hear more of this voice, they were seized with fear and said to Moses, "Let us not die, then, [for . . . if we hear the voice of the Lord our God any longer, we shall die]. . . . You go closer and hear [all that the Lord our God says]" (Deut. 5:22,24). Then Moses heard the rest of the Ten Commandments one at a time, and he repeated them to Israel. That is what is meant by the verse, "As Moses spoke, God answered him with His voice" (Exod. 19:19).

We conclude that in the case of the first two commandments, Israel heard the same voice that Moses did, only they did not hear distinct phonemes, whereas Moses did. As for the rest of the Ten Commandments, they did not hear them from the Lord at all, but rather received them as part of Moses' prophecy like all the other commandments. Thus it is said at the beginning of Song of Songs Rabbah, " 'Moses charged us with the Torah' (Deut. 33:4), meaning commandments equivalent in number to the word *Torah* [611]. They heard [the first two of the Ten Commandments,] 'I [the Lord am your God]' and 'You shall have no [other gods],' directly from the All-Powerful," both in one burst of His voice. That is what is meant by the verse, "One thing God has spoken; two things have I heard." Thus far the view expressed by the author of the *Guide,* may his memory be a blessing.

But Nachmanides, may his memory be a blessing, is of the opinion that Israel heard all of the Ten Commandments directly from the Lord. This, [he says,] is the meaning of the verse, "God spoke all these words." Similarly, it says in Deuteronomy, "The Lord spoke those words . . . to your whole congregation" (Deut. 5:19), and it is written, "He inscribed them on two tablets of stone" (Deut. 5:19). From this we learn that what Moses inscribed on the tablets God had said "to your whole congregation." As for the saying of our Sages, may their memory be a blessing, that "they heard 'I [the Lord am your God]' and 'You shall have no [other gods]' directly from the All-Powerful," implying that they did not hear the other commandments from the All-Powerful: the word "heard" includes both the hearing of the ear—as in the verse, "He whose ear heeds the discipline of life" (Prov. 15:31)—and the understanding of the heart—as in the verse, "Grant, then, Your servant a hearing heart" (1 Kings 3:9). It was only the first two commandments that Israel understood as well as heard directly from the All-Powerful; the rest they heard from the Lord but did not understand, so that Moses had to help them understand what the Lord had meant. That is what is referred to in the verse, "I stood between the Lord and you at that time to convey the Lord's words to you" (Deut. 5:5). It also explains the verse, "As Moses spoke, God answered him with His voice" (Exod. 19:19)—Moses spoke to Israel, the term "answered" referring to an initiation of speech, something that precedes speech, as in "Job answered and said" (Job 3:2 *inter alia*). Thus far the view of Nachmanides.

According to the Kabbalah, when it says "God spoke" [in this passage], it means the Lord;* scripture only uses the name "God" to indicate Israel's [low] level of perception. This is the message of the prophet, peace be to him: "The deep [rather than heaven] gives forth its voice" (Hab. 3:10). It is also referred to earlier, in the verse, "Moses went up to [the level of] God" (Exod. 19:3). That is why it is said, "We heard 'I [the Lord am your God]' and 'You shall have no [other gods]' directly from the All-Powerful [i.e., from God]."

Thus Onkelos in his marvelous wisdom translates "God" as "the Glory of the Lord" or "the Word of the Lord" each time it occurs in this *parashah* [in relation to Moses], not to conceal but to reveal [that it was the Lord Himself who spoke to Moses]. . . . And wherever the Unique Name [Lord] is mentioned in the *parashah,* he translates it directly, without his usual [euphemisms] "the Glory" or "the Word." Thus, "The Lord came down on Mount Sinai" he translates as "the Lord was revealed"; and "On the third day the Lord shall come down" he translates as "the Lord shall be revealed." The reason is that the Lord is revealed in all His glory on Mount Sinai, and it is He Himself who speaks with Moses. This is the same Divine presence that appeared to the Patriarchs as *El-Shaddai* (Almighty God); they had not as yet learned the Unique Name [Lord] through prophecy. This is the so-called dark glass through which all the prophets saw what they saw.

Now ponder this: Since it was the Lord Himself who was speaking [to Israel], scripture might well have said, "The *Lord* [rather than God] spoke all these words," as in the verse, "The Lord spoke those words—those and no more—to your whole congregation at the mountain, with a mighty voice out of the fire and the dense clouds" (Deut. 5:19); or as in the verse, "The Lord spoke to you out of the fire" (Deut. 4:12). But since it says earlier, "The Lord had come down upon it in fire" (Exod. 19:18)—meaning that the highest form of His name is the Unique Name, which is the Attribute [*sefirah*] of Splendor [*Tif'eret*] dwelling in the fire—scripture had to say *"God* spoke," these words

---

*The two Divine names, *Elohim* (God) and *YHVH* (Lord), are taken here to refer to lower and higher manifestations, respectively, of the Divinity.

being an explanation of what is meant by "out of the fire" [i.e., a lower manifestation]. For Israel heard His voice "out of the fire," as scripture says, "The Lord our God has just shown us His majestic Presence, and we have heard his voice out of the fire" (Deut. 5:21). Therefore, when it says "The Lord spoke to you" (Deut. 4:12) and when it says "The Lord spoke those words" (Deut. 5:19), it immediately adds "out of the fire," [to tell you at what level He spoke].

The Hebrew text [of Exod. 20:1] reflects Israel's level of perception, and thus it says *"God* spoke." Onkelos's translation, on the other hand, follows Moses' level of perception. Hence he renders [the scriptural clause] "God spoke" as "the Lord spoke," rather than [using the euphemisms] "the Glory of the Lord spoke" or "it was spoken from before the Lord" and rather than translating it as he translates the verse "Let not God speak to us" (Exod. 20:16)—"Let it not be spoken to us from before the Lord"—where he follows Israel's level of perception. But Moses' perception was deeper than that of Israel. Hence it is written, "For in Yah the Lord [you have an everlasting Rock]" (Isa. 26:4): the Lord, who is the Rock of All the Worlds, is in the name Yah, and it is with this name that He speaks and says, "I the Lord am your God." The name is within Him, as it is written, "My Name is in him" (Exod. 23:21). That is the hidden meaning of the verse, "I am the Lord in the midst of the land" (Exod. 8:18). And it says "[I the Lord am your God] who brought you out [of the land of Egypt]," because the act of bringing out was accomplished by the Unique Name. Hence it is written, "It was with a mighty hand that the Lord brought us out"; and it is written further, "It was the Lord who brought you out of the land of Egypt" (Exod. 16:6). —RABBENU BAHYA

Although there are many differences in wording between the two versions of the Ten Commandments [in Exodus and in Deuteronomy], it is the Lord who is speaking in all Moses' words. —MISHNEH KESEF

WE SHALL PLAY HIS MELODIES ALL OUR LIVES

For most of the Ten Commandments there are two different cantillations. The reason for this is as follows: on Shavu'ot, when we re-enact the Giving of the Torah and translate the Ten Commandments aloud, [the second and fourth commandments,] "You shall have no [other gods beside Me]" (Exod. 20:3–6) and "Remember [the sabbath day]" (Exod. 20:8–11) are chanted in longer musical phrases, making each commandment sound as though it were all one verse, while "You shall not murder," "You shall not commit adultery," "You shall not steal," and "You shall not bear false witness" (Exod. 20:13) are chanted in shorter musical phrases that render them as though they were four separate verses, one for each commandment.

However, when we read the Ten Commandments during the month of Shevat as part of the annual cycle of weekly Torah readings, "You shall have no [other gods beside Me]" and "Remember [the sabbath day]," are chanted in shorter musical phrases that render each commandment as four distinct verses, while "You shall not murder," "You shall not commit adultery," "You shall not steal," and "You shall not bear false witness" are chanted in longer musical phrases that combine all four into a single verse. For in the entire Bible there is no other instance of a verse that has only two words except for these [three: "You shall not murder," "You shall not commit adultery," "You shall not steal," each of which, in Hebrew, is made up of two words].

There is also in the Shavu'ot reading a more extended melody for "I [the Lord am your God who brought you out of the land of Egypt, the house of bondage]" and "You shall have no [other gods beside Me]" (Exod. 20:2–3), which renders them as a single verse, to remind us that they were [first] spoken in a single utterance. How so? The word "I" is chanted with the accent *pashta;* "your God" is chanted with *zakef katon;* "Who brought you out" with *telisha;* "from the land of Egypt" with *kadma ve'azla;* and "bondage" with *revi'i.**
—HIZKUNI, Yitro

THE VOICE OF GOD

I, Hizkiyahu, swear that I heard in a dream the voice of God pronouncing the Ten Commandments, sweetly and softly, to the world and all its inhabitants.
—HIZKUNI, Introduction

I have heard it said in the name of the Ba'al Shem Tov, may his memory be a blessing, that if Israel sanctify and purify themselves, they shall always merit hearing the voice of the Lord speaking to them as He did at Sinai. —KETER TORAH, Yitro

*The Masoretic accents, indicated by signs in the printed text of the Bible, signify melodic elements and at the same time serve as a form of punctuation. This particular sequence of five accents, ending with what amounts to a semicolon rather than a period, is appropriate for the first clause in a compound sentence. The rest of the sentence would then be the verse that follows (v. 3).

The disciples of our teacher and master Yisra'el ben Eli'ezer [the Ba'al Shem Tov], may the memory of the righteous be a blessing, testified that they purified themselves to such an extent that they heard the Sinai revelation, in "thunder and lightning" and "a very loud blast of the horn" (Exod. 19:16). They heard "I the Lord am your God" and the rest of the Ten Commandments directly from the Holy One, blessed be He. —HEIKHAL HABERAKHAH, Beshalah 94b

Whoever hallows himself will merit hearing the voice of the Lord, which persists forever, just as the Ba'al Shem Tov, may his memory be a blessing, and his disciples [merited]. Indeed, they merited hearing [even] the "thunder and lightning" and the "blast of the horn" in the uttering of "I [am the Lord]," with all the deep, supernal secrets [contained therein]. —SHA'AREI HA'EMUNAH

I heard from a pious man who was present in the synagogue of the Seer [of Lublin] at the hour of the reading of the Ten Commandments that it seemed to him that the synagogue was empty, that there was not another person there, for all those who heard the reading had left their bodies and become disembodied souls that took up no space at all. —GEDULAT HAZADDIKIM

HENCEFORTH

Once, on Shavu'ot, before the reading of the Ten Commandments, Rabbi Menahem of Riminov ordered his assistant Reb Zvi Meshores to announce that anyone who had not fulfilled the Ten Commandments should leave the synagogue during the reading. [When the time came,] Rabbi Naftali of Ropschitz, may his memory be a blessing, got up and left. When the other worshipers saw that this pious man had walked out, they did so as well, leaving Rabbi Menahem and Reb Zvi, his assistant, alone in the synagogue. Since there was no quorum, Rabbi Menahem said to Reb Zvi, "I see they have not fulfilled the Ten Commandments. Nevertheless, go tell them that if they undertake to fulfill them henceforth, [they can come back in]." He went out and told them, and the whole congregation returned. Then Rabbi Menahem read the Ten Commandments. —SIPPURIM NIFLA'IM

EXODUS 20:15

All the people saw the sounds* and the lightning,
the blare of the horn and the mountain smoking;

*See note, p. 143.

*and when the people saw it, they fell back
and stood at a distance.*

ALL THE PEOPLE SAW THE SOUNDS

We pointed out above that according to Nachmanides, Rabbenu Bahya, and others, the sounds in the scriptural phrase "saw the sounds" were identical with the sounds mentioned before the Giving of the Torah. The Gemara (Berakhot 6b) supports this view, saying that the Torah was given by five sounds, for the word "sound" is mentioned five times in the narrative of the Giving of the Torah. This does not include the sounds that "all the people saw," for these preceded the Giving of the Torah. In other words, scripture is speaking [here, in 20:15] of the same sounds mentioned in Exod. 19:16: "There were sounds and lightning."

As for the fact that here [in 20:15] the lightning is called *lapidim* rather than *berakim* [the word in 19:16], the Zohar says: "First scripture called it *berakim;* now it calls it *lapidim;* but it is the same thing. Once the [*berakim*] were fully formed and therefore visible, they were called *lapidim.*"

The same point is implied in *Targum Yonatan:* "All the people saw the sounds"—as they reverberated in everyone's ears. [They saw] the commandments issue forth from the lightning. They saw how "the blare of the horn" revived the dead. [And they saw] "the mountain smoking." Seeing all this, the people recoiled twelve miles. . . .*

However, there are those who say that these sounds were something new. They interpret the Gemara according to the view expressed by the sage Rabbi Menasheh of Ilya in his work *Alfei Menasheh,* namely, that the five sounds include only those that preceded the Giving of the Torah, not those that followed it.

According to Rashi, " 'All the people saw the sounds' issuing forth from the mouth of the All-Powerful." In *Ha'amek Davar,* Rashi's comment is explained as follows: What he means is that the "sounds" refer, not to the thunder that accompanies lightning but to the sound of the Ten Commandments, which is what is meant by the verse, "The voice of the Lord is power; [the voice of the Lord] is majesty" (Ps. 29:4). This sound was accompanied by sparks of fire and flashes of lightning like the letters of the commandments.

---

*Here Agnon cites a source appearing again immediately below as the last paragraph of the excerpt from *Yalkut Shim'oni.* He identifies it as a quote by *Yalkut Shim'oni* from *Pirkei de-Rabbi Eli'ezer.*

"All the people saw the sounds [and the lightning]"—They saw what is visible and heard what is audible, according to Rabbi Yishma'el. Rabbi 'Akiva said: They saw what is [normally only] audible and heard what is [normally only] visible. They saw the fiery word issuing forth from the mouth of the All-Powerful and being engraved on the tablets, as it is written, "The voice of the Lord engraves flames of fire" (Ps. 29:7).

"All the people saw"—sounds of thunder and flashes of lightning. How many sounds could there have been, and how many flashes of lightning? Rather, what it means is, each person heard according to his capacity, as it is written, "The voice of the Lord is power"* (Ps. 29:4).

Rabbi [Yehudah Hanasi] said: This is meant in praise of Israel, for when they all stood at Mount Sinai to receive the Torah, they heard God's word and interpreted it, as it is written, "He encompassed it, he understood it" (Deut. 32:10)—they interpreted God's word as soon as they heard it. Rabbi Eli'ezer said: This is meant in praise of Israel, for when they all stood at Mount Sinai to receive the Torah, there were no blind people among them, as it is written, "All the people saw." How do we know none of them was dumb either? From the verse, "All the people answered as one" (Exod. 19:8). We can also infer that none was deaf from the verse, "All that the Lord has spoken we will do and we will hear" (Exod. 24:7). And how do we know none of them was lame? From the verse, "They stood at the foot of the mountain" (Exod. 19:17). And we can infer that none of them was a fool from the verse, "You have been shown to know [that the Lord alone is God]" (Deut. 4:35). —MEKHILTA

"All the people saw" teaches us that there were no blind people among them. Since it is written, "You have been given to know that the Lord alone is God" (Deut. 4:35), we can infer that none of them was a fool. Since it is written, "All the people answered as one" (Exod. 19:8), we can infer that none of them was dumb. Since it is written, "From the heavens He let you hear His voice" (Deut. 4:36), we can infer that none of them was deaf. Since it is written, "You stand [this day, all of you, before the Lord your God]" (Deut. 29:9), we can infer that none of them was lame. And how do we know that not one of them suffered from headaches or toothaches? From the verse, "None among their tribes faltered" (Ps. 105:37).

"[All the people saw] the sounds and the lightning"—Normally, one cannot see a sound, but here they saw both the sounds and lightning. Just as

*The word koah can mean power or capacity.

they saw the lightning they saw the sounds. "When the people saw it"—What did they see? They saw great majesty. —MEKHILTA DE-RABBI SHIM'ON BAR YOHAI

Rabbi Eli'ezer said: How do we know that [at Sinai] the humblest Israelite maidservant saw more than the greatest of the prophets [saw in later times]? Because it is written, "When the people saw it." What did they see? They saw great majesty.

"They fell back (vayanu'u)"—The term "to fall back (ni'ah)" connotes madness, as in the verse, "The earth is swaying (no'a tanu'a) like a drunkard" (Isa. 24:20), and the verse, "Their hearts and the hearts of their people trembled (vayana') as trees of the forest sway (keno'a) before a wind" (Isa. 7:2).

"All the people saw the sounds"—Rabbi Yehudah said: When people speak to one another they hear the vibrations of each other's voices but they do not see any visual manifestation. Israel, however, not only heard the voice of the Holy One, blessed be He, but also saw it issuing forth from the mouth of the All-Powerful in the form of lightning and thunder, as it is written, "All the people saw the sounds." —YALKUT SHIM'ONI

"Saw the sounds"—Bar Kappara said: The Holy One, blessed be He, made invisible things visible, gave the power of hearing to things that do not hear— "See, this very stone shall be a witness against us, [for it heard all the words that the Lord spoke to us]" (Josh. 24:27)—and gave the power of speech to things that do not speak—"Then the Lord opened the ass's mouth" (Num. 22:28). How do we know He made invisible things visible? [From the verse,] "All the people saw the sounds and the lightning." —MIDRASH SHMUEL 9

"All the people saw"—It is not written, "All the people heard," because [at first the sounds] were not heard at all. Rather, as the utterances came forth, everyone would [greet each utterance] by kissing it softly, lovingly. Only then would [the commandment] speak out and proclaim itself. —ZOHAR HADASH, Exodus 41b

When the Holy One, blessed be He, revealed Himself at Mount Sinai, all Israel was able to see [the Divine] as one sees light through the glass of a lamp. And in that light, each of them could see what even the Prophet Ezekiel could not. How so? All those celestial sounds were revealed [to them] at once, as we have

said, and "all the people saw the sounds." But only the Shekhinah in her chariot
was revealed to Ezekiel, and he saw it as though through many barriers.
—ZOHAR, Exodus 82a

"All the people saw the sounds"—miraculously. It must be explained, however, that knowing, hearing, and seeing are essentially all one thing, as in the
verse, "Do you not see? Return to the city" (2 Sam. 15:27). What is meant is
perception. —BEKHOR SHOR

"Saw the sounds"—Meaning hail and stones, as in the verse, "God's sounds
and hail" (Exod. 9:28). —RASHBAM

"Saw the sounds"—As I have explained, the phrase can be understood as the
application of a single verb to all the senses. —IBN 'EZRA

[This comment of Ibn 'Ezra's can be understood] by reference to the verse,
"She [got a wicker basket for him] and caulked it with bitumen and pitch"
(Exod. 2:3). Scripture might have been expected to say, "All the people saw the
lightning and *heard* the sounds," just as there scripture might have been ex-
pected to say, "She . . . caulked it with bitumen and *tarred it* with pitch."
However, one verb suffices for both actions. —A COMMENTARY ON IBN 'EZRA

Maimonides, may his memory be a blessing, wrote: In Hebrew, comprehen-
sion through one sense is sometimes expressed in terms of another. Thus it is
written, "See the word of the Lord!" (Jer. 2:31), meaning, "Hear the word of
the Lord"; for what is meant is perception of His word. Similarly, "See the
smell of my son" (Gen. 27:27), meaning "Smell the smell of my son"; for what
is meant is recognizing the smell. Hence it is written, "All the people saw the
sounds and the lightning." —GUIDE OF THE PERPLEXED I:46

"Saw"—What is meant is not literally seeing but rather comprehending.
—SHEM TOV

"All the people saw"—understood. —EFODI

"Saw"—comprehended the sounds, as in the verse, "Esau saw that Isaac had
blessed Jacob" (Gen. 28:6), or "Jacob saw that there were food rations to be had
in Egypt" (Gen. 42:1), or "I see that your father's manner toward me is not as
it has been in the past" (Gen. 31:5). —RABBI MEYUḤAS BEN ELIYAHU

"Saw the sounds"—What is meant is inner vision. —ME'OR HA'AFELAH

"Saw the sounds"—The plain sense is that they were able to see even invisible things. However, knowledge that something is true can also be expressed in terms of seeing, as in the verse, "See, this is what I found, said Koheleth" (Eccles. 7:27). —HIZKUNI

"Saw the sounds"—There are instances [in scripture] where seeing is substituted for hearing, as in, "Jacob saw that there were food rations to be had in Egypt" (Gen. 42:1). But our Sages, may their memory be a blessing, say Israel actually saw the [Divine] voice. —TUR

"Saw the sounds"—"They saw sound, something that normally cannot happen" (Mekhilta). In other words, the meaning of this phrase is not that they *heard* the sounds, as some commentators, may their memory be a blessing, have said, pointing out that in a number of places [in scripture] one kind of sense perception takes the place of another; for example: "My heart has seen" (Eccles. 1:16), "My ear has heard and understood it" (Job. 13:1), "See the smell of my son" (Gen. 27:27). Rather, through a miracle they were actually able to see sound, something that is not otherwise possible. Thus our Sages, may their memory be a blessing, said: "They affixed two crowns to each word that issued from the mouth of the Holy One, blessed be He" (Shabbat 88b); and Rashi, may his memory be a blessing, explains: "[They affixed them] to tangible, visible words, as it is written, 'Saw the sounds.' " —Rabbi Avraham Bakarat Halevi, SEFER ZIKKARON

"All the people saw the sounds"—They saw them reverberating in each other's ears and emerging from the fire, and they saw the sound of the horn bring the dead to life. —YONATAN

GOD THUNDERS MARVELOUSLY WITH HIS VOICE

"God thunders marvelously with His voice" (Job 37:5)—What is meant by "thunders"? When the Holy One, blessed be He, gave the Torah at Sinai, He displayed great marvels to Israel with His voice. How? The Holy One, blessed be He, spoke, and His voice reverberated throughout the world. Israel, hearing the voice coming from the south, ran southward to greet it. But then it shifted to the north, so they ran northward. Then it shifted to the east, so they ran eastward. Then it shifted to the west, so they ran westward. Then it came from heaven, so they looked up. Then it came from the earth, so they looked down. Thus it is written, "From the heavens He let you hear His voice to discipline you" (Deut. 4:36). Then Israel said to one another, "Where can wisdom be found; [where is the source of understanding]?" (Job 28:12). What Israel was saying was, "Where is the Holy One, blessed be He, coming from, the east or the south? For it is written, 'The Lord came [to] Sinai; He shone upon them from Seir [i.e., the east]' (Deut. 33:2); and it is written, 'God is coming from Teman [i.e., the south]' (Hab. 3:3)."

It is written, "All the people saw the voices"—not "the voice" but "the voices." Rabbi Yohanan said: [God's] voice split into seventy different voices, one for each of the seventy languages, so that all the nations could hear [Him] in their own languages. And when they did so, they died [of fright]; but Israel heard and was unharmed.

How did the voice issue forth? Rabbi Tanhuma said: It issued forth in dual fashion, slaying the idolaters who did not accept the Torah and giving life to Israel who did accept it. This is what Moses meant when he said to them forty years later, "For what mortal ever heard the voice of the living God speak out of the fire, as we did, and lived?" (Deut. 5:23)—You heard the voice and lived, but the idolaters heard it and died.

Observe how the voice issued forth. It came to each Jew according to his capacity [to hear]: the elderly, the young men, the children, the infants, the women—each according to his capacity. Even to Moses himself, as it is written, "As Moses spoke, God answered him with a voice" (Exod. 19:19)—meaning, a voice he was capable of hearing. Similarly, it is written, "The voice of the Lord is power" (Ps. 29:4)—not "His power" but simply "power," meaning, according to the power of each [listener to hear]. Even pregnant women heard according to their capacities. In other words, everyone according to his capacity.

Rabbi Yose bar Rabbi Hanina said: If this surprises you, consider the matter of the manna, which came down according to each Israelite's [appetite]. The young men would eat it like bread, as it is written, "I will rain down bread for you from the sky" (Exod. 16:4). The old men would eat it like honey wafers, as it is written, "It tasted like waters in honey" (Exod. 16:31). Infants would eat it [as they drank] their mothers' milk, as it is written, "It tasted like rich cream" (Num. 11:8). The sick would eat it like flour mixed with honey, as it is written, "The food that I had given you—the choice flour, the oil, and the honey, which I had provided for you to eat" (Ezek. 16:19). But to the idolaters it tasted bitter, like coriander seed, as it is written, "Now the manna was like coriander seed" (Num. 11:7).

Rabbi Yose bar Rabbi Hanina said: If the manna, which was one kind of food, turned into many kinds in order to suit the needs of individual people, how much more so did the Divine voice, so filled with power, have to adapt itself to each listener so that he would not be harmed by hearing it. How do we know the voice split into many different voices so that the listeners would not be harmed by it? From the verse, "All the people saw the voices." Hence, "God thunders marvelously with His voice." —EXODUS RABBAH 5:9

AN EXPLANATION

God's voice sounded from one end of the world to the other, to teach you that the Glory of the Lord and His sacred word are not limited to one spot but fill the whole world, encompassing all the corners of the earth at once.

"Coming from the south"—That is, the Holy One, blessed be He, tried to persuade the people of the south to accept the Torah. "It shifted to the north"—so that the northerners would hear it. The same applies to the east and the west, as explained by our rabbis in their interpretation of the verse, "The Lord came [to] Sinai; [He shone upon them from Seir; He appeared from Mount Paran, and approached from Rivevot-kodesh]" (Deut. 33:2). For people living at the equator [i.e., closer to heaven] to hear it, "it came from heaven." And to reach the outlying area where we live, "it came from the earth."

Now, there is more to this matter, for the main purpose of the Torah is to achieve perfection of the soul, but it is also beneficial for people in their earthly lives—for example, in civil matters and the like. Thus it is written that the voice came first from the south, for this is the right-hand side,* an allusion to the well-being of the soul, as in the verse, "In her right hand is length of days" (Prov. 3:16). Then the voice shifted to the left [north], which has to do with wordly well-being, as in the verse, "In her left, riches and honor" (Prov. 3:16).

[The Torah] contains all kinds of practical wisdom—such as logic, geometry, fractions—upon which the light of human intelligence shines (yizrah). Therefore the Midrash says the voice shifted to the east (mizrah), for these [sciences] illuminate the sources of knowledge. [The Torah] also contains

*The cardinal directions were reckoned facing east.

Divine wisdom, which is quite obscure, and most people who delve into it must grope in the dark rather than explore it in the light. Therefore the Midrash says the voice shifted to the west, where the sun sets and the light of knowledge is extinguished, leaving faith alone to illuminate its path.

Referring to astronomy and the calculations of the seasons and the months, which are also quite obscure, the Midrash says the voice shifted to heaven. And referring to the sciences of nature and the earth, it says the voice shifted to the earth.

This, then, is the meaning of the verse, "Where is the source of understanding?" (Job 28:12). Israel saw that the Lord's voice brought with it all sorts of wisdom, and they did not know which to take hold of and concentrate on, for all of them seemed conducive to spiritual well-being.

"Hence it is written, 'From the heavens He let you hear His voice. . . . [On earth He let you see His great fire]' (Deut. 4:36)"—This verse supports the view of Rabbi Yishma'el in the *Mekhilta,* who taught as follows: One verse says, "I spoke to you from the very heavens" (Exod. 20:19), while another says, "The Lord came down upon Mount Sinai" (Exod. 19:20). The difficulty is resolved by a third verse, which says, "From the heavens He let you hear His voice. . . . [On earth He let you see His great fire.]" This differs from the view of Rabbi 'Akiva, who said: We can infer [from the two verses in Exodus] that the Holy One, blessed be He, inclined the highest heavens down to touch the top of the mountain and spoke to them [there] from heaven.

"As explained by our rabbis in their interpretation of the verse, 'The Lord came [to] Sinai' (Deut. 33:2)"—[In this connection] Sifrei (314) cites the verse, "Like an eagle who rouses his nestlings . . . [so spread He His wings]" (Deut. 32:11). The effect [of juxtaposing these two verses] is: "the Lord came [to] Sinai; [He shone upon them from Seir; He appeared from Mount Paran, and approached from Rivevot-kodesh]," i.e., from three of the four directions, "like an eagle who rouses his nestlings." The eagle does not enter his nest without first flapping his wings among the surrounding trees and branches, so as to awaken his young and get them ready to receive him. In like manner, when the Holy One, blessed be He, revealed Himself in order to give the Torah to Israel, He did not reveal Himself from one direction only, but from all four, as in the verse, "He said: The Lord came [to] Sinai; He shone upon them from Seir; He appeared from Mount Paran, and approached from Rivevot-kodesh." What is the fourth direction? "God came from Teman [i.e., the south]" (Hab. 3:3).

"It is written, 'All the people saw the voices' "—The Midrash takes the view that these were not the voices referred to earlier—"There were voices [i.e., thunder], and lightning, and a dense cloud" (Exod. 19:16)—but rather another voice that issued forth from the All-Powerful and spoke to them, the voice of God out of the fire, engraving itself on the tablets. This is the view of Rabbi 'Akiva, as we learn in the *Mekhilta*.

"[God's voice] split into seventy different voices"—See *Tanhuma* and Nachmanides on Parashat Yitro.

"They died"—A hyperbole referring to their fear. Similarly, when it says, "The idolaters heard it and died," it simply means they were seized with a great trembling, as if they were dying of fright. But the voice brought Israel new life and healing.

"So that the listeners would not be harmed"—See Nachmanides on Parashat Va'ethanan.

"The elderly . . . according to [their] capacity"—Bedersi writes: The Divine words were couched in such a way that anyone who examined them could understand them as well as if they were his own familiar thoughts, and thus he could agree to fulfill them and could take issue with anyone who contradicted them. This was equally true for the prophets, who were privy to God's counsel (hence, "even to Moses himself [according to his capacity]"); for the sages (hence, "[to] the elderly . . . according to [their] capacity"); and for the masses, with their received opinions (hence, "[to] the children [according to their capacity]"). —YEFEH TO'AR

THE VOICES THROUGH WHICH THE TORAH WAS GIVEN

"All the people saw the voices"—Can voices be seen? In fact, what they saw were the voices to which David [traditional author of the Psalms] referred:

—"The voice of the Lord is over the waters; the God of Glory thunders, the Lord, [over the mighty waters]. The voice of the Lord is power" (Ps. 29:3–4). And it is written, "By the power of my hand have I wrought it" (Isa. 10:13); and it is written, "My hand founded the earth" (Isa. 48:13); [i.e., Israel at Sinai saw the work of Creation].

—"The voice of the Lord is majestic" (Ps. 29:4). And it is written, "His deeds are majestic and glorious; His beneficence is everlasting" (Ps. 111:3); [i.e., they saw His deeds].

—"The voice of the Lord breaks cedars" (Ps. 29:5)—It is a bow [so powerful that it can] split cedar and cypress trees.

—"The voice of the Lord kindles flames of fire" (Ps. 29:7)—It makes peace between fire and water. Having kindled the fire, it prevents it from boiling away the water, but it also prevents the water from putting out the fire.

—"The voice of the Lord convulses the wilderness; [the Lord convulses the wilderness of Kadesh]" (Ps. 29:8), as it is written, "He shows kindness to His anointed, with David and his offspring forever" (Ps. 18:51).

—"The voice of the Lord causes hinds to calve, and strips forests bare; while in His temple all say 'Glory!' " (Ps. 29:9); and it is also written, "I adjure you, O maidens of Jerusalem, by gazelles or by hinds of the field" (Song 3:5).

We have thus seen that the Torah was given through seven voices, in all of which they saw the Lord of the World revealed. That is what is meant by the verse, "All the people saw the voices." —SEFER HABAHIR

"The voice of the Lord is over the waters"—an allusion to the supernal waters of Grace.*

" 'The voice of the Lord is power,' and it is written, . . . 'My hand founded the earth' "—referring to the left hand [of God], which means the Divine Attribute of Strength.* Hence the verse continues, "My right hand spread out the skies" (Isa. 48:13).

"The voice of the Lord kindles flames of fire"—referring to Peace and Truth,* for it makes peace between the fire and the water.

"The voice of the Lord convulses the wilderness"—and then a prooftext is brought, "He shows kindness to His anointed," an allusion to Eternity,* which stems from Grace.*

The seventh voice is in the verse, "The voice of the Lord causes hinds to calve," to which is adduced the verse, "by hinds of the field." As you know, the hind is a symbol of the Shekhinah,* and the field referred to is the Apple Orchard [i.e., paradise]. This is also the meaning of the verse, "Even the hind in the field foresakes her newborn fawn" (Jer. 14:5), a metaphor for the exile of the Shekhinah. So is the phrase "morning hind" (Ps. 22:1), for [the Shekhinah] is like a hind at dawn, as in the verse, "Hear my voice, O Lord, at daybreak" (Ps. 5:4).

But because Israel did not perceive [God Himself] until the very end [of the Ten Commandments], [the Torah] refers to lightning, the horn, and the mountain smoking, [which were, at first, all that they perceived]. —RECANATI

*Sefirot.

One verse says, "All the people saw the voices," while another says, "You heard the sound of words [but saw no shape]" (Deut. 4:12). How can this be? At first they "saw the voices." What did they see? The seven voices referred to by David [in Psalm 29]. And finally they heard the utterance coming from all of them. —SEFER HABAHIR

And since at this moment they actually saw Him, our Rabbis, may their memory be a blessing, say they fainted away, either in the sense of "no spirit remained in me"* or in the sense of the prophetic [trance]. —RECANATI

"In the sense of 'no spirit remained in me' "—The force of the perception so completely overwhelmed Daniel's senses that it was as if his soul had departed and ascended on high. Now it might be objected that Israel's perception [at Sinai], being prophetic, was higher than Daniel's. But even prophetic visions bring with them trembling and shaking and a blackout of the senses, as we see in the case of Abraham: "A deep, dark dread descended upon him" (Gen. 15:12). —EVEN YEKARAH

"No spirit remained in me," as in the verse, "No spirit is left in me" (Dan. 10:17). The full verse is, "How can this servant of my Lord speak with my Lord, seeing that my strength has failed and no spirit is left in me?" As Ibn 'Ezra explains, these words are spoken by the angel [in Daniel's vision], and since at the moment [of the revelation at Sinai] [the people] Israel were like angels, the expression is fitting. But if the reference is to the verse, "[His illness grew worse,] until he had no spirit [lit., breath] left in him" (1 Kings 17:17), Rabbi David Kimhi has explained this as referring to a case of [a child] who had not, in fact, died, but whose illness was so severe that his vital signs, both breathing and pulse, were undetectable, so that his mother thought he was dead. And the same is said of Daniel, that he had no more breath in him. But the correct explanation [of the verse in Kings] is that [the child] had in fact died. [Thus a comparison with this verse is inappropriate.]

Now I will tell you something wondrous. It is my understanding from the words of our Rabbis, may their memory be a blessing, that human speech resounds in the air, penetrating layer upon layer of atmosphere and firmament until it reaches heaven. If it is virtuous and upright, expressed in holiness, it is carried to Him-Who-Spoke-and-the-World-Came-Into-Being. The speech is praised, its speaker is praised, and it is recorded there forever. But if the speech

*Cf. Dan. 10:17, discussed below.

is wicked or corrupt or libelous, woe to its speaker, for it will be recorded most unfavorably on high. This is alluded to in the verse, "The guilt of Judah is inscribed [with a stylus of iron, engraved with an adamant point on the tablet of their hearts, and on the horns of their altars]" (Jer. 17:1). Consequently, Jews have always bemoaned their troubles in a loud voice, so that their words resound in the air and penetrate the layers of atmosphere. Indeed, the great scientific genius Rabbi Sa'adyah Gaon wrote something akin to this in relation to the verse, "All the people saw the sounds," that the voice [of God] penetrated the air and resounded there, as if it had been written in actual letters that could be seen. —Rabbi David ben Zimra, MAGEN DAVID

OF TWO KINDS

The frightening sights [Israel] saw at Sinai were of two kinds: (a) prophetic visions that they were able to see in their mind's eye and perceive with inner senses, much like the sounds and sights the prophets saw in their visions; and (b) actual sounds and sights that they saw and heard with their physical eyes and ears.

The Sages, may their memory be a blessing, said: With every utterance that they heard from the mouth of the Lord, they fainted away [lit., their souls left them] (Shabbat 88). What this means is that because they were not prepared for prophecy, their physical bodies posing a block between them and the Holy One and holding back their souls, the latter broke away altogether from their bodies, as occurs at the time of death. It was at that moment that they saw the sounds and the lightning, with the inner, prophetic eye of their souls. This is what is described by the verse, "All the people saw the sounds and the lightning." Our Sages, may their memory be a blessing, said they saw what is [normally only] audible and heard what is [normally only] visible, for their perception was through the inner senses.

Then, when God finished speaking to them, their souls returned. It was as our Sages, may their memory be a blessing, said: The Holy One, blessed be He, let flow the dew of resurrection, restoring souls to lifeless corpses. Then they were able to see the sounds and the lightning with their physical eyes, for there were real sounds and lightning to be witnessed. It was then that they recoiled twelve miles,* as our Sages, may their memory be a blessing, said (Shabbat 88). Concerning this it is written again, "[when] the people saw [it]"—meaning physically—"they fell back and stood at a distance]" (Exod.

*See note, p. 24.

20:15). And because this happened all through the proclamation of the Ten Commandments, the subject precedes the verb [at the beginning of the verse], indicating a prior action.

Concerning the words "['You speak to us,'] they said to Moses" (Exod. 20:16), there is disagreement in the Midrash. According to the view that they heard all the Ten Commandments directly from the All-Powerful, they said this only after the ten were finished. According to the view that they only heard the first two of the ten directly, they said this after the second. Neither view is in accord with that of Nachmanides, who maintains that they said it before any of the Ten Commandments was uttered. But if that had been the case, why did the Lord say to Moses, "Go down, warn the people" (Exod. 19:21)? They themselves would already have pulled back and stood at a distance before the commandments began! —MALBIM

Rabbi Abba said: It is written, "All the people saw the sounds." Saw? Should it not be "heard"? Rather, this is what we have learned: the sounds etched themselves into the darkness, the cloud, and the fog, becoming visible there, as visible as something corporeal. [Hence] they [both] saw visible things and heard audible things out of that darkness and fog and cloud. And the sight brought them a celestial illumination, so that they came to know things subsequent generations could not know: they all saw [the Divine] face to face. This is what is meant by the verse, "Face to face the Lord spoke to you" (Deut. 5:4). What was it that enabled them to see what they did? Rabbi Yose taught: It was the light shed by the voices, all of which shone brightly. By this [light] they saw all the secrets and mysteries and all the generations that were to come until the time of the King Messiah. Thus it is written, "All the people saw the sounds"— they actually saw them. —ZOHAR, Exodus 81–82

"All the people saw the sounds"—I heard a parable from my master and grandfather [the Ba'al Shem Tov], may his memory be a blessing: A musician was playing very sweetly, giving his listeners such pleasure they could not contain themselves and began to dance. In their delight at the sweetness and pleasantness of the music, they danced with great abandon. The closer one stood to the music, the greater his delight and the more enthusiastic his dancing. Along came a deaf person, who heard nothing. Seeing people dancing this way, he thought they had gone mad. Why are they so happy? he thought. Had he been able to hear, he would have understood that it was because of the great delight and enjoyment they derived from the sound of the instrument, and he too would have begun dancing.

That is the meaning of "All the people saw the sounds." They saw that the blessed Lord was making Himself manifest to all of them equally in the full light of His divinity, which they could all perceive together. When they saw how great the joy was [all about them]—"The angels of the hosts were skipping about" (Ps. 68:13)—they understood that it was on account of the sweetness and pleasantness of the light of the holy Torah, and they tried very hard to hear its sound, even though they were hard of hearing. Until that point they had not heard any sounds—that is, they had not heard the sweetness and pleasantness of the sound of the Torah. Then, although they did not perceive it directly, they inferred it from the celebration, which they understood was occasioned by the great delight of the Torah, and so they tried very hard to hear the sound, in hopes of experiencing it directly and understanding it. —DEGEL MAHANEH EFRAYIM

"Angels *(mal'akhei)"*—in the verse, it actually says "kings *(malkhei)."* See Shabbat 88b and Pa'neah Raza on Parashat Yitro.

"All the people saw the sounds"—The people were looking at the external manifestations: the thunder, the lightning, etc. —EMET VE'EMUNAH, citing Rabbi Menahem of Kotzk

"All the people saw the sounds"—It should have said, "All the people *heard.*" [What is the explanation?] It is said that all "seeing" is in the mind's eye [i.e., entails understanding]. These "sounds" were thunder, the *"lapidim"* (lit., torches) were lightning, and as for the horn sounded at the top of Mt. Sinai, it is said that it was the left horn of Abraham's ram [the one that appeared at the Binding of Isaac], the great right horn being held in reserve for blowing when King Messiah comes, as it is written, "A great ram's horn shall be sounded" (Isa. 27:13). The significance of this is that the awakening at Mount Sinai shall find its counterpart at the time of the coming of the Messiah, but it shall be even greater. —ME'OR HA'AFELAH

Concerning the "voices" of the Giving of the Torah it is written, "[The Lord spoke those words] . . . with a mighty voice *(velo yasaf)"* (Deut. 5:19). [Onkelos] renders *velo yasaf,* "He did not stop." For the voices remain today as they were then, only, as then, we need preparation in order to hear them. Thus it is written, "Now then, if you will hear My voice" (Exod. 19:5). —SIAH SARFEI KODESH, citing Rabbi Yizhak Me'ir of Gur

Rabbi Natan said: Whence do we know that the Omnipresent showed our Father Abraham Gehinnom,* the Giving of the Torah, and the splitting of the Reed Sea?

"When the sun set and it was very dark, there appeared a [smoking] oven, [and a flaming torch]" (Gen. 15:17)—this teaches us about Gehinnom, as it is written, "[His rock shall melt with terror . . . —declares the Lord, who has a fire in Zion,] who has an oven in Jerusalem" (Isa. 31:9).

"There appeared a smoking oven and a flaming torch (lapid)" (Gen. 15:17)—this teaches us about the Giving of the Torah, as it is written, "All the people saw the voices and lightning (lapidim)."

"[A flaming torch which passed] between those pieces (hagezarim)" (Gen. 15:17)—this teaches us about the splitting of the Reed Sea, as it is written, "Who split apart (gozer . . . ligezarim) the Sea of Reeds" (Ps. 136:13).

He showed him the Temple and the order of the sacrifices, as it is written, "Bring Me a three-year-old heifer, [a three-year-old she-goat, a three-year-old ram, a turtledove, and a young bird]" (Gen. 15:9).

He showed him the four empires that would one day subjugate his children, as it is written, "As the sun was about to set, a trance fell on Abram, and a deep, dark dread descended upon him" (Gen. 15:12). "Dread" refers to the Babylonian empire; "dark" refers to the Median empire; "deep" refers to the Hellenistic empire; and "descended" refers to the fourth, the wicked empire of Rome. Others reverse the order: "descended (naflah)" refers to the Babylonian empire, as it is written, "fallen (naflah) is Babylon" (Isa. 21:9); "deep (gedolah)" refers to the Median empire, as it is written, "King Ahasuerus promoted (giddal) [Haman]" (Esther 3:1); "dark" refers to the Hellenistic empire, which brought the gloom of fasting [to end their sufferings] upon Israel; and "dread (eimah)" refers to the fourth empire, [that of Rome], as it is written, "As I looked on in the night vision, there was a fourth beast—fearsome, dreadful (eimtani), and very powerful . . . —that devoured and crushed, and stamped the remains with its feet" (Dan. 7:7). —MEKHILTA, Yitro

---

Thus far the words of the Mekhilta. What follows are the words of Rabbi 'Akiva and the other sages as they appear in the twenty-eighth chapter of Pirkei de-Rabbi Eli'ezer, words that do not appear in the censored versions.

---

*The Valley of Ben-Hinnom in Jerusalem, a place of human sacrifice in pre-Israelite times, later synonymous with hell.

Rabbi 'Akiva said: At [the making of the Covenant of] the Pieces, the Holy One, blessed be He, showed our Father Abraham the empires that would come to power and then fall.

Thus it is written, "Bring Me a three-year-old heifer" (Gen. 15:9). This refers to the fourth empire, that of the Arameans [Rome], which was like a trampling heifer.

"A three-year-old she-goat" (Gen. 15:9)—This refers to the Hellenistic empire, as it is written, "Then the he-goat grew very great" (Dan. 8:8).

"A three-year-old ram" (Gen. 15:9)—This refers to the empire of Media and Persia.

"A turtledove (tor)" (Gen. 15:9)—This refers to the Ishmaelites. Tor is not the biblical [Hebrew] word [meaning turtledove], but the Aramaic word meaning ox. When a male and a female ox are yoked together they will begin ploughing up the ground in all the valleys [cf. Isa. 28:24].

"And a young bird" (Gen. 15:9)—This refers to Israel, who are compared to a young bird in the verse, "O my dove, in the cranny of the rocks" (Song 2:14), and in the verse, "Only one is my dove, my perfect one" (Song 6:9).

Rabbi Aḥa ben Ya'akov said: These references to "three" allude to mighty men, as it is written, "A threefold cord is not readily broken" (Eccles. 4:12). Said Rabbi Mesharshia: It means [the empires] will come in three stages; they will rule Israel three times. The first time each will rule separately, the second time they will rule in pairs, and the third time all three together will do battle with the Son of David,* as it is written, "Kings of the earth take their stand . . . [together against the Lord and against His anointed]" (Ps. 2:2).

Rabbi Yehoshu'a said: Abraham took his sword and sliced them all in two, as it is written, "He . . . cut them in two" (Gen. 15:10). Had he not done so, the world could not have endured; in doing so, he sapped their strength. He then brought the pieces together, as it is written, "Placing each half opposite the other" (Gen. 15:10). He left a young dove alive, as it is written, "He did not cut up the birds (hazippor)." (This teaches that wherever the Torah speaks of "birds" [zippor], it means doves.)

A vulture swooped down to separate and devour the pieces, the vulture being the Son of David, who is compared to a vulture in the verse, "My inheritance acts like a speckled vulture" (Jer. 12:9). From sunup to sundown, Abraham would sit and wave his kerchief back and forth over them, to keep the vulture from getting hold of them. Rabbi El'azar ben 'Azaryah said: This teaches us that the entire period when these four empires rule will seem like

---

*The Messiah, who will re-establish the Jewish kingdom.

a single day to the Holy One, blessed be He. Rabbi El'azar ben Arakh said to him: You are undoubtedly right—for it is written, "He has left me forlorn, in misery the whole day long" (Lam. 1:13)—save for two-thirds of an hour. You will be convinced of this if you consider that when the sun has declined in the west to within two-thirds of an hour of sunset, its strength is spent and it no longer shines brightly. Thus before nightfall the Son of David, Israel's light, shall appear, as it is written, "There shall be light at evening" (Zech. 14:7).

Abraham arose and prayed to the Holy One, blessed be He, that his children not be subjugated to these four empires. A deep sleep came over him, as it is written, "[As the sun was about to set], a trance fell on Abram" (Gen. 15:12). Can a person pray lying down? Rather, what we learn from this verse is that it was the power of his prayer, asking that his children endure the rule of the four empires, that caused Abram to lie down and fall asleep, as it is written, "A deep, dark dread descended upon him" (Gen. 15:12). "Dread" refers to the fourth empire [Rome], of which it is written, "[There was a fourth beast]—fearsome, dreadful, and very powerful" (Dan. 7:7). "Dark" refers to the Hellenistic empire, which darkened Israel's eyes by [forbidding the observance of] all the commandments in the Torah. "Deep (gedolah)" refers to the empire of Media and Persia, which could afford (gadlah) to sell Israel for nothing.* "Descended" refers to the Babylonian empire, into the hands of which the crown of Israel fell. "Upon him" refers to the Ishmaelites, over whom the Son of David will arise, as it is written, "I will clothe his enemies in disgrace, while upon him his crown shall sparkle" (Ps. 132:18).

Rabbi 'Azaryah said: These empires were only created to serve as firewood for Gehinnom [Hell], as it is written, "There appeared a smoking oven, and a flaming torch which passed" (Gen. 15:17), "oven" and "torch" being references to Gehinnom, as it is written, "[Thus] declares the Lord, who has a fire in Zion, who has an oven in Jerusalem" (Isa. 31:9). —PIRKEI DE-RABBI ELI'EZER 28

AND THE MOUNTAIN SMOKING

"And the mountain smoking"—Smoke results when light [i.e., fire] takes hold of a material object derived from earth. Similarly, the conversion of the animal soul from something potentially holy† into something actually holy is called smoke. The nature of smoke is that it rises, and when it approaches fire, the

*A reference to the story of Esther.
†Nogah. See note, p. 137.

object that is producing the smoke is ignited. Similarly, the smoking mountain brought about thunder and lightning, which are the ebb and flow of holiness.
—TORAH OR

THEY FELL BACK AND STOOD AT A DISTANCE

"When the people saw it, they fell back *(vayanu'u)*"—The verb *no'a* denotes staggering, as in the verse, "The earth is swaying [like a drunkard]" (Isa. 24:20).

"And stood at a distance"—More than twelve miles away. What this tells us is that Israel recoiled twelve miles and came back twelve miles, altogether twenty-four miles, after each of the Ten Commandments, so that on that one day they walked 240 miles.* At that hour the Holy One, blessed be He, said to the ministering angels, "Go help your brethren along," as it is written, "The angels† of the hosts help them along" (Ps. 68:13)—they help them walk away and help them come back. And not only do the ministering angels help, but the Holy One, blessed be He, does so as well, as it is written, "His left hand was under my head, his right arm embraced me" (Song 2:6).

Rabbi Yehudah ben Rabbi Ila'i said: As [the Israelites] were being scorched by the sun above, the Holy One, blessed be He, said to the Clouds of Glory, "Shower the dew of life on My children," as it is written, "The earth trembled, the sky rained because of God" (Ps. 68:9); and it is written, "You released a bountiful rain, O God" (Ps. 68:10). When was all this glory manifest? When Israel was the most beautiful of the nations and respected the Torah, as it is written, "Housewives are sharing in the spoils" (Ps. 68:13), "spoils" meaning the Torah, as it is written, "I rejoice over Your promise as one who obtains great spoil" (Ps. 119:162). —MEKHILTA

"The people . . . fell back and stood at a distance"—They left their camp, which was twelve miles across, and they trembled. This happened after they heard the first two commandments. This is also what happened to the prophets: when they were seized with prophecy they trembled and quaked with fear lest their senses be overwhelmed and their bodies grow weak. And when [the people Israel] felt unable to go on listening to the rest of the commandments, they said to Moses, "You speak to us . . . and we will obey" (Exod. 20:16),

*See note, p. 24.
†See note, p. 211.

which is explained in Deuteronomy. He said to them, "God has come only in order to test you" (Exod. 20:17); in other words, He tested them in this confrontation, giving them direct experience of prophecy, so that if someone were to come along one day claiming to be a prophet, they would know what prophecy was like and could tell whether he was a true or a false prophet. Hence it is written concerning the false prophet, "The Lord your God is testing you" (Deut. 13:4). —ME'OR HA'AFELAH

"They . . . stood at a distance"—out of humility, as in the verse, "Moses hid his face" (Exod. 3:6). And having pulled back from the perception [of God's word], they then drew nearer and perceived even more. This is what is meant by "The people remained at a distance" (Exod. 20:18). It is similar to "The Lord revealed Himself to me from afar" (Jer. 31:3). And it says, "they fell back *(vayanu'u)*" to indicate that they swayed *(nitna'ne'u)* [in intense concentration] in order to focus their minds and perceive more clearly, as one does in prayer.

This was one of the three questions the Christian asked Rabbi Shim'on: "Why do the Jews, more than any other people, sway when they read?" [The second was,] "Why do you say you cleave to the Lord, even though you are beaten and chastised more than any other people? (Such treatment) does not befit those who cleave to the King!" And the third was, "You hope for the building of the Third Temple; yet the Torah says, 'The glory of this latter House shall be greater than that of the former one' (Hag. 2:9), alluding to the First and Second Temples but not the Third! What do you say to that, old man?" [Rabbi Shim'on] looked at him, and he turned into a pile of bones.

The questions this wicked man asked have already been asked above [in the previous section]. The swaying shows Israel's distinction, for they derive from fire, and it is written "The lifebreath of man is the lamp of the Lord" (Prov. 20:27). Just as lamplight always wavers and then flares up, Israel sways from the strength of its [inner] fire, as it is written, "O you, the Lord's remembrancers, take no rest" (Isa. 62:6); and it is written, "O God, do not be silent" (Ps. 83:2). But the other nations flicker and die down, like the bone in the fire that is still and does not move. Israel retains this [practice] from the time of the Giving of the Torah, as it is written, "When the people saw it, they swayed."

As for the fact that, while we are close to the King, we are beaten and tortured, the explanation is that we are like the heart, which, being in the center of the body, is prescient, for it is very delicate and pure. Thus it is written, "More than all that you guard, guard your heart, for it is the source of life" (Prov. 4:23). Israel, then, being compared to the heart, feels all sorrow and pain more keenly than the other nations, which are compared to the body.

As for the question about the First and Second Temples, had Israel not sinned they would only have [needed] the First Temple. It would have been more fitting for it to have been built by the Holy One, blessed be He, Himself, as it is written, "[You will bring them and plant them in Your own mountain,] . . . the sanctuary, O Lord, which Your hands established" (Exod. 15:17). But since Israel sinned, the [first two] Temples had to be completed by human beings, and so they did not last, as it is written, "Unless the Lord builds the house, its builders labor in vain on it" (Ps. 127:1). But [in the End of Days] the Holy One, blessed be He, will Himself build Jerusalem, fulfilling the verse, "The sanctuary, O Lord, which Your hands established," and in accordance with the verse, "I myself—declares the Lord—will be a wall of fire all around it, and I will be a glory inside it" (Zech. 2:9). It is concerning this that scripture says, "The glory of this latter House shall be greater than that of the former one." —ZEROR HAMOR

"All the people witnessed the thunder and lightning, the blare of the horn and the mountain smoking; and when the people saw it, they fell back and stood at a distance"—They saw the face of the Shekhinah and reached the level of fully conscious prophecy, things not attained by any prophet except Moses our Teacher, peace be to him. [How is it that] when the Lord spoke to them face to face, they were not frightened, but when they saw "the thunder and lightning, the blare of the horn," they were frightened? This comes to tell us how strong and virtuous [the people] Israel were: they witnessed tremendous sounds, fiery lightning, and "a very loud blast of the horn" (Exod. 19:16), without seeing the horn itself or the blower; they saw the mountain smoking; and they saw wonders that had not previously come into the world—yet they were not afraid. When did they become afraid ("They fell back and stood at a distance")? At the second sight, that of the face of the Shekhinah. Hence it says again, "when the people saw it," referring to them seeing the face of the Shekhinah. On that day all of them, from the youngest to the oldest, were privileged to reach the level of the prophet, as it is written, "Face to face the Lord spoke to you on the mountain out of the fire" (Deut. 5:4). On this, Rashi, may his memory be a blessing, writes: " 'All the people witnessed the thunder, etc.'—issuing forth from the mouth of the All-Powerful." That is how he answers the question. —SHEMEN TOV

"When the people saw it, they fell back"—The people referred to at the beginning of the verse—"All the people saw the thunder"—are Israel; but those referred to here—"When the people saw it, they fell back"—are the Mixed Multitude [of gentiles who came out of Egypt together with Israel], who did not "[see] the thunder" but only "stood at a distance."

The explanation of this is: thunder is an extension of the light of the Infinite One, be He blessed. That is, the light of the Infinite One, be He blessed, flows and is revealed to those who efface themselves before Him, be He blessed. This self-effacement takes place when the soul is stirred from within, from the depths. But since the soul is a created and therefore limited thing, yet it is stirred by the Infinite One, be He blessed, who is unlimited and utterly incomprehensible, [the stirring] is like a voice from the Unlimited and Boundless, which draws that which is bounded. But the Mixed Multitude did not have the capacity to be stirred by contemplation of the greatness of the Infinite One, be He blessed, Himself, as it were. Rather, they were mainly stirred by the movement of the heavenly spheres, their size and great height— merely material things; but by the Infinite One, be He blessed, Who is boundless, they were not stirred at all. It was the Mixed Multitude, then, who said, "Make us a god who shall go before us" (Exod. 32:1). They wanted something they could physically see. —TORAH OR

"When the people saw it, they fell back"—For they saw how enormous their distance from Him still was, and they were shaken by the awesome things [they had seen] and could not bear [to go on watching] them. —'AKEDAT YIZHAK

"All the people saw . . . and when the people saw it, they fell back"—[Why does "saw" occur twice in this verse? To tell us two different things.] In the first instance "[the people] saw"—it means they had been deemed worthy of perceiving something holier and more exalted than an angel, something most people are not privileged to see. In the second instance—"When the people saw it, they fell back (vayanu'u)"—it means that [they realized that] the sight was too much for them, much like a person who is carrying something too heavy for him and who begins to stagger (mitno'e'a) under the load. The weight of all this holiness was too much for them, and they began to stagger. —HA'A- MEK DAVAR

"When the people saw it, they fell back (vayanu'u) and stood at a distance"— Rabbi Menahem of Kotzk said: One can see [visions] and sway (velanu'a) [in prayer], and yet stand at a distance [from God]. —'AMUD HA'EMET

"When the people saw it, they fell back and stood at a distance"—The word "saw," [occurring here for a second time in the sentence,] appears to be redundant. What it means, however, is that they saw how far away they were standing. —LIKKUTIM HADASHIM

We must try to understand what point there was in standing at a distance. After all, it is said of the blessed Lord that "His presence fills all the earth!" (Isa. 6:3). I would maintain that every Jew must believe with perfect faith, on the basis of true tradition, that there is one Lord in the world and that miracles demonstrating the uniqueness and greatness of the Creator are only for those of little faith. Hence when Israel saw that the Holy One, blessed be He, at the time of the Giving of the Torah, was manifesting His uniqueness and greatness in a miraculous way, they realized that they still stood "at a distance" and had not yet reached true faith. This is what scripture means by "When the people saw it"—when they saw the miracles—"they fell back and stood at a distance"— they knew that they still stood "at a distance." —BEIT YISRA'EL, citing Rabbi Avraham Ya'akov of Sadgora

"When the people saw it, they fell back and stood at a distance"—As is well known, a righteous person, in his great awe and dread of [God], may His name be blessed, feels that he is still distant [from Him], that he has hardly begun to serve Him, may His name be blessed. That is what is meant by "When the people saw it, they fell back and stood at a distance." —AHAVAT SHALOM

A REMEMBRANCE OF SINAI

" 'When the people saw it, they staggered (vayanu'u)'—Thus we sway (mitna'ne'im) when we study the Torah; for the Torah was given amidst fear, trembling, and shaking" [Ba'al Haturim]. The sage Rabbi Profian Duran writes, "The reason students of the Torah sway (yitno'u) is to arouse the senses and sharpen the memory. Perhaps this is why it says, 'When the people saw it, they staggered (vayanu'u).' " But the sage [Rabbi Yehudah Halevi], author of The Kuzari, gives a different explanation: habit and custom. For in ancient times, [several people] would read from one book, so that each of them would constantly have to pull back [to give the others the opportunity] to read and return; and so this became a custom. —SEFER SHA'ASHU'IM

EXODUS 20:16

"You speak to us," they said to Moses,
*"and we will obey; but let not God
speak to us, lest we die."*

" 'You speak to us,' they said to Moses, 'and we will obey' "—This teaches us that they only had the strength to receive the Ten Commandments, as it is written, "If we hear the voice of the Lord our God any longer, we shall die" (Deut. 5:22). [As for the rest,] "You go closer and hear [all that the Lord our God says]" (Deut. 5:24). From that time on, [the people] Israel were deemed worthy of having the Omnipresent raise prophets from their midst, as it is written, "I will raise up a prophet for them [from among their own people]" (Deut. 18:18). "I was planning to raise up a prophet from among them eventually, but they proved worthy of being given one sooner, as it is written, 'The Lord said to me, ["I have heard the plea that this people made to you;] they did well to speak thus" ' " (Deut. 5:25).

Fortunate are those of whose words the Omnipresent approves. Thus scripture says, "The plea of Zelophehad's daughters is just" (Num. 27:7), and "The plea of the Josephite tribe is just" (Num. 36:5). Fortunate are those of whose words the Omnipresent approves. Thus scripture says, "I pardon, as you have asked" (Num. 14:20).

"May they always be of such mind . . . forever" (Deut. 5:26)—[God says,] "Were it possible to do away with the Angel of Death, I would do so, but I have already issued My decree." Rabbi Yose said: [The people] Israel stood at Mount Sinai on condition that the Angel of Death would have no power over them. Thus it is written, "I had taken you for divine beings, sons of the Most High, all of you" (Ps. 82:6), "but you have undermined yourselves by your deeds, [and so] 'you shall die as men do, fall like any prince' (Ps. 82:7)." —MEKHILTA

When they said, "You go closer and hear" (Deut. 5:24), they believed Moses had been set apart and was fit for prophecy. This is what is meant by the verse, "I will raise up a prophet for them" (Deut. 18:18)—"I had planned to raise up a prophet for them even if they had not asked for one, but now that they have asked, their merit has brought it about sooner," as it is written, "They did well to speak thus" (Deut. 5:25). —BEIRUREI HAMIDDOT

"[The people] Israel stood at Mount Sinai on condition that the Angel of Death would have no power over them"—According to Rabbi Yose, the decree of death that had been issued at the time of Adam's sin was cancelled, so that no Jew thenceforth would die except for his own sins. Thus it is said, "There is no death without sin" (Shabbat 55a).

" 'You speak to us,' they said to Moses, 'and we will obey' "—Thus did they merit being given [other] prophets. And so scripture says, "The Lord your God

will raise up for you a prophet from among your own people, like myself"
(Deut. 18:15). But when they mocked the messengers of God, the holy spirit
[of prophecy] left them. Thus scripture says, "They mocked the messengers of
God [and disdained His words and taunted his prophets until the wrath of the
Lord against His people grew beyond remedy]" (2 Chron. 36:16).

   "Let not God speak to us, lest we die"—Had they heard one more word,
they would have died. But why did they wait to tell Moses this until after the
Ten Commandments had been spoken? (The latter had already been given by
this point.) They thought something else was going to be said. —MEKHILTA
DE-RABBI SHIM'ON BAR YOHAI

Had they heard the entire Torah directly from the Holy One, blessed be He,
they would have said, "The words of the Prophets and the Writings are
worthless; for if the Holy One, blessed be He, had thought they were of value
He would have taught them all to us at Sinai." Therefore they were given to
hear [most of it] from Moses, so that they would know they had to pay
attention to prophets like him as well. —YALKUT DAVID

AND INSCRIBE IT UPON THEIR HEARTS

"You speak to us . . . and we will obey"—Rabbi Yehudah said: From the time
Israel heard the words "I the Lord am your God" on, the Torah they learned
stuck in their minds, so that they would study it and not forget anything. They
came to Moses and said, "Moses, our teacher, be our go-between"—as it is
written, "You speak to us . . . and we will obey"; "Let us not die" (Deut.
5:22)—"what good would there be in our perishing?" [As soon as he began to
do so] they went back to forgetting what they had learned. They said, "Just as
Moses, a man of flesh and blood, is transitory, so are his teachings transitory."
So they returned to Moses and said, "Moses, our teacher, if only [God] would
reveal Himself to us again! If only He would 'give me of the kisses of his mouth'
(Song 1:2)! If only the Torah we learned could stick in our minds as it did!"
He said to them, "Not now, but in the future." This is what is meant by the
verse, "I will put My Torah into their inmost being and inscribe it upon their
hearts" (Jer. 31:33). —SONG OF SONGS RABBAH 1:15

THE SOUND OF GOD

"They heard the sound (kol) of the Lord God [moving about in the garden]"
(Gen. 3:8)—when they approached Mount Sinai. This is what is meant by the

verse, "Has any people heard the voice *(kol)** of a god speaking from out of a fire, [as you have, and survived?]" (Deut. 4:33).

The Mixed Multitude [of gentiles who came out of Egypt with Israel] then died, those who had said to Moses, "Let not God speak to us, lest we die," and thus, [by insisting that the rest of the commandments be revealed through an intermediary,] caused [Israel] to be forgetful of what they would learn of the Torah. These were the [forerunners of the] ignoramuses, of whom it is written, "Cursed be he who lies with any beast" (Deut. 27:21);† for they partake of the character of the Serpent, of which it is written, "Cursed shall you be of all the beasts" (Gen. 3:14). [Israel was subject to] many forms of miscegenation, like those among animals and beasts. There was miscegenation involving the Serpent; miscegenation involving the idolatrous nations, who resemble animals and beasts of the field; miscegenation involving goblins, which are the ghosts of the wicked; and miscegenation involving spirits and ghouls. All these had become intermixed with Israel.

But there is none so accursed as Amalek, who is the evil Serpent, the "alien god" [of Ps. 81:10], the embodiment of all fornication. He is a murderer, and his mate is the poison *(sam)* of idolatry. All [these evils] describe Sama'el [as well]. Now there is more than one Sama'el, and they differ from one another; but it is their descent from the Serpent that makes them the most accursed of all. —ZOHAR, Genesis 28b

"They said to Moses"—after hearing the Ten Commandments—"You speak to us"—and if they had not said this, the Holy One, blessed be He, would probably have told them the rest of the commandments directly. —RASHBAM

" 'You speak to us,' they said to Moses, 'and we will obey; but let not God speak to us, lest we die.' " "Lest we die"—for our failings and our unworthiness to see His Glory and hear His words. Similarly, Manoah said, "We shall surely die, for we have seen a divine being" (Judg. 13:22). Concerning this, it is written in Deuteronomy, "Has any people heard the voice of a god speaking from out of a fire, as you have, and survived?" (Deut. 4:33). —GERSONIDES

---

*See note, p. 143.
†A reference to Pesahim 49b: "Let [a man] not marry the daughter of an ignoramus, because they are detestable, and their wives are vermin, and of their daughters it is said, 'Cursed be he who lies with any beast.' "

" 'You speak to us,' they said to Moses, 'and we will hear' "*—They changed their minds, for originally they had asked to hear the entire Torah from the mouth of the Lord Himself, without a mediator. But then they saw they were not prepared for this, so they said, " 'You speak to us,' so that we can hear, 'but let not God speak to us, lest we die' "—after having fainted away at the utterance of each commandment. Miracles do not happen every day. —MALBIM

The Prophets only heard the voice according to their individual capacities (koḥam), as it is written, "The voice of the Lord is power (koaḥ)" (Ps. 29:4). But Moses our Teacher heard it as it was, as it is written, "He would hear the voice" (Num. 7:89)—the voice as it was. Similarly, when our forefathers stood at Mount Sinai they said, "If we hear the voice of the Lord our God any longer, [we shall die]" (Deut. 5:22), but Moses our Teacher did hear it. Great was Moses' strength, to be able to bear what six hundred thousand people could not, as it is written, "You speak to us . . . and we will obey; [but let not God speak to us, lest we die]." —MISHNAT RABBI ELI'EZER 6

THOUGH GOD HAS SPOKEN TO HIM

"We have seen this day that man may live though God has spoken to him. Let us not die, then, for this fearsome fire will consume us; if we hear the voice of the Lord our God any longer, we shall die" (Deut. 5:21–22)—Having just said that "man may live though God has spoken to him," how is it that they thought they would die, and therefore said, "Let us not die"? What they meant [by these two statements], however, was, "We have seen this day that *you* may live though God has spoken to you; why then do you want us to die? You go closer (Deut. 5:24), for you are not afraid, having survived all these things."

I have heard a beautiful interpretation [of this passage]. Our Sages, may their memory be a blessing, said: No one departs this world without seeing the face of the Shekhinah, though until the time of death one cannot see it. And when they said, "We have seen this day that man may live though God has spoken to him," what they meant was, "We have now proven worthy of seeing the face of the Shekhinah while still alive. Perhaps, then, we shall not die!" In other words, one is [normally] given to see the face of the Shekhinah only at the hour of one's death. " 'Why, then, should we die,'† for we have been

*See note, p. 110.
†An alternative reading of the words translated above as "Let us not die, then."

allowed to see Him while still very much alive? But 'if we hear the voice of the Lord our God any more,' that is, if we are allowed to see more in death than we saw in life, 'we shall die,' that is, we choose to die, since this would be an ascent to a higher level." —Joseph Caro, SERMONS, in OR ẒADDIKIM (Salonica edition)

THEY DID WELL TO SPEAK THUS

"You speak to us . . . and we will obey; [but let not God speak to us, lest we die]." "The Lord said . . . , 'They did well to speak thus. May they always be of such mind, to revere Me and follow all My commandments' " (Deut. 5:25–26). There are two kinds of worship: Sometimes a person's heart is filled with great fervor from above, without any awakening from below. And sometimes preparation and [inner] fervor are needed in order to worship, and one must clothe oneself in love and great awe in order to contemplate and fathom the exaltation of the Creator, be He blessed. Only then can one connect with the higher worlds.

What happened at the time of the Giving of the Torah was the first kind of worship. The Holy One, blessed be He, filled [the people Israel] with love and awe. Therefore they said to Moses, "You speak to us," meaning, "We do not want to go on worshiping [God] without an awakening from below, 'lest we die.' " That is, [they were afraid of] falling some time from this high level and not knowing how to climb back up. "Rather, 'you speak [to us]' "—for Moses represented [acquired] knowledge, and "By knowledge are its rooms filled [with all precious and beautiful things]" (Prov. 24:4). [Having this kind of knowledge] they would never be shamed, for though they might fall from their high level they could go on worshiping out of inner conviction, following in [Moses'] footsteps. Concerning this, the Holy One, blessed be He, said, "They did well to speak thus." "May they always [be of such mind]"—to serve Him, always, out of [an inner] awakening and contemplation. —DEGEL MAHA-NEH EFRAYIM

"The Lord said to me, 'I have heard the plea that this people made to you; they did well to speak thus' " (Deut. 5:25)—This would appear surprising. Would it not have been better for them to hear [the Torah] from the master [i.e., God, rather than the pupil, Moses]? As for their plea, "Lest we die," this is not a valid reason [not to hear God directly]. On the contrary, it is by self-sacrifice that our worship [of God] is elevated. The desire of the soul is to be sacrificed, for thus is it lifted up. Rather, in saying "they did well to speak thus," He was mainly praising them for being truthful and speaking frankly. Such [praise is not due] to those who flatter and cajole without sincerity. Thus He says, "May they always be of such mind" (Deut. 5:26). —OHEV YISRA'EL

One Shavu'ot, as Rabbi Moshe of Kobrin was sitting at his holy table among his followers, he began to expound the verse, "You speak to us . . . and we will obey; but let not God speak to us, lest we die." "Is it possible," he asked, "that Israel, that people of saints, that knowledgeable generation that was privileged to attain the holiness of being present when God revealed Himself at Mount Sinai—is it possible that, out of fear of dying, they refused to hear Him? Would [hearing God] not be our greatest joy, our deepest desire, our fondest pleasure? Do we not hope and pray that we may merit the help of the blessed Lord in drawing near to the supernal Glory, our souls leaving behind their shells and cleaving to the Light of Life?" He repeated his question again and again, with such intense longing and devotion that he eventually collapsed and appeared to have died. The frightened assemblage set about trying to revive him with cold water and at last, by dint of great effort, succeeded in bringing him around. Resuming his seat, he concluded by saying, "What Israel mainly feared when they said, 'Lest we die,' was having to leave off serving the blessed Lord."

EXODUS 20:17

Moses answered the people, "Be not afraid;
for God has come only in order to test you,
and in order that the fear of Him may be
ever on your faces, so that you do not sin."

IN ORDER TO TEST YOU

"Moses answered the people, 'Be not afraid' "—Moses was encouraging them, which shows us his great wisdom, his ability to stand before all those thousands and tens of thousands of people and placate them. Concerning him, later scripture comments, "Wisdom is more of a stronghold to a wise man than ten magnates" (Eccles. 7:19).

"In order to test you"—God's purpose is to make you great.

"And in order that the fear of Him may be ever on your faces"—meaning shamefacedness, a good sign in a person.

"So that you do not sin"—This teaches us that shame leads to fear of sin, as it is written, "They have acted shamefully; they have done abhorrent things" (Jer. 6:15). —MEKHILTA

It is taught: "In order that the fear of Him may be ever on your faces"— meaning shame. "So that you do not sin"—This teaches us that shame leads to fear of sin. Hence it is said that shame is a good sign in a person. Others say: He who is slow to feel shame is a sinner; and if one has no shame, it is clear that his ancestors were not present at Mount Sinai. —NEDARIM 20a

The Holy One, blessed be He, gave Israel three gifts: mercy, shame, and kindness. How do we know about mercy? From the verse, "[That the Lord may] . . . show (lit., give) you compassion" (Deut. 13:18). How do we know about shame? From the verse, "In order that the fear of Him may be ever on your faces." When a person does not sin, it is a sign that he has shame. And if one has no shame, it is clear that his ancestors were not present at Mount Sinai. —PALESTINIAN TALMUD, Kiddushin 4:1

"His ancestors were not present at Mount Sinai"—For it is from there that the heritage of shame derives. —ROSH

Rabbi Nehora'i said: Whoever shames another will in the end be shamed. Moreover, the ministering angels will hound him out of this world and hold him up to universal ridicule. But he who is capable of shame does not readily sin, as it is written, "In order that the fear of Him may be ever on your faces, so that you do not sin." —KALLAH

"Moses answered the people, 'Be not afraid' "—He said to them, "God only gave you the Torah and performed wonders and mighty deeds for you 'in order to test (nassot) you,' to make you greater than all others," as in the verse, "Evil-merodach [of Babylon] raised (nassa) [the head of King Jehoiachin]" (2 Kings 25:27).
   Another interpretation of "in order to test (nassot) you": to make you great through the fulfillment of the commandments, as in the verse, "[The Lord their God shall prosper them on that day; . . . (They shall be)] like crown jewels glittering (mitnosesot) on His soil" (Zech. 9:16); and the verse, "Give those who fear You a banner (nes) for waving (lehitnoses)" (Ps. 60:6).
   Another interpretation of "in order to test you": Until now you have sinned unwittingly; now when you sin it will be intentional. Until now you

did not know the reward of the righteous or the punishment that will be meted out to the wicked in the Time to Come; now you do. —MEKHILTA DE-RABBI SHIM'ON BAR YOHAI

"Will be meted out *(maḥat)*" means "will strike *(makkat)*." Until now you have not been put to the test; now that you know, you will be put to the test.
   "Be not afraid"—For the Holy One, blessed be He, has not performed all these wonders to harm you but only to benefit you, to test whether your hearts would submit to serving Him, and make you fear Him so that you would not sin. All this is for your good. —BEKHOR SHOR

"Moses answered the people, 'Be not afraid' "—for the Lord, may He be exalted, did not reveal these wonders to you, descending in His glory in the cloud, in order to kill you; He did it to raise you up with this wondrous Torah. For [it is the wonders that] will persuade you to accept it. And He showed you terrifying sights so that you would fear Him and follow His Torah. —GERSONIDES

I am surprised to see Nachmanides write, concerning the verse "All the people saw the voices" (Exod. 20:15), "Everything that is mentioned in this passage took place before the Ten Commandments [were given]." . . . . None of the other commentators takes this view. [As they see it,] all this transpired *after* Israel heard the Ten Commandments. And this is correct, for having heard all [the commandments] directly from the All-Powerful, they were not upset by the voices or the terrible lightning or the even more frightening blare of the horn or the smoking mountain, nor did they ask Moses to do anything about them. They pulled back of their own accord, without any command from above, retreating until they were further from the mountain than Moses had placed them. And the reason it says they "stood at a distance" (Exod. 20:15) is that they were afraid the fire and smoke would consume them, and they thought they would be spared that by standing further away. . . .
   It was to explain their fear and trembling at the sound of the Divine voice that they said to Moses, "You speak to us . . . and we will obey; but let not God speak to us, lest we die." In other words, "we regret having asked to hear the voice of the Lord, for it is dangerous to do so." It is as if they had said, "We are not asking that anything be done about the thunder or the lightning or the blare of the horn or the smoking mountain, frightening though they are; we only ask [not to hear] the Divine voice." For they knew it was the Lord's will to proclaim all His commandments and His Torah to them in that same voice.

Thus, after hearing the Ten Commandments [from Him], they felt compelled to ask Moses to prevent the Holy One, blessed be He, from speaking to them further in His own voice. Moses then replied, "Be not afraid; for God has come only in order to test you." In other words, "Do not fear death—you said, 'Lest we die'—for this tremendous Divine voice has only come to you for two precious reasons: 'in order to test you, and in order that the fear of Him may be ever with you, so that you do not sin.' " —ABRABANEL

"To test you"—to enhance your standing in the world. You will acquire a reputation among the nations as the one to whom He revealed Himself in all His glory. "Test *(nassot)*" connotes lifting up and making great, as in the verses, "Raise an ensign *(nes)* [over the peoples]" (Isa. 62:10); "I will . . . lift up My ensign *(nisi)* [to peoples]" (Isa. 49:22); and "[like] a pole *(vekhanes)* upon a mountain" (Isa. 30:17)—something that stands tall. —RASHI

"To test you *(nassot)*"—The word is probably related to "exaltation" *(hit-nas'ut)*, even though it is spelled with the letter *samekh* and the latter with the letter *sin*.* Thus the *Mekhilta* says God came to enhance [Israel's] standing. His intention was that, having received the Torah, they would be exalted above the other nations. Hence it is written in a previous passage, "You shall be My treasured possession among all the peoples" (Exod. 19:5). Furthermore, the Torah would make them "a kingdom of priests" (Exod. 19:6). This is the exalted stature that comes to those who live by the Torah. —GERSONIDES

"For God has come only in order to test you"—God has come to accustom you to the ways of faith. Now that He has shown you the Shekhinah, His faith has entered your hearts, so that you will cleave to Him and never abandon your faith in Him.

"And in order that the fear of Him may be ever on your faces"—Having seen that He alone is God, in heaven and on earth, you will fear Him greatly. Or it might mean: The fear of "this great fire" (Deut. 5:22) will be on your faces, preventing you from sinning.

The language here ["test *(nassot)*"] is akin to that of the verse, "He tried to walk but he was not used to *(nissah)* it. . . . ['I cannot] walk in these, for I am not used to *(nissiti)* them' " (1 Sam. 17:39)—a matter of becoming accustomed. The Master [Maimonides] writes in *The Guide of the Perplexed* that [what Moses means by] "Be not afraid" is this: "What you have seen is only in order

---

*The two letters for the "s" sound are sometimes etymologically interchangeable.

[to prepare you for a time] when the Lord God will test your faith by sending you a false prophet who will contradict what you have heard. You will never stray from the true path, however, now that you have seen the truth with your own eyes." What the verse is saying, then, is: "God has come now so as to be able to test you in the future and so that you will pass every test."

In my view, however, the present test is a real one, and what Moses is saying is this: "God wishes to test your readiness to observe His commandments. He has removed all doubt from your hearts, and now He will be able to tell whether you love Him and want Him and His commandments." The term *nissayon* always refers to a test. Thus, "['I cannot] walk in these, for I am not used to *(nissiti)* them' " actually means, "I have never tested my ability to walk in them."

One can also be tested by something good. A master will sometimes test his servant with a difficult task, to see if, out of devotion to him, he bears up under it; but he may also do his servant a kindness, to see if the latter returns the favor by working harder or honoring him more. In this connection, the Sages said, "Fortunate is the man who passes his tests, for there is no one whom the Holy One, blessed be He, does not test. The test of the rich person is whether he opens his hand to the poor; the test of the poor person is whether he accepts his tribulations; etc." [Exodus Rabbah 31:2].

This is why scripture says God dealt kindly with you in showing you His Glory, something He has not done for any other nation. In doing this, He was testing whether you would repay His kindness by being His special people, as in the verse, "Do you thus requite the Lord . . . ?" (Deut. 32:6); and "You alone have I singled out of all the families of the earth—that is why I will call you to account for all your iniquities" (Amos 3:2). "The other nations," He was saying, "do not owe Me the same obligation you do, for it is you whom I have gotten to know face to face." —NACHMANIDES

"In order to test you"—That is, the reason the Omnipresent, blessed be He, revealed Himself was to subject you to tribulations so as to find out whether you would accept them gladly.

"And in order that the fear of Him"—that you might remember the greatness of His glory forever and so fear Him, as is written further on, "The day you stood [before the Lord your God at Horeb, when the Lord said to me, 'Gather the people to Me that I may let them hear My words, in order that they may learn to revere me as long as they live on earth]' " (Deut. 4:10).

"On your faces *('al peneikhem)*"—meaning, in your faces *(bifneikhem)*. This refers to shamefacedness and awe [*Mekhilta,* Yitro 9]. We learn here that

Israel has shame and is humble, and those who have no shame cannot be descendants of those who stood at Sinai. —Rabbi Meyuḥas ben Eliyahu, COMMENTARY

"In order to test *(nassot)* you"—to prove your mettle, as in the verse, "God put Abraham to the test *(nissa)*" (Gen. 32:1)—He provoked and afflicted him. Similarly, it is written: "If one ventures *(hanissa)* a word with you, will it be too much?" (Job. 4:2); "Because they tried *(nassotam)* the Lord" (Exod. 17:7); "[The place was named] Massah [trial] and Meribah" (Exod. 17:7); and "Probe me, O Lord, and try me *(venasseni)*" (Ps. 26:2). —RASHBAM, Genesis 22

"Be not afraid; for [God has come] only in order to test you, etc."—What [Moses] means to tell them in saying "Be not afraid" is this: "At the Giving of the Torah, God revealed His Shekhinah to you and cast His fear over you 'so that His fear will be ever with you.' Then, when you are tempted to violate 'You shall not murder' or 'Remember the sabbath day,' His fear will be ever with you, and you will say, 'One who, [like me,] merited seeing the face of the Shekhinah with the utterance of each Commandment ought not to sin.' "

Another interpretation of "to test *(nassot)* you": "to get you used to His Torah and His commandments," as in the verse, "[And she who is most tender and dainty among you, so tender and dainty] that she would never venture *(nista)* to set a foot [on the ground, shall care nothing for the husband of her bosom]" (Deut. 28:56); and the verse, ['I cannot walk in these, for] I am not used to *(nissiti)* them' " (1 Sam. 17:39). "[God] wants to accustom you to the Ten Commandments, which contain all the other commandments, so that, being used to them, His fear will be with you on all other occasions and you will not sin." It is according to this line of reasoning that Moses decides to tell them it is a test: the blessed Lord wishes to see whether they can bear up under numerous other commandments. —ZEROR HAMOR

"For God has come only in order to test you"—The fact that the Holy One, blessed be He, Himself uttered the words, "I [the Lord am your God]" and "You shall have no [other gods]" [to the people] made a deep impression in the heart of every Jew, so much so that even the least observant among them was willing [thereafter] to give his life for the sanctification of His Name, be He blessed. That is the meaning of "in order to test you"—to prepare you to stand the test. —KEDUSHAT LEVI

"['You speak to us,'] they said to Moses, '. . . lest we die.' Moses answered the
people, 'Be not afraid; [for God has come only in order to test you,] and in
order that the fear of Him may be ever with you, so that you do not sin' "—It
is not the fear of death that is the [true] fear of the Lord but the fear of sin.
—AMUD HA'EMET, citing Rabbi Menahem of Kotzk

"In order to test *(nassot)* you"—All this is "a banner to wave *(nes lehitnoses)*"
(Ps. 60:6) in the exaltation of the knowledge and recognition of the Divine.
—OHEL YA'AKOV

"Moses answered the people, 'Be not afraid; for God has come only in order
to test you, and in order that the fear of Him may be ever with you, so that
you do not sin' "—Our teacher Rabbi Yosef Jabez poses the following difficulty: [Moses] begins by saying "Be not afraid" and ends by saying "that the
fear of Him may be ever with you," an apparent contradiction. But, writes
Rabbi Ya'akov Yosef of Polonnoye, there is more than one kind of fear in the
world, and all of them have their roots in the fear of the Lord. Those who cling
to this root fear are spared all the other kinds, which are merely guises for the
primary, inner fear. This is what Moses meant by "Be not afraid": "[These
other fears] are merely apparent, but let 'the fear of Him,' which is the only real
fear, 'be ever with you.' Then you will be spared all other kinds of fear." This
is what is meant by the verse, "The fear of the Lord prolongs life" (Prov. 10:27).
—TOLDOT YA'AKOV YOSEF

"All the people witnessed the thunder and the lightning . . . and . . . they fell
back and stood at a distance. 'You speak to us,' they said to Moses. . . . Moses
answered the people, 'Be not afraid; for God has come only in order to test you,
and in order that the fear of Him may be ever with you.' . . ."—It is well known
that if Israel had not said to Moses, "You speak to us," but had heard all the
commandments directly from the Holy One, blessed be He, they would have
lost their evil impulse and would never have sinned from then on. But in saying
"You speak to us," they brought about [their own sin]. Our Sages, may their
memory be a blessing, expounded this passage as implying that Moses felt let
down [by the people's lack of courage].
　　This matter was made clear by my master and grandfather [the Ba'al Shem
Tov], may his memory be a blessing, [who said]: Learning from a saint is a great
thing; how much more so learning from the Creator Himself. Certainly the
Master [God] gives strength to His disciples; just as He and His words are alive,
His disciples [i.e., the people Israel], too, would have lived indefinitely, never

reneging on [their acceptance of the Torah]. But that could not be the case if the words came from a mere mortal.

They heard "I [the Lord am your God]" and "You shall have no [other gods beside Me]" directly from the All-Powerful. And their request to Moses, that "you speak to us"—that is, that they not hear any further from the Holy One, blessed be He, directly—is explained by scripture itself as follows: "All the people witnessed the thunder and lightning . . . and the mountain smoking" (Exod. 20:15), [and were therefore afraid]. On this the *Zohar Hadash* says: Some of them looked at the thunder and lightning, but a few looked directly at the commandment, "I [the Lord am your God]," thus raising a screen between themselves and "I [the Lord]." Having this, "they fell back and stood at a distance," that is, behind the screen that separated them, at some distance, from the Creator, be He blessed. It was this that led them to say to Moses, "You speak to us."

And Moses our Teacher, peace be to him, said to them, "Be not afraid; for God has come only in order to test you." "Test" *(nassot)* connotes lifting up, as in the expression, "they raised a banner *(nes)*." In other words, "The Holy One, blessed be He, wants to raise you up to an exalted plane 'so that you do not sin.' That is, just as He is eternal and lives forever, so shall you remain whole and alive forever through the 248 positive commandments and the 365 negative ones." —DEGEL MAHANEH EFRAYIM

"I am sending an angel before you [to guard you on the way and to bring you to the place which I have made ready]" (Exod. 23:20)—Blessed be the Omnipresent, blessed be He, for having chosen Israel out of all the world's inhabitants, the work of His hands that He created; for having acquired Israel irrevocably as His children and servants.

Consider what is written about them: "Say, therefore, to the Israelite people: I am the Lord. I will free you. . . . And I will take you to be My people, [and I will be your God]. . . . I will bring you into the land [which I swore to give to Abraham, Isaac, and Jacob, and I will give it to you for a possession, I the Lord]" (Exod. 6:6–8). And it is written, "I am sending an angel before you." May it be Your will, Father in heaven, that You never put us into the hands of an intermediary.

This is explained by a parable. To what may it be compared? To a mortal king who arrived [in a certain city] with horses and riders and a great army. When his servants and retainers [who lived in that city] heard it, they quaked and trembled in great fear. But the king was wise and intelligent and clever. Settling himself in the city, which was near his own place of residence, he said,

"How many householders are there here? Give them so much wheat and so much barley and clothe them in so much wool. How many poor people are there here? How many blind and lame people? Give them so much wheat and so much barley and clothe them in so much wool. How many deaf people are there? Give them so much wheat and so much barley and clothe them in so much wool. How many children and adolescents are there? Give them so much wheat and so much barley and clothe them in so much wool and flax. How many old men and women are there? Give them, ..."

Thus, when the Holy One, blessed be He, revealed Himself in order to give the Torah to His children, He was preceded by 248 [myriads of angels], and another 248 before them.* How do we know He sent 248 [myriads of angels] before Him? Because it is written, "God's chariots are myriads upon myriads, thousands upon thousands; [the Lord is among them as in Sinai in holiness]" (Ps. 68:18); and it is written, "God is coming from Teman, [the Holy One from Mount Paran. His majesty covers the skies (at Sinai) . . . and there His strength (Torah) which was hidden is revealed]" (Hab. 3:3–4).

Similarly, when He came down upon Mount Sinai, with the ministering angels appointed [to look after] each and every Jew, the angels took them back twelve miles† [upon hearing each commandment] and returned them twelve miles [afterward], twenty-four miles in all for each commandment, as it is written, "Like an eagle who rouses his nestlings, [gliding down to his young, so spread He His wings and took him, bore him along on His pinions]" (Deut. 32:11). [The angels were told to do all this, because] when our ancestors stood at Mount Sinai ready to accept the revealed Torah, they were seized with a great fear and trembling, as it is written, "On the third day, [as morning dawned, there was thunder, and lightning, and a dense cloud upon the mountain, and a very loud blast of the horn; and all the people who were in the camp trembled]. . . . The blare of the horn [grew louder and louder. As Moses spoke, God answered him in thunder]. . . . And all the people witnessed the thunder [and lightning, the blare of the horn and the mountain smoking]. . . . 'You speak to us,' they said to Moses, ['and we will obey']" (Exod. 19:16,19; 20:15–16). Seeing that they had been seized with dread of the Holy One, blessed be He, Moses said to them, "Be not afraid," as it is written, "Moses

---

*Parallel texts in the Talmud and Midrash read, in each instance, 22 instead of 248. This reading, suggests the commentary *Yeshu'ot Ya'akov*, would explain the use of Ps. 68:18 as a prooftext, for *ribbotayim* ("myriads upon myriads") can be understood to mean "two myriads," technically 20,000, and *alfei shin'an* ("thousands upon thousands") can be understood to mean "two thousand"—hence 22,000 in all.

†See note, p. 24.

answered the people, 'Be not afraid. . . .' " (Exod. 20:17). He first reassured them and then set before them the civil laws and the rules for the dispensation of justice. —SEDER ELIYAHU RABBAH 22

EXODUS 20:18

So the people remained at a distance,
while Moses approached the thick
cloud where God was.

"So the people remained at a distance, while Moses approached the thick cloud where God was"—Moses did the opposite of what they did. When they remained at a distance, he approached the thick cloud. —IBN 'EZRA

"So the people remained at a distance"—This refers to the twelve miles. The text is telling us that the camp of Israel was twelve miles across. Thus scripture says, "They encamped by the Jordan from Beth-jeshimoth as far as Abel-shittim, in the steppes of Moab" (Num. 33:49)—a distance of twelve miles. —MEKHILTA (Yalkut Shim'oni version)

"Moses approached the thick cloud"—How did he merit this? By being humble, as it is written, "Now Moses was a very humble man, [more so than any other man on earth]" (Num. 12:3). What scripture is telling us is that whoever is humble helps bring the Shekhinah down among men. Thus it is written, "For thus said He who high aloft forever dwells, whose name is holy: I dwell on high, in holiness; yet with the contrite and the lowly in spirit" (Isa. 57:15); and it is written, "The spirit of the Lord God is upon me, because the Lord has anointed me; He has sent me as a herald of joy to the humble" (Isa. 61:1); and it is written, "All this was made by My hand, . . . Yet to such a one I look: to the poor and broken-hearted" (Isa. 66:2); and it is written, "True sacrifice to God is a contrite spirit" (Ps. 51:19).

But whoever is haughty defiles the land and drives the Shekhinah away. Thus it is written, "I cannot endure the haughty and proud man" (Ps. 101:5). The haughty are called an abomination, as it is written, "Every haughty person is an abomination to the Lord" (Prov. 16:5). Idolatry, too, is called an abomination, as it is written, "You must not bring an abomination into your house" (Deut. 7:26). Just as idolatry defiles the land and drives away the Shekhinah, so does the haughty person cause the land to be defiled and the Shekhinah to be driven away.

"Moses approached the thick cloud"—going past three barriers: darkness, cloud, and thick cloud. There was darkness without, cloud within, and thick cloud within that, as it is written, "Moses approached the thick cloud [where God was]." —MEKHILTA

"With the contrite (ve'et dakka) and the lowly in spirit" (Isa. 57:15)—Rav Huna and Rav Hisda differed about this verse. One read it, "The contrite person is with Me (iti dakka)," and the other read it, "I am with the contrite person (ani et dakka)." But the latter view is more plausible, for the Holy One, blessed be He, rejected all the other mountains and hills to pour His Shekhinah down onto Mount Sinai, [the lowest of the mountains]. —SOTA 5a

"I am with the contrite person"—I incline My Shekhinah toward him. This teaches that, following the example of our Lord, we should love lowliness.
    "All the other mountains and hills"—such as Tabor and Carmel, which came there [to compete], as scripture says, "Why so hostile, O jagged mountains . . . ?" (Ps. 68:17). —RASHI

"I cannot endure [the haughty and proud man]" (Ps. 101:5)—Read it not oto lo ukhal (I cannot endure) but iti lo ukhal (I cannot abide with Me). Said the Holy One, blessed be He, "He and I cannot live in the same world." —'ARAKHIN 15b

"Moses approached the thick cloud ('arafel)"—We would not have known whether the inner or the outer cloud was meant had scripture not added, "where God was." We can infer that there were two walls of cloud, [an outer one and an inner one,] and Moses went through the one until he reached the other. Similarly, Solomon says, "The Lord has chosen to abide in a thick cloud (ba'arafel)" (1 Kings 8:12). Hence it is said that the Prophets all prophesied through dark glass, while Moses our Teacher saw through clear glass. Fortunate are you, O Moses, fortunate are you, son of Amram, in what has been granted you! —MEKHILTA DE-RABBI SHIM'ON BAR YOHAI

"Moses approached the thick cloud"—The Kabbalists said: No one ever reached the spiritual level known as Yehidah* except Moses at Mount Sinai and Adam. That is what is meant by the verse, "[You went up to the heights, . . .] having received the tribute of man (adam)" (Ps. 68:19). —HEMDAT YAMIM

*The highest capacity of the soul.

[God] elevated Moses greatly, for not even the angels and *seraphim* were allowed to enter the inner precinct to which Moses was admitted. Thus it is written, "The people remained at a distance, while Moses approached the thick cloud where God was." Rabbi Yose said: The thick cloud was in juxtaposition to the Temple [on high], which is why the Temple is called "a thick cloud," as in the verse, "Then Solomon declared, 'The Lord has chosen to abide in a thick cloud' " (I Kings 8:12). What is more, [Moses was allowed] to take hold of the Throne of Glory, as it is written, "He grasps the front of His throne, over which He spread His cloud" (Job 26:9)—that is, the Holy One, blessed be He, had him take hold of it. —MISHNAT RABBI ELI'EZER 8

"Moses approached the thick cloud"—as it says later, "You remain here with Me" (Deut. 5:28). The "thick cloud *('arafel)*" is the same as the "thick cloud *('av he'anan)*" referred to earlier (Exod. 19:9). It is called this because it was a rain cloud, as in the verse, "[under heavens] dripping dew *(ya'arfu tal)*" (Deut. 33:28). —Meyuḥas ben Eliyahu, COMMENTARY

There is a kind of visible thick cloud called *'arafel,* the word being composed of *'erev* (mixture), meaning a condition in which forms are indistinct, and *afel* (darkness). Hence, the Musaf service for the New Year says, "You were revealed to them in clouds *('arpelei)* of purity," referring to the harsh, bright light of the Divine Glory, which obscures Him and prevents Him from being gazed upon.

"Clouds of purity *(tohar)*"—as in the verse, "[And they saw the God of Israel: under His feet there was the likeness of a pavement of sapphire,] like the very sky for purity *(latohar)*" (Exod. 24:10). —MAHZOR OHALEI YA'AKOV

"Moses approached the thick cloud"—Why was the Torah given in the dark? He should have given it in the light! But since the Holy One, blessed be He, knew that [Israel] would one day worship other gods, He did not want to give it in the light, lest there be too much joy. —BA'ALEI HATOSAFOT

"Moses approached the thick cloud [where God was]"—Past the cloud *('anan)* there was thick cloud *('arafel),* and one might have thought Moses approached only the nearest part of the latter. Hence, scripture tells us Moses our Teacher, peace be to him, attained a higher level of experience, in that he [was permitted to] go to the furthest reaches of the thick cloud, where God Himself—may His name be blessed and His Glory exalted—was to be found. —Rabbi Joseph Caro, SERMONS

HAPPY IS THE ONE YOU CHOOSE AND BRING NEAR

"The Lord called to him from the mountain" (Exod. 19:3)—Rabbi Yizhak began his discourse with the verse, "Happy is the man You choose and bring near to dwell in Your courts" (Ps. 65:5): Happy is the lot of the person whom the Holy One, blessed be He, desires and brings near "to Him" to dwell in His holy palace. For whomever He desires for His service bears a heavenly stamp that lets everyone know that he is among those chosen by the supreme and holy King to dwell with Him. And whoever bears this stamp can pass through all the celestial gates unhindered.

Rabbi Yehudah said: Happy was the lot of Moses, of whom it is written, "Happy is the man You choose and bring near," and of whom it is written, "Moses approached the thick cloud" and "Only Moses shall come near the Lord, but they shall not come near" (Exod. 24:2). —ZOHAR, Exodus 79b

YOU YOURSELVES SAW*

EXODUS 20:19
The Lord said to Moses: Thus shall you
say to the Israelites: You yourselves saw
that I spoke to you from the very heavens.

"The Lord said to Moses: Thus shall you say"—just as I dictate to you.

"Thus shall you say to the Israelites"—in the holy tongue [Hebrew]. Wherever in scripture we find the words "thus *(koh)*" or "so *(kakhah)*" with variations on "answered and spoke," it means in the holy tongue.

"You yourselves saw that . . . from the very heavens"—There is a difference between what a person sees with his own eyes and what others relate to him. When others relate something to him, he may react ambivalently. But here, "you yourselves saw."

Rabbi Natan said: Why does it say "you yourselves saw"? Because it is written, "All the kings of the earth shall praise You, O Lord, for they have heard the words You spoke" (Ps. 138:4). Now, we might have thought that if they heard they also saw; therefore scripture says, "You yourselves saw," meaning, you saw, but the other nations of the world did not.

"That I spoke to you from the very heavens"—One verse says, "[I spoke to you] from the very heavens," while another says, "The Lord came down upon Mount Sinai" (Exod. 19:20). Do these verses not contradict one another? The difficulty is resolved by a third verse: "From the heavens He let you hear His voice to discipline you; [on earth He let you see His great fire; and from amidst that fire you heard His words]" (Deut. 4:36). Thus far the view of Rabbi Yishma'el. Rabbi 'Akiva said: One verse says, "[I spoke to you] from the very heavens," while another says, "The Lord came down upon Mount Sinai, on the top of the mountain." This teaches us that the Holy One, blessed be He, inclined the highest heaven down to the top of the mountain and spoke to

*The Hebrew phrase was the original title of this book.

them from [that] heaven, as it is written, "from the very heavens." Thus scripture says, "He bent the sky and came down, thick cloud beneath His feet" (Ps. 18:10). Rabbi [Yehudah Hanasi] said: "The Lord came down upon Mount Sinai . . . and the Lord called Moses to the top of the mountain and Moses went up"—One might have understood this literally, but it can be read as follows: If a servant of servants [the sun] can be [felt] in one place and yet be in another, surely it is even easier for the Glory of Him-Who-Spoke-and-the-World-Came-Into-Being. —MEKHILTA

"From the heavens He let you hear His voice to discipline you; on earth He let you see His great fire" (Deut. 4:36)—His Glory was in heaven, but His fire and His power were on earth. —RASHI

"The Lord said to Moses: Thus shall you say to the Israelites"—in the holy tongue [Hebrew]. "Thus"—concerning the following matters; "thus"—in the following order; "thus"—in the following verses; "thus"—in the following chapters. [In other words,] "just as the Lord had commanded [him]" (Exod. 40:16), neither more nor less.

"You yourselves saw"—You did not hear it second hand or read it in books—"that I spoke to you from the very heavens."

We have here two verses that seem to contradict one another. One says, "The Lord came down upon Mount Sinai" (Exod. 19:20), and the other says, "You yourselves saw that I spoke to you from the very heavens." How can it say "[The Lord] came down" when it also says "I spoke to you from the very heavens"? The difficulty is resolved by the verse, "From the heavens He let you hear His voice to discipline you; on earth He let you see His great fire" (Deut. 4:36). This teaches us that the Omnipresent, blessed be He, inclined the highest heaven down to the top of the mountain and spoke to them from that heaven, which rested on the top of the mountain. Thus scripture says, "He bent the sky and came down, thick cloud beneath His feet" (2 Sam. 22:10). —MEKHILTA DE-RABBI SHIM'ON BAR YOHAI

"The Lord said to Moses: Thus shall you say"—"in the holy tongue [and] just as I dictate to you"—so the Mekhilta teaches us. It would seem that the blessed Lord insisted on the use of certain words and no others, for these words had a special significance and could yield multiple interpretations. For example, the words "With Me (iti) . . . you shall not make [any gods of silver]" (Exod. 20:20) are interpreted by our Rabbis, may their memory be a blessing, as "You shall not make Me *(oti)* [into gods of silver]"; and had a different word been used, one that [did not yield these two readings* but] could only mean "with," there would be no room for the other interpretation. And there are many other examples.

"I spoke to you from the very heavens"—One verse says, "I spoke to you from the very heavens," while another says, "The Lord came down upon Mount Sinai" (Exod. 19:20). To resolve the difficulty, a third verse is brought: "From the heavens He let you hear His voice to discipline you; on earth He let you see His great fire; [and from amidst that fire you heard His words]" (Deut. 4:36). But does this really resolve the difficulty? One could raise the same question concerning this third verse, which seems internally contradictory. First it says, "From the heavens He let you hear [His voice]," and then it says, "From amidst that fire you heard His words," [the fire] that had appeared on earth! Thus the difficulty remains.

My teacher, God protect him, explains that the difficulty is to be resolved in terms of the language of this third verse: when it uses the word "voice" it means heaven, and when it says, "From amidst that fire you heard His words," it means earth. Thus, "the voice of the Lord is power" (Ps. 29:4) refers to God speaking to His people from heaven. Having asked that the blessed Lord speak to them [directly], they would be taught a lesson: [so overwhelmed were they] when He spoke that they fainted away, never having heard such a voice, that spoke without distinct words. But He had only spoken to them [from heaven] in order "to discipline [them]." "On earth He let you see His great fire [and from amidst that fire you heard His words]"—The voice had now been toned down so that Israel could bear listening to it and could understand the words. Hence, "from amidst that fire you heard His words." Thus the two verses sit well with each other: He did indeed speak to them from heaven, His voice then descending to earth, so that Israel heard the *voice* from on high, but the *words* they heard only from the fire below.

Our Sages, may their memory be a blessing, said further that the Holy One, blessed be He, inclined the highest heavens down and spread them over the mountain, as scripture says, "He bent the sky and came down" (2 Sam. 22:10). —Rabbi Moshe Najara, LEKAH TOV

"You yourselves saw that I spoke to you from the very heavens"—All [the people of] Israel were witnesses to the things they had seen with their own eyes, the signs and great wonders, beginning with the Ten Plagues and extending

*The letters can be read either way.

through the Giving of the Torah. Thus the Holy One, blessed be He, reminded them of what "you yourselves saw," both at the beginning and at the end. Earlier, in the passage describing the conditions of the covenant, He began by saying, "You have seen what I did to the Egyptians" (Exod. 19:4), and now He tells them, "You yourselves saw that I spoke to you from the very heavens"— "for My glory rested on Mount Sinai, but My speech was from heaven."
—RABBENU BAHYA

"I spoke to you from the very heavens"—Scripture teaches us that the words of the Torah may be compared to fire. Just as fire was given from heaven, so were the words of the Torah given from heaven, as it is written, "You yourselves saw that I spoke to you from the very heavens." Just as fire lives forever, so do the words of the Torah live forever. Just as one can be burned by getting close to fire and chilled by keeping away from it, so it is with the words of the Torah: as long as a person labors over them, they give him life, but when he puts them aside they can kill him. Just as fire has its uses in both this world and the next, so do the words of the Torah have their uses in this world and the next. —SIFREI, Vezot Haberakhah

"Give ear, O heavens" (Deut. 32:1)—because the Torah was given from heaven, as it is written, "You yourselves saw that I spoke to you from the very heavens." "Let the earth hear the words I utter" (Deut. 32:1)—for it was on earth that Israel stood when they said, "All that the Lord has spoken we will do and we will hear!" (Exod. 24:7).

Another interpretation of "Give ear, O heavens": They did not fulfill the commandments that were given to them concerning the heavens. Which were these? The laws concerning the leap year and the fixing of the months, as it is written, "They shall serve as signs for the set times—the days and the years" (Gen. 1:14). "Let the earth hear"—Nor did they fulfill the commandments that were given to them concerning the earth: the laws of the gleanings, the forgotten sheaves, and the corners of the field, the laws of the tithes, the sabbatical year, and the jubilee year.

Another interpretation of "Give ear, O heavens": They did not fulfill all the commandments that were given to them from heaven. "Let the earth hear"—Nor did they fulfill the commandments that were given to them on earth. . . . Moses said, "I am but flesh and blood, and tomorrow I will die. If one day they claim they did not accept the Torah, who will dispute them?" Therefore he appointed to testify against them two witnesses that would endure throughout eternity, [heaven and earth]. But the Omnipresent appointed to testify against them the Song of Moses, as it is written, "In order that this song may be My witness against the people of Israel" (Deut. 31:19). He said, "This song shall bear witness from below, and I shall bear witness from above." How do we know the Omnipresent is to be called a witness? From the verse, "I will step forward to contend against you, and I will act as a relentless witness . . . said the Lord of Hosts" (Mal. 3:5); and the verse, "I am He who knows and bears witness—[declares the Lord]" (Jer. 29:23); and the verse, "Let my Lord God be your witness" (Mic. 1:2). —SIFREI, Ha'azinu

"It has been clearly demonstrated to you that the Lord alone is God; there is none beside Him" (Deut. 4:35). "It has been clearly demonstrated to you"— According to Rashi: " 'You have been shown.' When the Holy One, blessed be He, gave them the Torah, He opened up seven heavens before them." For the Holy One, blessed be He, Himself sits above the seven heavens, and when He descended onto Mount Sinai He tore away the upper six and inclined the seventh, on which He was sitting, down to the mountain. "Then, just as He had torn the upper six heavens away, He tore away the lowest one, the seventh, as well, so that they could see that He alone was God. Hence it is written, 'It has been clearly demonstrated to you [that the Lord alone is God].' " —Rabbi Nahman of Bratslav, BEI'URIM

"The Lord said to Moses: Thus shall you say to the Israelites: You yourselves saw that I spoke to you from the very heavens: With Me, therefore, you shall not make any gods of silver, nor shall you make for yourselves any gods of gold"—This passage comes to teach us what a high degree of merit Israel attained at the time of the Giving of the Torah. Before the Giving of the Torah, He had spoken to them only of temporal benefactions, saying, "You have seen what I did to the Egyptians" (Exod. 19:4) and "You shall be to Me a kingdom of priests" (Exod. 19:6). But now, after the Giving of the Torah, He tells them of the true reward that is hidden away for the righteous: enjoying the sight of His splendor. This is usually attained only after death, but they have now attained it while yet alive.

That being the case, " 'with Me, . . . you shall not make any gods of silver,' for now that I have appeared to you face to face, how could anyone refute you? If they tell you to worship false gods or not to believe in Me, you can tell them, 'We do not need to put our trust in any prophet, for the Holy One, blessed be He, Himself has told us, "I the Lord [am your God]" and "You shall have no [other gods beside Me]." ' " This is the meaning of the words, "that the fear of Him may be . . . on your faces": "you have seen Him face to face and [so] will not sin, for you will say [to the false prophets], 'If He does not appear to us again as He once did [and confirm your words], we shall not believe you.' " This, then, is the meaning of the words, "[You yourselves saw] that [I spoke to you] from the very heavens," and therefore, "with Me, you shall not make any gods of silver." —ZEROR HAMOR

"The Lord said to Moses: Thus shall you say to the Israelites: You yourselves saw that I spoke to you from the very heavens: With Me, therefore, you shall not make any gods of silver, nor shall you make for yourselves any gods of gold. Make for Me an altar of earth and sacrifice [on it]"—As you know, the users of talismans would make such images, saying that they themselves were not worthy of receiving the flow of Divine bounty directly from the First Cause. This was the reason they made such images, as an intermediary between themselves and the blessed Creator.

They were like those who worshiped the Golden Calf, who said to Aaron, "Come, make us a god who shall go before us, for that man Moses, who brought us from the land of Egypt—we cannot tell what has happened to him" (Exod. 32:1). These people certainly did not think Moses our Master was divine, God forbid. Rather, they said, "Until now it was Moses who received the Divine bounty, and it then flowed on to us; now that he is lost, make us another image through which the Divine bounty can flow, an intermediary between us and the blessed Creator." Therefore scripture says, "Do not think this way, God forbid, for 'you yourselves saw' with your own eyes 'that I spoke to you from the very heavens,' face to face, without any intermediary. Therefore, 'with Me, you shall not make any gods of silver, nor . . . any gods of gold' to be an intermediary between Me and you, saying that in My greatness and exaltation I shall not deign to relate to you." —SHEMEN TOV

"You yourselves saw that I spoke to you from the very heavens"—"and not from the earth. Nevertheless, you did not see any image of My Glory." Thus scripture says, " 'You saw no shape when the Lord your God spoke [to you at Horeb]' (Deut. 4:15). That being the case, you must not make gods of silver or gold, images of anything in the world, and say that they represent the image of the Divine Glory." —HIZKUNI

"You yourselves saw that I spoke to you from the very heavens"—"I bypassed all the hosts of heaven to speak to you and take pleasure in your company. I did not speak to the heavenly hosts, for you are dearer to Me than all the angels on high. Thus it is self-evident that there is no need for an intermediary between us, for you are near to Me." —MA'AGELEI ZEDEK

THE HOLY ONE, BLESSED BE HE, SAYS, "YOU YOURSELVES SAW THAT I SPOKE TO YOU FROM THE VERY HEAVENS," AND THE ASSEMBLY OF ISRAEL SAYS, "LOOK DOWN FROM YOUR HOLY ABODE, FROM HEAVEN."

"Look down from Your holy abode, from heaven, and bless Your people Israel and the land You have given us, [a land flowing with milk and honey,] as You swore to our fathers" (Deut. 26:15). "Look down from Your holy abode, from heaven, and bless Your people Israel. Do it for our sake. And [bless] the land You gave us, for the land's sake. Do it in the name of our Torah, as You swore to our ancestors. Do it for the sake of Your great name, by which we are called, as it is written, 'You are in our midst, O Lord, and Your name is attached to us—do not forsake us' (Jer. 14:9)." —MEKHILTA ON DEUTERONOMY

GLOSSARY

Aggadah. Lit., "lore." The nonlegal genres of Rabbinic literature, encompassing midrash (q.v.), wisdom, theology, legends, homilies, and anecdotes.

'Amidah. A series of benedictions, said standing, in silent meditation, which make up the most solemn section of the service of worship.

Ari. Lit., "lion." An acronym for *Ha-elohi Rabbi Yizhak* (the divine Rabbi Yizhak), the name by which the great Safed mystic Yizhak Luria (1534–72) is known.

Baraita (pl., *beraitot*). In the Babylonian Talmud, a rabbinic text of the period of the Mishnah but not included therein.

Earlier Authorities. Heb. *rishonim*. Codifiers of Jewish law between the close of the Talmud and the compilation of Rabbi Joseph Caro's *Shulhan Arukh,* in the sixteenth century.

Gemara. The discussions of the Mishnah, which make up the bulk of the Talmud.

Gematria. An ancient hermeneutic system in which the import of a word or phrase is derived from the numerical value of its letters, often in juxtaposition to another word or phrase of equal value.

Haggadah. Lit., "narration." The text of the Passover-night table ceremony *(Seder),* in which the Exodus from Egypt is commemorated.

Halakhah (pl., *halakhot*). Lit., "way." The body of Jewish law; or, a particular law.

Haver (pl., *haverim*). Originally, in the tannaitic period, a member of a group that took upon itself extra stringency in the observance of the laws of tithes and purity that obtained in the Land of Israel; later, a scholar in general.

Kabbalah. Lit., "tradition." Here and in scholarly English usage: the Jewish esoteric and mystical tradition.

Later Authorities. Heb. *ahronim*. Codifiers of Jewish law after Joseph Caro (sixteenth century).

Masorah. Lit., "transmission." The ancient tradition by which the division, wording, spelling, and punctuation of the biblical text were handed down.

Megillah. Lit., "scroll." The Book of Esther. Sometimes also applied to the Song of Songs, Ruth, Lamentations, and Ecclesiastes.

Midrash (pl., *midrashim*). Lit., "search" or "investigation." (1) The ancient rabbinic homiletical interpretation of the Bible, involving amplification of the text well beyond its plain sense; (2) a particular instance of such interpretation; (3) a volume of *midrashim* (e.g., Midrash Tanhuma); (4) the entire literature of midrash ("the Midrash").

Min (pl., *minim*). In the Rabbinic period, a Jewish sectarian. Sometimes refers to Jewish Christians.

Onkelos. Second-century C.E. author of an Aramaic translation of the Bible, known as *Targum Onkelos* or simply the *Targum* (translation), which appears in many standard editions of the Hebrew Bible and has long been regarded as a kind of commentary upon it.

Oral Torah. The body of law believed to have been revealed at Sinai along with the Written Torah and eventually set down in the Talmud.

Parashah (pl., *parshiot;* construct, *parashat*). A section of the Torah, comprising several chapters, read publicly in the synagogue as part of the annual cycle of weekly readings. In traditional usage, a passage in the Torah is often cited according to its *parashah* rather than by chapter and verse.

Rabbis, The. When capitalized, the Sages (q.v.).

Rebbe. In Hasidism, the spiritual leader of a sect, regarded in some respects as an intermediary between his followers and the divine. An equivalent Hebrew term is *zaddik* (righteous one).

Sages, The. The Palestinian and Babylonian Jewish scholars of the first five centuries of the Common Era whose discussions make up the Talmud and much of the Midrash. Often referred to in Hebrew by the acronym *HaZaL (hakhameinu zikhronam livrakhah,* "our Sages, may their memory be a blessing").

Sefer. Book; in traditional usage, a book dealing with sacred matters.

Sefirot. The ten Divine emanations or manifestations that form the cosmos in kabbalistic doctrine.

Shavu'ot. Pentecost; one of the three Pilgrimage Festivals, occurring in late spring, seven weeks after Passover, and considered the anniversary of the Giving of the Torah.

Shekhinah. The Divine presence in the world.

She'ilta. A halakhic ruling couched in the form of a question and answer and usually grounded in a narrative passage in the Torah, as in the *She'iltot* of Aha of Shabha (Babylonia, eighth century).

Siddur. The Jewish prayer book.

Talmud. The body of teaching concerning the Mishnah (the code of law of Rabbi Yehudah Hanasi) expounded by the sages of the third to fifth centuries C.E. in the academies of Palestine and Babylonia. Unless specified, "Talmud" generally refers to the Babylonian Talmud, the larger and more authoritative of the two compilations.

Tanna. A sage of the period of the Mishnah.

Targum. See Onkelos.

Torah. (1) The Pentateuch; (2) the Pentateuch together with all other sacred literature that supplements or comments upon it.

Written Torah. The Pentateuch.

Zaddik. See Rebbe.

BIBLIOGRAPHY

No bibliography was provided by the editor, S. Y. Agnon, for *Present at Sinai: The Giving of the Law*. The following listing, prepared by the translator, is based in part on bibliographies supplied by the editor to two similar compilations of his, *Yamim Nora'im (Days of Awe)* and *Sefer, Sofer, Vesippur (Book, Author, and Story)*, in which references to some of these titles appear.

Wherever known, the century and country of composition are given, along with the year and place of publication mentioned by Agnon. In the case of many works, the date of composition remains approximate or uncertain.

As for works not listed in Agnon's two bibliographies, most have gone through numerous printed editions, and it is not always possible to ascertain which edition Agnon is citing in the present work. This information is not supplied, then, unless Agnon himself provides it. In a few cases, it is not even certain which *book* is meant, there being several distinct works with the same title that are similar in content and style to the excerpt quoted.

Because Agnon sometimes identifies a text by author and sometimes by the title of the work and the reader cannot be expected easily to differentiate between the two—rabbinic writers are frequently known by the titles of their works and vice versa—we have combined authors and titles into a single alphabetical list. In most cases, Agnon refers to authors by the title "rabbi," generally omitted in the present translation and in this bibliography.

The symbol (E) indicates books for which English translations have been published as well as authors at least some of whose works are available in English.

Abrabanel, Yizhak ben Yehudah. 15th- to 16th-century Portuguese-Spanish-Italian biblical exegete, philosopher, and statesman.
Abudarham, David. 14th-century Spanish liturgical commentator.
Adler, Nathan. 18th-century German rabbi.
Aggadat Bereshit. Aggadic midrash on Genesis; ed. Solomon Buber, pub. Cracow, 1903.
 See *Seder Eliyahu Rabbah*.
Ahavat Shalom. Kabbalistic commentary on the Torah by Menahem Mendel ben Ya'akov Kopel of Korets, Poland–Ukraine, date unknown; pub. Lwow, 1833.

'Akaviah, Avraham Aryeh. 19th- to 20th-century Polish-Palestinian-Israeli Yiddish and Hebrew writer and authority on the Jewish calendar.

'Akedat Yizhak. Allegorical and homiletical commentary on the Torah by Yizhak ben Moshe Arama, Spain, 15th century.

Alshekh, Moses. 16th-century Palestinian Bible commentator.

'Amar Neke. Supercommentary on the Torah commentary of Rashi, by 'Ovadiah di Bertinoro, Italy, 15th to 16th century.

'Amud Ha'emet. Teachings of the hasidic master Menahem Mendel of Kotsk, Poland, 18th to 19th century.

Apirion. Homilies on the Torah and Aggadah, by Solomon Ganzfried, Hungary, 19th century; pub. Ungvar, 1864.

'Arakhin. Tractate of the Talmud (E).

'Ateret Yeshu'ah. Compendium of quotations from the Talmud, Midrash, and Zohar, by Yoel ben Yehoshua Heshl; pub. Vilna, 1799.

Avnei Eliyahu. Hasidic commentary on the Torah, by Eliyahu Frankel; pub. Munkacs, 1889.

'Avodat Yisrael. Homiletical work by Yisra'el ben Shabtai of Koznitz, Poland, 19th century; pub. Lwow, 1850.

Avot. Tractate of the Mishnah, also referred to as Pirkei Avot (E).

Avraham Ya'akov of Sadgora. 19th-century Ukrainian hasidic master.

Ba'al Haturim. Ya'akov ben Asher, 13th- to 14th-century German-Spanish halakhic authority, author of the code *Arba'ah Turim* and of a popular commentary on the Torah; also known as "the Tur."

Ba'alei Hatosafot. 12th- to 14th-century French-German school of Talmudic and biblical exegetes who based their work upon the commentaries of Rashi.

Baba Batra. Tractate of the Talmud (E).

Bacrat, Avraham. Avraham ben Solomon Levy-Bacrat, 15th- to 16th-century Spanish–North African poet, known for his supercommentary on the Bible commentary of Rashi, *Sefer Zikkaron* (q.v.).

Bahya. *See* Rabbenu Bahya.

Beirurei Hamiddot. Ethical treatise based on talmudic and kabbalistic sources, by Aharon Shlomo Maharil; pub. Jerusalem, 1923.

Beit Aharon. Collection of hasidic homilies on the Torah, by Aharon of Karlin. Lithuania, 19th century; pub. Brody, 1875.

Beit Halevi. Responsa, talmudic glosses, and homilies by Yosef Dov Soloveichik, Lithuania, 19th century; pub. Vilna and Warsaw, 1863–74.

Beit Yisrael. Teachings of the hasidic master Yisrael Ruzhin, Ukraine-Moldavia-Bukovina, 19th century; ed. Reuven Zak, pub. Piotrkow, 1913.

Beiur Vehagahot Hagra. Commentary on the Zohar by Eliyahu ben Shlomo Zalman (the Vilna Gaon), Lithuania, 18th century.

Bekhor Shor, Yosef ben Yizhak. 12th-century French commentator on the Torah.

Bekhorot. Tractate of the Talmud (E).

Ben Porat Yosef. Hasidic commentary on the Torah by Ya'akov Yosef of Polonnoye, Ukraine, 18th century; pub. Korets, 1781.

Ben Zimra, David. David ben Shlomo Ibn Abi Zimra (Radbaz), 15th- to 16th-century Spanish-Egyptian-Palestinian halakhist and kabbalist.

Berakhot. Tractate of the Talmud (E).

Binyan Shlomo. Commentary on Tractate Avot, by Me'ir Yehudah ben Shlomo; Przemysl, 1896.

Caro, Joseph. 16th-century Spanish-Turkish-Palestinian halakhist and mystic.

Degel Mahaneh Efraim. Sermons on the weekly Torah readings, by the hasidic master Moshe Hayyim Efraim of Sudylkow, Poland, 18th century.

Derekh Erez. A Minor Tractate, appended to the Talmud (E).

Derekh Zaddikim. Sayings of the hasidic masters; ed. Avraham Yellin, pub. Piotrkow, 1912.

Deuteronomy Rabbah. 8th- to 9th-century homiletical midrash (E).

Devash Hasadeh. Hasidic stories and homilies; ed. Dov Baer Meir, pub. Bilgoraj, 1909.

Divrei Emet. Commentary on the Torah, by Ya'akov Yizhak (the Seer) of Lublin, Poland, 18th to 19th century; pub. Sudylkow, 1836.

Divrei Hayyim. Ethical treatise, with commentary on Genesis, by Yeruham of Buczacz, Poland, date unknown; pub. Munkacs, 1906.

Dover Shalom. Teachings and tales of Shalom Roke'ah (founder of the Belz hasidic dynasty), Russia, 18th to 19th century; pub. Przemysl, 1910.

Efodi. Profiat Duran, 14th- to 15th-century Spanish scholar, physician, polemicist and author of the grammatical work *Ma'aseh Efod.*

'Einei Kol Hai. Halakhic argumentation and commentary on the Aggadah, by Hayyim Palache (Palaggi), Turkey, 19th century; pub. Izmir, 1878.

'Emek Hamelekh. Treatise on kabbalistic theology, by Naftali ben Ya'akov Elhanan Bacharach, Germany, 17th century; pub. Amsterdam, 1648.

Emet Ve'emunah. Homilies by Menahem Mendel of Kotsk, Poland, 19th century; pub. Jerusalem, 1940.

Even Yekarah. Responsa on the Shulhan Arukh, by Binyamin Aryeh Weiss; pub. Lwow, 1894.

Exodus Rabbah. Name applied to two collections of midrashim on Exodus, one homiletical, from the 9th century, the other exegetical, from the 10th century or later (E).

Gedulat Hazaddikim. Hasidic teachings, compiled by Gerson Staschevsky; pub. Warsaw, 1934–37.

Gedulat Mordekhai. Hasidic teachings, compiled by Gerson Staschevsky; pub. Warsaw, 1934–37.

Genesis Rabbah. 5th-century exegetical, aggadic midrash (E).

Gersonides. Levi ben Gershom (Ralbag), 13th- to 14th-century French Bible commentator, philosopher, mathematician, and astronomer.

Guide of the Perplexed. Philosophical work by Moses Maimonides (Rambam), Egypt, 12th century; pub. Venice, 1551, and numerous subsequent editions (E).

Gur Aryeh. Commentary on the Torah and Tractate Avot by Yehudah Aryeh Leib of Gur (Sfat Emet), Poland, 19th century; combining comments by his grandfather Yizhak Meir Rothenberg Alter (Hiddushei Harim, q.v.).

Ha'amek Davar. Commentary on the Torah, by Naftali Zvi Berlin (Neziv) of Volozhin, Belorussia, 19th century.

Hafez Hayyim. Yisrael Meir Hakohen Poupko, 19th- to 20th-century Belorussian halakhist, known by the title of his ethical work, *Hafez Hayyim.*

Hagigah. Tractate of the Talmud (E).

Hanoten Imrei Shefer. Commentary on the Torah and the festivals, with hasidic teachings, by Yeshayah Naftali Herz Shapira, 19th century; pub. Przemysl, 1887.

Harokeah. El'azar ben Yehudah of Worms, 12th- to 13th-century German rabbinical authority, author of a halakhic work bearing this name.

Hashavah Letovah. Halakhic work by Hanokh Henikh Alexandrow, Poland, 19th century; pub. Piotrkow, 1929.

Heikhal Haberakhah. Commentary on the Torah by Yizhak Yehudah Yehiel of Komarno, Poland, 19th century.

Helkei Avanim. Supercommentary on Rashi's commentary on the Torah, by David Lida, Netherlands, 17th century.

Hemdat Yamim. Kabbalistic work on Jewish ritual, written by an anonymous late 17th-century Sabbatean; pub. Zolkiev, 1732.

Hiddushei Harim. Yizhak Meir Rothenberg Alter, 18th- to 19th-century Polish founder of the Gur (Ger) hasidic dynasty and author of a halakhic work bearing this title, by which he is known.

Hiddushei Hatorah. Novellae by Mordekhai Leib Klein, Bohemia, 19th to 20th century; pub. Cracow, 1904.

Hizkuni. Commentary on the Torah and on Rashi by Hizkiyahu ben Manoah; France, 13th century.

Hoffmann, David Zvi. Prominent 19th- to 20th-century German rabbi, halakhist, and philologist.

Ibn 'Ezra, Avraham. 12th-century Spanish-Italian-French Bible commentator, poet, grammarian, philosopher, and physician (E).

Ibn Shu'aib, Yehoshu'a. 14th-century Spanish scholar, known for his *Derashot*, a volume of sermons on the Torah.

'Ir Gibborim. Sermons by the prominent rabbi Efraim Shlomp ben Aharon of Luntshits (Leczyca), Poland-Czechoslovakia, 16th to 17th century.

Kallah. A Minor Tractate, appended to the Talmud (E).

Kara, Yosef. 11th- to 12th-century French Bible commentator, a student and colleague of Rashi.

Kedushat Levi. Sermons on the Torah by the hasidic master Levi Yizhak of Berdichev, Poland, 18th to 19th century; pub. Hrubishov, 1818, Lemberg, 1850.

Keter Torah. Commentary on Maimonides, Genesis, and Exodus, by Me'ir ben Levi Yizhak of Berdichev, Poland, 18th to 19th century; pub. Zhitomir, 1803.

Ketoret Hasamim. Commentary on the Torah based on *gematria*, by Aharon Tannenbaum; pub. Warsaw, 1868.

Kiddushin. Tractate of the Talmud (E).

Kimhi, David. 12th- to 13th-century Provençal grammarian and exegete, known as Radak.

Kimhi, Yosef. 12th-century Spanish-French grammarian, exegete, translator, and polemicist.

Kli Hemdah. Commentary on the Torah by Me'ir Dan Refa'el Plotsky, 19th to 20th century; pub. Piotrkow and Warsaw, 1906–38.

Knozel, Ya'akov. Author of a supercommentary on Rashi.

Kobrin, Moshe. Moshe ben Yisra'el Polier of Kobrin. 18th- to 19th-century Belorussian hasidic rabbi.

Kohen-Zedek, Avigdor. Author of a commentary on the Song of Songs.

Kol Dodi. Pseudonymous title applied by Agnon to his own comments.

Kol Yehudah. Commentary on the Torah, by Yehudah Leib ben Shim'on of Yanov; pub. Piotrkow, 1906.

Lekah Tov. See Midrash Lekah Tov.

Leket Yosef. Alphabetical collection of laws, by Yosef Nissim Burla, Palestine, 19th century; pub. Jerusalem, 1900.

Lev Aryeh. Commentary on the Torah and the Scrolls, by Yehudah Aryeh Leib ben Yehoshu'a Hoeshke; pub. Wilhermsdorf, 1674.

Leviticus Rabbah. 5th-century (amoraic) homiletical midrash (E).

Likkutei 'Ezot Hadash. Teachings of the hasidic master Nahman of Bratslav, compiled by Natan of Nemirov, Ukraine, 18th to 19th century; pub. Lwow, 1874.

Likkutim Hadashim. Collection of hasidic teachings by Yehiel Moshe of Yadimov; pub. Warsaw, 1899.

Ma'agelei Zedek. Teachings of the hasidic master Nahman of Bratslav, Ukraine, 18th to 19th century; pub. Josefov (Prague), 1850.

Ma'aseh Efod. Grammatical work by linguist Profiat Duran (*see* Efodi), Spain, 14th to 15th century; pub. 1403.

Ma'ayan Hahokhmah. Kabbalistic midrash concerning Moses and the angels, date unknown; pub. Shklov, 1784.

Magen David. Kabbalistic work on the letters of the Hebrew alphabet, by David ben Shlomo Ibn Avi Zimra, Palestine-Egypt, 16th century.

Maggid Meisharim. Homiletical, kabbalistic commentary on the Torah, based on the mystical diary of Joseph Caro (q.v.); pub. Amsterdam, 1708.

Maharan. Natan Neta Shapira. 17th-century Polish-Palestinian kabbalist and author of *Tuv Ha'arez;* pub. Venice, 1655.

Maharsha. Shmuel Eliezer Edels, 16th- to 17th-century Polish Talmud commentator.

Maharzu. Ze'ev Wolff Einhorn, 19th-century author of a commentary on Midrash Rabbah.

Mahazeh Avraham. Section of the Zohar dealing with Exodus 18, accompanied by the commentary *Or Hahamah,* by Avraham Azulai, Morocco-Palestine, 16th to 17th century.

Mahzor Ohalei Ya'akov. Festival prayer book; ed. Ya'akov Yizhaki; pub. Jerusalem, 1908–10.

Maimonides. 12th- to 13th-century Spanish-Moroccan-Egyptian philosopher and halakhist (E).

Makkot. Tractate of the Talmud (E).

Malbim. Meir Loeb ben Yehiel Mikhael, 19th-century Ukrainian-Polish-Romanian rabbi and preacher, known for his Bible commentary (E).

Matnot Kehunah. Commentary on Midrash Rabbah, by Yissakhar Ber ben Naftali Katz of Szczebrzeszyn, Poland, 16th century; pub. Vilna, 1878.

Megaleh 'Amukot. Kabbalistic exposition of Moses' prayer in Deuteronomy 3:23ff, by Natan Spira, Poland, 16th to 17th century; pub. Cracow, 1637.

Mei Marom. Series of pietistic works by Ya'akov Moshe Harlap, Palestine-Israel, 19th to 20th century.

Mei Menuhot. Commentary on the Bible and Aggadah, by El'azar Hayyim Yadman; pub. Piotrkow, 1910.

Mekhilta. See Mekhilta de-Rabbi Yishma'el.

Mekhilta de-Rabbi Shim'on bar Yohai. Halakhic exegetical midrash on Exodus, dating from the tannaitic period but redacted after the 4th century.

Mekhilta (de-Rabbi Yishma'el). Halakhic exegetical midrash on Exodus, dating from the tannaitic period but redacted after the 4th century (E).

Mekhilta on Deuteronomy. Selections from *Hamidrash Hagadol*; also called *Midrash Tanna'im*; ed. David Hoffman; pub. Berlin, 1908–9.

Mekor Hayyim. Homilies by Hayyim of Zanz, Poland, 19th century; ed. Avraham Simhah Bunem Michelson, pub. Bilgoraj, 1912.

Mekor Mayim Hayyim. Novellae on the Talmud and Shulhan Arukh, by Ya'akov Meir Padua, Lithuania, 19th century.

Melekhet Mahshevet. Zerah ben Meir Eidlitz, Czech rabbi and preacher, 18th century, referred to by the title of a Hebrew-Yiddish mathematics textbook he wrote.

Menahem of Kotzk. Menahem Mendel of Kotzk, 19th-century Polish hasidic master.

Menahot. Tractate of the Talmud (E).

Menorat Hama'or. Ethical compendium by Yizhak Aboab, Spain, 14th century; pub. Constantinople, 1514.

Me'or Ha'afelah. Midrash by Netanel ben Yeshayah, Yemen, 14th century; pub. Jerusalem, 1957.

Meshekh Hokhmah. Commentary on the Torah, by Meir Simhah Hakohen of Dvinsk, Russia, 19th to 20th century; pub. Riga, 1927.

Meyuhas ben Eliyahu. Turkish exegete, author of a commentary on Exodus; pub. Budapest, 1929.

Midrash 'Aseret Hadibrot. Collection of stories from the gaonic period (7th to 11th century.)

Midrash Hadash. Minor midrash appearing in *Torah Shlemah* (q.v.).

Midrash Hadash 'Al Hatorah. Minor midrash appearing in *Torah Shlemah* (q.v.).

Midrash Hagadol. Anonymous 13th-century anthology of exegetical aggadic midrashim on the Torah and Scrolls; pub. New York, 1930.

Midrash Hane'elam. Section of the Zohar (q.v.) (E).

Midrash Haser Veyater. Anonymous 9th-century homiletical work explaining defective and plene writing in the Bible; also known as *Midrash Haserot Viyterot;* ed. Wertheimer, pub. Jerusalem, 1930.

Midrash Lekah Tov. Anonymous 11th-century collection of aggadic, exegetical midrashim on the Torah and the Scrolls, also known as *Pesikta Zutarta.*

Midrash on Proverbs. Exegetical midrash, probably completed in the gaonic period; ed. Solomon Buber, pub. Vilna, 1893.

Midrash on Psalms. Collection of aggadic midrash, comprising material thought to date from the 3rd to the 13th centuries; ed. Solomon Buber, pub. Vilna, 1891 (E).

Midrash on Samuel. Compilation, probably Palestinian, dating from the 11th century or later, of homiletical midrashim of various periods; pub. Warsaw, 1852.

Midrash on the Song of Songs. 11th-century collection of extracts from various midrashim (E).

Midrash Sekhel Tov. Halakhic and aggadic midrashic anthology, arranged according to the weekly scriptural readings in Genesis and Exodus, by Menahem ben Shlomo, Italy, 12th century; ed. Solomon Buber, pub. Berlin, 1900.

Midrash Shmuel. See Midrash on Samuel.

Midrash Tadshe. 10th-century mystical, aggadic midrash; pub. Warsaw, 1924.

Midrash Tanhuma. See Tanhuma.

Mikhlal Yofi. Philosophical commentary on various midrashim, by Shmuel Zarza, Spain, 14th century.

Milin Yekirin. Hasidic homilies on the Torah; ed. Avraham Yizhak Dzubes, pub. Piotrkow, 1902.

Mishnat Rabbi Eli'ezer. Exegetical aggadic midrash on Proverbs 30:1–3, probably dating to the 8th century; also known as *Midrash Agur.*

Mishneh Kesef. Torah commentary and other material, by Yosef ben Abba Mari ibn Kaspi, France and Spain, 13th to 14th century.

Moshav Zekenim. Collection of comments on the Bible by the Ba'alei Hatosafot (q.v.); pub. in *Torah Shlemah* (q.v.).

Nachmanides. Moshe ben Nahman, 13th-century Spanish Bible exegete and philosopher (E).

Nahal Eshkol. Commentary on *Sefer Ha'eshkol* (q.v.), by Zvi Binyamin Auerbach, Germany, 19th century; pub. Halberstam, 1868.

Nahal Kedumim. Homiletical commentary on Genesis and related *aggadot,* by Aryeh Nahum Lubetzky; pub. Piotrkow, 1931.

Nahman of Bratslav. 18th to 19th-century Ukrainian hasidic master.

Najara, Moshe. 16th-century Syrian-Palestinian kabbalist and rabbi.

Narboni. Moshe ben Yehoshu'a of Narbonne, 14th-century French philosopher and Bible commentator.

Natan of Grodno. Natan ben Shimshon Shapira, 16th-century Polish author of *Beiurim shel Maharan,* a supercommentary on Rashi.

Nedarim. Tractate of the Talmud (E).

Nefuzot Yehudah. Sermons by Yehudah ben Yosef Moscato, Italy, 16th century.

Neta' Sha'ashu'im. Identity of source uncertain.

Netiv Mizvotekha. Introduction to the halakhic work *Ozar Hahayyim,* by Yizhak Yehudah Yehiel Safrin, Ukraine, 19th century; pub. Lemberg, 1858.

Nifla'ot Hatif'eret Shlomo. Epigrams, stories, and homilies of the hasidic master Shlomo Rabinowitch of Radomsko, Poland, 19th century; ed. Zvi Silberstein, pub. Piotrkow, 1923.

No'am Elimelekh. Sermons on the weekly Torah readings, by Elimelekh of Lizensk, Poland, 18th century; pub. Lwow, 1849.

No'am Megadim. Hasidic teachings by Eli'ezer ben Ya'akov Halevi Horovitz of Tarnogrod, Poland, 18th to 19th century; pub. Lemberg, 1873.

Ohel Ya'akov. Homilies on the Torah, by Ya'akov Kranz, the Maggid of Dubno, Poland, 18th to 19th century.

Ohev Yisrael. Hasidic teachings by Avraham Yehoshua Heschel of Apta (Opatow), Poland, 18th to 19th century; pub. Zhitomir, 1863.

Or Hahayyim. Kabbalistic commentary on the Torah, by Hayyim ben Moshe Ibn Attar, Morocco and Palestine, 18th century; pub. Venice, 1742.

Or Torah. Textual notes on the Torah, by Menahem ben Yehudah di Lonzano, Turkey and Palestine, 16th to 17th century; pub. Amsterdam, 1659.

Or Yesharim. Hasidic teachings, by Moshe Hayyim Kleinman; pub. Piotrkow, 1924.

Or Zaddikim. Homilies on the Torah, by Joseph Caro (q.v.); pub. Salonica, 1797.

Ozar Hakavod. Kabbalistic interpretation of *aggadot* in several tractates of the Talmud, by Todros Halevi Abulafia, Spain, 13th century.

Ozar Midrashim. Anthology of midrash, by Yehudah David Eisenstein, United States, 19th to 20th century; pub. New York, 1915.

Pa'aneah Raza. Commentary on the Torah based on *gematria,* by Yizhak ben Yehudah Halevi, Germany, 13th century; pub. Tarnopol, 1813.

Pekudat Halevi'im. Codification of laws in the tractates Berakhot and Ta'anit, by Yizhak ben Ya'akov Alfasi (Rif), Morocco, 11th century; pub. Mainz, 1874.

Penei David. Commentary on the Torah, by Hayyim Yosef David Azulai, Palestine, 18th to 19th century; pub. Leghorn, 1792.

Pesahim. Tractate of the Talmud (E).

Pesikta de-Rav Kahana. 5th- to 6th-century homiletical midrash for festivals and special sabbaths; ed. Solomon Buber, pub. Lyck, 1868 (E).

Pesikta Hadeta. Anonymous medieval collection of homilies on the festivals; place and date unknown; pub. in Adolph Jellinek (ed.), *Beit Hamidrash,* Leipzig, 1853–57.

Pesikta Rabbati. 8th- to 9th-century midrash for festivals and special sabbaths; ed. Meir Friedmann, pub. Vienna, 1880 (E).

Pirka de-Rabbenu Hakadosh. Anonymous numerological midrash, probably medieval; pub. in Gruenhut, *Sefer Halikkutim,* Jerusalem, 1899.

Pirkei Heikhalot. Mystical treatise, attributed to the 2nd-century tanna Rabbi Yishma'el; pub. Shklov, 1785.

Pirkei de-Rabbi Eli'ezer. Aggadic work on the Torah, attributed to the 1st-century tanna Rabbi Eli'ezer ben Hyrkanos; pub. Warsaw, 1852 (E).

Pleitat Sofrim. Appendix, by Menahem Mendel Krengel (Poland, 19th to 20th century), to H.J.D. Azulai's bibliographical dictionary *Shem Hagedolim Hashalem;* pub. Piotrkow, 1930.

Rabbenu Bahya. Bahya ben Asher ben Hlava, 13th-century Spanish exegete and Kabbalist, known for his commentary on the Torah.

Rabbenu Efraim. Efraim ibn Avi Alragan, 11th- to 12th-century Algerian halakhist and commentator on Alfasi.

Radak. *See* Kimhi, David.

Ramatayim Zofim. Hasidic commentary on *Tanna Devei Eliyahu* by Shmu'el of Sieniawa (q.v.).

Rashbam. Shmuel ben Meir, 11th- to 12th-century French commentator on the Bible and Talmud.

Rashi. Shlomo ben Yizhak, 11th- to 12th-century French commentator on the Bible and Talmud (E).

Recanati. Menahem ben Binyamin Recanati, 13th- to 14th-century Italian mystic and halakhist, author of a kabbalistic commentary on the Torah.

Rosh. Asher ben Yehiel, 13th- to 14th-century German talmudist and halakhic authority.

Ruah Hayyim. Commentary on Tractate Avot, by Hayyim Berlin of Volozhin, Belorussia, 19th century; pub. Vilna, 1859.

Seder Eliyahu. Exegetical aggadic midrash, compiled in the 7th to 10th century; ed. Meir Friedmann, pub. Vienna, 1902 (E).

Seder Eliyahu Rabbah. First part of *Seder Eliyahu* (q.v.) (E).

Seder Eliyahu Zuta. Second part of *Seder Eliyahu* (q.v.) (E).

Seder 'Olam. Midrashic chronicle, later known as *Seder 'Olam Rabbah,* ascribed to the 2nd-century tanna Yose ben Halafta; pub. Mantua, 1513; ed. B. Ratner, pub. Vilna, 1894 (E).

Seder Ruhot. Part of *Sefer Heikhalot (Sefer Hinukh),* a short, early, kabbalistic midrash; pub. in Adolph Jellinek, *Beit Hamidrash,* Leipzig, 1853–57.

Sefer Habahir. First work of Kabbalah, ascribed to the tanna Nehuniah ben Hakanah; appeared in France, 12th century; pub. Vilna, 1883.

Sefer Ha'eshkol. Halakhic commentary by Avraham ben Yizhak of Narbonne (Rabi Abad), France, 12th century.

Sefer Hapeli'ah. 14th-century kabbalistic commentary on Parashat Bereshit (Gen. 1:1–6:8); pub. Korets, 1784.

Sefer Haredim. Spiritual manual by El'azar Azikri, Palestine, 16th century; pub. Vilna, 1922.

Sefer Hasidim. Ethical, mystical, and ascetic teachings by Yehudah ben Shmuel he-Hasid of Regensburg, Germany, 12th to 13th century; pub. Bologna, 1538; another version, ed. J. Wistinetzki, pub. Berlin, 1891, and Frankfurt am Main, 1924.

Sefer Hamizvot Hagadol. Digest of the precepts of the Torah by Moshe of Coucy, France, 13th century.

Sefer Hazikkaron. Supercommentary on the Bible commentary of Rashi, by Avraham Bacrat *(q.v.).*

Sefer Sha'ashu'im. Anthology of Jewish folklore following the sequence of the Scriptures, by Nehemiah Shmuel Leibovitch; pub. New York, 1925.

Sefer Zikkaron. See *Sefer Hazikkaron.*

Sekhel Tov. Aggadic and halakhic midrashic anthology, arranged according to the weekly Torah readings, by Menahem ben Shlomo; Italy, 12th century; pub. Berlin, 1900.

Sforno. 'Ovadiah ben Ya'akov Sforno, 15th- to 16th-century Italian Bible commentator.

Sha'arei Ha'emunah. Collection of novellae on the Torah, ed. Natan Nata of Kolbial (?); pub. Piotrkow, 1928.

Shabbat. Tractate of the Talmud (E).

Shekalim. Tractate of the Talmud (E).

Shem Shmuel. Also called *Shem mi-Shmuel;* hasidic teachings of Avraham of Sochaczew, Poland, 19th century; edited by his son Shmuel; pub. Piotrkow, 1932.

Shem Tov. Shem Tov Ibn Shem Tov, 14th- to 15th-century Spanish rabbi whose *Sefer Ha'emunot* attacks Maimonides' *Guide of the Perplexed.*

Shemen Hatov. Commentary on the Torah, by Shlomo Ohev, Croatia, 16th century; pub. together with *Zekan Aharon* (q.v.), Venice, 1657.

Shibbolei Haleket. Halakhic and other teachings of Yehudah ben Binyamin Harofe 'Anav, Italy, 13th century, compiled by Zidkiyah ben Avraham Harofe; ed. Solomon Buber, pub. Vilna, 1887.

Shmu'el of Sieniawa. 19th-century Polish rabbi, author of *Ramatayim Zofim* (q.v.).

Shnei Luhot Habrit. Theological treatise by Yeshayah Halevi Horowitz of Prague, 16th to 17th century; pub. Amsterdam, 1649.

Shtei Yadot. Collection of philological, liturgical, and poetic writings by Menahem ben Yehudah de Lonzano, Turkey and Palestine, 16th to 17th century; pub. Venice, 1618.

Siah Sarfei Kodesh. Compilation of the teachings of various hasidic masters; ed. Yoez Kaddish, pub. Lodz, 1927–28.

Siah Sefunim. Homiletical commentary on the Five Scrolls, by Eli'ezer ben Reuven Kahana; pub. Zholkva, 1749.

Sidrei Hazemanim. Chronology of Jewish history by Avraham Aryeh Leib Akavya, Poland and Israel, 20th century; pub. Tel Aviv, 1946.

Sidrei Zemanim. See Sidrei Hazemanim.

Sifra. Halakhic midrash on Leviticus, composed of materials from the tannaitic period; pub. Vienna, 1862.

Sifrei. Halakhic midrash on Numbers and Deuteronomy, composed of materials from the tannaitic period; ed. Meir Ish-Shalom, pub. Vienna, 1864.

Siftei Kohen. Commentary on the Torah, by Mordekhai Hakohen, 16th century, Palestine; pub. Wannsbeck, 1690.

Siftei Zaddikim. Hasidic commentary on the Torah, by Pinhas of Dinovitz; pub. Lwow, 1863.

Sippurim Nifla'im. Anthology of hasidic stories, ed. Hayyim Yizhak Malik, pub. Satu-Mare, 1940.

Song of Songs Rabbah. 6th- or 7th-century exegetical midrash (E).

Sota. Tractate of the Talmud (E).

Ta'amei Haminhagim. Encyclopedia of Jewish practices, by Avraham Yizhak Shub Sperling; pub. Lemberg, 1928.

Tamid. Tractate of the Talmud (E).

Tanhuma. 8th- or 9th-century midrash on the Torah (E).

Tanhuma Hayashan. Variant version of Tanhuma (q.v.); ed. Solomon Buber, pub. Vilna, 1885.

Tanna Devei Eliyahu Zuta. See Seder Eliyahu.

Tif'eret Yisrael. Sayings of Yisrael of Chortkov, Ukraine, 19th century; pub. Husiatyn, 1904.

Tikkunim. Part of the Zohar (q.v.), also known as *Tikkunei Hazohar;* pub. Belgrade, 1851 (E).

Toldot Aharon. Concordance of biblical verses cited in the Babylonian Talmud, by Aharon of Pesaro, Italy, 16th century; pub. Freiburg, 1583–84.

Toldot Kol Aryeh. Biography of the 19th-century Hungarian rabbi Avraham Yehudah Schwartz, by Dov Beer Spitzer; pub. Kleinwardein (Kisvarda), 1940.

Toldot Ya'akov Yosef. Compilation of the teachings of Yisrael Ba'al Shem Tov, by Ya'akov Yosef of Polonnoye, Ukraine, 18th century; pub. Korets, 1780.

Torah Or. Hasidic homilies on Genesis, Exodus, Esther, and the festivals of Hannukah and Passover, by Shneur Zalman of Lyady, Belorussia, 18th to 19th century.

Torah Shlemah. Compendium of Rabbinic commentary on the Torah, by Menahem Mendel Kasher, Poland-Israel, 20th century; pub. Jerusalem, 1927.

Torat Emet. Hasidic homilies on the Torah and the festivals, by Yehudah Leib Eger of Lublin, Poland, 19th century; ed. Avraham Eger, pub. Lublin, 1889–90.

Torat Ha'olah. Treatise on the Temple and the sacrificial cult, by Moshe Isserles of Cracow, Poland, 16th century; pub. Prague, 1569.

Tosafot. Comments on the Talmud that take the commentary of Rashi as their point of departure; France and Germany, mainly 12th and 13th centuries, included in all printed editions of the Talmud.

Tosfot Harosh. Commentary on the Talmud, by Asher ben Yehiel; France-Germany-Spain, 13th to 14th century; included in printed editions of the Talmud.

Tractate Derekh Erez. *See* Derekh Erez.

Tur. See Ba'al Haturim.

Vayelaket Yosef. Comments on the Torah by various hasidic masters, collected by Ben-Ziyyon Rabinovitz (Ostrover); ed. Y. Mandelkern, pub. Jerusalem, 1946.

Vehizhir. 10th-century Palestinian halakhic midrash, following the method of the *she'iltot* (see Glossary).

Yadav Shel Moshe. Halakhic and homiletical work by Moshe Prisco, Turkey, 18th to 19th century; pub. Salonica, 1812.

Yalkut David. Sermons and eulogies by David Tevl Yaffe; pub. Cracow, 1896.

Yalkut Reuveni. Compendium of kabbalistic homilies on the Torah, by Reuven ben Hoeshke Katz, Bohemia, 17th century; pub. Amsterdam, 1700.

Yalkut Shim'oni. 13th-century anthology of exegetical, aggadic midrash.

Yedei Moshe. Commentary on Midrash Rabbah, by Ya'akov Moshe ben Avraham Hellin Ha'ashkenazi, Germany, 17th century; pub. Frankfurt am Main, 1692.

Yefeh To'ar. Commentary on Genesis Rabbah (q.v.), by Shmuel ben Yizhak Ashkenazi Jaffe, Turkey, 16th century; pub. Venice, 1597.

Yeshu'ot Ya'akov. Commentary on *Seder Eliyahu* (q.v.), by Ya'akov Naftali Herz of Brody, Poland, date unknown; pub. Zolkiew, 1796.

Yismah Moshe. Hasidic homilies by Moshe ben Zvi Teitelbaum of Ujhely, Hungary, 18th-to 19th century; pub. Lemberg, 1848.

Yoma. Tractate of the Talmud (E).

Yonatan. Targum Yonatan, also known as *Targum Yerushalmi I* and *Pseudo-Yonatan;* an Aramaic translation of the Torah, probably compiled in the 7th or 8th century.

Zayit Ra'anan. Responsa and interpretations of aggadah, by Moshe Yehudah Leib Zilberberg, Poland, 19th century; pub. Warsaw, 1851–69.

Zeh Yenahamenu. Homily on the Creation, by Avraham Bibago, Spain, 15th century; pub. Salonica, 1523.

Zekan Aharon. Commentary on *Shemen Hatov* (q.v.), by Aharon Hakohen of Ragusa (Dubrovnik), Croatia, 16th to 17th century; pub. Venice, 1657.

Zekhuta de-Avraham. Sermons by the hasidic master Avraham Landau of Ciechanow, Poland, 19th century; pub. Warsaw, 1895.

Zera' Barekh. Homilies on the Pentateuch by Berakhiah Barekh Shapira; pub. Cracow, 1646.

Zeror Hamor. Commentary on the Torah, by Avraham ben Ya'akov Saba, Spain-Portugal-Morocco, 15th to 16th century; pub. Venice, 1522.

Zevahim. Tractate of the Talmud (E).

Zikkaron Larishonim. Hasidic tales and teachings, compiled by Moshe Hayyim Kleinman; pub. Piotrkow, 1912.

Ziyyoni. Mystical commentary on the Torah, by Menahem Ziyyoni, Germany, 14th to 15th century; pub. Korets, 1785.

Zohar. Kabbalistic commentary on the Torah, by Moshe de Leon, Spain, 13th century; pub. Cremona, 1560, Sulzbach, 1684 (E).

Zohar Hadash. Teachings of the medieval Safed kabbalists, included as an appendix to printed editions of the Zohar; pub. Jerusalem, 1953.

INDEX OF CITATIONS

The following is an alphabetical listing of the principal passages that make up the body of this book, as opposed to brief quotations (mainly biblical verses) within passages. As in the foregoing text, the passages are generally identified in this listing as Agnon identifies them— by title or author or both—and, occasionally, by chapter, page, or paragraph as well. Italicized numbers are those supplied in the original citations; other numbers refer to pages in the present translation. Citations from the Mishnah and the Palestinian Talmud are marked (M) and (P) respectively; otherwise, names of talmudic tractates refer to the Babylonian Talmud.